The Sonoran Dynasty in Mexico

Confluencias

SERIES EDITORS

Susie S. Porter
University of Utah

María L. O. Muñoz
Susquehanna University

Diana Montaño
Washington University in St. Louis

THE SONORAN DYNASTY IN MEXICO

Revolution, Reform, and Repression

JÜRGEN BUCHENAU

University of Nebraska Press | Lincoln

© 2023 by the Board of Regents of the University of Nebraska. Portions of the manuscript were previously published as "'La Bola': Corruption and Power in Revolutionary Mexico," *Südosteuropa-Forschungen* 77, no. 1 (2018): 51–73. All rights reserved.

The University of Nebraska Press is part of a land-grant institution with campuses and programs on the past, present, and future homelands of the Pawnee, Ponca, Otoe-Missouria, Omaha, Dakota, Lakota, Kaw, Cheyenne, and Arapaho Peoples, as well as those of the relocated Ho-Chunk, Sac and Fox, and Iowa Peoples.

Library of Congress Cataloging-in-Publication Data
Names: Buchenau, Jürgen, 1964– author.
Title: The Sonoran dynasty in Mexico : revolution, reform, and repression / Jürgen Buchenau.
Description: Lincoln : University of Nebraska Press, 2023. | Series: Confluencias | Includes bibliographical references and index.
Identifiers: LCCN 2023019868
ISBN 9781496236135 (hardback)
ISBN 9781496236142 (paperback)
ISBN 9781496236982 (epub)
ISBN 9781496236999 (pdf)
Subjects: LCSH: Mexico—Politics and government—1910–1946. | Obregón, Álvaro, 1880–1928—Relations with generals. | Calles, Plutarco Elías, 1877–1945—Relations with generals. | Mexico—History—Revolution, 1910–1920. | Generals—Mexico—Sinaloa (State) | BISAC: HISTORY / Latin America / Mexico
Classification: LCC F1234 .B88 2023 | DDC 972.08/2—dc23/eng/20230522
LC record available at https://lccn.loc.gov/2023019868

Set in Vendetta by K. Andresen.

To Anabel

Contents

List of Illustrations   viii

Preface   ix

List of Abbreviations   xi

Introduction   1

Part 1. The Sonorenses in the Revolution, 1910–1915

   1. The Making of a Faction   21

   2. The School of War   47

Part 2. The Road to Power, 1915–1920

   3. Inside the Revolutionary Regime   77

   4. The Triumph of the Sonoran Alliance   103

Part 3. The Sonoran Triangle, 1920–1924

   5. The Sonorenses in Power   133

   6. The Triangle Broken   163

Part 4. The Duarchy, 1924–1928

   7. On Trial before the World   193

   8. Almost Porfirio   221

Part 5. The Maximato, 1928–1934

   9. From Caudillos to Institutions   249

   10. The End of an Era   275

Epilogue   301

Notes   313

Bibliography   359

Index   383

Illustrations

1. Map of Sonora in 1935   7
2. Mexican states and territories in 1935   18
3. Maytorena, Madero, and other Maderistas   40
4. Calles, Gómez, and the revolutionaries of Sonora in Hermosillo, 1913   51
5. Alvarado, Calles, and Obregón with Yaqui commanders, April 1913   55
6. Five-peso note issued by the Maytorena state government, 1915   57
7. Constitutionalist troops at the train station in Silao, Guanajuato   70
8. Diéguez and Obregón as wounded warriors   71
9. Calles, de la Huerta, and students from the Cruz Gálvez school   80
10. Obregón and Hill   105
11. Carranza, Bonillas, and Pesqueira   115
12. Governor de la Huerta takes office, 1919   119
13. Calles reads the Plan de Agua Prieta   121
14. De la Huerta, Calles, and Hill celebrate Independence Day   125
15. President de la Huerta flanked by Hill, Calles, and Alvarado   126
16. Alvaro Obregón and María Tapia Monteverde on their wedding day   158
17. Abelardo L. Rodríguez's family   159
18. Calles, Morones, and CROMistas   164
19. Obregón, Serrano, and Calles confront the rebellion   184
20. Gómez and other generals at Calles's inauguration   188
21. Fallen Cristeros in Colima   210
22. Serrano and Fernando Torreblanca   229
23. The jefe máximo   253
24. Rodríguez and Cárdenas pay homage to the jefe máximo   281

Preface

This book marks the end of a long journey begun more than three decades ago. Research conducted on Mexican international history as a graduate student left me eager to learn more about the politics of the turbulent period between 1920 and 1934. Two generals from the northwestern state of Sonora, Álvaro Obregón and Plutarco Elías Calles, dominated the scene after rising to prominence in the course of the Mexican Revolution. Torn between popular demands for social reform and opposition at home and abroad, Obregón and Calles—themselves aspiring entrepreneurs—mixed radical rhetoric with the accommodation of entrenched interests, as they sought to modernize the nation and reconstruct national political authority. Their group from Sonora begs further study. What was the worldview of a group that accounted for four out of six presidents of that period? How did leaders from a remote northern state suddenly find themselves in the epicenter of what the intellectual Martín Luis Guzmán famously called the "fiesta of bullets"?[1] How did they negotiate power with various constituencies, and at what cost? After forays in the form of biographies of Calles and Obregón, this volume represents the culminating synthesis of my engagement with these questions.[2] These questions still appear important today, at a time when the drug war wracks Mexico in another cycle of violence and when the current president, Andrés Manuel López Obrador, fashions himself as the architect of a new period of renovation and reconstruction.

I owe a lot of thanks. First and foremost, I appreciate the help of Bridget Barry, editor in chief of the University of Nebraska Press, as well as Emily Casillas, associate acquisitions editor, and the two external readers of the manuscript, including Tim Henderson, who identified himself to me. I am very honored to have this book included in the press's new Confluencias series and appreciate the support of the editors, Diana Montaño, María L. O. Muñoz, and Susie Porter. Financial assistance from the National Endowment of the Humanities, UNC Charlotte, and the American Philosophical Society provided release time from teaching and helped defray the cost of numerous research trips. I also acknowledge the invaluable assistance of Norma Mereles de Ogarrio, the director of the Fideicomiso Archivos Plutarco Elías Calles and Fernando Torreblanca in Mexico City, and her excellent staff, especially Amalia Torreblanca and Alejandra Alquicira. This book would be unthinkable without this archive, probably the finest private collection in Mexico City, which holds the personal papers of four of the protagonists examined herein. Pedro Boker alerted me to the existence of a private archive once belonging to General Abelardo L. Rodríguez, one of the subjects of this study. With his help, we transferred that collection to the Fideicomiso, and I was one of the first scholars to consult it.

Bill Beezley recruited this manuscript to the University of Nebraska Press. Four graduate students, Sarah Beckhart, Xenia Wirth, Sean Kane, and Sarah Walker, provided valuable assistance with primary source research. Two cohorts of my graduate reading colloquium provided feedback on drafts of the manuscript, and I especially thank John Catton for his candor in suggesting some improvements. My friend Carol Hartley read the entire manuscript from the vantage point of a generalist reader and made many valuable suggestions.

I am lucky to work at a place that values research. I benefited from the counsel of my colleagues at UNC Charlotte, especially Lyman Johnson, David Dalton, John David Smith, Carmen Soliz, and Greg Weeks. A special thanks to our Latin American Studies writing group, which included Vanessa Castañeda, Dan Cozart, Oscar de la Torre, Maria Labbato, and Andrea Pitts.

I am deeply indebted to the friendship and advice of Mexicanist colleagues at other institutions; for example, Ignacio Almada, Luis Anaya, Matthew Butler, Barry Carr, Pedro Castro, Carmen Collado, Gregory Crider, Ben Fallaw, José Alfredo Gómez Estrada, Paul Gillingham, Alan Knight, Martha Loyo, Pablo Mijangos, Sarah Osten, Monica Rankin, Douglas Richmond, Bill Schell, Jackie Sumner, and Daniela Spenser. Robert Weis and Barbara Tenenbaum provided insightful comments on conference papers that triaged some of the arguments made in this volume. I especially cherish the lifelong mentorship and friendship of Gil Joseph, who suggested further work on the Sonorenses three decades ago. Finally, the love of my family (Anabel, Nick, and Julia) made it all worthwhile.

Abbreviations

ACJM	Asociación Católica de la Juventud Mexicana (Catholic Association of Mexican Youth)
AF of L	American Federation of Labor
BNCA	Banco Nacional de Crédito Agrícola (National Agricultural Credit Bank)
CCCC	Cananea Consolidated Copper Company
CGOCM	Confederación General de Obreros y Campesinos Mexicanos (General Confederation of Mexican Workers and Campesinos)
COM	Casa del Obrero Mundial (House of the World's Worker)
CROM	Confederación Regional Obrera Mexicana (Mexican Regional Workers' Confederation)
CTM	Confederación de Trabajadores Mexicanos (Confederation of Mexican Workers)
ICAM	Iglesia Católica Apostólica Mexicana (Mexican Catholic Apostolic Church)
ICBM	International Committee of Bankers on Mexico
JFCA	Junta Federal de Conciliación y Arbitraje (Federal Board of Conciliation and Arbitration)
LNC	Liga Nacional Campesina (National Campesino League)
LNDLR	Liga Nacional Defensora de la Libertad Religiosa (National League for the Defense of Religious Liberty)
LNDR	Liga Nacional de la Defensa Religiosa (National League of Religious Defense)
PCM	Partido Comunista Mexicano (Mexican Communist Party)
PCN	Partido Católico Nacional (National Catholic Party)
PCP	Partido Constitucional Progresista (Constitutional Progressive Party)
PLC	Partido Liberal Constitucionalista (Liberal Constitutionalist Party)

PLM	Partido Laborista Mexicano (Mexican Labor Party)
PNA	Partido Nacional Agrarista (National Agrarian Party)
PNC	Partido Nacional Cooperatista (National Cooperatist Party)
PNR	Partido Nacional Revolucionario (National Revolutionary Party)
PRI	Partido Revolucionario Institucional (Institutional Revolutionary Party)
PSS	Partido Socialista del Sureste (Socialist Party of the Southeast)
PSY	Partido Socialista de Yucatán (Socialist Party of Yucatán)
UDCM	Unión de Damas Católicas Mexicanas (Union of Catholic Mexican Ladies)

The Sonoran Dynasty in Mexico

Introduction

War consisteth not in battle only, or the act of fighting; but in a tract of time, wherein the will to contend by battle is sufficiently known.
—Thomas Hobbes, *Leviathan*

On August 15, 1914, a cool and cloudy day, Mexico City's puzzled inhabitants watched General Álvaro Obregón's army enter the city. A bystander noted that the force looked nothing like the Federales, the government army styled in French fashion that had just surrendered to Obregón. The officers "all dressed in a dissimilar manner. Many wore suits similar to those worn by Texan cowboys . . . : wide-winged felt hat with chinstrap and braided bristle headgear, . . . ; olive green cloth camisole with patch pockets on both sides of the chest; khaki-colored riding pants, brown cowhide leggings, carrying a dagger in one of them and on the belt a revolver hanging from its respective cartridge belt." Most troops "wore brand-new American shoes; the rest wore sandals; almost all of them wore jeans, and their armor was the same as that of the U.S. Army. . . . They were dusty, their faces were sunburned; their lips, parched and cracked. They were dirty, sweaty and disheveled, with their beards grown out." The observer also noted Yaqui officers and soldiers, "the marrow" of Obregón's army.[1]

For the first time, a force from the distant northwestern border state of Sonora had occupied the Mexican capital, bringing the rough-and-tumble culture of the borderlands with it. For the next twenty years, *los sonorenses* would play a crucial role in the world's first social revolution of the twentieth century. This book helps understand that revolution more generally. The emergence of the Sonorenses from primarily middle-class origins and their relationships with their allies, families, and subordinates provides a lens through which to study the negotiation of power and state formation in revolutionary Mexico.[2]

The Sonorenses brought their own priorities to a revolution in which Mexico's poor rural majority did most of the actual fighting. Between

1910 and 1915 they participated in a series of three civil wars under the overall umbrella of a revolution. The two terms are not mutually exclusive: as one historian has noted, "all violent revolutions are civil wars, not all civil wars are revolutions."[3] Fought by diverse factions of regional origins, the first of these wars broke out with no common purpose beyond the removal of a dictator. But over time, the fighters produced a push for social and economic reforms codified in the Mexican constitution of 1917. This constitution was the first in the world to postulate social rights, such as the right to an education, a plot of land, and collective bargaining. Sharply anticlerical and nationalist, it curtailed the rights of the Catholic Church and foreign proprietors. Between 1920 and 1934 governments under the Sonorense aegis helped determine how far the revolution would go in implementing the constitution. Rejecting the Indigenous and Catholic past and using repressive methods, the Sonorenses aimed to reform Mexico along the lines of the modern, secular societies in western Europe and the United States. They promoted social reforms in alliance with worker and campesino organizations and then helped create an official revolutionary party that held on to the presidency under three iterations until 2000.

Using the constitution selectively, and developed in negotiation with Congress, governors, the military, and ordinary Mexicans, the Sonorense program featured three broad aims: nationalism, modernization, and centralization. Nationalism included the establishment of a secular, Spanish-speaking society achieved at the expense of the Catholic Church and Indigenous communities and curbs to the legal and tax privileges of foreign investors. Modernization, or "roads and schools, Fords, and books,"[4] meant an improved financial system, an upgraded infrastructure, commercial agriculture, and an emphasis on education and public health. That goal also addressed some of the constitution's promises of land reform and better working conditions via patronage of rural and urban labor. Centralization involved the construction of a political machine around allied caciques and revolutionary social movements, the reconstruction of the state apparatus that had disintegrated in the cycles of violence in the 1910s, an effort to police the nation and its borders, and the defense of national sovereignty.[5] This program evolved in a dialogue with U.S. Progressivism and European social democracy.[6]

The Sonorenses were the second of two region-based dynasties in postindependence Mexico. Benito Juárez and Porfirio Díaz, leaders from the southern state of Oaxaca, dominated the mid-to-late 1800s. Mexico's only Indigenous president in history, Juárez governed from 1858 to 1872, interrupted by a Conservative uprising and then the French Intervention. Díaz (1876–80 and 1884–1911) ruled with an iron fist until Francisco I. Madero's coalition overthrew "the Porfiriato" in the first phase of the Mexican Revolution (1910–11).

The Sonorenses' road to power began during Madero's revolution. Fought in the field by the agrarian insurgencies of Pascual Orozco and Emiliano Zapata, the six-month uprising featured Sonora as a sideshow. Most of the fighting occurred in those leaders' home states: Chihuahua, in the North, and Morelos, in the South. Sonorenses only fully mobilized when the unrest from Chihuahua threatened to spill over into their neighboring state, at the height of Orozco's unsuccessful rebellion against his former master, President Madero, in 1912. In the words of one historian, the Sonorenses conducted a "revolution by administration"—a carefully planned, centrally organized response to an external threat rather than an inchoate popular uprising such as the ones that characterized Chihuahua and Morelos.[7]

This well-provisioned army fought against the counterrevolutionary regime of the Porfirian-era general Victoriano Huerta, whose men had ousted and murdered Madero in February 1913. Sonora played a critical role as the only state ruled by a sitting governor who defied Huerta's authority and as the headquarters of the "Constitutionalists" under the leadership of "First Chief" Venustiano Carranza, a prosperous landowner and governor of Coahuila until Huerta's forces chased him out of his state. Another member of the Constitutionalist coalition was Pancho Villa, a sharecropper's son formerly allied with Orozco and commander of the largest army in the coalition. This much more destructive war ended with Obregón's seizure of the capital in August 1914, months after Villa had scored decisive victories in central Mexico.

United only in its opposition to counterrevolution, this coalition fell apart after Huerta's demise. In the War of the Winners (1914–15), the Carranza and Obregón factions defeated Villa's vaunted army, which was allied with that of Zapata, an indefatigable advocate for the restitution of village lands usurped by large haciendas and plantations during Díaz's rule. Obregón's forces struck decisive blows against Villa's army in 1915, while Sonora featured a war between Obregón's and Villa's clients. Under Carranza's leadership, the winning factions reconstructed a central national government, but the victorious alliance disintegrated once more. In 1920 Obregón assembled a new coalition that led Mexico's last successful coup d'état, one resulting in Carranza's death.

Thus began the Sonoran Dynasty. The six presidents of the next fourteen years included four Sonorenses—Adolfo de la Huerta, Obregón, Plutarco Elías Calles, and Abelardo L. Rodríguez. From 1928 to 1934, after his own presidential term, Calles played a powerful role as the *jefe máximo* (supreme chief) of the revolution; hence those years are still known as the Maximato. By then, the Sonorenses had entrenched themselves in national politics. In 1930 a state with less than 2 percent of Mexico's population accounted for an estimated 11.4 percent of the governing elite.[8]

The Sonorenses ruled over a revolutionary regime. In the words of two scholars, such regimes emerge "out of sustained, ideological, and violent struggle from below." They establish their authority in a process "accompanied by mass mobilization and significant efforts to transform state structures and the existing social order."[9] Revolutionary regimes often define the legacy of a revolution, as they put into practice reforms that address the social, economic, and political conditions that gave rise to the revolution in the first place. In Mexico's case, the tremendous death toll of the upheaval (estimated variously between 1.9 and 3.5 million) produced a weak revolutionary regime devoted to a significant degree to tasks of reconstruction.

This concept of a revolutionary regime invites a reconsideration of the chronology of the Mexican Revolution. Most scholars believe it to have ended in May 1920, when the final violent change of government ushered in "postrevolutionary authoritarian rule."[10] However, that final successful coup did not end the Mexican Revolution any more than the Bolsheviks' victory in 1917 finished the Russian Revolution. Wars tested and defined both regimes. Whereas in Russia a civil war culminated in the formation of the Soviet Union in 1922, Mexico suffered three major wars between 1923 and 1929. A minimalist interpretation posits the revolution's end in 1920 as concluding "effective threats to the new regime."[11] In that case, "effective" means successful. But per Thomas Hobbes, a seventeenth-century English philosopher familiar with violent upheaval, war "consisteth not in battle only, or the act of fighting; but in a tract of time, wherein the will to contend by battle is sufficiently known."[12] This "will to contend by battle" continued at least until 1929, when the emergence of a ruling party and the utter exhaustion of nineteen years of war combined to set the nation on a "postrevolutionary" course. In addition, the 1920s and 1930s witnessed important reforms, including a rural education campaign, land redistribution, and the incorporation of organizations representing workers and campesinos (defined as poor rural dwellers, whether small farmers, sharecroppers, or debt peons) into the new regime.[13] Antonio Gramsci's concept of a "catastrophic equilibrium," in which "the old is dying and the new cannot yet be born," is useful for understanding the state of the revolution under the Sonorenses.[14] To obtain and keep power, they sought a fragile compromise between contending forces in a society in upheaval.

Taking these factors into consideration, this study of the Sonorenses provides arguments for positing a later end to the revolution in Mexico. One historian aptly refers to the 1930s as the "latter stages of the first social revolution of the twentieth century."[15] Another scholar proposes 1940 as an end date.[16] Some even push the end of the revolution past the end of World War II.[17] By 1950 the reform drive was spent, a new generation of leaders had assumed control, Mexico had become a Cold War ally of the United States, and the specter of coups had faded away in a country that had by then become what one scholar has dubbed "unrevolutionary Mexico."[18]

This book focuses on eleven Sonorense leaders, five of them major figures after 1920. The primary patriarchs, Obregón and Calles, loom largest, followed by two interim presidents, de la Huerta and Rodríguez. Two others—Benjamín G. Hill and Francisco R. Serrano—were close Obregón allies with prestige at the national level, but Hill's career was cut short by his untimely death in 1920. Five leaders will receive more cursory attention: Salvador Alvarado, Manuel M. Diéguez, José María Maytorena, and Ignacio L. Pesqueira, all of whom split from the group before Obregón's ascent to power, as well as Arnulfo R. Gómez, a presidential hopeful in the late 1920s. All these leaders were either presidential candidates or state governors, or both.

The Sonorenses represented different sectors of society. Hill and Maytorena were affluent landowners; Calles and Obregón both came from formerly wealthy clans in decline; and the others were upwardly mobile members of the middle class. By necessity, this study is selective, limiting itself to Sonorenses who figured as state governors and/or presidential candidates.[19] Some were not Sonora natives but had acquired their formative political experiences in that state. Alvarado, Hill, and Serrano came from neighboring Sinaloa. In fact, northern Sinaloa, southwestern Chihuahua, and southern Sonora formed a tristate area dubbed "Sochiloa." The home of Gómez, Hill, Obregón, and Serrano, Sochiloa was one of the two cradles of the Sonora group; nearby Guaymas (Calles, de la Huerta, Maytorena, and Rodríguez) was the other. Diéguez arrived from Jalisco, in central Mexico; while his inclusion in the group is arguable, he did spend his formative political years in Sonora. Notably, all four Sonorense presidents hailed from Sonora's fertile coastal strip, between the city of Guaymas and the Mayo River.[20]

Paradoxically, a new ruling elite that professed to centralize via institutionalization continued the series of wars and revolts that had wracked Mexico since the beginning of the revolution. Torn apart by unbridled ambitions, the group was never cohesive to begin with. The Sonorenses joined the revolution in two cohorts. Some fought with Madero in 1910; others, including the two patriarchs, only took up arms in 1912, in defense of Sonora against Orozco's invading rebel force. Unsurprisingly, the Maderistas always resented those who (as they thought) had only belatedly and opportunistically joined the fighting. Calles and Obregón often worked at cross-purposes, and Sonorenses more broadly disagreed over the role of the military and the extent of anticlerical policies. In 1923 the De la Huerta Rebellion pitted one Sonorense presidential aspirant against another. In 1927 Serrano and Gómez challenged Obregón's effort to win a second term as president and paid for this challenge with their lives. Two years later, the Escobar Rebellion set the Sonora governor against the federal government.

The Sonoran Dynasty disintegrated in a series of internecine conflicts, including two (the De la Huerta and Escobar Rebellions) equally or more

1. Map of Sonora in 1935. Patrick Jones, UNC Charlotte Cartography Lab.

destructive than Madero's revolution. Rather than the "unraveling" of the group in power, a "great man" interpretation that suggests that personal rivalries led to national conflicts, the conflicts featured opposing social and political movements that fractured a divergent group.[21] Six of the Sonorenses had died by 1928: Alvarado, Diéguez, Gómez, and Serrano by execution; Obregón by assassination; and Hill from a mysterious illness.

In a diverse and divided nation in which political stability had been the exception rather than the rule, the Sonorenses also ruthlessly employed repressive and corrupt methods that presaged the abuses of the official ruling party founded by Calles and his allies in 1929. From modest beginnings, the party slowly but surely reduced violent conflict but used authoritarian, corrupt, and repressive methods. The revolution also provided the Sonorenses opportunities for personal enrichment.

❧ ❧ ❧

Historians often judge processes by their end result. Hence the memories of the Maximato (and secondarily, the conflict between church and state) have loomed large in shaping perceptions of the Sonorenses, and specifically Calles, the last man standing with the exception of Rodríguez. Amid growing social ferment in the Great Depression and a time of global ideological polarization, Calles appeared to make and unmake entire presidential administrations and had publicly announced his opposition to further land distributions to dispossessed campesinos. Scholars thus remember the scathing opinions expressed during and after the Maximato more so than the more balanced ones from the 1910s and 1920s.[22]

A sampling will illustrate this point. Tamaulipas native Emilio Portes Gil, the first of three presidents who operated under the jefe máximo's aegis, referred to this era as *sonorismo*, with reference to the group's overweening power.[23] The novelist Martín Luis Guzmán ridiculed a group whose members had placed ambition over friendship: "In politics, the most bitter, the cruelest enemies, often start as the most intimate of friends."[24] José Vasconcelos, Obregón's secretary of public education, opposed what he saw as Yankee imperialism and materialism. He sarcastically mocked the "men from the northern frontier, carriers of civilization."[25] Catholics and Communists lamented the persecution of the church and the repression of radical social movements, respectively. Finally, Calles's and Rodríguez's palatial homes in Cuernavaca led critics to assail corruption. They called the neighborhood "Ali Baba Street" or "Street of the Millionaire Socialist."[26] An Austrian American observer, Frank Tannenbaum, depicted the Calles era as "debased and clouded."[27]

These negative portrayals of the Sonorenses made historians inclined to forgo in-depth analyses of the group or its members. Eager to tell the story of popular movements in a revolution that preserved the capitalist mode of production, scholars first focused on the defeated agrarian forces, including the biographies of two of their icons, Villa and Zapata.[28] Only then did they turn their attention to the Sonorenses.[29] This study is the first archivally based analysis of the group and its role in revolutionary Mexico.

Published at a time when historians did not have access to relevant archival materials, John W. F. Dulles's *Yesterday in Mexico* (1961) remains the only English-language work on the topic. The son of former U.S. secretary of state John F. Dulles, "Jack" Dulles was a mining engineer who spent extensive time in Mexico and Brazil as part of his work and then refashioned himself as a professor of Latin American studies. On the basis of published sources and interviews, Dulles portrayed a chaotic political system in which business interests played only a minor role. He credited the Sonorenses with rebuilding the Mexican state but criticized them for their repression.[30] The author saw himself as a chronicler and paid close attention to the opinions of his interviewees. Indeed, he revised his unpublished manuscript based on the feedback of prominent subjects. As Dulles put it, "The project is endless since most of the actors are still living and they have strong points of view, which differ very directly with [*sic*] each other."[31]

In general the historical literature is not kind to the Sonorenses. Winning the revolution came at the price of blame for its shortcomings, including the persistence of authoritarian governance and widespread corruption; the failure to achieve social justice; and the inability to diminish the influence of the United States. The more radical revolutions in Cuba (1959) and Nicaragua (1979), the Socialist government of Salvador Allende in Chile (1970–73), and Mexico's own Zapatista Rebellion (1994) eclipsed the Mexican Revolution in their commitment to social reform. In his seminal 1972 book written from prison, Adolfo Gilly—an Argentine immigrant and member of the Trotskyist Fourth International—called it an interrupted revolution.[32] Gilly's work portrays Carranza and the Sonorenses as agents of this interruption; in his telling, the revolution had taken a wrong turn. Gilly's perspective influenced Héctor Aguilar Camín's history of the revolution in Sonora. In 1977 Aguilar described the rise of modernizing agricultural entrepreneurs imbued with what he considered the capitalist work ethic of the neighboring United States. He portrayed the group's rise to power as an invasion from the North and the Sonorenses as rugged individualists from the borderlands who did not understand the Catholic, multiethnic culture of central and southern Mexico.[33] With good reason, Ignacio Almada has rejected these generalizations by pointing out significant differences in the Sonorense leadership and, specifically, the divergence between the revolutionaries who joined the fighting with Madero in 1910 and those who took up arms against Orozco in 1912.[34]

Much of the criticism specifically targeted Calles, as Obregón, the most powerful Sonorense until his murder in 1928, escaped similar historiographical scrutiny by virtue of his early and violent demise. The Calles administration faced the devastating Cristiada as a result of its repressive policies, which also included the ruthless elimination of Serrano and Gómez, most likely with Obregón's assent, if not upon his initiative. After Obregón's assassination, Jefe Máximo Calles played a significant role in constructing a ruling party that monopolized the presidency for the rest of the century. The political scientist Arnaldo Córdova dubbed the Maximato "the revolution in crisis."[35] For his part, Aguilar Camín labeled Calles the "architect of one of the most corrupt political systems in Latin America."[36] One historian has maintained that Calles was "hated far and wide."[37] A leading U.S. textbook on Mexican history concludes that "something drastic had happened to the Revolution and its leaders. Honest, idealistic men . . . had been not only diverted from tasks of high priority, but corrupted as well."[38]

Sonorense rule stood in unfavorable contrast with the subsequent presidency of Lázaro Cárdenas. Over a period of six years, the Cardenistas redistributed more land than all of the previous revolutionary regimes combined, and their expropriation of the foreign-owned oil industry remains an iconic event in national memory. Cárdenas also went out of his way to show ordinary people that he wanted to hear their concerns and identified with them.[39] According to Córdova, "when one compares [Calles] to Cárdenas or studies the conflict between the two, [Calles] appears like a monster of conservative evil."[40] Not surprisingly, the Cardenistas made a clean break with the Sonoran Dynasty, and the sons of the Sonorenses were never able to reclaim the power that their fathers had once held. Just two of the numerous children of the Sonorense presidents served in prominent political positions thereafter: Álvaro Obregón Tapia, as governor of Sonora from 1955 to 1961, and Adolfo de la Huerta Oriol, as a federal senator from 1979 to 1982.

However, the widespread notion that Cárdenas revived a revolution that the Sonorenses had abandoned deserves close scrutiny. Cardenismo arose on Sonorense foundations. At the cost of a severe crisis in U.S.-Mexican relations, the Calles administration crafted petroleum legislation seeking national control over a significant resource. The Maximato governments approved land and labor codes that paved the way for Cardenismo.[41] Finally, the historian Sarah Osten has demonstrated that Obregón's and Calles's alliances with Socialist movements in southeastern Mexico provided an early model for the national ruling party and Cardenista political mobilization.[42]

Revisionist historians have depicted both Sonorismo and Cardenismo as stages in a broader trajectory of an authoritarian state. After the massacre of student protesters on the eve of the Mexico City Olympics in October 1968, scholars inquired into the roots of the repressive Partido Revolucionario Institucional (PRI, or Institutional Revolutionary Party). They concluded that the inclusion of popular movements in the Cardenistas' corporatist apparatus was a stepping stone toward a cynical party that parroted revolutionary phraseology while trampling human rights.[43] With reference to the National Palace on Mexico City's main square, one historian has argued that the Sonorenses and Cardenistas built a "Leviathan on the Zócalo."[44]

However, the revisionists went too far in their teleological quest to read the PRIato backward into the 1920s and 1930s. So far as there was a "state" as a historical actor, it was weak indeed. With good reason, historian Alan Knight has warned against "statolatry," the tendency to exaggerate its agency in a regionally and socially fragmented country undergoing cyclical waves of violence.⁴⁵ Subsequent "regional" and "cultural" historiographical turns demonstrated the ways that ordinary Mexicans negotiated state formation in a highly contested process.⁴⁶ Indeed, the state as a historical agent needs deconstruction. As a sociologist once wrote, "The state is not the reality . . . behind the mask of political practice. It is itself the mask."⁴⁷

What are historians to make of Aguilar's assertion that Calles and the other Sonorenses were singularly corrupt, especially compared to Cárdenas, who was known for his probity? An answer requires a definition of "corruption." With reference to Mexico, Knight defines corruption as "the use of political power and office in ways that are geared to some individual or collective self-interest and that are illegal and/or considered corrupt, improper, or self-serving."⁴⁸ The Sonorenses did in fact use political office for financial gain. As "roving bandits" in the wars against Huerta and Villa, they seized the properties of their vanquished enemies for themselves and their supporters. Once entrenched as "stationary bandits" after 1915, these leaders defended existing property rights.⁴⁹ The Sonorenses made most of their fortunes in new sectors beyond the scrutiny of a public focused on the large haciendas targeted by land reformers: garbanzo farms, vineyards, orchards, fisheries, spas, casinos, and movie theaters.⁵⁰

Still, Sonorense corruption was not extraordinary in the broad sweep of what Mexicans have called the *robolución* with reference to the theft of public funds.⁵¹ Díaz, Madero, and Carranza packed their governments with loyalists and members of their extended families, and their camarillas fed from the public trough. During the 1920s and 1930s, other new plutocrats (for example, Generals Maximino Ávila Camacho and Juan Andreu Almazán) far exceeded the wealth of the Sonorenses, even that of Rodríguez, who was known as Mexico's first "millionaire president." After the Sonorense era came rampant graft in the administrations of Miguel Alemán Valdés (1946–52), José López Portillo (1976–82), and Carlos Salinas de Gortari (1988–94).⁵² At the time of his inauguration in 1920, Obregón owned thirty-five hundred hectares and employed an estimated fifteen hundred workers. As president, he could no longer personally tend to his businesses. By 1926 he was deeply in debt. As illustrated in the mantra attributed to him that "no general can resist a cannon shot of 50,000 pesos,"⁵³ maintaining political power required cash outlays that might have otherwise been employed to build more wealth. Witness, for example, Obregón's comment to de la Huerta, who had not enriched himself and only had a small family of four: "I have to maintain more than seventy people who have gathered around me. I have become a milk cow!"[54]

It is therefore fair to say that while the Sonorenses indeed contributed to the corruption, repression, and social inequality that left most observers disappointed in the outcome of the revolution, their rule also brought important reforms and innovations, in addition to defending Mexican sovereignty and political stability. Historians have taken note. In 1997 Aguilar Camín retracted some of his conclusions, blaming a national penchant for history's losers: "The pantheon of the Mexican Revolution prefers ... to celebrate its fallen eagles rather than its victorious caudillos."[55]

✥ ✥ ✥

This study of the "victorious caudillos" primarily relies upon Mexican documentary sources and especially the vast holdings of the Fideicomiso Archivos Plutarco Elías Calles y Fernando Torreblanca in Mexico City (FAPEC). FAPEC houses the private papers of the four Sonoran presidents as well as those of longtime secretary of war and the navy Joaquín Amaro. Unavailable to Dulles and Aguilar Camín, these sources have informed Pedro Castro's and Ignacio Almada's more nuanced recent studies.[56] Materials from U.S. and European government archives and published sources, including newspapers and memoirs, round out the source base.

The book contains five sections separated by significant historical moments. The first is the victory of Carranza's and Obregón's Constitutionalist coalition in 1915. The second turning point is the Sonorense seizure of power in 1920. The third watershed is the bloody conflict that divided the Sonorenses (1923–24). Obregón's assassination on July 17, 1928, and the subsequent creation of an official revolutionary party constitutes the fourth disjuncture. Each section has two chapters: some organized chronologically; others, thematically.

Chapter 1, "The Making of a Faction," traces the origins of the Sonorenses in a border state that became one of Mexico's most rapidly growing regions during the late 1800s. They were all Yori, a term that the Indigenous Yaqui population gave to the Spanish-speaking descendants of the

Introduction 13

colonial settlers. In a region with weak government and an even weaker church, the Yori relied on familism, the priority of the family and kinship networks in social positioning. The Porfiriato brought material benefits to many of the Sonorense protagonists, some of whom held local office. They entered the revolution divided. Some fought to end Porfirian rule. Others took up arms to keep outsiders out of Sonora. Under Governor Maytorena, the latter vision prevailed, especially in Sonora's response to the Orozco Rebellion of 1912.

The next chapter, "The School of War," outlines the role of the Sonorenses in both the war against Huerta (1913–14) and the War of the Winners. Nationally, the latter conflict pitted the Constitutionalist alliance of Obregón's and Carranza's factions against the armies of Villa and Zapata, under the Conventionist banner. While the Sonorenses fought together to defeat Huerta, they divided in the War of the Winners, with Maytorena joining Villa in a war against Sonorenses allied with Carranza. The main argument of the chapter is that the goals of the Sonorenses transformed from narrowly regional concerns with the autonomy of their state to a commitment to broader economic and social change at the national level.

The third chapter, "Inside the Revolutionary Regime," analyzes the Sonorenses' role in assembling and establishing the new Constitutionalist government after their victory over Villa and Zapata. It argues that a quartet of Sonorense governors (Calles and Diéguez in Sonora, Alvarado in Yucatán, and Diéguez in Jalisco) experimented with reforms and anticlerical measures, some of which the revolutionary constitution of 1917 then enshrined at the national level. On the other hand, their direct influence in the Constituyente was minimal. Calles's influence in de la Huerta's governorship also provided an early example of his role in the Maximato. Finally, Calles's hostility to the Yaqui and their repressive methods also presaged the political methods of the nascent revolutionary regime.

Chapter 4, "The Triumph of the Sonorense Alliance," traces Obregón's rise as a national leader and the first Sonorense presidency after Carranza's bloody overthrow. It argues that the caudillo's opposition to parties and parliamentary rule foreshadowed the persistence of personalism and authoritarianism under his leadership. Carranza's selection of the civilian Ignacio Bonillas as his successor led to a break with Obregón's faction. His subsequent attack on the sovereignty of Sonora under de la

Huerta's leadership brought forth Mexico's final successful coup d'état, punctuated by Carranza's murder. The chapter ends with an analysis of de la Huerta's brief interim presidency, marked by an attempt to pacify a nation that had been at war for ten years.

The fifth chapter, "The Sonorenses in Power," demonstrates that Obregón's new government presided over a weak state. It took almost three years to negotiate U.S. diplomatic recognition, at a steep price. Similarly, an understanding with the Catholic Church papered over a growing chasm between anticlerical popular movements and increasingly dynamic Catholic mass organizations. Domestically, Obregón mixed coercion with negotiation. He also gave new impulse to land reform featuring *ejidos* that he imagined as individually held plots; he reduced the size of the army; and his government sponsored an ambitious educational program. In the process, the Sonorenses became part of a new revolutionary elite with significant entrepreneurial ambitions.

Chapter 6, "The Triangle Broken," analyzes the disintegration of the Sonorense group over the presidential succession. Calles enjoyed the support of popular organizations such as the CROM association of labor unions and self-styled southeastern Socialists. The civilian de la Huerta, who originally refused to challenge his friend, had support from much of the military and members of Congress who favored parliamentary over strongman rule. This conflict separated Obregón's inner circle (which also included Calles, Serrano, and Gómez) from de la Huerta and Alvarado. The resultant De la Huerta Rebellion involved a majority of the armed forces but ultimately failed due to its lack of unity and U.S. support for the Obregón administration. Espousing a worker-campesino platform, Calles won the election.

The seventh chapter, "On Trial before the World," argues that the Calles government consisted of one phase dedicated to reform and another devoted to crisis management. In its first eighteen months, the Calles administration fulfilled some of his promises to workers and campesinos, including stepped-up agrarian reform and laws that curtailed the privileges of foreign oil companies and landowners. At the same time, it built a financial infrastructure and intensified the country's rural education program. After June 1926 the conflict with the Catholic Church and an economic crisis sapped the administration's momentum. But its prominent opponents exiled in the United States, including de la Huerta, were never able to mount an insurgency. Despite strained relations, the U.S. and Mexican governments cooperated in keeping the Mexican opposition at bay.

Chapter 8, "Almost Porfirio," analyzes Obregón's decision to run for a second term, made amid the decline of his business emporium. It argues that Obregón's candidacy further destabilized the political landscape. It antagonized the candidates Serrano and Gómez, both of whom assailed it as a violation of the constitutional principle of no reelection. With rumors of an insurrection swirling, Mexican army officers killed Serrano in October 1927 and Gómez a month later. Obregón won another term, but on July 17, 1928, a Catholic activist assassinated the caudillo. Calles responded with a vow to end the era of strongman rule—which Obregón had personified—and usher in an era of institutions.

The ninth chapter, "From Caudillos to Institutions," traces the incipient transition from the direct rule of the Sonorenses to the authority of a new ruling party, the Partido Nacional Revolucionario (PNR). This transition featured Calles's status as the jefe máximo of the Mexican Revolution. This status was symbolic as well as substantive. While Calles played a significant role from behind the scenes, his sway was more limited than other historians have described. Presidents Emilio Portes Gil (1928–30) and Pascual Ortiz Rubio (1930–32) confronted the Great Depression and increasing political polarization, but only the latter faced constant interference from Calles, who became more conservative and called for an end to land redistributions. These administrations responded to the economic crisis with measures that indicated an incipient return to reform in other areas, including a federal labor law that implemented (at least in theory) protections for organized labor.

Chapter 10, "The End of an Era," continues along the same lines of argument in showing that the transition from Sonorismo to Cardenismo was more gradual than most historians have imagined. The final Sonorense administration under Rodríguez (1932–34) enshrined an agrarian code and a national minimum wage. The PNR approved a six-year plan that, like Franklin D. Roosevelt's New Deal in the United States, presented the state as an active agent of economic and social development. When Calles criticized the wave of strikes in Cárdenas's first year in office, the new president sidelined many of the remaining Callistas. In April 1936 Calles's exile to the United States ended the last vestiges of Sonorismo.

This book, then, focuses on influential men who steered the Mexican Revolution as what one historian has called a "patriarchal event."[57] Aiming to steer clear of the pitfalls of the "great man approach"—a myopic focus on the achievements of these male leaders—I use the group as a way to study Mexican political culture. A return to the scene in Mexico City after Obregón's arrival there illustrates this point.

On August 18, 1914, Obregón visited Madero's grave. In the company of congressional deputies who had once collaborated with Huerta, he beckoned the schoolteacher María Arias Bernal, an activist who had protected the grave from Huerta's henchmen. Obregón offered her his pistol and said, "There is no excuse for the men who could have carried a rifle and did not do so for fear of abandoning their homes. I abandoned my orphaned children, and as I admire valor, I cede my weapon to Señorita Arias, because she is the only one worthy of wielding it."[58] Obregón was not calling for female mobilization. Rather, he questioned the masculinity and patriotism of the congressional deputies. While Arias lived on in popular lore as "María Pistolas," the men from Sonora went on to win the Mexican Revolution, with Obregón as their caudillo.

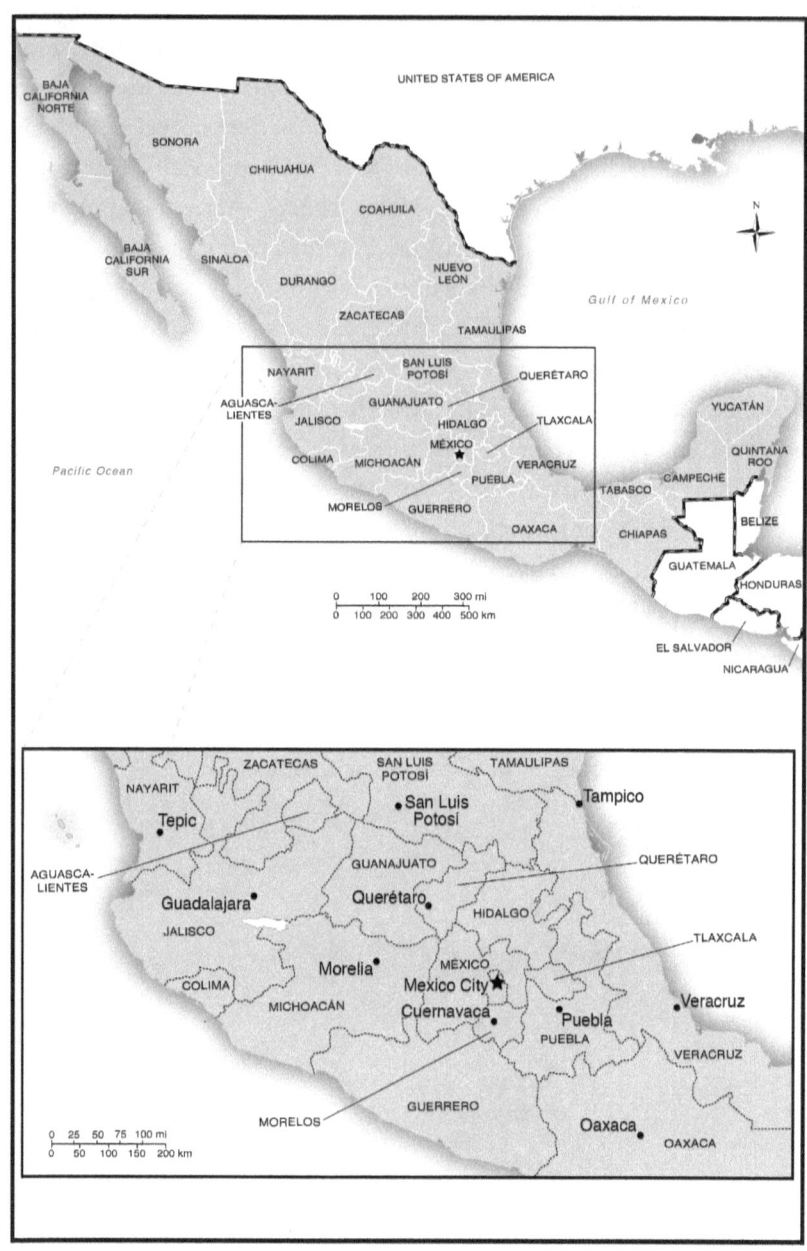

2. Mexican states and territories in 1935. Patrick Jones, UNC Charlotte Cartography Lab.

Part 1 ∻ The Sonorenses in the Revolution, 1910–1915

1 ∻ The Making of a Faction

Sonora is the state most distant from us.... [In] our national history, written in blood and tears, one will not find a single act ... that would reveal the least solidarity with our many pains and our few pleasures.... They ... never cried with us. —Federico Gamboa, 1923

The country's second-largest state, Sonora is geographically isolated within Mexico: from Baja California by the Sea of Cortez, and from Chihuahua by the towering Sierra Madre Mountains. The state features four distinct geographical regions: the mountains, the foothills, the Sonoran Desert, and a southern coastal stretch in the vicinity of the Yaqui and Mayo Rivers. Water—not land—is the most coveted resource. In the words of one historian, "Here, people know water because of thirst."[1] Within an arid climate, storms and torrential rainfalls have produced periodic floods that devastate swaths of farmland and even redirect the course of rivers. The Sonorenses knew a world of binaries: mountains and coast; sand and water; Indigenous and Spanish.[2]

Some would say that the Sonorenses came from a different region of the Americas than the rest of Mexico. In 1943 an archaeologist excluded the North from what he called Mesoamerica: an area he defined as the footprint of interconnected city-building Indigenous civilizations such as the Maya, Toltecs, and Mexica (Aztecs).[3] The idea of Mesoamerica suggests that central and southern Mexico share more commonalities with Central America than with the northern states. In the 1890s Matías Romero, the Mexican ambassador in Washington DC and a native of Oaxaca, labeled his nation a Central American state.[4] Indeed, Sonorans (and Baja Californians) appeared even more isolated from the rest of Mexico than their neighbors in the other border states. Witness the epigraph to this chapter by a famous novelist and former Porfirian diplomat who served with Vice President Ramón Corral, a native of Álamos.[5]

Both Gamboa and Romero exaggerated the gulf between the North and central Mexico, a gulf that was narrowing as new technologies connected the United States and Mexico as well as Mexican states to one another. The parents of the Sonorenses remembered a calamitous world of warfare, Indigenous revolts, U.S. land grabbing, and population decline—a frontier society structured primarily by armed individualism and the family unit. But the Second Industrial Revolution turned the frontier into a border, and political stability arrived in Sonora at long last in the 1880s. The Sonorenses therefore grew up in a rapidly modernizing region marked by some of the highest economic and demographic growth in Mexico. When the revolution came, some went to fight dictators and oppressors; and others went to defend their state.

A Frontier Society

On the eve of the Spanish conquest, the Northwest and the heartland were different indeed. Tenochtitlán, the capital of the Mexica Empire, featured some 150,000 inhabitants, and Emperor Moctezuma ruled over more than five hundred states with a population of at least five million people. The area that forms Sonora today included a population of no more than three hundred thousand. Many communities in the region's desert north and northwest, including the Pima, Seri, and Tohono O'odham, lived nomadic lives, following the water. In the south and east, where conditions permitted more intensive agriculture, the Mayo, Yaqui, and Ópata lived in small towns and villages. There were no Indigenous empires on the northwestern periphery.[6]

The Spaniards brought conquistadors and contagion. While building a new capital, Mexico City, upon the ruins of Tenochtitlán, they sent expeditions to the far north that reached Sonora in 1533. In search of seven legendary cities of gold, they failed to find mineral riches of the kind that the Mexica and Inca Empires had accumulated. The conquistadors made slow progress against fierce Native resistance. Just as they did in Mesoamerica, the conquistadors introduced Old World diseases such as smallpox. One estimate puts the resulting population decline in the Northwest at 90 percent, disrupting trade routes and depopulating many towns and villages.[7] By 1600 Spaniards referred to Indigenous communities as the ranchería people, due to the scattered settlements left after the epidemics.[8]

Amid this demographic crisis, the Jesuit order became the main agent of colonization west of the Sierra Madre. The Jesuits first founded missions in the fertile coastal stretch and then extended into the arid North and the mountains. They provided the kind of spatial and social organization that the Indigenous communities had lost as a result of the epidemics. Thus, the Yaqui and Jesuits struck a pact that lasted until the Yaqui revolt of 1740. Sensitive to local conditions, the Jesuits' Christian teachings also provided a salve (however imperfect) for the suffering. Unfortunately, the missions also served as a conduit for the further spread of disease.[9]

Settlers came on the trail of the mission system and brought the kinds of coercive labor systems that characterized the rest of New Spain. A conservative estimate counted approximately five hundred Spanish families by 1678.[10] The region got a name: in 1637, "Nueva Andalucía," and then in 1648, "Sonora." In 1691 Sonora combined with Sinaloa to form the Provincias de Sonora, Ostimuri y Sinaloa. There are a number of origin stories for the name. Two have "Sonora" as an adaptation of the word "Señora" (lady) that explorers used to name two rivers for female saints: "Nuestra Señora de Rosario," referring to the Yaqui River, or "Nuestra Señora de Angostura," referring to the Sonora River. According to legend, the local population did not pronounce the diacritic, and so "Señora" became "Senora" and then "Sonora." A third story refers to a cenote, or well, near present-day Huépac. According to an early eighteenth-century source, the Ópata community knew the place as "sonot," which Spaniards heard as "Sonora."[11]

The eighteenth-century Bourbon Reforms targeted northwestern New Spain in an effort to increase control and revenue generation from silver mining, which had begun in the 1680s near the southern town of Álamos. As part of these reforms, the Crown expelled the Jesuits in 1767. The expulsion left religious practice in the hands of lay leaders, and particularly women, in what one historian has called "Christianity without priests."[12] Popular religiosity was especially strong among the Yaqui, who referred to themselves as Pascua Hiaki (Easter People). The Crown also mounted a concerted attempt to secure greater control over the empire's contested frontiers. The Apaches posed a formidable threat. In 1680 they had begun to launch periodic raids from their base near the Gila River, prompting the building of the first *presidio* (fort) in 1692, followed by many others throughout the Northwest. The Crown invited military colonists, offering them as much land as they could defend. The Bourbons also promoted mining and the construction of urban centers (including Guaymas, the state's principal port), as well as an administrative bureaucracy that tied Sonora more closely to the viceroyalty. The reforms and the silver boom spurred immigration from northern and eastern Spain. Between 1750 and 1830 the population increased from ninety to two hundred thousand.[13] Economic growth highlighted deep social inequalities, as elsewhere in New Spain. Wrote the Prussian adventurer, Alexander von Humboldt, "Mexico is the country of inequality. Nowhere does there exist such a fearful difference in the distribution of fortune, civilization, cultivation of the soil and population."[14]

While the devastating Wars of Independence (1810–21) barely touched Sonora, their aftermath threw it into prolonged chaos. Most of the settler elite (a group known as the notables) had sided with the Crown, except for the faction of the insurgent José María González Hermosillo. Independence brought warfare and instability, due in part to the disintegration of the presidio system. Mirroring events in central Mexico, the region witnessed incessant strife between Centralists and Federalists. Sonora y Sinaloa broke apart, and the state capital relocated from Ures to Álamos to Hermosillo to Arizpe back to Ures.[15] Sonora then suffered the consequences of the war with the United States (1846–48). The state lost territory in the Treaty of Guadalupe Hidalgo and then again in the Gadsden Purchase (1853). After the war U.S. freebooters tried to seize more land, attacking Guaymas and other towns.[16] After a brief respite under Liberal governor Ignacio Pesqueira, French troops invaded as part of their support for the Austrian-born emperor Maximilian. The French Intervention (1861–67) prompted expressions of a distinct regional identity. As one newspaper exclaimed, "Sonorans, we do not have among us cowards as do the corrupt cities of the center of the republic."[17] Yet Pesqueira's rivals eagerly collaborated with Maximilian, for example, the business partner of one Francisco Obregón, whose youngest son would figure as one of the protagonists of this story.[18] From 1830 to 1869 Sonora's population declined by half.[19]

The years of chaos witnessed growing conflict with Indigenous communities. For example, in the north, Apache raids kept the local population on high alert. In the south, the Yaqui opposed the obligation to pay taxes after the constitution adopted in 1824 had ended the colonial *fueros* (the special legal status of the church, army, and Indigenous communities). In 1828 they launched a rebellion aiming to unite the state's Indigenous peoples. Like other Indigenous communities, they supported Maximilian against the Pesqueiras and President Juárez—a Zapotec whose government had put Indigenous land at risk by means of legislation favoring private landholdings. In 1868 the victorious Liberals exacted revenge in the form of a massacre of 120 Yaqui inside a church. The Yaqui kept on fighting under the leadership of José María Leyva, also known as Cajemé, who had won Pesqueira's trust after fighting the empire as a member of the army. In 1872 Pesqueira named him *alcalde mayor* (regional magistrate). But Cajemé led the Yaqui into rebellion once again, establishing control over much of the coastal stretch. In 1882 the Mayo joined this revolt.[20]

On the other side stood the Yori, a contemptuous Yaqui term for "outsiders."[21] Like *ladino* in Chiapas and Guatemala, Yori stands for a Westernized, Spanish-speaking individual. The Yori united in their rejection of Indigenous culture and communal patters of landownership. However, they were a diverse group, including creoles, mestizos, and acculturated Indigenous people, as well as members of different social classes. The middle-class and poor majority featured a large number of fluid and often insecure families. Approximately one in six children was born out of wedlock. Warfare and the departure of thousands of men during the California gold rush left a large number of households headed by women, especially in northern Sonora, where their share of the adult population exceeded 70 percent in some places. Many of these women served as merchants, moneylenders, and faith leaders.[22] The notable class—many of them descendants of Spanish immigrants who had come to the Northwest in the eighteenth century—concentrated in the urban centers, from where they dominated state politics and the economy. Familism, defined as "the hegemony of the family in the positioning of oneself with regard to a conflict or to defend one's interests," structured their world.[23]

Friendship networks and familism served as organizing principles in a Hobbesian world in which powerful clans pursued their objectives. In the words of one historian, deep friendships "played a foundational role in the regional development of a ... remarkably nuanced, fragile, and sporadic form of civil society."[24] Kinship networks controlling food production worked through both family and friendship ties to govern their communities, often with brute force carried out by their armed retainers. Their aims included ruthless tactics: "faits accomplis, the idea of lawful killing, the desire for plunder,... [and] the de facto occupation—without legal titles—of the assets of disappeared or annihilated Indians, missions, and neighbors."[25]

Many Yori considered themselves white and were regarded as such by outsiders. By the time of the revolution, Sonora's share of inhabitants who constructed their identity as "white" far exceeded the national average. In the 1921 census 59 percent self-identified as mestizo, 29 percent as Indigenous, and 10 percent as white.[26] In Sonora 43 percent listed themselves as white, 41 percent as mestizo, 14 percent as Indigenous, and 2 percent as foreign.[27] Obregón was often described as white. Consider, for example, Spanish novelist Blasco Ibáñez's description:

> It would be ... erroneous to imagine him as a Mexican chieftain of the type which we so frequently see in the movies ... a copper-colored personage with slanting eyes and thick, stiff hair, sharp as an awl; in short, an Indian dressed up like a comic-opera General. Obregón is nothing of the sort; he is white, so positively white that it is difficult to conceive his having a single drop of Indian blood in his veins. He is so distinctively Spanish that he could walk in the streets of Madrid without any one guessing that he hailed from the American hemisphere.[28]

Or witness the testimony of Eduardo Iturbide, prefect of Mexico City under the Huerta dictatorship and a distant relative of Emperor Agustín de Iturbide (1822–23). In his words, Obregón "resembled one of Cortés's conquistadors more so than a mestizo, and his physiognomy did not reveal any evidence of indigenous ancestry."[29] These assertions stand out when compared to depictions of Calles, whom many Mexicans called "Turk," "Jew," and "Arab" despite the lack of any evidence of his descent from the eastern Mediterranean, or de la Huerta, whose Yaqui ancestry on his grandmother's side led another Sonorense to describe him as *moreno* (dark).[30]

Landowning Yori often practiced endogamy in order to preserve their status in an existence often only one bad harvest, drought, or flood away from financial ruin. Endogamy included marriages between relatives, including first cousins, as well as the practice of two close relatives marrying two members of a different family. Other unions strategically linked important families: for example, the Obregóns and the Hills were related through the Salido clan. Later on, marriages connected the Obregóns to the Elías Calleses and the Serranos, as well as Arnulfo R. Gómez to the Elías family.[31] The notables ruled through firearms rather than institutions and laws. Their actions reflected a defense of their livelihoods and privileges in a rough-and-tumble world, as well as a focus on local rather than national politics. This world changed beginning in 1876 with the growth of a strong central state under General Porfirio Díaz. The changes wrought during the Porfiriato proved to be important formative experiences for the men who would lead the Sonoran variant of the Mexican Revolution.

The Old Regime in Sonora

The Porfiriato brought a neo-Bourbon effort to centralize power and secure borders and the development of the national economy in concert with the industrializing economies of the North Atlantic. As a result, the erstwhile frontier became a rapidly transforming border region.[32] Until the turn of the century, this transformation brought benefits to many middle-class and notable Sonorense families, including several of the protagonists in this story. After 1905 the crisis of the Porfiriato turned some—but, crucially, not all—Sonorenses against the regime.

The leadership style of the principal protagonist, General Porfirio Díaz Mori, would leave a lasting impression on the Sonorenses. Díaz was born into a poor family in Oaxaca City on September 15, 1830, to a creole father and mestiza mother. He trained for the priesthood but left the seminary to offer his services to the army at the outset of the war with the United States. After a term of service during which he did not see any action, he studied law and began a close association with then-governor Benito Juárez. After Juárez's accession to the presidency, Díaz proved his abilities as a military leader during the Wars of Reform and the French Intervention. He led his troops to victory in the first Battle of Puebla on May 5, 1862, an event his regime later commemorated on what is still known as Cinco de Mayo. His victory in the final Battle of Puebla (1867) sealed Emperor Maximilian's fate and made Díaz the nation's most powerful military leader. Over the next nine years, Díaz angled for power, portraying himself as a rustic outsider opposed to urban elites. He claimed fraud after Juárez's reelection in 1871 and launched an unsuccessful rebellion. After Juárez's death in 1872, Sebastián Lerdo de Tejada became the new president and, in 1876, sought reelection, just as Juárez had done. Díaz proclaimed an uprising under the motto of "effective suffrage, no reelection." In November 1876 his forces took Mexico City. True to his motto, Díaz allowed a confidant, Manuel González, to succeed him after his first term. But after returning to power in 1884, he held on to it until the revolution.[33]

The longevity of the Díaz regime rested upon three strategies. First, it managed to end the bitter rivalry between the nation's main political camps as well as within the Liberal Party. Díaz blended the Conservative quest for order with the Liberal zeal for economic development and foreign investment capital, and he mended fences with the Catholic Church. His marriage to Carmen Romero Rubio—his English tutor thirty-four years his junior—forged kinship ties to the Lerdo clan, which had opposed his seizure of power. Second, the regime understood the importance of infrastructure for political centralization and the production of commodities as the Second Industrial Revolution picked up steam in the United States. Third, Díaz believed that foreign investment could forestall future annexations. Although he allegedly once exclaimed, "Poor Mexico, so far from God and so close to the United States," he viewed trade as the best strategy to prevent further land grabbing. Sure enough, the "American colony" in Mexico grew in symbiosis with the Porfiriato and often advocated for it in Washington DC.[34] Sonora and the other border states played a crucial role in this strategy. As the railroad made neighboring Arizona accessible by train, the resultant population growth of a once-remote territory brought more U.S. visitors to Sonora. Border posts such as Nogales grew into towns on both sides of the line.[35]

The Porfirians wrought a realignment in Sonoran politics. At the national level, they transitioned the government from Liberal machine politics to the rule of one man. Conversely, in Sonora, they constructed a political machine after the disintegration of Pesqueira's rule. In 1875 Pesqueira had attempted to set the stage for his son José to succeed him. The resultant outrage among the notables finally forced him out of power.[36]

In 1879 General Luis E. Torres began the first of four terms as governor but never achieved the dominance that Pesqueira had enjoyed. Along with Rafael Izábal and Ramón Corral, Torres formed part of a triumvirate that dominated state politics.[37] Corral alone was a native of the state, although Izábal's mother, Dolores Salido, hailed from one of the most prominent notable families. Likewise, Díaz's man in Chihuahua, Luis Terrazas, was the son of a wealthy butcher who also came from outside his state's elite. But while Chihuahua featured an enormous concentration of wealth and power in the Terrazas-Creel clan, the elite in Sonora remained divided.[38]

The Porfiriato also effected changes further down the political ladder, and especially with regard to the district prefects, or *jefes políticos*. Since independence, the prefects had served as crucial intermediaries between the state government and the municipalities.[39] The Liberal Reform of the 1850s had made the prefectures elective positions, but the Porfirians restored the state governors' power to appoint these officials. The prefecture became a "midget dictatorship" dependent on the national and state governments but also powerful in its own right.[40] In charge of public order and public lands, the prefects played a crucial role in the Porfirian project. Farthest down the line were the *jefes municipales*, local bosses caught between elected councils and the dictates from prefects, governors, and the national government. It was at the local level that the Sonorenses would gain firsthand experience with the Díaz regime.[41]

The Porfirian project entailed the repression of the state's Indigenous communities. In 1885 the Yori crushed Cajemé's semiautonomous state and opened the Yaqui Valley to commercial farming.[42] During this war, Corral earned a reputation as a brutal oppressor. After Cajemé's execution in 1887, the new Yaqui chief, Tetabiate, led an intermittent guerrilla war until his death in battle in 1901. The failure of these wars of resistance ultimately led to a split strategy, as *bronco* (or "wild") Yaqui continued to fight for their ancestral lands via guerrilla tactics, while *manso* (or "tame") Yaqui sought accommodation.[43] The Mayo also opposed Yori encroachments while irrigation techniques turned the Mayo Valley into a thriving agricultural region. At the same time that the triumvirate asserted control over the south, it also confronted the Apaches in the north. As the Yaqui with Cajemé, the Apaches had a formidable leader in Gerónimo. They suffered devastating defeats at the hands of the U.S. and Mexican armies, and in 1886, Gerónimo gave himself up and spent the rest of his life in confinement or under government supervision in the United States.[44]

The defeat of Sonora's Indigenous communities facilitated the flow of foreign investment, helping economic growth that doubled state revenue per capita between 1888 and 1907. Foreign investment funded railroads. For example, the Southern Pacific Railroad connected Arizona to Guaymas and then to Sinaloa, although the line did not link up with the nation's central railway system until the 1920s. In the Northeast, U.S.-financed copper mining provided 30 percent of the copper used for the electrification of the United States. By the early 1900s Cananea had become the state's largest city, a company town of William Greene's Cananea Consolidated Copper Company (CCCC), with fifteen thousand inhabitants. J. P. Morgan and the Guggenheims also invested in mining properties. In a cautionary tale, the Sinaloa and Sonora Land Irrigation Company obtained a wide-ranging concession for railroad building and irrigation in the Yaqui Valley. In 1904 the Compañía Constructora Richardson acquired the irrigation rights after the bankruptcy of that company. The Richardson failed to meet the promised targets and exacerbated the conflict with the Yaqui, whose lands formed part of the concession. All of these companies took advantage of generous tax exemptions offered to foreign capital.[45]

Closer relations with the world market also brought new opportunities for small entrepreneurs and a burgeoning middle class. For example, the production of garbanzo (chickpeas), wheat, and tomatoes burgeoned during the first decade of the 1900s. The farming boom created ancillary opportunities for lawyers, teachers, doctors, distillers, and bankers. Like the landowning elite, the middle classes professed a secular outlook. Commercial activity contributed to the growth of a Masonic movement. For example, in 1897 one Guaymas newspaper published the Masonic Code on its front page in defiance of the bishop.[46] Calles, a son of that city, most likely became a Mason during those years.

Economic growth led to a population boom: from 1871 to 1910 the population increased from 108,000 to 265,000. Better sanitary conditions reduced the incidence of cholera and other diseases, and railroad building, copper mining, and intensive agriculture encouraged national and international migration.[47] The burgeoning Chinese population was a case in point. The 1910 census estimated the Chinese community in Sonora at 4,486 individuals—by far the largest foreign community, ahead of the combined total of U.S. citizens (3,164), Spaniards (259), and Germans (183). Engaged in money lending, trading, and many other professions, the Chinese became targets of xenophobia.[48]

An expansion of primary education followed on the heels of economic and demographic growth. Public education brought the positivist ideas espoused by the *científico* (scientist) faction. The científicos were a group of some twenty educated individuals close to Díaz who enjoyed a near-monopoly on the most important political positions and obtained great wealth as a result. They viewed politics from the vantage point of outcomes rather than process. In their minds, meaningful reform came from above, dispensed by those with power and knowledge. Sharing the hegemonic faith in modernity common among Latin American elites at that time, Porfirian Sonora saw the Yaqui as impediments to modernization, redeemable only by education in the Yori culture.[49] By 1910 Sonora numbered among the most literate states in Mexico. Official (inflated) figures estimated literacy at 46 percent overall and 44 percent for women, compared to 28 and 24 percent nationally and 30 and 29 percent in Sinaloa.[50] High school education became available upon Corral's inauguration of the Colegio de Sonora in 1889, although university education did not arrive until 1942. Many affluent Sonorans sent their offspring to boarding schools in California.[51]

The Porfirian transformation benefited several of the leaders whom we will introduce in detail in the succeeding sections. In particular, the repression of Indigenous communities in the south provided agricultural opportunities to Álvaro Obregón, Benjamín G. Hill, and Francisco R. Serrano. Salvador Alvarado and Manuel M. Diéguez found employment in the boom town of Cananea. However, some struggled even in the boom years. After high school in Mexico City, Adolfo de la Huerta took over the administration of the family store in Guaymas, which went bankrupt in 1906. A trained schoolteacher, Plutarco Elías Calles failed in his attempt to farm his family's lands in the northeast. And Ignacio L. Pesqueira found himself among the "outs" after the ouster of his clan from the governorship.[52]

De la Huerta's and Calles's travails mirrored the crisis of the Porfirian program after 1900. A steep drop in the price of silver and copper produced a sharp economic contraction, illustrating the disadvantages of an economic model that relied on globalization. The contraction highlighted the overweening role of foreigners in the economy. Taking advantage of plummeting land prices, foreign-owned companies gobbled up usable land: the Richardson owned more than 230,000 hectares in the Yaqui Valley and William Greene controlled 500,000 hectares of pasture land and forest in the northeast. In fact, Calles only undertook his unsuccessful foray into farming because he worried about losing fallow properties to the Cananea Cattle Company, the agricultural arm of the CCCC.[53] Generally speaking, then, the Porfirians and their foreign allies diminished the economic opportunities of the ascendant middle class.[54]

The economic crisis led to harsh tactics that rank among the worst abuses of the Old Regime. To simultaneously break Yaqui resistance and furnish cheap labor to export economies in the Southeast, the government removed fifteen thousand Yaqui (or half of the population) to tobacco plantations in Valle Nacional, Oaxaca, and henequen-growing estates in Yucatán. An Indigenous population that had constituted one-fourth of Sonora's inhabitants in 1840 only made up approximately 6 percent in 1910.[55] Another example was the bloody suppression of a strike in Cananea. The CCCC's foreign-born workers received higher wages than Mexicans for performing the same work. In June 1906 miners struck for better wages and working conditions. Federal troops and Arizona Rangers—the latter acting as "volunteers"—helped crush the strike only a day's ride away from the U.S. border.[56] This strike showed the influence of the anarcho-syndicalist Partido Liberal Mexicano. Opposed to both capitalism and authoritarianism, the party found adherents among the cosmopolitan workforce in the mines. Its newspaper, *La Regeneración*, was one of the few publications widely available in the Northwest, and most literate Sonorans read it on a regular basis. *La Regeneración* spread news of the strike and the U.S. role in suppressing it.

By 1910 the Sonoran triumvirate and its associates had acquired the reputation of a sclerotic and authoritarian group of leaders. As in other states, the Porfirians monopolized political power, choking off challenges from the Pesqueiras and other notable clans. These clans bided their time, waiting for their opportunity. After three decades in which the triumvirate had held the state in a tight grip, an opposition alliance emerged under the leadership of a landowner directly affected by the Yaqui deportations.

The Sonorenses and the Revolution

As the only city in Sonora that enjoyed connections to central Mexico via its port, Guaymas harbored opponents to the Díaz regime familiar with the national political scene. In particular, it served as the home base of the patriarch of the opposition: José María "Pepe" Maytorena Tapia (1867–1948). Educated at Santa Clara College in California, Maytorena descended from a prominent notable family. His father had unsuccessfully challenged the Porfirians in the 1887 gubernatorial elections, costing the family its political influence but not its wealth. The Yaqui removal robbed the clan of cheap labor, and Don Pepe sheltered fugitive Yaqui from the authorities.[57]

Like other disenchanted northern leaders, Maytorena first joined the circle of General Bernardo Reyes, the modernizing governor of Nuevo León. During Reyes's long tenure, Monterrey transformed into an industrial city, home to a steel foundry and a major brewery. By 1900 he and his allies, equally authoritarian and hungry for a share of power at the national level, had become the principal rivals of the científico faction. Following the publication of Díaz's interview with U.S. journalist James Creelman, in which the dictator promised to step aside in 1910, Reyes set his sights on the vice presidency then occupied by Corral. To build support in Sonora, Reyes had his eldest son, Rodolfo, approach Don Pepe. As Rodolfo Reyes wrote to Maytorena, the triumvirate's selfish pursuits undermined Díaz. The message was that the elder Reyes would be a better Porfirian than Corral. Reyes represented hope for Maytorena and other notables who desired to open up the encrusted political scene while preserving existing socioeconomic structures. In 1909 Maytorena helped found the Club Reyista of Guaymas. However, Díaz reversed course, kept Corral on his ticket for the elections, and sent Reyes on diplomatic assignment.[58]

Reyes's departure opened the door for Francisco I. Madero, another northern landowner frustrated by Porfirian tactics but less willing to accept repressive methods. His family had benefited from a cotton boom facilitated by irrigation and also held stakes in ranching, mining, banking, and many other ventures. Madero witnessed Reyes's violent crushing of a demonstration in Monterrey. He resented the preferential oil and mining concessions, which involved tax breaks unavailable to Mexican entrepreneurs. His Spiritist faith made him look upon his nation as a human body sickened by the Díaz system. His book, *La sucesión presidencial de 1910* (The presidential succession of 1910), identified several symptoms. Above all, Madero hailed the principle of "effective suffrage, no reelection," espoused by none other than Díaz himself in 1876. Hence his followers became known as "anti-reelectionists." He also cited the Yaqui deportations and the bloody suppression of the Cananea strike. The book announced the creation of an opposition party.[59] In January 1910 Madero received an enthusiastic reception in Guaymas, one of many stops on a nationwide campaign tour.

The successful Madero visit edged Maytorena toward the opposition to Díaz. With Rodolfo Reyes's endorsement, Maytorena formed an anti-reelectionist club from among the remnants of the Reyes club. But he remained careful not to antagonize Díaz and declined Madero's invitation to run for governor on the anti-reelectionist platform. Díaz validated this caution when he had Madero thrown in jail and coasted to reelection. On November 20, 1910, Madero's Plan de San Luis Potosí—issued from exile in San Antonio—called for Díaz's overthrow. This step formally began the Mexican Revolution, focused initially on the dictator's removal and the holding of free elections. From Nogales, Arizona, Maytorena directed the Junta Revolucionaria, a state government in waiting.[60]

Sonora saw only sporadic fighting compared to Chihuahua and Morelos, where rebel forces mobilized among the poor rural population. In Chihuahua the former mule skinner Pascual Orozco gathered an impromptu army composed of small farmers and sharecroppers. South of Mexico City Emiliano Zapata called upon the Indigenous population to revolt. These rough-hewn rebels taxed Maytorena's upper-class sensibilities. Witness Orozco's famous message to Díaz that accompanied the uniforms of federal soldiers killed in an ambush: "Here are your wrappings. Send me more tamales!"[61]

True to form, from Arizona Maytorena focused on administrative matters and only ordered military action as a preventive measure against the Orozquistas, who had set up a separate rebel nucleus in the district of

Sahuaripa in eastern Sonora. Wary of connections with lower-class rebels from Chihuahua, he approached Salvador Alvarado and Juan G. Cabral, leaders of a rebel group in Cananea. While these forces ostensibly supported Madero, Maytorena intended to use them to remove the Orozquistas. After rebels carried out sporadic attacks without his authorization, he belatedly heeded the call to coordinate the uprising. Maytorena's Plan de Caborca of April 11 limited itself to supporting the goal of "no reelection, effective suffrage."[62]

Another elite opponent of the Díaz regime was Ignacio Leandro Pesqueira Gallego. Born March 13, 1867, in the northeastern town of Huépac, he was the same age as Maytorena and also—as the nephew of the famed Juarista strongman Ignacio Pesqueira—a member of a clan identified with the Liberal Party. Both the Maytorenas and the Pesqueiras shared adverse experiences with the Sonoran triumvirate and Porfirian politics more generally, but they also had specific grievances. While the forced removal of the Yaqui reduced the Maytorenas' labor supply, the Pesqueiras lost land to the Cananea Cattle Company. Pesqueira grew up in Cananea, where he worked as a mining agent. In 1907 he became a *regidor* (alderman) of that city. He had also experimented with gold mining, but his small mine ceased operations in 1906. Pesqueira joined the anti-reelectionist movement in late 1909.[63]

Yet another rebel in favor of the social and economic status quo was Benjamín Guillermo Hill Pozos. Hill was the grandson of a doctor in the U.S. Confederate army; he was also Obregón's cousin once removed on his grandmother's side. Born in Choix, Sinaloa, on March 31, 1874, Hill completed his secondary education in Hermosillo before embarking on a trip to Austria, Germany, and Italy, where he enrolled in a military academy and pursued his interests in music and adventure. He also won the affections of an Italian countess and took her to the Yaqui Valley, where she passed away during childbirth. Hill then married a farmer's daughter from the Mayo Valley and acquired the four-hundred-hectare hacienda of Mochibampo near Navojoa. He did well for himself by growing wheat—a staple in high demand during a time of rapid population growth. Due to the success of his agribusiness, the size of his holdings increased sixfold, and Hill became a *síndico*, the judicial representative of the municipality of Navojoa. This position gave him significant influence over the allocation of the water supply. In 1909 Hill won election as regidor of Navojoa.⁶⁴

As someone with a cosmopolitan mindset, Hill turned against Díaz despite his own privilege. In 1908 he published a letter in a Mexico City newspaper calling for free elections and new office holders at the level of president, vice president, and all governorships. Hill demanded "an influx of new blood to replace the stagnant blood which, existing in the veins of the Republic, has fallen ill with doddering old fools, no doubt for the most part honorable relics of the past, but now mummies which effectively hinder the march of our progress."⁶⁵ He became one of Madero's earliest adherents in Sonora, accompanying him on his tour in January 1910 and founding anti-reelectionist clubs in Álamos and Nogales. One of Madero's companions described Hill as "robust, muscular, energetic, and of high intelligence" and also commented upon his "atheist philosophy" and rebellious spirit.⁶⁶ The Porfirians imprisoned Hill in Hermosillo until the rebels freed him in April 1911. Due to his military training, Maytorena named him *jefe de operaciones* (zone commander) in the south of Sonora.

Maytorena's, Pesqueira's, and Hill's commitment to the socioeconomic status quo contrasted with the sentiments of many other Sonorense insurgents. Adolfo de la Huerta, Salvador Alvarado, Manuel M. Diéguez, Francisco R. Serrano, and Arnulfo R. Gómez came from lower- and middle-class origins. Influenced by various degrees by the anarcho-syndicalism of the Flores Magón brothers, they viewed the rebellion as the first step in a struggle for economic and social reforms.

Felipe Adolfo de la Huerta Marcor was born on May 26, 1881, in Guaymas. His father, Torcuato de la Huerta, was a well-to-do shopkeeper. The son of a Yaqui mother and a Spanish father, Torcuato maintained excellent relations with the Yaqui community. His mother, Carmen Marcor, also came from a merchant family. Helped by his privileged background, de la Huerta grew up as one of the few Sonorans with a high school education, and his brother studied in Europe. Adolfo studied accounting, violin, and singing at the Escuela Nacional Preparatoria (ENP) in Mexico City. Despite this immersion in the elite, de la Huerta retained a genuine concern with the Yaqui and Indigenous Mexicans in general. Other Sonorenses later made light of his heritage: Obregón referred to his children as *yaquesitos*, or "little Yaqui."⁶⁷

In 1900 de la Huerta returned to administer the family store after his father's death, a position he held until its bankruptcy six years later. He then worked as an accountant at a local bank, followed by a job as the administrator of a tannery in the vicinity of the city. De la Huerta was a critic of the Porfirian social and economic system. At least early on, he called himself a Socialist. In 1906 he became a member of the Partido Liberal Mexicano and subsidized *La Regeneración*. His musical abilities made him a popular guest at local groups opposed to the Díaz regime. De la Huerta joined Guaymas's anti-reelectionist club and served as its secretary. The group assembled in a building managed by Plutarco Elías Calles, whom he had met in secondary school in Hermosillo. After the outbreak of the revolution, the man who came to be known as "Fito" (for the diminutive, Adolfito) joined Maytorena's Junta Revolucionaria and worked as its chief liaison to other Maderista groups, thus showing his skill as a negotiator.[68]

Salvador Alvarado Rubio was born in Culiacán, Sinaloa, on September 16, 1880, and moved to Sonora at the age of eight. According to his birth certificate, his parents were unmarried when he was born, although Alvarado's marriage certificate states the opposite. The son of a dry cleaner, Alvarado grew up in Pótam near the Yaqui River and became a pharmacist's assistant and small merchant. Like de la Huerta, whom he met in nearby Guaymas, Alvarado called himself a Socialist. He experienced the Cananea strike as a shopkeeper in the city. In July 1910 Alvarado and several others gathered arms and ammunition for a planned uprising in Cananea. However, one of the collaborators betrayed the group, and Alvarado and the other leaders fled to Arizona. In November, he and Cabral launched their first sortie across the border, and in December, his men attacked the army headquarters in Hermosillo—one of the first revolutionary acts in the state.[69]

Manuel Macario Diéguez Lara was born on March 10, 1874, into a lower middle-class family in Guadalajara. His father was a notary, a job that paid so little that he supplemented his income by peddling. After elementary school, Diéguez moved to Mazatlán, Sinaloa, to work as a day laborer and carpenter. In 1897 his service on the military transport *Oaxaca* brought him to Guaymas. In 1901 he began work at the Cananea mine, rising to the position of assistant to the paymaster. Diéguez developed close ties

The Making of a Faction 37

with Alvarado in the local chapter of the Partido Liberal Mexicano. A few months before the strike, he founded the Unión Liberal Humana, an association dedicated to advocacy for the mine workers. As one of the foremost strike leaders, he received a fifteen-year prison sentence for his role. The Maderistas freed him from prison in Nogales upon their capture of the town in April 1911.[70]

Francisco Roque Serrano Barbeytia was born on Rancho de Santa Ana, Sinaloa, on August 16, 1889. His large, poor family moved to Huatabampo in the Mayo Valley in 1894. Eight years later, "Pancho" moved back to Sinaloa to learn accounting from one of his father's friends, who introduced him to the anarchist writings of Peter Kropotkin. In 1904 he began the first of a number of jobs along the Sonora-Sinaloa border. Serrano turned against the Old Regime early on. In 1907, barely eighteen years old, he authored a letter published in a local newspaper that opposed the reelection of Sinaloa's Porfirian governor, an action that landed him in jail. But the governor released him after a brief interview with the young oppositionist, impressed with his courage. The following year, Serrano began working for the Southern Pacific Railroad as a construction worker. In 1910 he joined an anti-reelectionist club in Navojoa and followed its lead into the uprising. After Díaz's fall, he served as Maytorena's private secretary.[71]

We know little about the origins of Arnulfo R. Gómez, the youngest of the Sonoran Maderistas. He was born in Navojoa on April 3, 1890. Like Cabral and Diéguez, he worked in the Cananea mine in 1906 and participated in the strike, but at sixteen years of age, he did not have a leadership position. Along with his brother, Gómez participated in the fight against the Díaz regime as a member of Maytorena's forces. He gained a reputation for faithfully carrying out his commands, as well as plaudits for his sobriety.[72]

The Sonorenses ultimately played only a minor role in the war. Acting against Madero's orders, Orozco's forces captured the border town of Ciudad Juárez on May 10, and the Zapatistas took Cuautla, Morelos, nine days later. Díaz resigned on May 21. The Porfirians exacted a high price for their surrender, however, as the treaty ensured the survival of the Federales while ordering the disarmament of the rebels. Interim president Francisco León de la Barra scheduled nationwide elections for October.[73]

Nonetheless, this diverse cast of characters took advantage of the political opening that the demise of the Díaz regime provided. Some ran for office, and others sought to further nascent military careers. In the July 1911 statewide elections, Maytorena won the race for governor and de la Huerta, a seat in the state Congress. Diéguez became mayor of Cananea, and Hill won appointment as prefect of Álamos.[74] These rebels had been united in their opposition to the Díaz regime and shared a commitment to representative government, but they held widely divergent views of the future. This divergence presaged the group's later fragmentation, but for now, Maytorena rewarded them for their participation in the revolution. He defied Madero in not disarming the rebels, instead integrating them in a "Sección de Guerra" under the governor's command.[75]

The Defense of State Sovereignty

The new regime disappointed. Madero won election as president but did not fulfill expectations, in part due to his timid leadership and in part due to the terms of the Treaty of Ciudad Juárez. His order to the rebel forces to lay down their arms incited a wave of protests. Madero also temporized on the issue of land reform. Furious, Zapata declared himself in revolt within six weeks of the president's inauguration. His Plan de Ayala called for Madero's overthrow and a land reform program that would return hacienda lands to the dispossessed. Madero sent the federal army back to Morelos, where it employed the harsh tactics of the Díaz regime until a former Porfirian general, Felipe Ángeles, took over military operations in August 1912. Ángeles employed the carrot and the stick. He offered an amnesty to rebels willing to lay down their arms but meted out harsh punishment to those who did not. Other former rebels kept their arms and contributed to a spree of banditry not seen since the early 1870s.[76]

In Sonora, Maytorena was equally reluctant to undertake meaningful social reform. Although he inherited a state where the interim government had successfully disarmed the rebels, high debt and a revenue shortfall limited his ability to address economic and social problems. Like Madero, Maytorena thus focused on political and judicial matters, especially electoral reform and the independence of the judicial branch. The governor also inaugurated a modest education program.[77] The state government offered scant recompense to the veterans of the uprising.

3. Maytorena, Madero, and other Maderistas. Fideicomiso Archivos Plutarco Elías Calles y Fernando Torreblanca (FAPECFT), Fototeca Colección de Álbumes Fotográficos de los Archivos Plutarco Elías Calles y Fernando Torreblanca, Fondo Plutarco Elías Calles, álbum 60, *Recuerdos de Agua Prieta, Sonora, 1910–1915*, fotografía 2, inventario 139. Used with permission.

Like the president, Maytorena used force to defend entrenched interests, authorizing municipal authorities to suppress mine-worker strikes. This professed ally of the Yaqui did not make progress on land reform, which Madero had promised Yaqui leaders in a meeting in August 1911.[78] Madero's offer of fifty privately owned hectares for each head of household fell short. The Yaqui demanded full autonomy, communal ownership of land, and the removal of the Yori. In a letter to Madero, Maytorena labeled the demands "impossible to achieve." In another letter, to de la Barra, he called the Yaqui "natural thieves."[79] In two respects, however, Don Pepe's accomplishments were more impressive than Madero's, simply by virtue of his ruling over a state distant from Mexico City. The state maintained its own military forces under the Sección de Guerra, and Maytorena also replaced the Porfirian bureaucracy in the state government.[80]

Just when the new order appeared caught between the vestiges of the Old Regime and the unfulfilled expectations of the insurgents, a threat from outside united the Yori. In March 1912 Orozco, who had vainly hoped to be rewarded with a plum government position, called for another revolt. His Plan de la Empacadora disavowed Madero's government, abolished the prefectures, and called for the restitution of illegally acquired hacienda land. Supported by wealthy landowner Luis Terrazas yet composed largely of lower-class troops, a rebel force of six thousand dealt the Federales a crushing defeat. Exasperated, Madero sent his best military leader into the field: General Victoriano Huerta, a Porfirian career officer from a poor Huichol family in Jalisco. Huerta did not make much progress, either, and the violence spilled over into Sonora.[81]

Maytorena considered this an "invasion" of his state, and indeed, there may have been as many as four thousand Orozquistas involved, although many of them were local converts to the cause rather than invaders from Chihuahua.[82] Through the Sección de Guerra, the state government commissioned local governments to put together state-sponsored militia forces. The result was the recruitment of Álvaro Obregón and Plutarco Elías Calles, men who had not fought in Madero's revolution. Obregón and Calles deserve an extended introduction due to their later emergence as the primary patriarchs of the Sonorense group.

Álvaro Obregón Salido was born on February 17, 1880, on a farm in the Mayo Valley. His mother descended from one of Sonora's wealthiest families, the Salidos, through whom he was related to Hill and the Porfirista Rafael Izábal. His father had once been a prominent landowner associated with a supporter of Emperor Maximilian with whom he jointly held properties in Cuernavaca and Mexico City. In 1867 the Juárez government impounded these properties. The senior Obregón died when Álvaro was an infant, and a few years later, flooding destroyed Siquisiva, the family's last remaining farm. Obregón grew up poor as the youngest of eighteen children in Huatabampo, upriver from Siquisiva. He was self-taught and spoke Mayo; later on, he learned some Yaqui as well. In 1906, after working as an agricultural mechanic on his maternal uncles' properties, he acquired a small farm and started chickpea production.[83] During those years, Francisco's sister, Amalia, married Álvaro's oldest brother, Lamberto, connecting the Serrano and Obregón clans. Thus began a close relationship.[84]

As a farmer on the rise, at the age of twenty-five Obregón became a regidor in Huatabampo, giving him a chance to experience Porfirian politics at the local level. As in many other towns, a *cacique*, or local boss, held sway. Content with his status, Obregón stayed on the sidelines during Madero's revolution. Once that revolution had triumphed, however, he took advantage of the new political order. Against the wishes of the cacique, he ran for *presidente municipal*, supported by the Mayo in the surrounding areas. His opponent, Pedro Zurbarán, lost the overall vote due to Obregón's support in the Mayo community and specifically that of their leader, who had personally delivered their votes to the local *ayuntamiento* (town council). Still, the council awarded victory to Zurbarán. Obregón appealed the case to the state legislature, where a committee of three, including de la Huerta, overturned the decision of the ayuntamiento.[85]

Obregón might have remained presidente municipal for a long time if Maytorena had not decided to defend his state against the Orozquista threat by mobilizing impromptu militias organized by local strongmen.[86] Without formal military training, Obregón accepted this task enthusiastically and recruited fellow landowners from the Navojoa area into one of these militias. The force initially mirrored his middle-class background so much that it was dubbed "the rich battalion." However, the "Fourth Irregular Battalion" that marched east in June 1912 included a large number of Mayo, most of them using bows and arrows. Serrano accompanied Obregón.[87]

As Obregón's men traveled east, their leader provided evidence of a strategic mind that would help him emerge on top of the factional struggle three years later. His superior ordered Obregón to dig collective trenches and wait until the arrival of federal reinforcements. Aware that his enemies knew the territory too well to allow a successful stationary defense of his outnumbered troops, Obregón disobeyed and resorted to guerrilla warfare, ordering his men to dig foxholes from where they launched a series of surprise attacks. When the reinforcements arrived, the combined troops drove the Orozquistas across the Sierra Madre into Chihuahua, where Obregón met General Huerta. After this successful campaign, Maytorena promoted Obregón, who returned to his position in Huatabampo, to the rank of colonel.[88]

Obregón's success required the help of leaders such as the police chief of the border town of Agua Prieta. Born on September 19, 1877, in Guaymas, Francisco Plutarco Elías Campuzano descended from a notable family fallen upon hard times. The Elíases numbered among the notables of Arizpe, where they had once owned more than one million acres. Struggling with alcoholism, the boy's father squandered much of the family fortune, and Apache raids and other calamities claimed most of the remainder. His mother came from lower middle-class origins and died when Plutarco was four years old. His maternal aunt and her husband, Juan Bautista Calles, raised the boy, who was born out of wedlock. Plutarco adopted "Calles" as his last name and only added back the patronymic "Elías" years later.[89] Calles trained as a teacher and spent his early adult years in that profession. He enjoyed the job but not the low pay, so he dabbled in various occupations as a hotel manager, mill operator, and farmer. This itinerant life in three different districts (Guaymas, Hermosillo, and Arizpe) had disappointing results. One of his daughters declared, "My father was an awful entrepreneur. He had ambition for power, but not for money."[90] Just like Hill and Obregón, Calles became an officeholder at the local level, serving as regidor of the northeastern town of Fronteras. In 1909 he coauthored a letter to the prefect stating, "We are people of property and work, unconditional friends of the government, and we only wish to avoid . . . difficulties and to protect our interests."[91]

Unlike Obregón, however, Calles at least sympathized with the Maderistas, perhaps in part because of his ongoing struggles to earn a living commensurate to his status as a Yori of notable origins. Following the bankruptcy of a flour mill that he had operated together with a business associate in Fronteras, Calles moved back to Guaymas, where he and his associate opened a store that sold flour and agricultural supplies. There, he renewed acquaintance with de la Huerta, whom he had met in 1894 when he served as a teacher's assistant. Both cooperated in the local anti-reelectionist movement in a hotbed of anti-Porfirian sentiment.[92]

After Madero's triumph, Calles ran for a state congressional seat. He lost to none other than de la Huerta. This friendship nevertheless paid off, as Calles was reportedly gracious in defeat, and at his request, de la Huerta recommended him for the post of police chief of Agua Prieta.[93] After years of failures, Calles demonstrated his aptitude for administration. He helped bring electricity and running water to the town (his family was the first to enjoy these new amenities). Calles also opened a school and reorganized the local prison. The inhabitants of Agua Prieta came to know him as a tough and sometimes ruthless authority figure. Endowed with these responsibilities, and in charge of a border town strategically located between Nogales and the Orozquista theater of operations, Calles organized an irregular battalion of some one hundred volunteers. However, unlike Obregón, he did not personally participate in the fighting. The police chief informed Maytorena that "the state can count on a great number of citizens in this district who are ready to defend the legally constituted government."[94] Calles also had the other side of the border at his disposal, where he gathered weapons, intelligence, and matériel.[95]

Along with Obregón and Calles, one must introduce Abelardo L. Rodríguez. He was born May 12, 1889, in San José de Guaymas, a hamlet outside the eponymous port city. Rodríguez's family, too, had fallen upon hard times. Whereas his paternal grandfather had been a lawyer in Durango, his father operated a small transportation business in the Sierra Madre before losing the mules that were indispensable to his livelihood. His mother was from a poor family. Young Rodríguez thus grew up poor as one of eleven children. As he wrote in his memoirs, "As a six-year-old, I only used shoes for special occasions."[96] Rodríguez spent part of his childhood in Nogales, where he learned English during summer vacations. He dreamed of becoming a professional athlete, especially after sustaining an injury at the hands of two U.S. youths. In 1903 Rodríguez went to work in a hardware store, and three years later, he moved to Cananea with the intention of preparing to avenge his injury by steeling his body in the copper mines. He witnessed the miners' strike before returning to Nogales, where he learned to his dismay that his adversaries were no longer there. He dabbled in baseball and singing before working for a railroad until he discovered that he was colorblind. Rodríguez's early efforts presaged his eventual business strategy centered on recreation.[97]

Having lived on the border as a child, Rodríguez was more familiar with U.S. culture than any of the other Sonorans.[98] Although his memoirs often profess his advocacy for the proletariat and the dispossessed, rugged individualism *à la estadounidense* defined his outlook: "I insist that a humble boy, no matter his origin, can become a capable and useful man, and even an important one. A small acorn will turn into a large, strong, and leafy oak tree."[99] A 1939 article in Mexico City's *La Prensa* looked back on Rodríguez's early years thus: "His youth shows him as a valiant sportsman and fortunate lover. In photographs of that period, we can see him, an agreeable, elegant, and beefy European Don Juan type, next to a beautiful brown-haired lady."[100] Due to his age, Rodríguez did not participate in Porfirian politics. Like Calles, he gained a fortuitous appointment after the triumph of the rebels—in his case, as police chief of Nogales in 1912.[101]

The campaign against the Orozquistas resulted in victory but also in a state under martial law. At the height of the campaign, Maytorena had taken advantage of new federal regulations that addressed the nation's worst wave of armed crime since the 1860s to curtail the very rights of free assembly and expression that he and Madero had trumpeted.[102] His state government had built a militia of almost three thousand troops. The militarization of Sonora would have lasting results. Unlike Chihuahua and Morelos, where ordinary people constructed makeshift armies that refused to lay down their arms after winning fights for Madero, Sonora featured a revolution organized from above. In the next phase, this revolution by administration would encounter first the Huerta dictatorship and then the war between the revolutionary factions.

2 ❖ The School of War

> Something much greater and much more sacred is at stake: the creation of justice, the pursuit of equality, the disappearance of the powerful, and the creation of equilibrium in our national economy.—Venustiano Carranza

In 1915 physician and writer Mariano Azuela published a short novel from exile in El Paso, Texas. *The Underdogs* encapsulates the worst years of the fighting like no other literary piece. The novel represents the revolution as a school of war that imprints a political ideology upon participants who joined without a common motive. The protagonist, Demetrio Macías, begins fighting after suffering a personal outrage. Through the influence of an intellectual, he learns that he is part of a larger struggle against oppressors. But Macías rejects these efforts to turn him into a social rebel and takes a cynical view of the revolution:

> The men threw out their chests as if to breathe the widening horizon, the immensity of the sky, the blue from the mountains and the fresh air, redolent with the various odors of the sierra. They spurred their horses to a gallop as if in that mad race they laid claims of possession to the earth. What man among them now remembered the stern chief of police, the growling policeman, or the conceited cacique? What man remembered his pitiful hut where he slaved away, always under the eyes of the owner or the ruthless and sullen foreman, always forced to rise before dawn, and to take up his shovel, basket, or goad, wearing himself out to earn a mere pitcher of *atole* and a handful of beans?[1]

Azuela's tale shows that widespread violence led the survivors to question the value of an individual life and often, of moral norms altogether. Indeed, the period 1913–15 brought new cycles of violence much more destructive than the rebellion against Díaz.

But the crucible of war also forced each contending faction to consider why Mexicans had taken up arms in the first place, including yearnings for land reform; democracy; social justice; regional and local autonomy; better working conditions; and an end to the privileges of foreigners. Like all the other factions, the Sonorenses emerged from this school of war with ideas different from those with which they had entered it. Their shared experience conditioned the Sonorenses to the "logic of the revolution," which impelled them toward supporting social reform, if not out of genuine conviction, then for survival.[2]

The Sonorans and the Huerta Coup

The second phase of the revolution began in February 1913 during the "Decena Trágica" (the tragic ten days) in Mexico City. After defeating several rebellions, the Madero government confronted a conspiracy involving General Reyes and Don Porfirio's nephew, Félix Díaz. Following their imprisonment after separate attempts to topple the government, Reyes and Díaz plotted from their cells in different prisons. In the wee hours of February 9, cadets forced their release. Reyes and his troops marched to the National Palace. Arriving early for work, the commander of the Palace Guard alerted his men, who thwarted the coup attempt, killing Reyes in the process. Meanwhile, Díaz seized the Ciudadela (armory) a mile west of the city center. General Huerta offered Madero his services as military commander. The Federales bombarded the heavily fortified armory, while its occupants used its provisions to return fire. Eager to effect regime change, U.S. ambassador Henry Lane Wilson blamed Madero for the bloodshed. He informed President William H. Taft that the Madero government was about to fall and received authorization to negotiate a new order. With Wilson and Huerta plotting behind the scenes, on February 18, Huerta's men entered the National Palace and arrested Madero and Vice President José María Pino Suárez. Huerta secured their resignations at gunpoint and then procured the presidency from a frightened legislature. On February 22 the Huertistas assassinated Madero and Pino Suárez en route to the penitentiary. Adolfo de la Huerta (the Sonorense and no relation to General Huerta), who had recently arrived to meet with Madero, witnessed firsthand the return of dictatorial rule.[3]

By itself, this coup d'état might not have elicited another rebellion. Weary of the unrest as well as of the restrictions on personal liberty that the federal Congress had adopted in response to it, many believed that Huerta represented a better alternative. Middle- and upper-class Mexicans were willing to support anyone who would close the Pandora's Box of social unrest and rebellions that Madero's revolution had opened.[4] Indeed, the Huerta regime quickly garnered recognition among most state governors. Most landowners supported the coup, as did some of the archbishops and legislators. Major foreign powers, including Austria, France, Germany, Great Britain, Spain, and Russia, recognized Huerta. Even Orozco tendered his endorsement.[5] However, Madero's and Pino Suárez's murders produced widespread popular outrage and antagonized incoming U.S. president Woodrow Wilson and two northern governors. Wilson opposed a regime brought to power by the force of arms, and the governors of Chihuahua and Coahuila, Abraham González and Venustiano Carranza, disavowed Huerta.[6]

Governor Maytorena did not know what to do. In contrast to the situation in polarized Chihuahua, a majority of Sonorenses united in their disdain for Huerta. As evidenced by spontaneous demonstrations and sporadic violence, the region's inhabitants were not inclined to acquiesce to a new status quo abetted by Orozco, whose troops had invaded the state twice in the last two years. However, the developments in other states gave Maytorena pause. The federal government counted on well-armed garrisons, including one in Guaymas easily reinforced by sea. On February 23 the Federales ousted González, followed by his assassination two weeks later.[7] Carranza held firm but the Federales forced him to flee to Monclova, 122 miles north of the state capital. Therefore, Maytorena temporized. He knew that a war would require levies on the wealthy and the confiscation of private property from the supporters of the new dictatorship. As he reportedly told Adolfo de la Huerta, "In this struggle, I would have to pressure the rich into giving up their money because one can only make this revolution with the help of money, and I have made a lot of promises."[8] Meanwhile, his old friend, Rodolfo Reyes, a member of Huerta's administration, pleaded with Maytorena to support the new regime in order to prevent further bloodshed.[9]

Ultimately, Maytorena decided to leave the decision to others. Citing poor health, he took a leave of absence and relocated to Tucson, Arizona.[10] The state legislature appointed one of their own as interim governor—Ignacio L. Pesqueira, one of Maytorena's rivals. The appointment angered the Sonorense military officers, especially Cabral, Hill, Alvarado, and Obregón, all of whom considered themselves worthy of the governorship. Pesqueira initially waffled in regard to Huerta's recognition, soliciting the mediation of the U.S. consul. The consul came close to persuading him to recognize Huerta, but Pesqueira feared that the dictator would oust him regardless of his stance.[11]

It fell to the Sonoran militia and legislature to push the state toward rebellion. Following Mayor Diéguez's lead, the Cananea town council denounced the coup. Obregón gathered his battalion near Navojoa.[12] Accompanied by an armed posse, Alvarado interrupted the state legislature in session and demanded a formal break with Huerta. On March 4 Pesqueira recommended Huerta's disavowal. The legislature quickly followed suit.[13]

The war against Huerta revealed emerging differences among the Sonorense leadership. Pesqueira was reluctant to call for violence. His March 7 manifesto invoked state sovereignty: "I have not wanted to subject the state to the contingencies of a military campaign. The people have decided the issue. Let's carry out the popular will!"[14] Obregón was more militant, warning the Federales that his forces would "smother them in their own thirst for blood, and we will then have proved worthy of the land that gave birth to us."[15] He also promised the Yaqui and Mayo the restitution of usurped lands, thus incurring a debt toward communities that sent thousands of fighters into the campaign. Huerta realized that he had a dangerous enemy in Obregón, reportedly stating, "Well, we will buy him off. And if we cannot, we will just have to kill him!"[16]

The mobilization also spawned early rivalries. Pesqueira appointed Obregón the foremost Sonorense commander as chief of the Sección de Guerra. In an army of three thousand troops, Obregón had three direct reports: Cabral in the north; Alvarado in the center; and Hill in the south. While Hill acquiesced to serving under his cousin's direction, Cabral and Alvarado resented Obregón's authority. As leaders who had fought Díaz's army, they viewed Obregón as an opportunistic Porfirista who had sat

4. Calles, Gómez, and the revolutionaries of Sonora in Hermosillo, 1913. *Bottom row, second and third from left*: Arnulfo Gómez and Plutarco Elías Calles. Fideicomiso Archivos Plutarco Elías Calles y Fernando Torreblanca (FAPECFT), Archivo Fernando Torreblanca, Fondo Plutarco Elías Calles, Oficial, serie *Pre-Constitucionalismo, 1913–1915*, mfn 75, imagen 18, inventario 164. Used with permission.

at home while they had put their lives at risk. Alvarado also considered Obregón a shameless self-promoter who did not recognize the contributions of other leaders in his campaign against Orozco.[17] Recognizing the significance of the copper mining district, Pesqueira gave Calles the command in the northeast and awarded him the rank of lieutenant colonel. For his part, Calles closed his store in Agua Prieta and moved to Nogales (where he ensconced his family on the U.S. side of the border). On March 13 his Nacozari Manifesto proclaimed, "The storms provoked by a popular rebellion are preferable to a peace sustained by the guns of military dictatorship."[18] Farther down the chain of command, Abelardo L. Rodríguez joined the rebels as a lieutenant.[19]

Pesqueira's appointment of Calles appeared to have been a mistake. Lacking combat experience, Calles rushed into military action without coordinating with the other commanders. Ignoring Obregón's warning, he sent his four hundred troops against the well-provisioned garrison in Naco. The Federales went on the offensive and chased the rebels to Agua Prieta, where de la Huerta later claimed to have found a sleeping Calles hidden under an automobile.[20] Obregón would never let Calles

The School of War 51

forget this disastrous beginning, labeling his ally Plutarco Elías "Corres" (You run). U.S. intelligence officers called Calles "weak, vacillating, and not fond of fighting."[21] The failed engagement of Naco also inaugurated Calles's cooperation with Gómez, who served in his forces as a captain, anointed by none other than Calles himself.

Even before the Sonoran contingents had won a single battle, some already worried about the role of the military. On March 17 Serrano, Maytorena's private secretary, pleaded with his boss to return. In describing the increasing mobilization of soldiers, Serrano asserted that "the military element is assuming such hegemony that it considers itself the exclusive owner of the situation; and it wants to dominate all branches of the administration by any possible means."[22]

The revolutionary army would indeed go on to dominate, beginning with a campaign that featured four primary revolutionary factions. Despite Serrano's misgivings, he would soon thereafter join Obregón's army. In addition to the Sonorenses, this campaign included a northeastern coalition under Venustiano Carranza, Pancho Villa's army based in the center North, and the Zapatistas in the South.

José Venustiano Carranza de la Garza was born in Cuatro Ciénegas, Coahuila, on December 29, 1859. Historians have often compared him to Madero due to their shared background as wealthy Díaz opponents from the same state. However, Carranza's cattle-ranching family was not nearly as rich as the Maderos. Still, Don Venustiano turned his ranch into a booming agribusiness. In 1893 he allied with Reyes to oust the incompetent governor of his native state. From 1903 to 1908 Carranza served in the federal senate. Aiming for the governorship, he got firsthand experience with the trammels of the Porfirian system. Although Carranza initially received the dictator's support, Díaz changed his mind in one of the reversals that became more common as he aged. Consequently, Carranza backed Madero and traveled to San Antonio to join him in exile. In recognition of Carranza's support, Madero named him minister of war in his provisional government, and in August 1911 Carranza won the gubernatorial election in Coahuila.[23] As the only elected governor among the rebel coalition still in charge, he claimed the mantle of the resistance. His Plan de Guadalupe of March 26, 1913, proclaimed him first chief of the Constitutionalist army, a movement that aimed to restore democratic rule under the 1857 constitution. The Carrancista leadership featured some formal military training: three commanders had attended the prestigious Colegio Militar. The Coahuilan coalition resembled the Sonorense one in its top-down organization; further, the two were similarly diverse in origin. General Pablo González Garza, for example, had worked as a field hand in Texas, and Carranza's son-in-law came from a family of small farmers in Veracruz.[24]

Doroteo Arango a.k.a. Pancho Villa was reportedly born on June 5, 1878, into a family of sharecroppers in the hamlet of La Coyotada, Durango. His father worked for a wealthy *hacendado*. Legend has it that a member of the hacendado's family raped Arango's sister, and that the sixteen-year-old avenged the act by killing the perpetrator. Whatever the truth, Arango crossed over into Chihuahua, where he became a social bandit known as Francisco, or "Pancho" Villa. At the beginning of the revolution, Villa joined Orozco's forces and distinguished himself by his bravery. He remained loyal to Madero during the Orozco Rebellion and fought his former comrades-in-arms. Huerta feared Villa and ordered his arrest on fabricated charges. Villa only avoided execution when Madero commuted his sentence to a prison term. He fled to El Paso, Texas, and then Arizona, where he first met Maytorena and de la Huerta, who encouraged him to join the fight in Sonora.[25] Villa demurred, reportedly saying, "No, *muchachito*, no. In your state, I'm worth nothing."[26] He was worth a lot, however, in the Chihuahuan revolution, which had sprung from grassroots popular mobilization rather than a state-sponsored militia.

Emiliano Zapata was born on August 8, 1879, in the village of Anenecuilco, Morelos, south of Mexico City. A mestizo farmer with intimate knowledge of the region's agriculture, Zapata aimed to reverse decades of land grabbing by the state's large sugar estates, which had despoiled their communities of their ancestral lands. His heavily Indigenous world was different from that of the northern rebels. Landowners had usurped most of the land of the villagers with the help of corrupt Porfirian officials. Zapata pursued a clearer political program than the northern revolutionaries, one dominated by a single-minded advocacy for land reform.[27] Like Villa's army, Zapata's grew from the ground up.

The campaign against Huerta therefore brought together a diverse alliance, just like the rebellion against Díaz. On April 18, 1913, de la Huerta and Roberto V. Pesqueira (the brother of the interim governor) formalized Sonora's adhesion to the Plan de Guadalupe by means of the Monclova Convention, and the Chihuahuan rebels also joined.[28] Zapata never formally signed on but helped the Constitutionalist coalition by engaging a large share of the federal army.

The Monclova Convention subordinated the insurgents from Sonora to Carranza's embryonic government. This step handed over control of any federal installations that might fall to the Sonoran army. Thus, a war to protect Sonora against the federal government became subsumed into a broader effort that compromised state sovereignty. Second, Carranza's imperious personality made him a problematic ally. Within this context, de la Huerta soon realized that Carranza represented interests divergent from his own. He later recalled that Carranza, as first chief, refused his request to address the needs of campesinos and workers.[29] Another sticking point was the organization of the Constitutionalist army. It included the División del Norte (Division of the North), under Villa's leadership; the Cuerpo de Ejército del Noreste (Corps of the Army of the Northeast), under González's command; and the Cuerpo de Ejército del Noroeste (Corps of the Army of the Northwest). Carranza awarded the leadership of the Ejército del Noroeste to Pesqueira. Obregón and the other Sonoran military leaders bitterly resented the governor's authority, but their complaints fell on deaf ears. For his part, the first chief saw Pesqueira as a figure of legitimacy in Sonora; even though he was an interim governor, he had been selected by the state legislature.[30]

Defeating the Dictatorship

The Sonoran campaign first aimed at the capture of border towns in order to seize customs revenue, control trade with the United States, and forestall federal reinforcements. After Calles's early disappointment, Obregón commanded successful attacks on Nogales and Naco. On March 25, he took Cananea, assuring its tax revenues for the Constitutionalists. To further boost revenues, the Constitutionalists imposed levies on businesses and expropriated Huerta supporters.[31] In the border area, Calles played an administrative role as a "border broker," taking advantage of his extensive personal contacts along the U.S. border.[32] As the rebels could not legally procure U.S. arms and ammunition under Wilson's policy of "watchful

5. Alvarado, Calles, and Obregón with Yaqui commanders, April 1913. *From right to left*: M. Martínez, Francisco Bule, Álvaro Obregón, Plutarco Elías Calles, Francisco Urbalejo, Salvador Alvarado. Fideicomiso Archivos Plutarco Elías Calles y Fernando Torreblanca (FAPECFT), Fototeca, Archivo Fernando Torreblanca, Fondo Plutarco Elías Calles, Oficial, serie *Pre-Constitucionalismo, 1913–1915*, mfn 85, imagen 2, inventario 148. Used with permission.

waiting," the border brokers played a crucial role. Calles and de la Huerta directed troop recruitment and training as well as arms smuggling across the border. Their men also took cattle confiscated from Huertista landowners and sold it in Arizona. Calles and Maytorena arranged to move a biplane across the border despite the attempts of U.S. authorities to keep it impounded in Arizona.[33]

Pushing farther south required confronting an enemy that proved hard to defeat, given its control over the Federal army and its installations. In July the Constitutionalist revolution suffered a setback when the Federales swept Carranza out of Coahuila. Rather than using U.S. territory, Carranza and his allies headed west on horseback toward Sonora, leaving González's army to contend in the Northeast. The Sonoran government stood alone in its defiance of Huerta even as popular rebellions assaulted the dictatorship from multiple directions.

By then, the Sonorenses had confronted a counteroffensive from the Guaymas garrison. But the Sonoran army had doubled in size. The state

The School of War 55

government had six thousand men under arms, including one thousand Yaqui and several hundred Mayo. With the help of this fighting force, Obregón drew the Federales away from their base, then defeated them midway to Hermosillo at the Hacienda de Santa Rosa. Another Federal commander tried his luck, only to suffer the same fate at Santa María, where Obregón's men routed a force of four thousand, killing three hundred and taking five hundred prisoners. The Federales soon found themselves reduced to Guaymas, and Alvarado's troops settled into a long-term siege.[34] The war effort in Guaymas impinged upon the Yaqui. Alvarado quartered his troops in their towns, and the new bosses on the haciendas seized from Huertista landowners exploited the communities just as their predecessors had done. As a result, the Yaqui leadership signed a manifesto asking for "freedom and land" in August.[35] To retain their allegiance, Obregón promised to return Yaqui land as soon as the "constitutional government was reestablished in the entire republic."[36]

With the Federales bottled up in Guaymas, Obregón encouraged Maytorena to resume the governorship. He knew that Alvarado and Calles were not eager to see the governor back in Hermosillo. But Maytorena had the law on his side in a movement that called itself "constitutionalist" and included all of the major northern revolutionary factions. Moreover, some leaders eagerly anticipated his return, including Yaqui chiefs Francisco Urbalejo and José María Acosta, who resented the anti-Yaqui Pesqueira. Urbalejo had a long-standing relationship with Maytorena, having reportedly helped chase down broncos who attacked Yori settlements.[37] Obregón brokered a compromise in which Calles and Alvarado supported Maytorena's return in exchange for expanded military roles.[38] Once he had returned, Maytorena hit the ground running, incorporating services of the federal government such as customs and telegraph under state auspices and issuing paper currency. By September 1913, six months into the war against Huerta, Sonora was practically a sovereign state.

That month, Obregón widened his campaign beyond Sonora. The political situation in Sinaloa had brightened following Huerta's decision to dismiss Governor Felipe Riveros, who had belatedly recognized his regime but now postured as an ardent Constitutionalist. In support of Riveros, Obregón led the bulk of his army into Sinaloa, including Cabral, Diéguez, Hill, and Serrano. Alvarado and Calles remained in Sonora; the former,

6. Five-peso note issued by the Maytorena state government, 1915. Museo Soumaya, Wikimedia Commons, https://commons.wikimedia.org/wiki/File:Billete_revolucionario_del_Estado_de_Sonora.tif (accessed July 2, 2022).

to continue the siege, and the latter, to ensure the flow of money and weapons from the United States.[39]

On September 18, after a trek of seventy-nine days, Carranza's entourage arrived famished and haggard in Sinaloa. Carranza was the most prominent among the anti-Huerta arrivals. Their ranks included a young Nuevo León attorney named Aarón Sáenz Garza, who would become one of Obregón's allies and business associates.[40] With their help, Carranza organized a federal government in Hermosillo. Carranza's appointments divided his allies against one another. For example, Carranza named Obregón the chief of the Cuerpo de Ejército del Noroeste and nominally subordinated Villa to his command.[41] As a counterweight, the first chief put Felipe Ángeles in charge of the Secretariat of War and the Navy (Secretaría de Guerra y Marina, hereafter abbreviated as Secretariat of War). This move subordinated Obregón to Ángeles. However, Obregón's opposition to reporting to a former Porfirista made the first chief demote Ángeles to undersecretary, a move that in turn convinced Ángeles to join the Villistas in January 1914. Subsequently, Ángeles designed a three-pronged attack along the northwestern, northern, and northeastern railroads while Zapata's rebels continued to fight the Federales south and southeast of Mexico City.[42] Notably, Carranza's cabinet did not contain any of Maytorena's closest allies, and the governor viewed it as a threat to his rule.[43] These maneuvers anticipated a split between Carranza and

The School of War 57

Obregón on one side, and Villa, Maytorena, and Ángeles on the other.[44] Carranza stayed in Hermosillo until December 1913.

In a less controversial move, Carranza appointed de la Huerta to the position of *oficial mayor* (chief clerk) in the Secretaría de Gobernación (Secretariat of the Interior), the agency in charge of elections, relationships with the states, and internal security. In this capacity, de la Huerta became the first Sonorense to think in national rather than regional terms. Many Constitutionalists saw their struggle as narrowly political rather than the social aims that de la Huerta and many of his cohort envisioned. For example, Obregón reportedly told Carranza, "We have no *agraristas* here, thank God! All those of us who are involved in this effort are doing it for patriotism and to avenge the death of Mr. Madero."[45]

Carranza himself appeared to have made a conversion to a commitment to social causes during his long trip on horseback. Initially, he had proclaimed his opposition to social reform since the war effort depended on the support of the wealthy: "The less resistance there is, the shorter the war will be. The large land owners, the clergy, and the industrialists are stronger than the federal government." But after his trek, he announced:

> At the moment when the armed struggle . . . has ended, the social struggle, the class struggle in all its power and its grandeur must begin. Whether they want it to happen or not, the new social ideas must win out among the masses against all opposition. It is not merely a question of dividing up the land and the natural resources, not merely a question of honest elections, not merely a question of opening new schools or of the equal distribution of the wealth of the land. Something much greater and much more sacred is at stake: the creation of justice, the pursuit of equality, the disappearance of the powerful, and the creation of equilibrium in our national economy.[46]

This speech marked an important initial step in the broadening of the Constitutionalist cause beyond the restoration of democracy to economic and social reform.

The turn toward supporting at least a modicum of social reform also reflected Carranza's awareness that the Huerta regime remained entrenched. At the end of 1913 the Constitutionalist rebellion had only made limited headway since its initial successes, with the exception of Villa's offensive in Chihuahua. Huerta remained in control of most of the country. Presidential elections in October 1913 reinstalled Huerta, even though he could not officially be a candidate. The dictator still enjoyed significant support, not least from prominent members of the high clergy, even though his manipulations to stay in power came at the expense of a Catholic Party candidate. At the same time, when U.S. president Wilson grew ever more determined to see regime change in Mexico, a group of bishops and archbishops enjoined Pope Pius X to help them keep Huerta in power. Pius X responded by consecrating Mexico to Christ the King (Cristo Rey) on January 6, 1914. The huge procession that wound its way through Mexico City seemed like a Holy See endorsement of the Huerta regime as well as confirmation of the belief held by many anticlericals that the church bore at least part of the blame for the dictatorship.[47]

After Wilson dropped the weapons embargo on February 1, the prospects of the Constitutionalists brightened. By the spring of 1914, Obregón's army was ready to push south, enjoying full access to supplies from the United States. Like Sonora, Sinaloa featured a heavily fortified garrison easily resupplied by sea, in Mazatlán. While Obregón's troops besieged this garrison, Diéguez's army took Tepic on May 18 and began an arduous trek up to the central highlands, joined by a local revolutionary contingent. In early June the rebels crossed into Jalisco, where the division reunited. Under Obregón's command, the Sonorenses prepared an attack on Guadalajara, Mexico's second-largest city and Diéguez's hometown.[48]

Victory appeared near. In April Villa and Ángeles had captured Torreón, Coahuila, a city that lay at the junction of two major railroads, in a battle that claimed more than fifteen hundred lives. The Zapatistas had taken Chilpancingo, the capital of Guerrero. Sensing that the tide had turned, U.S. president Wilson sent Marines to occupy Veracruz, thus denying the Huerta regime its supply route. The most nationalist leader in the Constitutionalist coalition, Carranza, decried this violation of Mexican sovereignty even though it helped his cause.[49]

At this critical juncture, the Constitutionalists began to consider the future after Huerta. Which army would capture the national capital? González's Ejército del Noreste could not win this race although the force occupied Monterrey on April 24. With Villa poised to advance through the center, Obregón's army faced long odds to reach Mexico City first. However, Carranza preferred the Sonorans to the Villistas, whom he considered a gang of bandits even though he knew that the División del Norte was more disciplined and better organized than any other on the rebel side. The first chief embargoed the shipment of coal and sent the division east toward Saltillo to support González's ineffective army. This order stopped Villa from marching straight toward Zacatecas, delaying his seizure of that city until June 23, 1914, in a hotly contested battle.[50] A livid Villa demanded an alliance against the first chief from Obregón, whom he considered his "friend." He threatened to move his army back north if the Sonorense refused, leaving his army alone to deal with a Federal counteroffensive. Obregón urged Villa to postpone the resolution of his concerns until after their victory.[51]

The Ejército del Noroeste seized its opportunity. On July 6 and 7—the same time as Zapata's capture of Cuernavaca—its seventeen thousand troops overwhelmed the twelve thousand Federales in Orendaín, Jalisco. A day later, Obregón's and Diéguez's men occupied Guadalajara. Providing an early glimpse of an uncompromising style, Obregón ordered the execution of the federal commander, and his men imprisoned five thousand Federales. He also collected five million pesos in forced loans and recruited fifteen thousand additional troops as reinforcements for his final offensive.[52] Diéguez stayed behind as zone commander and governor, exhorting all to "cooperate with the legions that have come from the remote lands of the north to re-conquer the rights of the people, so outraged [and] so oppressed."[53]

Obregón's troops therefore reached the capital first. In mid-July, Huerta resigned and fled to exile in Europe. As chief negotiator for the Constitutionalists, Obregón held peace talks with the governor of the Federal District, the representative of the national government. Signed on August 13 on the fender of an automobile, the Treaty of Teoloyucan surrendered Mexico City, and Obregón entered the capital two days later.[54] Carranza awarded Obregón the rank of General de División after his own arrival on August 20. Borrowed from the French classification system of officers, the divisional general marked the highest military rank under the secretary of war. It was a great honor indeed. The government had not promoted anyone to that rank since the aftermath of the French Intervention, in which Porfirio Díaz had earned that distinction. Carranza did not similarly reward Villa for his achievements.

The entry of Obregón's army frightened the *capitalinos*, with good reason. Like many other Sonorenses, Obregón retained a provincial perspective. He resented the national capital and its inhabitants. He reportedly once harangued a Maderista veteran who had lost an eye in combat for being a Mexico City native. Obregón and his chief of staff, Serrano, placed the capital under martial law and imposed the death penalty for disturbances of the public order. Angry at what he interpreted as the church's support of the Huerta regime, Obregón also levied a fine of 500,000 pesos on the office of Archbishop José Mora y del Río.[55]

In conflict with the Mexico City elite, Obregón and his commanders sought out allies in the former members of the Casa del Obrero Mundial (COM, or House of the World's Worker). The COM had emerged during the Madero presidency as an anarcho-syndicalist workers' organization, only to be suppressed by the Huerta regime. Obregón allowed it to reopen in the Casa de los Azulejos (House of Tiles), an iconic building that had housed the Jockey Club during the Porfiriato. He also gave the COM ecclesiastical real estate for their use, including a convent and a monastery. This step provided symbolic recognition of organized labor and showed the elite that there were new masters in town.[56]

The Sonorenses stood poised to play a major role in the formation of a new government. Obregón's long march had introduced his charges to regions very different from the one they knew. Along the way, the Sonorans encountered the Catholic Bajío and cosmopolitan Mexico City, as well as areas that had benefited less from Porfirian modernization than their own. In particular, they witnessed the desperation in much of rural Mexico, where the best land remained in the hands of wealthy hacendados. Their firsthand experience conveyed the importance of a national settlement that would restore political stability. Perhaps even more importantly, it also imbued the Sonorenses with a sense of the personal stakes of the revolution's participants. Informed by the "logic of the revolution," they had begun to appreciate the social dimensions of the fighting.[57] Yet the war did not change the provincial outlook of most Sonorenses. As the victorious factions got ready to deliberate the fate of their nation after Huerta, the Sonorenses still thought locally rather than nationally, focusing on the sovereignty of their own state. Soon thereafter, however, a new conflict would force them to think in bigger terms.

The Failure of Negotiation

At the national level, Carranza and Villa clashed over personal ambitions and contrasting political outlooks. Villa opposed Carranza's decision to continue serving as first chief rather than as an interim president, which would have rendered him ineligible to run in a future election. He disdained the Carrancistas as men from comfortable middle-class backgrounds, out of touch with ordinary Mexicans. For his part, Carranza considered Villa a bandit unable to solve complex national problems and criticized his failure to condemn the U.S. occupation of Veracruz as a bid for U.S. support. In July Carrancista and Villista military leaders had attempted a resolution, signing an agreement that recognized Villa as leader of the División del Norte and Carranza as first chief. The agreement also stipulated new coal and ammunition shipments to the Villistas and called for a convention of military leaders to negotiate Mexico's political future. However, neither Villa nor Carranza approved this accord.[58]

Meanwhile, Sonora featured more animosity between Maytorena and the military commanders. On May 29 Calles stripped Maytorena of his personal escort, which he considered responsible for gunshots in Hermosillo's central plaza.[59] Maytorena did not take this affront lying down. As he wrote to Urbalejo, "The militarism reigning in this capital continues to irritate in its brutal attacks against my person."[60] Through Obregón's and Alvarado's mediation, Maytorena obtained Calles's withdrawal to Nogales.[61] Alvarado's telegram to Carranza urged a "policy of conciliation," and another missive asserted that "public opinion rejects Col. Calles, . . . the only one responsible" for the unrest.[62] To no avail: Calles organized a new fighting force in July.[63] Recent events in the north of the state assured him that the first chief needed his services, as a strike in the Cananea Consolidated Copper Company threatened access to the tax revenues provided by workers in the copper mines. For his part, Ángeles brokered an alliance between Maytorena and Villa based upon their common opposition to Carranza, while Carranza encouraged Alvarado to purge his command of Maytorenistas such as Acosta and Urbalejo. A Carrancista agent indiscreetly leaked this scheme to the two Yaqui commanders, who imprisoned Alvarado. In response, Carranza named Hill provisional governor, and Maytorena attacked his and Calles's forces.[64] Thus, Sonora featured conflict between Carrancistas and Villistas months before the outbreak of hostilities at the national level. Calles and Hill faced off with Maytorena. Recalling the state's response to external threats from Orozco (1912) and Huerta (1913), the governor called his movement *soberanista*, postulating that his government defended Sonora's sovereignty against the first chief.[65]

Aware that Maytorena's offensive threatened to deprive him of influence in his home state, Obregón attempted mediation. On August 21 he left the capital for a conference with Villa in Chihuahua. Villa presented himself from his most amicable side: "The destiny of the fatherland is in our hands. In short order, we will dominate the country. I will be the power behind the scene, and you, the president." But Obregón distrusted Villa, sensing "a man who does not control his nerves well."[66] The two leaders then met with Maytorena and named him military commander of Sonora. This appointment gave Maytorena the command over Calles and Hill but subordinated him to Obregón—as chief of the Ejército del Noroeste—and, implicitly, First Chief Carranza. Enraged, Maytorena's partisans published a leaflet with incendiary charges against Obregón. In response, Obregón and Villa removed Maytorena's authority over Calles and Hill and ordered both sides to remain in their respective positions. They named Juan Cabral, one of the first insurgents against the Díaz regime in Sonora, governor and military commander and deployed Calles's forces to Chihuahua. Obregón and Villa then also signed a memorandum that largely accommodated the goals of the latter. Carranza was to assume the title of interim president followed by the election of another civilian president, the filling of judicial vacancies, and the naming of agrarian commissions at the state level.[67] However, the pieces on the chessboard would not move in accordance with these plans. Carranza rejected both the proposals regarding his own political future and agrarian reform. Since Cabral had not yet arrived, Maytorena consolidated his authority. Meanwhile, fearful of living in Villista territory, Hill and Calles did not comply with their orders.[68]

With the agreement unraveling, Obregón headed back to Chihuahua in the company of Serrano, whose past work for Maytorena gave him some credibility in the Villa camp. Obregón planned to ask for a unilateral concession in requesting Maytorena's removal. The ploy did not work, as Villa got word that Calles's and Hill's troops were marching toward Hermosillo in an effort to oust Maytorena. Suspecting that Obregón sought to sow divisions within Villa's inner circle by means of his visit, he ordered him shot. Obregón stoically declared that his execution would give him "a personality that I do not have, and the only one suffering from this will be you."[69] In the end, Luz Corral (Villa's wife), Serrano, and Ángeles successfully intervened on his behalf. Serrano made an impression by arguing that only a coward would assassinate a guest who had arrived at his quarters in good faith, and Corral made similar arguments. When Villa learned that Calles and Hill refused to obey Obregón's orders while their leader remained in his hands, he issued more death threats before allowing his party to leave. Both he and Maytorena disavowed Carranza.[70]

After the failure of mediation, Obregón joined a larger peacemaking effort on behalf of fifty generals who formed a pacification committee that pegged its hope on a national convention, an idea that all factions had embraced in principle. Obregón and other members of this committee journeyed to Zacatecas to confer with Villista representatives and Pánfilo Natera, a military leader neutral in the conflict. All agreed on a convention of military officers at Aguascalientes, a city under Natera's control but close to the División del Norte. Each of the factions would have representation in proportion to their numerical strength. Carranza initially instead convened a meeting in Mexico City stocked with his supporters. He disingenuously offered his resignation as first chief, but the assembly rejected his resignation and voted to disband to attend the convention in Aguascalientes.[71]

The convention opened its first session on October 10, 1914. Obregón attended, hoping that the dissension between and within the Villista and Carrancista camps might make him a crucial intermediary in what he knew would be a symbolic rather than substantive gathering. Carranza and Villa did not, even though the latter paid the convention a one-day visit during which he and Obregón embraced on the podium. Posing as a unifier, Obregón had all attendees sign a Mexican flag in solidarity and gave a theatrical speech: "I will not betray Carranza ... I will not betray Villa ... I will not betray my fatherland, and I will live my life in its service."[72] He also professed a political awakening. Before the struggle against Huerta, he said, "I was a cadaver, morally speaking, because I believed us unworthy of a free country."[73]

Early on in the convention, it appeared that the ideologically flexible Obregonistas and Villistas would be able to work together in limiting Carranza's influence. The two delegations resembled each other in their focus on regional autonomy, in contrast to the Carrancistas, a group dominated by leaders who thought about national solutions. First and foremost, both leaders wanted to protect their respective bailiwicks against outsiders: the central North, in Villa's case, and the Northwest, in Obregón's. However, Maytorena's control of Sonora and Villa's death threats ruled out an alliance.[74]

The arrival of a Zapatista delegation on October 26 shook up the convention. Like Carranza and Villa, Zapata did not accompany his delegation, which had marching orders to secure an endorsement of the Plan de Ayala. The Zapatistas had not come to be agreeable. To the shock of most present, Antonio Díaz Soto y Gama, an urban intellectual to whom Zapata had awarded a military rank so he could qualify as a delegate, gave an incendiary speech that insulted the Mexican flag as a symbol of reaction. When tempers cooled down, Obregón took stock of the new reality, which included a Villa-Zapata alliance. On his recommendation, the convention chose General Eulalio Gutiérrez as president, a man with a limited following but few enemies, and passed a resolution asking both Carranza and Villa to resign their positions. Delegate Diéguez strongly objected. This incident helped split Diéguez—head of the largest contingent within the Ejército del Noroeste—from his Sonorense comrades-in-arms. Diéguez strongly supported Carranza, who (for his part) would never forget Obregón's role in a proposal that would have ended his tenure as first chief.[75]

The convention disintegrated. Villa had no intention of giving up his position and moved his forces within striking distance of Aguascalientes. In response, Carranza asked his delegates to abandon the meeting and declared that he would not resign unless Villa left his command first. En route to Córdoba, Veracruz, where he set up an interim government, Carranza met with Obregón and other military leaders and asked them to allow him to stay in office until Villa resigned. When Obregón told

Carranza that he would oust Villa if he refused to give up his command, the first chief replied angrily that he, not Obregón, would be the one to remove him. In the absence of Carranza's faction, the majority named Villa the chief of military operations and approved a program of agrarian reform.[76]

The failure of the convention highlighted Carranza and Villa as the antagonists of the coming War of the Winners. Forced to choose between the two camps, Obregón allied with Carranza. Villa's death threats during their second meeting in Chihuahua and Maytorena's control over his home state made this the more palatable option: choosing Villa would have meant accepting a subordinate role. This decision aligned Obregón with the national, centralizing vision of the Carrancistas. A strongly worded manifesto that assailed the "cursed trinity" of Ángeles, Villa, and Maytorena repudiated Villismo but not Zapatismo.[77] Headquartered at Veracruz following the departure of U.S. Marines on November 23, the new Constitutionalist faction included approximately fifty-seven thousand men. Villa's and Zapata's Conventionists counted on seventy-two thousand troops.

In the War of the Winners

The prospects of the Carrancistas and Obregonistas initially appeared slim. Obregón briefly occupied the capital, then abandoned it again when Conventionist forces bore down on Mexico City at the beginning of December. Several days later, Villa and Zapata met in the National Palace, proud of having chased out, in Villa's words, "men who have always slept on soft pillows. How could they ever be friends of the people, who have spent their whole lives in nothing but suffering."[78] In mid-December, Alvarado lost Puebla to the Zapatistas. At the peak of their power, the Conventionists controlled most of the national territory while the Constitutionalists held redoubts in four different regions, including the port city of Veracruz, the new home of Carranza's interim government following the departure of the U.S. Marines in November 1914. Fearing disaster, Carranza suggested the dissolution of Obregón's army into guerrilla units. Obregón reportedly replied, "I did not leave Sonora to be a bandit on the run. I am the commander of the Constitutionalist Army, and that is how I will die if it is necessary."[79]

In Sonora, Maytorena's five thousand troops faced off against eighteen hundred Constitutionalists under Hill's command, all concentrated in Naco. According to Hill, Sonorans "violently and decidedly" supported Maytorena.[80] However, Naco was well fortified, and the U.S. border provided access to food and provisions. As early as October 1, thirteen hundred Conventionist troops had attacked the state's remaining Carrancista stronghold, but the attack failed, as did a number of subsequent attempts, before both sides settled into a prolonged siege. Calles and Gómez earned a reputation for bravery during the conflict, which turned into the longest standoff of the revolution in the harsh winter of northeastern Sonora.[81]

The Constitutionalists turned the corner in January 1915. At the national level, Carranza's base in Veracruz gave him access to the customs house, revenues from oil production, as well as weapons and ammunition that the U.S. armed forces had left behind. From that base, Obregón retook Puebla on January 5. The Constitutionalists also controlled Tampico, the isthmus of Tehuantepec, and, thanks to Diéguez's forces, portions of Jalisco. The Conventionists had overextended their positions and abandoned the capital in late January. On January 27 the Obregonistas marched into Mexico City without firing a shot. When they left the capital to the Conventionists once more on March 10, they did so to prepare for the final confrontation with Villa, having secured their supply lines to central Mexico, where they anticipated the decisive engagement.[82]

In Sonora Maytorena's dominance faltered. In early January the U.S. consul in Nogales brokered an agreement that turned Naco into a neutral zone, ordered the withdrawal of Maytorena's troops to Fronteras, and redeployed the Constitutionalists to Agua Prieta through U.S. territory. Agua Prieta was familiar territory for Calles, who had just taken over the defense of Naco after Carranza ordered Hill to join Obregón. In March Calles's forces took Fronteras while Gómez's troops seized Navojoa, forcing Maytorena into a two-front war.[83] Unable to pay his soldiers, Maytorena faced mass desertions. The long war had produced a state revenue shortfall of 75 percent, and the siege had drained the state treasury. Wheat prices surged, leading to a rise in inflation, and forged paper money flooded the state, rendering the soberanista currency worthless.[84]

Sagging morale cost Maytorena the services of one Lázaro Cárdenas del Río, a nineteen-year-old lieutenant who joined Calles's forces on March 27 along with his contingent of four hundred soldiers. Cárdenas presented himself to Calles and found a "man of character and firm convictions." He accepted Calles's command with "enthusiasm" and gushed, "Due to Calles, the excesses that happened in other states did not occur [in Sonora]. He was energetic, imposing moral standards upon his troops, and always stimulated the initiative of his subordinates."[85]

The conflict between the Constitutionalists and Conventionists featured a contrast in political ideas and styles. At the risk of oversimplification, the Constitutionalists represented an urban, centralizing political vision, and the Conventionists a rural and decentralized one. One difference in ideology pertained to attitudes toward the Catholic Church. The centralizing vision of the Constitutionalists took aim at the church. Many Constitutionalists, and especially the Sonorense faction, blamed the church hierarchy for its support for the Huerta regime. By comparison, Conventionists were less anticlerical, although Villa's attacks on foreign priests in Chihuahua had made headlines during the war against Huerta. Historians have also noted differences in social origins among the warring armies. For example, while all factions featured leaders from comfortable backgrounds, most of the lesser officers were of similar social station as the troops under their command. Villa's and Zapata's armies had grown from rural grassroots mobilization, while Obregón's came from a middle-class-based militia that defended state sovereignty.[86]

Despite these differences, the Conventionists and Constitutionalists ended up agreeing on many of the most important social questions, for example, the unequal distribution of land and the miserable situation of workers. Despite their middle-class background, the Constitutionalists' reliance on the rural and urban poor to fight their wars drove home the significance of addressing their grievances. Luis Cabrera, one of Carranza's most influential advisers, put it best when he declared that revolutions seek to "change the laws, customs, and the existing social structure for the purpose of establishing a more just order."[87] Cabrera's words reflected a political realignment wrought by the Confederación Revolucionaria (Revolutionary Confederation), an alliance of reform-minded Constitutionalist leaders that included Obregón and prominent Carrancistas.[88] First came the December 1914 additions to the Plan de Guadalupe, which included a long list of sketched promises, including land reform, fair taxation, improvements of the condition of the working classes, and the free *municipio*.⁸⁹ On January 6, 1915, Carranza issued the Veracruz Decrees authored by the former Villista Pastor Rouaix, who had crafted the first statewide land reform legislation as governor of Durango. These decrees promised the restitution of all illegally seized lands to Indigenous villages, the core demand of the Plan de Ayala.⁹⁰ On February 20 the Constitutionalists signed a pact with the COM, taking advantage of Obregón's prior alliance with that organization. Composed of seven thousand volunteers, the *batallones rojos* (red battalions) boosted Constitutionalist operations.

The alliance with the COM came in handy during Obregón's second occupation of Mexico City. He found widespread misery and starvation in the capital, where "illnesses and hunger had overpowered the lower classes."⁹¹ Obregón immediately ordered the closure of all casinos. His associate, Alberto J. Pani, organized the Revolutionary Junta for Aid to the Poor, which established a brigade staffed by women and youth to hand out food and necessities to the poor. To procure these goods, Obregón requisitioned 10 percent of the inventory from all wholesale merchants stocking food and other essential items.⁹² He railed against the "privileged classes..., headed by the clergy and hostile to the revolution, [who] raised prices and hid articles of primary necessity" and placed the Compañía Telefónica y Telegráfica Mexicana under the administration of a union of electrical workers affiliated with the COM.⁹³

The Mexico City elite responded with predictable outrage. Most of the merchants temporarily closed their stores, a move that prompted Obregón to levy a new tax on capital investments. Confident of protection from their consular representatives, the foreign merchants refused to pay the new tax. When the Mexican entrepreneurs followed suit, Obregón seized the opportunity for a grand demonstration. In late February Mexico City residents were treated to the spectacle of entrepreneurs sweeping the street in front of the National Palace before the bayonets of Yaqui soldiers. Although Obregón reassured the merchants that he meant them no harm, the symbolism was not lost on the common people.⁹⁴ Obregón portrayed himself as a champion of ordinary Mexicans, which increased popular support for the Constitutionalists.⁹⁵

As winter turned to spring, the Constitutionalists made strides on the battlefield. They focused on the national picture, in contrast to the regional

7. Constitutionalist troops at the train station in Silao, Guanajuato. Fideicomiso Archivos Plutarco Elías Calles y Fernando Torreblanca (FAPECFT), Fototeca, Archivo Fernando Torreblanca, Fondo Álvaro Obregón, Oficial, serie *Pre-Constitucionalismo y constitucionalismo, 1912–1915*, mfn 36, imagen 13, inventario 38. Used with permission.

perspective of the Conventionists. Obregón's army had undergone a conversion to Carrancista principles: while his army had combated Huerta in defense of regional autonomy, it fought the Villistas with the aim of establishing a national government. Enjoying better access to ammunition, clothing, and food than the Conventionists, the Constitutionalist commanders enforced strict discipline and paid their troops on time. In contrast, the Conventionist leadership squabbled and found themselves unable to meet their payroll. Obregón proved better prepared for the war than Villa. Aware that the German offensive on the Western Front in the first months of World War I had bogged down, he understood that modern technology, including machine guns, trenches, and barbed wire, maximized the advantage of defensive positions. He therefore drew the División del Norte toward central Mexico, stretching its supply lines, and then goaded their cavalry into attacks on his entrenched positions. From April to July 1915 Obregón's army won a series of overwhelming victories over the Villistas in Guanajuato and Aguascalientes.[96]

8. Diéguez and Obregón as wounded warriors. Fideicomiso Archivos Plutarco Elías Calles y Fernando Torreblanca (FAPECFT), Fototeca Colección de Álbumes Fotográficos de los Archivos Plutarco Elías Calles y Fernando Torreblanca, Fondo Fernando Torreblanca, álbum 2, *Historia política de México 1913–1920, Volumen II*, fotografía 452, inventario 72. Used with permission.

Still, Obregón himself did not emerge unscathed. On the morning of June 3, 1915, enemy fire greeted his group near the hacienda of Santa Ana de Trinidad, Guanajuato. A grenade knocked Obregón to the ground and ripped off the caudillo's right arm.[97] As an eyewitness reported, he got up, bleeding profusely, and shouted at his company, "Let's go, guys! Long live Mexico! Long live the Revolution!"[98] Obregón recounted the event

The School of War 71

as follows: "With the remaining hand, I took the small Savage pistol that I was carrying on my belt and fired it at the left side of my chest, trying to finish the work that the grenade had not been able to finish." But the chamber of the gun was empty. Certain of his impending death, Obregón told General Francisco Murguía, "Tell the first chief that I have fallen in battle in fulfillment of my obligation, and that I am dying wishing the Revolution well!" He went on to name his cousin, Hill, as his successor.[99] But Obregón recovered. His injury contributed to an emerging macho mystique of the undefeated caudillo of the revolution: the *manco* (one-armed) man of Celaya. Even as the Carrancistas celebrated the Constitutionalist victory, they knew that a new rival was on the horizon. As one of them noted, "Villismo dies at Celaya, but there rises up a new caudillo and with him, a new faction, Obregonismo. This is something against which precautions must be taken."[100] Diéguez, too, suffered an injury in battle.

Obregón's victory helped Calles go on the offensive in Sonora. He did so without any competition from any of the other Sonorense leaders. Hill and Serrano had joined Obregón in the showdown with the Villistas; de la Huerta served in Carranza's provisional government; and the first chief had sent Alvarado to secure Yucatán and its lucrative henequen crop. Diéguez fought the Villistas in his native Jalisco, where he commanded a force of ten thousand, the second-largest Constitutionalist contingent behind Obregón's own.[101] Thus it fell to Calles to claim Sonora from Maytorena, who postured as an "unblemished populist" who favored land reform and opposed U.S. influence.[102] In July 1915 Calles's troops routed positions decimated by massive desertions, swaying public opinion drastically in his favor.[103] These campaigns forged alliances between Calles and two leaders who would play important roles in the 1920s and 1930s: Luis L. León and Lázaro Cárdenas. He may have also made the personal acquaintance of Abelardo L. Rodríguez during the defense of Naco.[104]

These victories came with rewards. On August 4 Carranza appointed Calles provisional governor. Still controlling just a slice of the state's territory, the new Constitutionalist governor issued a manifesto outlining his goals. Like Madero and Maytorena, he emphasized effective suffrage, local autonomy, an independent judiciary, human rights, and public morality. The former schoolteacher also set a goal of establishing a public school in each community larger than five hundred inhabitants. His program included the redistribution of land, the establishment of a fair system of taxation, the founding of a rural credit institution, and improvements in working conditions. In a variation on Zapata's mantra, land and liberty, Calles ended his manifesto with a call for land and books for all.[105] Just like Carranza's Veracruz Decrees, his program represented a shift from political to social goals. The manifesto revealed that the Sonorans had completed their curriculum in the school of war. Their path to power would involve support for the goals for which ordinary Mexicans had fought and died on both sides of the factional struggle. Yet they would still benefit from Maytorena's foundations in the revolution by administration, a fighting force organized by and loyal to the state government.

Maytorena and the Conventionists still hung on. On August 30 one month before his term expired, Maytorena announced he would remain in power because the "tremendous revolutionary convulsions" made it impossible to conduct elections.[106] Meanwhile, Villa made preparations to invade Sonora against Maytorena's strenuous objections, giving Calles an opportunity to posture as a defender of his state: "Francisco Villa, whose movement ... does not have motives other than the venting of personal passions, does not ... deserve any title other than that of *bandido máximo*."[107]

Upon learning of Villa's march to Sonora, Maytorena decided he was done. On October 1 he went into exile in the United States. In the opinion of his biographer, Maytorena had represented the "defense of the state against its absorption into the nation" and the "autonomy of Sonora with regards to the center of the country."[108] His regional vision fit within the Conventionist perspective, although his privileged position provided a different optic from Villa and Zapata, one that regarded his enemies as parvenus bent on expropriating private property.

Then it was Villa's turn to face defeat in Sonora. In October the Wilson administration had awarded de facto recognition to the Carranza government. Formal recognition facilitated the provisioning of the Constitutionalists with U.S. weapons and matériel. In November, twelve thousand Villistas charged Agua Prieta and suffered a humiliating rout at the hands of eight thousand Constitutionalists under Calles and Serrano's command. Afterward, Obregón and Diéguez chased the Villistas back to Chihuahua. On the way out of the state, the Villistas committed a massacre in the village of San Pedro de la Cueva. Demoralized, they trudged east toward Chihuahua. Soon thereafter, Diéguez's forces occupied Hermosillo, and on November 26, Cárdenas's troops seized Nogales. On December 10 Calles's victory near Fronteras ended the War of the Winners in Sonora, months after it had finished in central Mexico.[109]

Yet, the conflict was by no means over. Villa and Zapata remained in the field. Porfiristas still wielded influence in much of the heavily Indigenous South, defying Constitutionalist efforts to control Campeche, Chiapas, Oaxaca, and parts of Tabasco, the area of operation of Félix Díaz after his return from exile in 1916. For example, a succession of Constitutionalist governors ruled in Oaxaca but relied upon the conservative *caciques* that had run the state for decades.[110]

Even within the victorious coalition, stability was tenuous. Allies of convenience, Carranza and Obregón barely tolerated one another. Armed conflict threatened in Puebla, San Luis Potosí, Veracruz, and several other states, where ambitious caciques vied for control. Mexico, and the Sonorenses, confronted an uncertain future.

Part 2 ~:· The Road to Power, 1915–1920

3 ❦ Inside the Revolutionary Regime

Far from wanting to destroy capitalism—and not even attack it—I always tried to give it the greatest facilities for its development so that it could occupy the social function that the community has the right to demand of it.—Salvador Alvarado

Although the Constitutionalists had won the War of the Winners, the direction of the revolution was not clear. Beginning in December 1914, Carranza had issued a number of decrees addressing popular demands, for example, the Veracruz Decrees, which demanded the return of lands seized illegally during the Porfiriato. The first chief also promulgated a decree that declared coal and oil the patrimony of the nation, as well as another reforming the judiciary, and yet another establishing the right to divorce.[1] However, land reform remained minimal, and the needs of labor awaited resolution. This unfinished revolution provided the backdrop to the Sonorenses' emergence as significant players in the national elite.

The cycles of violence between 1910 and 1915 had ravaged the country more than any other upheaval since the Wars of Independence. The death toll was in the millions. The economy suffered from the devastation, the consequences of banditry, forced loans imposed by warring factions, and the virtually limitless printing of worthless paper money. Agriculture had severely declined in the Bajío, the location of the showdown between Villistas and Obregonistas and the primary grain-producing area in the country. As a result, much of the nation faced a food shortage.[2]

At the same time, much of the export economy kept going strong. The oil companies had hired caciques such as Manuel Peláez to keep the violence away from their precious wells. Once the Constitutionalists took control, industrial and mining production rebounded to 1913 levels within two years, taking advantage of high demand for raw materials during World War I.[3]

In this context, members of the Sonorense group reached the governorship in three crucial states—Sonora, Jalisco, and Yucatán. As proconsuls appointed by First Chief Carranza during a time when the ongoing unrest did not permit elections, they turned their states into laboratories of political, economic, and social reform, but also of repression. Then, the Sonorenses contributed to building a new political system at the national level.

Sonora as a Laboratory of the Revolution

In 1915, Sonora exhibited the scars of a major military theater. Aside from thousands of deaths, families bemoaned the effects of pillage, rape, and robbery. Many farms lay abandoned, as their owners had made up the backbone of both contending armies, and others had fled from the violence. Damage to irrigation canals left formerly fertile land desiccated. Food was scarce, and prices had increased dramatically.[4]

While still bottled up in Agua Prieta, Governor Calles turned to social issues. His very first decree, the *ley seca* (dry law) outlawed the production, sale, and consumption of alcohol. The decree followed similar measures elsewhere, including Governor González's prohibition in 1912. But its language was more strident, correlating crime and the use of alcoholic beverages and aiming to "moralize the citizens that have fallen under their sway, and to attempt their betterment."[5] Not surprisingly, some observers mocked the law, pointing out that Calles himself abused alcohol. According to one story, the new governor celebrated the ley seca with a shot of brandy. A subsequent decree prohibited games of chance.[6] Enforcing one of Carranza's edicts, another measure legalized divorce. It favored men, who could divorce their wives for any reason, while a woman needed to demonstrate that her husband's adultery had dishonored her family.[7]

Once the Constitutionalists held effective control in Sonora, Calles addressed economic issues. First, he targeted the mining companies to remedy the dire situation of the state treasury. Under the standard Porfirian incentive package, foreign companies did not pay production taxes, instead contributing to the local economy through their payroll. Calles levied a tax of 1.5 percent on copper production.[8] Protesting that the revolutionary war had cost them millions, the mining companies made only partial payment, prompting another decree that terminated all Porfirian concessions. In response, the companies threatened a shutdown, an empty threat while copper prices were high in the era of World War I. The copper barons finally agreed to additional tax payments, handing Calles a political victory.[9]

Next, Calles's agricultural policy sought to aid smallholders. It proscribed repurchase agreements that had enabled large landowners to skirt progressive taxation by keeping newly purchased land titled to its former owners. The governor also imposed taxes on large estates. For example, a tax on fallow land targeted proprietors who withheld fields from cultivation to keep food prices high.[10] Further, Calles set up an agrarian bank to provide credit and finance repair to damaged irrigation works. Finally, he decreed a program of land reform that emphasized the *pequeña propiedad* (small family farm). This program rewarded supporters with property taken from the Constitutionalists' enemies, but it did not parcel out communal land to Indigenous communities.[11] While Cárdenas's claim that Calles was "the first governor with socialist ideas in Sonora" was exaggerated, it is true that his economic policies were advanced for their time.[12]

The educational initiatives were unquestionably the hallmark of the reform program of a teacher turned governor. To help illiterate migrants, the Sonoran state government opened municipal libraries and evening schools for adults and mandated the establishment of company-funded schools in mining towns and on large estates. Using his newfound revenue from production taxes, the governor hiked funding for primary education to 58 percent of the budget. Calles also opened the state's first normal school for teachers, as well as the Cruz Gálvez school for orphans of the revolution. The school reflected the influence of the U.S. educational reformer John Dewey, specifically the belief in practical education connected to workforce needs. Cruz Gálvez provided instruction in practical trades as well as in reading, writing, and arithmetic and became an industrial venture in its own right. By 1918 Sonoran public schools enrolled twice as many pupils as in 1910.[13]

Calles's tenure also provided examples of the repression that his faction meted out against their enemies. Just as Maytorena had anticipated, they expropriated the land of their adversaries.[14] Maytorena's own family lost almost all their property. In a similar spirit of retribution, Calles also launched a campaign against the Catholic Church. He expelled all

9. Calles, de la Huerta, and students from the Cruz Gálvez school. Fideicomiso Archivos Plutarco Elías Calles y Fernando Torreblanca (FAPECFT), Fototeca, Archivo Fernando Torreblanca, Fondo Plutarco Elías Calles, Oficial, serie *Gobierno de Sonora, 1915–1919*, mfn 93, imagen 4, inventario 178. Used with permission.

priests—a grand total of thirty-five—labeling them "bad elements" that had colluded with the Huerta dictatorship.[15] One historian has sought to explain the expulsion via a Vatican document that suggested that a priest from Hermosillo had seduced Calles's niece.[16]

Even as Calles's early anticlericalism contrasted with Carranza's desire to avoid conflict with the church, it was not unusually strident within the context of his time. By 1916 several other Constitutionalist governors had taken similar or even more radical steps against the Catholic clergy. Governor Calles's policies toward the church—similar to Obregón's measures during his occupations of Guadalajara and Mexico City—reflected the first wave of anticlericalism in the early Constitutionalist era (1914–15).[17] Calles and the other anticlerical governors blamed the Catholic hierarchy for the sins of the Old Regime. In Porfirian Mexico, Pope Leo VIII's encyclical *Rerum novarum* (1891) had found a limited echo. Although the social Catholicism inspired by the encyclical called for the formation of Catholic unions and better working conditions for Mexico's poor majority, as an alternative to the Socialist class consciousness that Catholics abhorred, much of the hierarchy supported the socioeconomic status quo. As one historian has observed, Catholic conservatives "represented an ideological inclination toward order, hierarchy, property, and stability; a preferential option for the well-to-do, one might say."[18]

The *bronco* Yaqui were in for worse treatment than the church. Here, Calles acted in agreement with Carranza and also with Obregón, who despised a group that sought "absolute dominion ... in the region that comprises the village lands that they had lost, with the intransigent condition of eliminating ... every element alien to their race."[19] Like the nineteenth-century Argentine leader Domingo Faustino Sarmiento, Obregón contrasted Yori "civilization" and Yaqui "barbarism."[20] For his part, Calles denied citizenship to the broncos and other "nomadic" peoples.[21]

The Villista raid on the border town of Columbus, New Mexico, on March 9, 1916, added fuel to the fire. The attack prompted President Wilson to send the so-called Punitive Expedition into Chihuahua to capture Villa. Eventually involving as many as forty-eight hundred troops, *la punitiva* resurrected Villismo as a nationalist movement. It also made Carranza prepare for possible additional military conflicts. The first chief appointed Obregón secretary of war and sent him to negotiate with the U.S. government, resulting in a vague commitment to withdraw the expedition in exchange for a promise to subdue Villa's forces. Because the verbal agreement never led to a signed treaty, the expedition forces remained in Mexico until February 1917.[22] Worried that the broncos would support the Villistas, Obregón appointed Calles zone commander.[23] In coordination with Serrano, the head of the Yaqui Column, Calles remobilized the state militia and scoured the state in search of new recruits. However, the broncos defied this effort to subdue them, just as they had the previous ones.[24]

Because Carranza had prohibited concurrent service as governor and zone commander in a move designed to weaken regional strongmen, Calles's assumption of a military role gave Carranza a reason to make a change in the governorship. Indeed, Carranza had been unhappy with Calles for some time, being particularly opposed to the latter's decisions regarding the anti-alcohol campaign and the expulsion of the priests. Furthermore, he remained close to the Calles critic Pesqueira, by all accounts his favorite Sonorense. With good reason, Pesqueira's portrait still graces Carranza's former private residence in Mexico City. Aware that the Yaqui would oppose Pesqueira's appointment, on April 16, 1916, Carranza appointed de la Huerta—the other Sonorense with whom he had worked closely. Calles expressed displeasure even though de la Huerta was a close friend. He feared that de la Huerta might have grown too close to the first chief in the course of his service in Carranza's administration.[25] However, the new governor emphasized his "intimate ... friendship" with Calles, whose "unconditional approval" he credited for his appointment.[26] As a result, according to an U.S. intelligence agent, "Sonora now [has] two governors. One, de la Huerta, has the name and absolutely no power. Calles, the 'deposed' governor, possesses all the pay, powers, and emoluments of the office."[27]

Thus began the "Sonoran Maximato," with de la Huerta as governor and Calles working behind the scenes in an unequal power relationship.[28] Calles expressed embarrassment regarding his friend's solicitude. As he wrote to de la Huerta, "I am disappointed that you are still being so childish, and that you are trying to give me explanations for your conduct that I do not need."[29] Dissatisfied with Calles's conduct of the Yaqui campaign, Obregón tested this system in October 1916 when he appointed Serrano zone commander and ordered Calles to report to Mexico City for reassignment.[30] At the time, Serrano asserted that Calles "gave every indication of being a whipped man. He was sullen and morose ... [, and] he asserted that he was at a loss to explain his recall."[31] However, Calles's strong network allowed him to continue to wield influence among army officers whom he had rewarded with positions and land taken from the enemies of the Constitutionalists.[32] For his part, Serrano took advantage of his new position by setting up an agricultural colony on the Colorado River, his first entrepreneurial venture.[33]

In October 1916 de la Huerta's term produced one of the most significant innovations in the pre-Constitutional period: the creation of a Cámara Obrera, or Workers' Chamber. Established to address what the governor called the "economic malaise of the working classes," the Cámara Obrera represented the interests of wage-earning employees. The chamber launched several reform initiatives, including worker's compensation, and also took an active role in mediating labor disputes. It functioned as a parallel legislature with a distinct set of responsibilities, or as a separate arm of the state government, and provided an early example of the Sonorenses' paternalistic approach to labor.[34] The decree countered Carranza's August 1916 closure of the COM, which had organized two large-scale strikes and claimed a membership of more than one hundred thousand workers. Without competition, the Cámara Obrera participated in formulating decrees that established the right of collective bargaining, employer-funded health care, and impartial boards of arbitration for labor disputes. The same decree that created the Cámara Obrera set maximum work hours, a minimum wage, and a mandatory weekly day of rest.[35] As such, Serrano's appointment as zone commander may have targeted de la Huerta as much as Calles. According to a U.S. intelligence report, Serrano opposed de la Huerta's "visionary... and utopian plans for the rule of Mexico by the masses" on Obregón's behalf.[36]

However, de la Huerta was hardly a radical firebrand. The governor cooperated with the U.S.-owned mining companies. Near the end of his term, de la Huerta announced plans to cut taxes. Following an order from Carranza, one decree forced Sonorans to use Constitutionalist paper money rather than the silver and gold specie that served as the only reliable method of payment.[37] De la Huerta also stimulated the state's capitalist economy. He started a fish cannery, ordered telegraph lines strung across the state, and decreed the opening of a technical school. In terms of culture, Calles later suggested that de la Huerta's artistic abilities brought U.S. music and dance to Sonora, including the foxtrot.[38]

Regarding the Yaqui, de la Huerta followed Calles's lead so long as his friend was zone commander. In his first four months in office, the governor attempted to use legal means to identify broncos who attacked Yori settlements. As of August 30, 1916, the Yaqui had to carry an identification card issued by the police, a requirement that did not extend to any other group. Anyone found without such a card would be considered a rebel.[39] Calles justified the decree as a measure to end "the refuge that the rebel Indians find among the *mansos* who live in the haciendas and villages, where they succeed in blending in with them whenever our troops... come close to annihilating them."[40]

The failure of the Yaqui campaign encouraged more conciliatory policies. Due to his Yaqui ancestry, de la Huerta gained a modicum of trust of the community.⁴¹ In January 1917 he promised to withdraw troops and to pay pensions to Yaqui ex-combatants in the Constitutionalist army. In response, the principal bronco leader ordered his rebels to leave the sierra and settle in the valley to dedicate themselves to agriculture: "We cannot be at peace living among bayonets or living with bayonets in our hands."⁴² Under this agreement, the Yaqui received land and self-governance in return for giving the state government the authority to keep them inside a confined area. Not surprisingly, the mansos resented life in a virtual concentration camp, and the understanding soon unraveled. Carranza recalled de la Huerta as governor in late March 1917, reportedly due to his "reckless and indiscriminate extravagance" in handling the state's finances—though the president reappointed him to his old position as chief clerk in the Secretariat of the Interior soon thereafter.⁴³ He then turned to Pesqueira after all, with predictable results, as Pesqueira's return as provisional governor fanned the flames of the Yaqui conflict once more. Agitated by reports that Pesqueira planned the execution of several hundred Yaqui "troublemakers," the broncos launched a new rebellion.⁴⁴

Meanwhile, Calles eyed the upcoming gubernatorial elections, scheduled for May 13, 1917. Obregón's older brother, José, was a candidate, and Calles suspected that Obregón had demoted him in part to clear the way. Unsurprisingly, José J. Obregón carved out an opposing position to Calles's, promising the abrogation of the ley seca and the return of the Catholic priests.⁴⁵ For his part, Calles feared that Álvaro Obregón's influence might be strong enough to ensure his brother's victory, even though José had little political experience. Nonetheless, Calles continued to communicate with his supporters via telegraph until Obregón permitted him to return to Sonora in December 1916. By then, Obregón's relations with Carranza had deteriorated, and Carranza decided not to support José's election, leading Obregón to abandon his own efforts on his brother's behalf.⁴⁶

Calles decided to seek broad-based support. He traveled throughout the state, giving speeches and handing out campaign literature in what a U.S. military intelligence officer called the "most approved American fashion."⁴⁷ In May 1917 Calles delivered a rousing speech, declaring his plan to establish a government "more radical than ever." The candidate claimed the support of the proletariat, which gave him a mandate for socialist policies. He announced a merciless approach to "the aristocracy" and other enemies of the state government. At the same time, Calles reassured U.S. diplomats that he had delivered a "sop to the Mexicans" and that his election would not result in major changes.[48] He also had the support of de la Huerta, who had exhorted the population to respect the outcome of the vote and encouraged local authorities to crack down on the sale of alcoholic beverages.[49] In the end, Calles rolled to an easy victory, gaining 76 percent of the vote to José Obregón's 22 percent.

Rather than antagonizing Don Álvaro, Calles's victory over his brother created an atmosphere of mutual respect. In demonstrating his own political weight, Calles had made an important point to someone who had underestimated his leadership abilities. Both Calles and Obregón knew that they needed to present a united front toward Carranza, who was developing a Porfirian propensity to intervene in state politics. The two leaders began addressing each other with the informal "tú" in their letters, after years of using the formal "usted."[50]

Calles's and de la Huerta's tenures as provisional governors showcased significant reforms. Contrary to the opinion of one historian that "it was not until the 1930s . . . that revolutionary change came to Sonora," the state numbered among the most progressive in the Constitutionalist era.[51] At least this was true from the Yori vantage point: as another historian has pointed out, "the history of the Yaqui in the period 1876 to 1930 should be written as if the revolution had not existed."[52]

The National Context of Reform

The reform program in Sonora reflected a national context. Several measures, including the Agrarian Law of October 1915 as well as decrees concerning administrative and judicial matters, implemented laws passed by Carranza's provisional national government. Calles and de la Huerta's reforms also resembled those of other provisional governors. For example, witness the anticlerical reforms of Governor Francisco J. Múgica in the southeastern state of Tabasco. A native of Michoacán in the center-west, Múgica was an outsider sent by Carranza to help control the strategic Isthmus of Tehuantepec. During his short tenure, Múgica changed the name of San Juan Bautista, the state capital, to Villahermosa and commenced a systematic "defanaticization" campaign against the church.

The two other governors from the Sonorense group—Diéguez in Jalisco and Alvarado in Yucatán—deserve a closer look.

Diéguez's first term as governor commenced with the Constitutionalists' entry into Jalisco in June 1914. Given the fact that the local government led by the National Catholic Party had continued in existence since Madero's rule, one historian has described the way that the event felt to many locals as an "occupation rather than a liberation." Consequently, Diéguez's first acts let the citizens of Guadalajara know that there was a new regime in town. Diéguez enforced the use of Constitutionalist paper currency, and, like Hill in Sonora, abolished the *jefaturas políticas*. On Carranza's orders, he dissolved the legislature and dismissed all state-level judges. In a parallel to Calles's first months as governor more than a year later, Diéguez only controlled Guadalajara and a few towns along the railroad. Most of the countryside did not recognize his authority as a Carrancista proconsul. And even in the state capital, the governor faced stiff resistance from the political Catholicism that his faction had ousted.[53]

Reforms and anticlericalism marked Diéguez's tenure in the area under his control. He took the demands of workers seriously. One decree fixed a nine-hour workday and Sunday as an obligatory day of rest; another established a minimum wage; and a third abolished all consumption taxes.[54] The Catholic Church played a far greater role in Jalisco than in Sonora: instead of a handful of priests, Jalisco featured thousands, led by a new archbishop, José Orozco y Jiménez. Although the Constitution of 1857 banned the church from ownership of land and real estate, the archbishopric skirted these provisions by means of front men. After Diéguez's arrival in Guadalajara, one of his aides found a reliquary made of gold, filled with more than seven hundred diamonds as well as sapphires and golden religious objects. Unlike Calles, who moved against the church from a position of strength, Diéguez governed in a Catholic stronghold, indeed, in a place that one historian has called "this un-revolutionary state."[55]

Diéguez confronted his formidable enemy head-on. He ordered the expulsion of the archbishop and impounded the gold found inside the cathedral. His faction melted works of art made of gold and later sold the metal to purchase arms and ammunition in the United States.[56] Mobs defaced religious symbols as state police looked on, and Diéguez closed most churches in Guadalajara. Authorities suppressed religious holidays, including Christmas, and forbade confessionals.⁵⁷ At one point, Diéguez ordered 120 priests arrested and imprisoned in a military jail. The governor characterized these priests as "those who, clothed as sheep, deceive the people." He accused them of violating their vows to "work in secret ... to bring down any government that valiantly and resolutely raises up the Liberal banner, lifts the people from their ignorance, and demands ample liberty of conscience and thought."⁵⁸

The ensuing War of the Winners challenged Diéguez's anticlerical project. His Constitutionalists in Jalisco hung on for dear life during the Conventionist offensive. Most locals enthusiastically welcomed the Villistas under the leadership of Julián Medina. Like Diéguez, Medina came from working-class origins, but he highlighted his local roots in contrast to the Sonorense carpetbagger who had become alien to his native state.⁵⁹ But in the end, the people found the Conventionists to be more of the same, as they, too, raided the assets of the church to pay their expenses and reward their supporters. According to a U.S. consular officer, a "feeling of deception set in, anxiety returned, and most of the good elements who had helped Villa against Diéguez ... drifted away." The two sides fought each other to a stalemate, and control over Guadalajara changed hands four times. During one of the spells when Diéguez occupied the capital, from January 19 to February 12, 1915, he instituted a veritable regime of terror, replete with extrajudicial executions and assassinations.⁶⁰

After helping Obregón obtain decisive victories in the Bajío, Diéguez tempered his image of a social radical. That became clear when his army returned north to help Calles finish off the Villistas in late 1915. Diéguez acquired the services of several prominent Huertistas. When the troops disembarked in Guaymas, the inhabitants recognized many of the same officers who had led Huerta's Federales in their defense against Alvarado.⁶¹ In the Yaqui Valley, Diéguez promised "every protection" to the Compañía Constructora Richardson and landowners.⁶² In March 1916 he visited Cananea, where he had been a strike leader inspired by anarcho-syndicalist ideas a decade before. This time, he came as a representative of the federal government, charged with enforcing the use of the new Constitutionalist paper money, the infamous *infalsificables* that formed part of Carranza's scheme to confiscate the silver or gold used as tender in everyday transactions. When the miners insisted on payment in silver, Diéguez exclaimed, "They are agitators and do not want to conform to our governmental wishes; I am afraid they will have to be disciplined presently."⁶³ After this visit, he commanded forces in the Yaqui campaign and earned an infamous reputation, as evidenced by his opinion that "the best Yaqui is a dead Yaqui."⁶⁴

Back in Jalisco, Diéguez mended fences with the entrepreneurs who had opposed him. As the U.S. vice consul in Guadalajara reported, he "sacredly promised the protection of myself and all other Americans in the district."⁶⁵ His rapprochement with the elite put Diéguez in a position to serve a second term as governor, this time elected. In charge of fifteen thousand troops, Diéguez played off his status as a preeminent military leader to turn a great personal profit. His men confiscated cattle from opponents, giving away free beef to the soldiers and selling much of the remainder on his account.⁶⁶

In his second term as governor, Diéguez remained a "hard-line anticlerical."⁶⁷ One of his decrees limited the number of priests to one per five thousand inhabitants and required all clergy to obtain a state license. But this offensive against the church failed. Diéguez left the implementation of this decree to an interim governor. He resumed military duties for sixteen months and returned just in time to give his final address as governor in 1919. By that time, the church had scored a major victory over the anticlerical state administration that Diéguez had left behind. Via an economic boycott and the suspension of worship, the Catholics managed to force the state government to back off from its anticlerical measures. This crisis presaged a struggle at the national level years later.⁶⁸

Yucatán constituted the final example of reform under the Sonorense aegis. The revenue from henequen, a lucrative export crop, gave the state a significant role in Carranza's campaign. After two failed attempts to impose a Constitutionalist proconsul, Carranza had sent Alvarado in March 1915 in the company of eight thousand troops.⁶⁹ Arriving in Yucatán after a brief stint as commander of the Federal District (Mexico City), Alvarado faced opposition from two fronts. The henequen barons—an entrenched elite also known as the *casta divina*, or divine caste—feared that the Constitutionalists would end their exploitation of the Maya. In addition, a powerful U.S. corporation stood in the way: International

Harvester controlled the processing of henequen and the distribution of the finished product, the binder twine used in harvesting wheat.[70]

A prolific writer, Alvarado—who styled himself the intellectual among the Sonorenses—inaugurated a significant reform program. Like Calles, he undertook a "moralization" campaign, highlighted by the prohibition of alcohol, gambling, and prostitution. As he later boasted, "I left Yucatán without alcohol, without games of chance, without bullfights, without cockfights, without raffles, without lotteries, without brothels, and without vagabonds."[71] Taking advantage of a full state treasury, he also launched an ambitious education campaign in a state with a low literacy rate even by Mexican standards. During Alvarado's term in office, the number of schools increased from 329 to 891, 65 percent of which were in rural areas.[72]

Anticlericalism was part and parcel of this campaign. The atheist Alvarado aimed to "defanaticize" the Maya "at all costs" and proposed no less than the eradication of religion. In his words, "The practice of religion...was purged...by the revolution...Defanaticization was completed by the foundation of competent lay schools and...one hundred libraries."[73] As Alvarado advised Carranza, "The only way to make this state a part of the nation is to organize these Indians, facilitating for them real interests that they will then owe to the revolution."[74]

In a significant difference from Calles and Diéguez, Alvarado helped Yucatecans build a novel political system that drew upon grassroots popular mobilization. In June 1916 his group founded the Partido Socialista Obrero, or Socialist Workers' Party. This party included two future governors among its first members: Carlos Castro Morales and Felipe Carrillo Puerto. A year later, the party changed its name to Partido Socialista de Yucatán (PSY). Yucatecan "Socialism" did not mean orthodox adherence to Marxist precepts; rather, it denoted a commitment to an inclusive, progressive, and secular society. In the words of one historian, "Alvarado's version of Socialism was always more about political practice than a clearly articulated ideology."[75] The *ligas de resistencia* (resistance leagues), which constituted the party's grass-roots connection, included campesinos, workers, and middle-class professionals. Furthermore, Alvarado professed particular interest in improving the situation of women. Under his tutelage, the state capital of Mérida hosted the country's first feminist congress in January 1916, only the second in all of Latin America. One of his decrees abolished domestic slavery, and women began to use the legal system to their advantage.[76] According to one historian, Alvarado's "approach to women's issues was revolutionary by the Mexican—and Western—standards of his time."[77]

Alvarado's "Socialist" economic program resembled that of his Sonoran colleagues in embracing state intervention in the economy, maximizing revenue, and carrying out social reforms without attacking the foundations of a robust export economy. While Calles had levied new taxes on the mining companies, Alvarado imposed a regulatory commission upon International Harvester. He planned to invest the proceeds in infrastructure improvements, particularly ports and railroads.[78] The price of henequen increased 300 percent between 1916 and 1918—in large part due to the world war—producing a windfall for the government as well as the planters.[79] Alvarado's agrarian measures included the legal end of forced labor, a widespread practice in Yucatán, where the Maya henequen cutters lived in conditions resembling slavery. This decree affected over one hundred thousand workers, many of whom left their haciendas, only to be replaced by contract workers brought in from other states.[80] The governor also taxed fallow land. As a result of the greater mobility of labor, the state witnessed significant growth in the production of foodstuffs such as beans, corn, sweet potatoes, peppers, and peanuts. Based on the Veracruz Decrees, an agrarian law redistributed some hacienda land in order to provide small plots for landless campesinos, "considering that no one is the exclusive owner of the earth any more than of light and air."[81] But Alvarado followed the Sonorense script in fostering smallholding rather than collective farming as practiced by the Maya peasants for millennia.

Just like his colleagues, Alvarado endeavored to keep his state's primary export economy profitable.[82] The sentiments in the epigraph to this chapter expressed his views as a social reformer rather than an enemy of capitalism: "Far from wanting to destroy capitalism—and not even attack it—I always tried to give it the greatest facilities for its development so that it could occupy the social function that the community has the right to demand of it."[83] Like the other Sonorenses, Alvarado aimed at a state-directed capitalist system.

Like Calles, de la Huerta, and Diéguez, Alvarado thus gained his first significant political experience as a military state governor. And like his colleagues, he distinguished himself by his reforms. Unlike them, however, Alvarado was an outsider who ruled over a heavily Indigenous state that he regarded as politically and socially backward. He was more interested than his colleagues in integrating his state into the nation, more focused on the incorporation of ordinary men and women into the revolutionary process, and more interested in agrarian matters. Aside from these reforms, his greatest contribution lay in assuring the continuous flow of cash from henequen. As Luis Cabrera proclaimed in 1919, "Yucatán has saved the revolution financially. Tabasco gave men ... to die in Tampico and Celaya ... Sonora gave lots of blood ... Yucatán gave lots of money."[84]

Although few sources have survived to document collaboration between them, we know that the three Sonorense governors communicated with each other about their respective programs. In August 1917, for example, Alvarado wrote to Calles, whom he dubbed "the great bandit of Agua Prieta, the republic." Two months later, responding to Calles's request for advice on how to deal with recalcitrant elites, he reported, "Here, the reaction contorts itself like a viper; it is much stronger than the one in your state, but especially because they have wanted to puff up their chests these days, I will tighten the screws a bit to end their good mood." For his part, Calles complained about the copper companies, and particularly his recent experience with the CCCC. In his words, "we have to fight openly against capital in order to take away all of its privileges, as [the mining companies] have handcuffed our people and ruined our government. We have needed to fight openly against foreign capital, against the most powerful companies in this country, which ... we have forced to respect the revolutionary government and its laws."[85] As a dark mark on both of their historical records, Calles and Alvarado also collaborated in resuming Yaqui deportations to Yucatán, albeit not nearly on the Porfirian scale.

The Constitution of 1917 and the Sonoran Leadership

Constitutionalist state-level theaters of reform and repression such as Sonora, Jalisco, and Yucatán informed the formulation of a new federal constitution, the world's first to promise social rights such as education and access to land. In the words of one historian, this constitution "set ideal goals rather than enforceable laws."[86] Although the Sonorenses played only a small role during the Constituyente, the resulting document would shape their policies at the national level.[87]

On September 15, 1916, Carranza called for a constitutional congress. In his opinion, the federal constitution from 1857 (which his faction had strenuously defended up to that point) had failed Mexico during the Díaz and Huerta dictatorships and needed significant updating. Hoping for a swift process, Carranza submitted a draft that included his additions to the Plan de Guadalupe, including the Veracruz Decrees and an effort to regulate the oil industry, as well as a significant strengthening of the executive branch at the expense of the legislature. In an effort to ram through his desired changes as quickly as possible, Carranza limited debate to two months.[88] On December 1, 1916, elected delegates met in Querétaro for what the first chief billed a "harmonious, one-party gathering."[89]

Although Carranza's draft already included a call for agrarian reform and fetters on foreign investments, many delegates sought more sweeping reforms than what the first chief envisioned. Unlike the Convention of Aguascalientes, which had been dominated by military leaders, the Constituyente included 62 lawyers and a mere 18 delegates with senior military rank among its 220 members. Although middle-class creoles formed the majority, the assembly also featured Indigenous and mestizo delegates. According to one estimate, 12 percent came from lower social origin. A proportional formula that allotted one delegate per seventy thousand inhabitants limited the influence of the North. Sonora had four delegates and Chihuahua, where fighting prevented voting in five districts, just one; in contrast, Jalisco sent twenty-one. Broadly speaking, the convention featured diverse political views, from cautious Maderistas to radical Socialists.[90]

In particular, an alliance of reform-minded delegates coalesced as the "Jacobins," a reference to the radical wing in the National Assembly during the French Revolution. Like their French antecedents, the Jacobins reflected a popular-minded, socially oriented perspective. Delegates like Múgica understood that the poor majority had fought to improve their livelihoods rather than merely to thwart dictatorships. Many Jacobin delegates hailed from rural areas ravaged by the fighting.[91] As such, these delegates understood this logic from their personal experience. Similarly, intellectuals within the group desired social reform as a part of their national vision. At the same time, while some had known poverty firsthand, many spoke of material deprivation in the abstract, as an ailment to be cured by a progressive and paternalistic state. A diverse group, the Jacobins coincided in their resolve to enshrine social rights in the constitution. Like the original Jacobins, they also held strongly anticlerical views.[92]

The Constituyente also served as a backdrop to a growing rivalry between Carranza and Obregón. As secretary of war, Obregón concentrated power at the expense of other generals. To fight "odious militarism," which he understood as the unchecked individual ambitions of military chiefs other than himself and his allies, he began to professionalize the revolutionary army. He also proposed barring leaders in active military service from holding political positions. Obregón's agency retired 30,000 soldiers and officers and reduced the army to 126,000 troops led by 206 generals, including 11 *divisionarios*, the highest and best-paid rank in the army.[93] Five of the eleven were Sonorenses: Obregón, Calles, Hill, Alvarado, and Diéguez. Three other Sonorenses—Gómez, Rodríguez, and Serrano—would attain that rank during the early 1920s. Aware of the growing Sonorense influence, Carranza did everything in his power to undermine Obregón.[94]

He had his work cut out for him. Obregón closely observed the proceedings. He traveled to Querétaro on various occasions, available to receive visitors who sought his advice—advice often adopted by his allies in the convention. True, the extent of Obregón's influence has been debated. In a 1938 panegyric, former delegate José Juan de Dios Bojórquez portrayed him as a champion of social rights who played an active role at the convention, a view that sought to draw a progressive arc from Obregón to Lázaro Cárdenas.[95] In fact, Obregón focused on a specific objective, opposing the seating of the so-called *renovadores*, who had served in Congress under both Madero and Huerta.[96] Those were the congressional representatives whom Obregón had insulted at Madero's grave in 1914, when he offered his gun to "María Pistolas." Only once did Obregón address the Constituyente. A December 20 letter to the delegates questioned the motives of his enemies and alluded to his own disability: "May men be mutilated and die for principles, but do not allow principles to die or be mutilated for [the benefit of] men."[97]

The other Sonorenses did not play any direct role. In his report to the state congress in May 1917, de la Huerta claimed having instructed the Sonoran delegates to advocate for a profit-sharing provision.[98] Years later, de la Huerta claimed being the "intellectual author" of the new constitution's article 123, which created protections for workers, and Bojórquez reported that de la Huerta asked his state's delegates to introduce a project similar to the eventual article. While de la Huerta remained in Sonora for the duration of the convention, these claims are an example of the type of indirect influence that reformist state governors wielded at the convention via their state's delegates. It is impossible to quantify this influence, but the examples at the state level mattered.[99]

The Sonoran delegation at the Constituyente did not include major political figures. Three out of the four delegates were part of Obregón's inner circle: the twenty-four-year-old Bojórquez, Flavio Bórquez, and Ramón Ross, a childhood friend. The fourth, Luis Monzón, was a schoolteacher inspired by Magonista anarcho-syndicalism who would go on to help found the Mexican Communist Party. Monzón did not share his colleagues' admiration for Obregón or, indeed, any propertied military leader. In addition to these delegates, there was one more Sonorense—Ignacio L. Pesqueira, who served for the Federal District, closely identified with the objectives of the first chief.[100]

The Constituyente amended Carranza's draft to bolster social rights. Two articles merit particular mention. Articles 27 and 123 severely limited the prerogatives of private and particularly foreign capital. The first of their kind in the world, these articles inspired other constitutions, such as that of Weimar Germany (1919). Article 27, which bore the influence of Pastor Rouaix, author of the Veracruz Decrees, declared land and the subsoil the patrimony of the nation. The article authorized the redistribution of land to those who worked it, and it restricted the extensive privileges of foreign nationals. It required government permission for the exploitation of subsoil resources and forbade foreigners from doing so close to the coast and national borders. This provision threatened foreign ownership of the copper mines in Sonora and oil wells near the Gulf Coast. In addition, the article required foreign companies to apply for permission from the federal government to operate and barred foreigners from owning large estates. For its part, article 123 advanced the interests of the working classes. It restricted the workweek to forty-eight hours, including a mandatory day of rest, and secured the right of collective bargaining as well as the right to strike. A strong contrast with Carranza's anti-labor measures such as his shutdown of the COM and a decree that made striking a federal offense, article 123 promised the world's most progressive labor code.[101]

The issue of church-state relations took up the most time at the convention. The Jacobins believed that the Díaz regime had violated the strict separation between church and state. In its desire to gain the Catholic hierarchy as an ally, the Porfirian regime had chosen to ignore the anticlerical provisions of the Constitution of 1857, such as its limits on public worship. And while the church was no longer the nation's largest landowner, it still played a significant role by means of its educational institutions and the influence of the Catholic hierarchy, not to mention popular religion.

The voice of the Jacobins reflected the apex of the aforementioned first wave of anticlericalism in Mexico, a wave that had begun in the wake of the Huerta dictatorship and found its final expression in the new constitution. Multiple articles aimed to diminish the role of the church. While article 3 of the Constitution of 1857 had established the freedom of education, the new version mandated universal lay education. Article 5 outlawed monastic vows and orders. Article 24 limited worship to the confines of church-owned buildings. It thus outlawed outdoors worship, through which Mexicans observed religious holidays, venerated local saints and the Virgin of Guadalupe, and expressed local culture and political commentary. Article 27 barred the influence of the church in educational or charitable institutions and further tightened the prohibition against ownership of real estate. Article 33, which allowed the president to expel foreign nationals whose presence had become "inconvenient" and also proscribed foreigners from interfering with political matters, targeted the high percentage of foreign-born priests among the clergy. Article 130 denied Mexican priests political rights such as voting and commenting on matters of public interest.[102]

The anticlerical articles elicited spirited debate. Differences in class, education, and faith produced a variety of attitudes contrary to organized Catholicism, ranging from popular iconoclasm to Marxist materialism and French-inspired irreligion. One scholar has differentiated among three sources of anticlericalism. Redemptive anticlericalism centered on the belief that the Catholic hierarchy should pay for its alleged role in sustaining the Díaz and Huerta dictatorships. Orthodox anticlericalism opposed organized religion of any kind and held the church responsible for a wide array of political and social ills. Finally, liberal anticlericalism sought nothing more than the strict separation of church and state.[103] These varieties correlate to ideological differences among the Sonorenses. Madero's program had espoused liberal anticlericalism: while the Madero administration favored lay education, it did not deny the church a role in public life, as the growth of a Catholic party demonstrated. De la Huerta, the preeminent Maderista among the Sonorenses, represented liberal anticlericalism, as did Serrano. By contrast, Obregón displayed redemptive anticlericalism in the waning days of the campaign against Huerta, levying stiff punishment on the church in Guadalajara and Mexico City. Finally, orthodox, or irreligious anticlericalism figured in the policies of the three military governors: Alvarado, Calles, and Diéguez.

To sum up, the Sonorenses influenced the deliberations of the Constituyente indirectly rather than directly, as the governors among them had pioneered social rights and nationalism in their states. Calles had levied production taxes on the copper companies. De la Huerta's establishment of a workers' chamber that served as a parallel legislature on labor issues presaged workers' rights in article 123. Alvarado's agrarian code foreshadowed the land redistribution provisions of article 27. Article 33 drew on Calles's and Diéguez's experience with undesirable foreigners, especially clergy.

As a final consideration, the interpretation of the new constitution was soon to intersect with a more radical revolution. Later that year, the Bolshevik Revolution in Russia created the Soviet Union, the world's first state founded on Marxist principles. In contrast to the updated capitalism embedded in the Mexican constitution, the Bolsheviks nationalized all industries, mines, and large estates. Although the Mexican example inspired the 1918 Soviet constitution, the Soviets far exceeded it in their radical negation of property rights. In turn, the Bolshevik model found admirers in Mexico. The Soviets provided an alternate development model for an agrarian society with a legacy of authoritarianism and great inequality of income.[104] But the triumph of the Soviets also prompted an anti-Communist backlash that would sharpen opposition to reforms that the Sonorenses and other capitalist revolutionaries considered too radical.

The Sonorenses in the Carranza Era

On May 1, 1917, the Chamber of Deputies (the lower house of Congress) certified Carranza's uncontested victory in the elections held on March 11. Bolstered by the enhanced presidential authority in the new constitution, Carranza's formal power created a new challenge for the Sonorense group. Carranza had made it clear that he intended to rein in the military, represented above all by Obregón. In response, the caudillo resigned from his post as secretary of war that same day, pleading poor health and a desire to return to farming; he had also recently gotten married. As he recalled his service in the military, "I kept my morality intact despite the mutilation of my body."[105] Few politicians thought they had seen the last of him. Reported a U.S. intelligence agent: "General Obregón . . . is about to play the Cincinnatus act. That he does not consider himself a soldier, but one who has been called from his plow to help free his country, and, having established it, to return to his . . . [farm, which] seems to be very much enlarged due to his official position."[106]

Indeed, in addition to undertaking a long trip to the United States that even included a visit with President Wilson, Obregón took advantage of his freedom from official responsibilities to further his fortunes. The estate satirically nicknamed "La Quinta Chilla," or the penniless farm, increased in size from 180 to 3,500 hectares. By 1919 he employed approximately fifteen hundred workers, most of them in the cultivation of chickpeas. While Obregón diversified into cattle breeding, mining, and an export/import agency in distant Nogales, it was the burgeoning chickpea production that most defined his business activity. In 1918 Obregón and associates founded the Sociedad Agrícola Cooperativa de Sonora Sinaloa, an association of chickpea growers known as the Garbanzo League. Through Obregón's agency, the Garbanzo League procured loans and coordinated export for its members. As of 1918 it controlled 90 percent of garbanzo production worth 8 to 10 million pesos in sales. The agency's monopoly allowed it to charge a commission of US$0.50 per bag, which provided Obregón an annual income exceeding US$50,000. The cooperative also helped all members by securing a high chickpea price. In Sinaloa, the value of the harvest doubled between 1917 and 1918.¹⁰⁷ The Garbanzo League was an excellent example of the Sonorense vision for agriculture, featuring privately held farms engaged in intensive production rather than large haciendas or communal ownership of land. Obregón's emporium illustrated a more general point of a foreign observer: "The Generals devote more time to mercantile pursuits than to combating banditry, they have trains and cars, and they attend to their own private business first."¹⁰⁸

Not everything was rosy, however. In Sinaloa, the league ran afoul of the Mayo, who saw invigorated chickpea growers grab their lands. The rush to grow garbanzos shortchanged food production in favor of an export commodity. As one local citizen remarked, "You, Obregón, are a traitor to our people ... You are to bring three million Yankee dollars with you; why don't you bring some food to your people. This treason will cost you your arm, you snake."¹⁰⁹ The year 1919 brought disappointing news as commodity prices plummeted after the end of the world war. In a letter to a business associate, Obregón acknowledged that it would not be cost-effective to plant cotton, maize, or frijol beans, all because of low prices and international competition.¹¹⁰ The following year, he told the Spanish journalist Blasco Ibáñez that he had been born to be a millionaire, but that his duties to the revolution had intervened: "You see, the revolution spoiled all that for me. I then became a soldier, and I rose to be a general." However, Ibáñez was quick to add that Obregón had done very well for himself, especially through his agency's monopoly on garbanzo exports.¹¹¹

Obregón's presence in Sonora overshadowed Calles's second term as governor. Finding the treasury depleted, Calles scaled back de la Huerta's initiatives, particularly in infrastructure improvements.¹¹² He also immediately confronted a serious crisis, as the CCCC suspended operations, citing the production taxes, the new laws protecting workers, and the creation of the Cámara Obrera. The CCCC hoped that Carranza would coerce Calles to relent, since taxation and labor once again fell under federal authority. El Tigre copper mine followed suit a few weeks later. The situation in Cananea turned desperate, as unpaid workers could not afford food, water, and housing. Municipal authorities even asked Calles to move the six thousand miners to other areas where they could find work.¹¹³ But the governor would not give in to the blackmail. He sent the miners away from Cananea, discouraging them from crossing over into

Arizona, where they would "encounter a difficult situation shameful to our race."[114] Sure enough, Arizona authorities broke a strike in Bisbee and arrested twelve hundred miners, most of them immigrants. Behind this bluster, Calles used the good offices of the manager of the Moctezuma Copper Company in Nacozari to negotiate. When the CCCC rebuffed these attempts, Calles traveled to Mexico City to consult with Carranza and left Cesáreo Soriano in charge as interim governor.[115]

Calles authorized Soriano to roll back some reforms to facilitate a solution. Arguing that the promulgation of article 123 of the new federal constitution made the Cámara Obrera obsolete, Soriano closed it to the acclaim of Calles, who believed that radical agitators from the Industrial Workers of the World had infiltrated the workforce of the copper mines.[116] The gesture worked: on November 17, 1917, the CCCC resumed operations. Calles rewarded the CCCC by cracking down on activists. In January 1918 he ordered the execution of Lázaro Gutiérrez de Lara, the vice president of the American Federation of Labor in Arizona.[117]

The ongoing Yaqui War also posed a serious challenge. In October 1917 state authorities massacred seventy broncos, and Yaqui rebels retaliated by attacking trains and stealing cattle from Yori farmers. On October 24 Soriano and Calles, who once again served as zone commander, promised an "energetic, definitive, and, if necessary, terrible campaign against that relatively insignificant group of individuals who are hostile to any civilizing influence."[118] They even resumed the deportation of Yaqui rebels, this time to central Mexico. But the Yaqui refused to be cowed. Borrowing from the Zapatistas' Plan de Ayala, in February 1918 Yaqui leaders published a manifesto under the motto of *Tierra y Libertad* (land and liberty).[119]

Calles's posture toward the Yaqui contrasted with a relatively tolerant position regarding the Chinese community, compared to that of other leaders in Sonora. As the home of one-third of all Chinese residents of the nation, Sonora became a hotbed of anti-Chinese sentiment at a time when popular xenophobia primarily targeted Spaniards and Chinese immigrants, especially merchants and moneylenders. In January 1918 Calles ordered the *presidente municipal* of the town of Magdalena to "give protection to those foreigners [or] you will suffer the consequences."[120] This statement questions the assertion of one historian that Calles "enthusiastically embraced anti-Chinese racism."[121]

By the summer of 1918 Calles had given up on his dream of subjugating the Yaqui and once again focused on reforms. Buttressed by the new federal constitution, his government promulgated three major reform laws. The Ley Agraria (agrarian law) favored small estates and limited the size of large land holdings. As the U.S. State Department noted, the law allowed expropriation without due process.[122] The Ley de Gobierno (government law) guaranteed the rights of local authorities vis-à-vis the state government, affirming the principle of the *municipio libre* (free municipality). Finally, the Ley de Trabajo (labor law) protected the right to strike and banned debt service beyond the wages a worker earned in a month; it also abolished the *tienda de raya*, the infamous company store that sold merchandise for scrip at inflated prices.[123] Calles's last annual address as governor in April 1919 expressed great satisfaction with the fact that "our workers organize in councils and societies, with ever greater enthusiasm, because we firmly believe that these will help the government resolve the vexing problems of the proletariat."[124] Also of note was Calles's foundation of the new Banco Mercantil y Agrícola de Sonora, an agricultural credit bank and a forerunner of the banking institutions created during Calles's presidency.[125]

Finally, Calles and the other Sonorenses had to come to terms with World War I. In late 1916 Germany had sought Mexico as a potential ally in case of war with the United States. Intercepted by British intelligence, the Zimmermann Telegram offering such an alliance ultimately contributed to the U.S. decision to join the war on the side of the Allies. Having offered German U-boats access to Mexican ports, the Carranza administration at least considered the proposal before its publication.[126] In the opinion of one historian, the telegram reflected the pro-German sympathies of the leading Constitutionalists.[127]

Indeed, some of the Sonorenses—and notably, Calles and de la Huerta—favored Germany, at least until the United States entered the war in April 1917. Calles treated Germans very well and allowed German spies to use Sonoran territory, including his own military trainer. Yet Calles maintained close business contacts with U.S. investors, assuring them that he favored Mexican neutrality.[128] De la Huerta also held Germans in high esteem. As governor, he established a German farming cooperative near the Sea of Cortez. He believed that "the good elements of that race could serve as an example and stimulation and educate our workers in the intensive cultivation and the good administration of their haciendas."[129] According to a U.S. agent, he effusively congratulated a German citizen regarding a report that the Kaiser's troops had won a significant victory on the Western Front. However, de la Huerta recognized the commercial opportunities of the U.S. entry into the war. Sent to Washington DC, in December 1917 with the charge of explaining Carranza's neutrality, he offered the Wilson administration access to raw materials for the war effort. De la Huerta then served as general consul in New York, where he looked after Calles's eldest son, Rodolfo, a student at a military academy.[130]

Yet at least three Sonorenses held pro-Allied sentiments. At the height of the slaughter at the Somme River in August 1916, Obregón informed a close friend that he would like to travel to the Western Front to help the French army. Whether or not he aired this idea as a real possibility, the desire to help the Allies rather than the Central Powers is noteworthy.[131] The following year, a U.S. military intelligence officer reported, "Obregón ... distrusts the German influence and propaganda in Mexico and has bitterly opposed those influences and the plans for an alliance with Germany and Japan for war with the United States."[132] Obregón also maintained significant connections with French and U.S. commercial interests, for example, the Clemente Jacques food cannery. Hill, due to his U.S. ancestry, and Alvarado also inclined toward the United States and the Western Allies.[133]

The Sonorenses experimented with reform in three states under their control in the first year after the Constitutionalist victory. In Jalisco, in Sonora, and in Yucatán, members of the Sonoran group served in governorships that pioneered economic, political, and social reforms. These reforms served as a blueprint for the social rights embodied in the Constitution of 1917. Although the Sonorenses played only a limited role in the formulation of that constitution, they became some of its most committed advocates, in the sense that they recognized its importance as the law of the land and a set of guideposts for social and economic reforms. They would appeal to it selectively in their bid for national power, and even more so after they took over the reins of the government.

4 ∴ The Triumph of the Sonoran Alliance

I have such good eyesight that I could see the presidency from Huatabampo.
—Álvaro Obregón

President Carranza had enjoyed a streak of good fortune. A landowner and former federal senator, he joined the opposition when President Díaz blocked his ambitions for the governorship of Coahuila, only to fulfill this dream after Madero's victory. Huerta's coup had provided him with an opportunity to assemble the Constitutionalist faction as first chief, capitalizing on his status as the only elected state governor opposed to the new regime after Maytorena's decision to go into exile. In his conflict with Villa, luck had remained on his side through his alliance with Obregón, whose military successes had contributed decisively to the Constitutionalist victory.

Carranza's success had masked a principal character flaw. According to a Villista intellectual, "nothing inside of him surpassed his obstinacy... [and] his inability to recognize his errors."[1] After so many lucky breaks, Carranza finally ran out of miracles, making the fateful decision to oppose Obregón's presidential ambitions. The resultant final violent change of government to date set the stage for Sonorismo at the national level.

Parties and Leaders in the Carranza Era

The presidential election of 1920 was to mark the full return to constitutional rule. Special elections in 1917 had installed a bicameral Congress and elected governors and state legislatures. The Carranza administration oversaw regular congressional elections the following year. De la Huerta won election to the Senate and Serrano to the Chamber of Deputies. Understanding the Sonorense rise to power requires appreciating their role in boss rule parties that primarily served individual ambitions in a landscape still dominated by warlords.[2]

The Carranza-era party system differed from that of Maderismo. The 1911 Congress had included a new governing party, the Partido Constitucional Progresista (PCP, or Constitutional Progressive Party) as well as the Partido Católico Nacional (PCN, or National Catholic Party), along with a host of smaller parties. Madero's decision to form the PCP at the expense of the Partido Nacional Antirreleccionista that had supported him had shown the supremacy of leaders over parties. The PCN emerged as a major party in the legislature.[3] Article 130 of the constitution forbade religious political activism and thus outlawed the PCN. In the absence of a Catholic party, the programmatic differences among the parties were minor, given their adherence to a constitution with mandates for social justice, anticlericalism, and economic nationalism.

In this political universe, leaders needed parties for the purpose of bidding for power. Prior to the Constituyente, Obregón, Hill, and several other generals founded the Partido Liberal Constitucionalista (PLC, or Liberal Constitutionalist Party) at Mexico City's Casa de los Azulejos (House of Tiles). The name linked Constitutionalism with the legacies of Juárez and Madero. In October 1916 the PLC held its constitutive meeting at the home of General Pablo González, one of Carranza's loyalists, and nominated the first chief for the presidency. Although Obregón and González both desired the position at this early juncture, Carranza's election was a foregone conclusion, and both generals pledged their support.[4] Hill and others then turned the party's focus toward working for Obregón for the 1920 contest. The March 1917 elections gave the party 80 percent of the seats in Congress. As the majority party, the PLC confronted Carranza's efforts to overrule the legislature by executive fiat. Leading up to the 1918 congressional elections, the PLC called for a strong and independent role for the legislature. The party's increasingly pro-Obregón leanings pushed out the Gonzalistas and Carrancistas.[5]

On August 1917 another party emerged in support of Obregón: the Partido Nacional Cooperatista (PNC, or National Cooperatist Party). In the words of one of its leaders, Jorge Prieto Laurens, a student at the national university, the PNC represented "the workers of the fields and the cities, and also a large percentage of the scorned middle class to which the majority of us belonged and continued belonging."[6] The party pledged the nationalization of land and public utilities as well as the substitution of

10. Obregón and Hill. Fideicomiso Archivos Plutarco Elías Calles y Fernando Torreblanca (FAPECFT), Fototeca Colección de Álbumes Fotográficos de los Archivos Plutarco Elías Calles y Fernando Torreblanca, Fondo Fernando Torreblanca, álbum 2, *Historia Política de México 1913–1920, Volumen II*, fotografía 515, inventario 72. Used with permission.

the revolutionary army with citizen militias. More importantly, however, it served as Obregón's second election club, as evidenced by the influx of some of Obregón's closest associates, including Serrano.[7]

It would be impossible to discuss these parties without referring to the phenomenon of *personalismo*, or allegiance to an individual leader, and caudillo rule, its ultimate consequence. Personal allegiances formed one vertex of Latin American republicanism in the century following independence, as evidenced by the frequent use of the suffix "-ista" in histories of the Mexican Revolution. Regional fragmentation, warfare, and the weakness of the new republican institutions combined to create the vertical structures that produced caudillos such as Argentina's Juan Manuel de Rosas, Mexico's Antonio López de Santa Anna, and Venezuela's José Antonio Páez. In the words of one historian, these caudillos inspired "intense devotion among a loyal personal following independent of any formal institution, leaders who became generals *after* acquiring an army of followers rather than the other way around."[8] They also personified "charismatic leadership" according to the definition by German sociologist Max Weber: "A certain quality of an individual personality, by virtue of which one is . . . treated as endowed with supernatural, superhuman, or at least specifically exceptional powers or qualities."[9]

Throughout Latin America, nineteenth-century modernization weakened caudillos and their counterparts at the regional and local levels. However, the dictatorship of Porfirio Díaz retained many characteristics of caudillo rule. The revolution shattered the central state but not personalismo. The Constitutionalist victory made Obregón into the preeminent caudillo, increasingly at odds with Carranza, who feared Obregón's popular appeal and strove to find a civilian to anoint as his successor.[10] Like other Latin American caudillos, Obregón invited comparisons to Napoleon Bonaparte, the great military leader who had emerged from the French Revolution only to crown himself emperor and conquer most of Europe. And it was not a coincidence that Obregón's supporters dubbed their chief the "Napoleon of the West."[11]

A charismatic leader, Obregón commanded great devotion among his followers. On the personal level, the caudillo exuded warmth and an irrepressible sense of humor. His prodigious memory allowed him to address by name virtually anyone whom he had ever met. Likewise, Obregón's public persona expressed authoritative confidence. His speeches commanded his audience as much as he had mastered the geography of the Bajío before the decisive battles against Pancho Villa's armies, even as he remained vague on his political ideas. As an eyewitness reminisced, "Agile intelligence and a privileged memory characterized the young warrior. Not all of what he said sprang from his own invention, but he flavored [the ideas of others] with his own seasonings, and his tales acquired an original quality."[12]

One example of Obregón's personality is the way he represented his injury to the public. Obregón suffered from the long-term effects of the loss of his right arm on his general health and well-being, experiencing weight gain and bouts of depression. The caudillo visited a number of hospitals in the United States, mixing medical appointments with business meetings and even political appearances such as his appointment with President Wilson. In public, however, Obregón made light of his injury by telling acerbic jokes about the loss of his limb. Referencing the corruption prevalent in the revolutionary elite, he told Ibáñez, "They have probably told you that I am bit of a thief... All of us are thieves, more or less, down here. The point is, however, that I have only one hand, while my opponents have two. That's why people prefer me. I can't steal so much or so fast."[13] He then shared how one of his aides found the arm on the battlefield. As Obregón put it, the aide held a ten-peso gold coin above his head. "At once a sort of bird, with five wings, rose from the ground. It was my missing hand, which had not been able to resist the temptation to fly from its hiding place and seize a gold coin."[14] Finally, San Luis Potosí strongman Gonzalo N. Santos recalled Obregón's reply to his condolences: "Thanks so much, my brother, but it would have been far worse if they had cut my dick off." For Santos, this reply proved that Obregón was a man of the people.[15]

Carranza's civilian authoritarianism and Obregón's caudillo style constituted two important legacies of the late 1910s for Mexico's future political history. One historian has called the PRIista governments "imperial presidencies," identifying the roots of the powerful executive in the failure of the revolutionary governments to break authoritarian and *personalista* traditions.[16] Even today, some textbooks periodize postrevolutionary history by *sexenios*, the six-year presidential terms.[17] Personality cults continued past the revolution: for example, witness the examples of Lázaro Cárdenas, president from 1934 to 1940, as well as President Andrés Manuel López Obrador.

As one historian has noted, there was a third legacy at the regional level, in the form of southeastern Socialist parties. Committed to state-led modernization and social programs and popular mobilization under an umbrella of greater social equality, "socialism" in the heavily Indigenous southeast resembled U.S. Progressivism or European social democracy more so than the Marxism of the Russian Revolution. A good example was the Partido Socialista de Yucatán (PSY, or Socialist Party of Yucatán), which became the dominant party in the state after Alvarado's governorship. The party helped the ambitions of its leader, Felipe Carrillo Puerto, but—unlike the election clubs that passed for "parties" elsewhere—relied on grassroots mobilization to achieve permanence. This effort included involving women, such as Carrillo Puerto's sister Elvia, in leadership, and the state featured one of the first women in political office. The Socialist parties foreshadowed the formation of the Partido Nacional Revolucionario (PNR, or National Revolutionary Party) a decade later, and even more so, the Cardenista refashioning of that party into the Partido de la Revolución Mexicana (PRM, or Party of the Mexican Revolution) in 1938.[18] In 1919 Hill reached out to the PSY and other regional parties on behalf of Obregón's candidacy. In exchange, Carrillo Puerto asked Obregón for his protection from Carranza's designs to dissolve the PSY and set up a new military government in his state.[19]

Foreshadowing later divisions, the Sonorenses differed in their opinion about legislatures and parties. Hill and de la Huerta regarded them as crucial elements in national political life. By contrast, Obregón and Calles displayed ambivalence toward the legislative branch in general and the PLC in particular. Obregón preferred the backing of several parties so that he would not depend on any one of them. From Carranza's own experience, he understood the fickle nature of partisan support and pronounced that a victory achieved with PLC backing would not equip him with the moral mandate necessary to confront his nation's problems. From his point of view, Hill and PLC president José Inés Novelo did not comprehend the political landscape. Years of war called for a strong hand rather than parliamentary debates. Similarly, Obregón had little regard for Congress.[20] Aware that Hill and Novelo aimed to enshrine parliamentary democracy, Calles criticized the PLC leadership for seeking conflict with Carranza and enjoined Hill to disown the party's "abominable" strategy that promised "disaster" for the Obregón campaign.[21]

This attitude reflected distrust of the metropolis. According to one of Calles's early biographers, "the courteous atmosphere" of high politics was "something new for Calles, who [had] not yet lost his provincial simplicity. It bothered him to ... subject himself to the rigors of etiquette on a daily basis."[22] Obregón lambasted "the eternal enemies of the Revolution, which in their majority live here in this city" and bet on the revolutionary army.[23] In his view, the military had fought and won the revolution and deserved to be rewarded with political positions, and particularly the ultimate prize: the presidency. In the words of one historian, "It was simply too much to expect that military men, convinced the army had made the Revolution, would accept the management of their handiwork by someone not authentically a revolutionary."[24]

Not all Sonorenses shared this perspective. Hill had acclimated to Mexico City. He knew that the Sonoran generals would need to work with the city's intellectuals, bureaucrats, and professionals. From 1916 to 1917 he served as the capital's zone commander. In that capacity, Hill had obtained first-hand knowledge of the urban elite. He was convinced that the Sonorans could only wield power by shedding their image as martial northern colonists. De la Huerta, too, had spent extensive time in Mexico City. For his part, Alvarado remained conspicuously absent from the deliberations, keeping his distance from Carranza and Obregón.[25]

Obregón's Presidential Campaign

A firm believer in civilian rule, Carranza distrusted the generals. As early as January 1919, he criticized "men of certain political prestige" for aiming to "extract premature promises before they have had time to reflect sufficiently." Alluding to Obregón's and González's preparations more than a year before the elections, Carranza cited the risk of "political effervescence" if candidates campaigned too early.[26] He worried with good reason. A few months later, an article in *El Universal* identified seven presidential hopefuls, including Generals Alvarado, Diéguez, González, and Obregón and three civilians (Luis Cabrera, Félix Palavicini, and Manuel Aguirre Berlanga). The article identified Obregón and González as the frontrunners.[27] Carranza made no bones about his preference for a civilian. As he reportedly told de la Huerta, "My friend, you should run for the presidency of Mexico ... We need a civilian, not a warrior like Obregón."[28] He also asked de la Huerta to serve his administration as secretary of the interior, something the Sonorense refused, citing his commitments to his friends. In reality, de la Huerta planned to run for the governorship in the 1919 elections.[29]

Carranza's rhetoric fired up a conflict that had thus far smoldered underneath the surface. Obregón and González considered the president's words an act of betrayal, believing that Carranza had promised them his noninterference with their ambitions in 1920 as a reward for their support in 1917.[30] Obregón called the president "a great man for little things and a small man for great things ... persistent and dogmatic as well."[31]

Carranza soon showed that his aim was to prevent rather than to delay the candidacies of the two generals. His first move consisted in enlisting one of his chief advisers, Secretary of Finance Luis Cabrera. In March 1919 *Excélsior*, a newspaper friendly to Carranza, published a long letter on the presidential succession authored by Cabrera, accusing Obregón and González of peddling favors in exchange for power. Obregón responded by means of a missive under the pseudonym of Clemente Reynoso. Published in newspapers friendly to him, the letter pointed out that candidacies could not succeed without popular support, regardless of clientelist dealings. "Reynoso" also alleged that Cabrera would partake in similar arrangements were he in a position to do so.[32]

González did not help his own ambitions when he took part in a cowardly conspiracy to kill Zapata. As the culmination point of a campaign to ensconce Constitutionalist rule in Morelos, where the Zapatistas had continued to fight since Villa's defeat, his minions gunned down Zapata on April 10, 1919, at the hacienda of San Juan in Chinameca. The heinous deed created the primary martyr of the revolution's agrarian movement, eternalized on countless murals, monuments, street names, and objects of mass culture. González had long sought to turn Morelos into his personal treasure chest. While many observers considered such graft standard operating procedure, it placed Zapata's murder in a particularly cynical light. Zapata's death strengthened Obregón's hand as the caudillo, whose forces had never fought the Zapatistas, intensified efforts to court the movement after the assassination.[33]

Adding to Carranza's worries, Mexico experienced a serious economic and demographic crisis. After a dramatic recovery in 1917, when wartime demand for raw materials fetched high prices for copper, oil, and other strategic products, another downturn buffeted the economy beginning in November 1918. The end of the world war reduced demand for exports. In addition, the worst epidemic of the twentieth century—the so-called Spanish flu—struck at that moment. Claiming more than sixty million lives worldwide, the epidemic proved particularly lethal in Mexico, where millions remained injured, sick, and malnourished. According to some estimates, the flu killed five hundred thousand people and particularly hit young, mobile workers without previous exposure to the H1N1 virus strain responsible for the outbreak. Combining the flu fatalities with war casualties, emigration to the United States, and births prevented by the upheaval, historians have estimated the human toll of the first decade of the revolution in the range of 1.9 to 3.5 million lives.[34]

As if these problems were not serious enough, the end of the war also freed up the U.S. government to pressure Carranza on the Constitution of 1917. The triumph of the Republican Party in the 1918 midterm elections placed the hawkish Albert B. Fall of New Mexico in charge of the Senate Foreign Relations Committee. Fall, who enjoyed close connections to oil companies, threatened the Carranza government with reprisals if it did not abrogate article 27 and resolve thousands of pending claims. For example, defaulted bonds posed a significant problem. In the absence of diplomatic relations with Great Britain, U.S. banks remained as the government's only viable creditors—and their bankers were loath to make additional loans.[35]

Carranza agreed to negotiate. His annual address to the legislature on September 1, 1918, had defended every nation's right to make its own laws: "All countries are equal ... No country may interfere ... in the internal affairs of others ... Nationals and foreigners are equal before the sovereignty of the country in which they live.... Diplomacy ... must not be used for the protection of private interests."[36] This "Carranza Doctrine" asserted the principle of national sovereignty against transnational capital. The doctrine projected a "moderate" alternative to the Soviet socialist model: instead of threatening expropriation, it focused on erasing the political clout of foreign investors. Armed with this doctrine, Carranza sent Secretary of Finance Alberto J. Pani to meet with representatives of U.S. claimants during the 1919 Paris Peace Conference. There, Pani attempted to enshrine principles of economic sovereignty in international law.[37]

Carranza believed that he could solve two problems at once by appointing Calles the new secretary of industry, commerce, and labor, a position that had remained vacant following Pani's transfer to the Secretaría de Hacienda (Secretariat of Finance) in July 1918. Pani had spent his time in the position focusing on economic development and especially industrial production. As Calles's handling of the Sonoran copper mines had drawn favorable reviews in Mexico City, the appointment appeared an appropriate step to address the economic downturn. The president also hoped to break up the emerging alliance among Obregón, Calles, and de la Huerta.

Carranza, who had reacted disdainfully to de la Huerta's campaign for governor of Sonora, hoped that Calles would become his ally once rewarded with a cabinet-level position.[38] On April 29, 1919, the president sent Calles a terse telegram, indicating that he "needed his services." Calles consented but informed Carranza that he would serve out his gubernatorial term.[39] Meanwhile, de la Huerta easily defeated Carranza's favorite, Ignacio L. Pesqueira. Once installed in the governorship, de la Huerta came to an agreement with the Yaqui without Carranza's authorization.

In view of Carranza's efforts to divide the Sonorenses, Obregón acted quickly to assert his future political role. On June 1, 1919, "Citizen Álvaro Obregón" announced his candidacy in Nogales. Seeking to counter Carranza's strategy of pigeon-holing him as a military caudillo, Obregón pointed out that he had resigned from the army and left the "trappings of a soldier" to live a life of "legitimate well-being" as a farmer. To give the appearance that he followed the call to duty rather than his ambition, he feigned reluctance to assume a task that would involve "anxiety, responsibilities, and danger." Obregón also promised his "absolute independence" from other leaders, parties, and interest groups.[40]

The Nogales Manifesto was a classic nineteenth-century political program. It referred to Mexico's old two-party system—divided between the Conservative and the Liberal parties. Obregón asserted that the Liberal Party had divided into several groups during the revolution (read: parties such as the PLC and PNC). Conservatives represented the Porfiriato and the "oppressors," and the successor parties to the Liberal Party, the revolution of 1910 and the "oppressed." Obregón depicted the clergy, landowning elite, and foreign investors as conservative, and the lower and middle classes s as liberal. As he put it, conservatives had remained in control because liberal leaders "prostituted their prestige, blinded by their ambition or by the defense of illicit fortunes."[41] Obregón called for the creation of a true conservative party so that the liberal one could purify itself and unify. The Nogales Manifesto endorsed capitalism and advocated the "complete recognition of the legitimately acquired rights . . . of foreigners."[42] This language aimed to put U.S. investors at ease about article 27. However, U.S. observers remained skeptical. In a private letter, the editor of the *Arizona Mining Journal* commended Obregón for his advocacy of property rights and pressed him for further guarantees lest "nothing short of intervention by the United States will ever settle conditions in Mexico."[43]

Within Obregón's camp, others went even further in distancing themselves from the economic nationalism in the constitution. Hill believed that it was "necessary to rescind the radical laws ... that threaten the development of trade and the great natural riches of Mexico" in order to assure Obregón of U.S. support.[44] He built an agribusiness emporium in Sinaloa, where he proposed the building of an irrigation system large enough to deliver water to two hundred thousand hectares. In that capacity, he hoped for the support of the Carranza administration, which had provided generous tariff benefits to him in the aftermath of the War of the Winners.[45]

While Obregón therefore found himself on Carranza's right concerning foreign property rights, he also cast himself as an advocate for the poor majority. Although he remained vague on specifics, he promised land reform. He also leaned upon Calles, whom he considered his ally in Carranza's cabinet. Three months later, Calles lamented to de la Huerta, "I have now confirmed ... that the president has brought me here not to gain my help as his collaborator, but to take me out of the state of Sonora.... I understand with total clarity that I am not ... favored by the people who surround the president."[46]

In collaboration with Obregón, Calles used his first national appointment to foster ties with potential allies in Congress as well as organized labor. In Congress, Calles worked with a group of legislators disaffected with the slow pace of implementation of the new constitution. In the factories, sweatshops, and mines, the nationwide economic crisis induced bosses to test the government's resolve to defend the rights of their workers, many of whom had unionized even in the absence of enabling legislation of article 123. A labor dispute in Orizaba, Veracruz, provided a litmus test. Home to a large brewery as well as numerous textile sweatshops, the area had a tradition of working-class militancy. In the War of the Winners, the COM's Red Battalions had included thousands of workers from this region. In 1916 the COM had negotiated collective bargaining contracts. After the wartime economic boom, the bosses in the Orizaba district attempted to abrogate these contracts, targeting particularly those workers who had served in the Red Battalions. In October workers at the

Moctezuma brewery and several other industrial enterprises walked out in protest, raising the possibility of a general work stoppage.[47] Calles conducted a mediation effort that resulted in a referral to the local arbitration board. Throughout this conflict, he postured as a workers' advocate: "The individual contract... signifies the death of the labor unions, which would put workers at the mercy of the industrialists."[48]

Calles's stance won the admiration of working-class leaders, and particularly Luis Napoleón Morones, the boss of the Confederación Regional Obrera Mexicana (CROM, or Mexican Regional Workers' Confederation). Born October 11, 1890, in Tlalpan near Mexico City to a working-class family, Morones worked as an electrician. After Madero's triumph, he founded his first labor union, one representing the employees of the Mexican Telegraph and Telephone Company. When Huerta dissolved the COM, Morones made a futile attempt at organizing a Socialist party. He played an important role in procuring labor support for the Constitutionalists. In 1916 Carranza had him imprisoned for his role in organizing a strike, but Obregón reportedly intervened to prevent his execution. In 1918 Morones helped found the CROM as an umbrella organization of unions. The CROM teamed up with the AF of L to form the Pan-American Workers Federation.[49]

On August 6, 1919, Morones and Obregón signed a secret pact, whereby Obregón promised to form a separate secretariat of labor, full implementation of article 123, and official recognition of the CROM as the entity that represented the interests of workers. In exchange, the CROM supported Obregón's presidential bid.[50] Obregón saw the CROM as the representative of urban labor (a population of no more than two hundred thousand). Morones, however, also aimed to include the three million rural workers in his organization, endeavoring to transcend the differences between the urban and rural proletariat that one historian has characterized as the "sandal and [the] shoe."[51] In December, Morones founded the Partido Laborista Mexicano (PLM, or Mexican Labor Party), which served as the political wing of the CROM.

Although the CROM and PLM figured as critical allies, the presidential candidate only gave them paternalistic support, as in the following campaign pronouncement: "True equality... cannot be realized in... the meaning of the word... There are men who are more vigorous, more

11. Carranza, Bonillas, and Pesqueira. Fideicomiso Archivos Plutarco Elías Calles y Fernando Torreblanca (FAPECFT), Fototeca Colección de Álbumes Fotográficos de los Archivos Plutarco Elías Calles y Fernando Torreblanca, Fondo Fernando Torreblanca, álbum 2, *Historia Política de México 1913–1920*, Volumen II, fotografía 396, inventario 72. Used with permission.

intelligent, better conditioned . . . than others; and they, without a doubt, are those who have to gain greater advantages from their efforts. . . . But it is necessary . . . that those up high feel more affection for those below; that they do not consider them as mere elements of labor at their service, but as coworkers and collaborators in the struggle for life."[52] Obregón embraced Mexico's capitalist system. In Mazatlán he explained that "the best ruler will be the one who establishes equilibrium between [labor and capital], so that both may find . . . reciprocal advantages." Without guarantees to capital, Obregón stated, it "will remain inside the safe deposit box or outside our borders, and then our workers will continue to have to leave the country, in hungry peregrinations, to look for bread in other countries where capital enjoys the sort of guarantees that it cannot find here." "We do not gain anything," Obregón concluded, "by giving felt hats and shoes to those who wear straw hats and sandals if we take them away from people who own them."[53]

Triumph of the Sonoran Alliance   115

The tour coincided with a worsening of the conflict with Carranza. On November 26, flanked by Calles and Hill, Obregón proclaimed that he could not "hook up his car to the train of Señor Carranza."[54] In January new variables entered the equation in the form of the candidacies of González and Carranza's handpicked choice, Ignacio Bonillas Frajio, a native of Hermosillo and ambassador to the United States. Along with de la Huerta, Bonillas had served as a state legislator during the Madero years. He had subsequently numbered among those who supported Pesqueira's efforts to curb Obregón's military authority. Married to an Irish American woman, the candidate known as "meester Bonillas" depended on Carranza's support. In Obregón's inimitable sarcasm, "Bonillas [is] . . . serious, honest, and hard-working. The world has lost a magnificent bookkeeper. If I become president of the republic, I will offer him the management of a bank."[55] Behind this sarcasm lay anger at Bonillas's nomination.[56]

The growing conflict induced Calles's resignation from the national government on February 1, 1920. Calles was keenly aware of his precarious position in a cabinet dominated by Carranza's son-in-law, General Juan Barragán, whom he later labeled as the head of a "corrupt camarilla" that had transformed the general staff into a "cove of coyotes."[57] His letter of resignation referred to his involvement in Obregón's campaign as "incompatible" with his service in the Carranza administration.[58] As he wrote to de la Huerta, he resented the "small circle that surrounds Don Venustiano, . . . the most corrupt people in the country."[59] Calles's departure set the stage for a final confrontation.

The Road to Agua Prieta

The Sonorenses were far from a monolithic faction. At its core was the Obregón group, consisting of the caudillo and five leaders whose goals appeared to be closely aligned: Calles, de la Huerta, Gómez, Hill, and Serrano. Obregón shared family ties with Hill and Serrano, and Calles and de la Huerta were close friends. With the exception of the disagreement regarding the role of the PLC referenced above, this group operated in concert. Pesqueira, the losing candidate in the Sonoran gubernatorial elections in 1919, remained identified with Carranza. Alvarado and Diéguez—two Maderista comrades in arms—assumed different positions in the conflict.

Alvarado had traveled a long separate road since his departure from Sonora in late 1914. In 1917 Carranza ended Alvarado's time as Yucatán governor for fear of his independent power base. Alvarado then served a brief stint as secretary of public works before Carranza appointed him military commander of Chiapas and Tabasco under the leadership of his son-in-law, Cándido Aguilar, with primary responsibility for the ongoing campaign against the rebel faction commanded by Félix Díaz. Alvarado resented his subordination to Aguilar in view of his own long-standing service.[60] During those years, his political ideology shifted to the right, frustrated by his inability to break the power of the *casta divina* elite in Yucatán and jaded by his experience as a military commander. After a year chasing Felicistas, pragmatism had won out over idealism.[61]

Alvarado manifested his disenchantment via an open letter to Carranza, González, and Obregón. He called articles 27 and 123 of the new constitution "beautiful concepts" that had been formulated with "the best of intentions, but without the meditation and study needed for a work of such importance … It has not been the fruit of prolonged efforts of a group of capable … experts, and that is why in many cases, its precepts are inapplicable, contradictory, and obscure." Alvarado then enjoined González, Obregón, and all other divisional generals to forswear their presidential ambitions and to join him in a party of unification that could select a candidate via democratic means.[62]

The Obregonistas did not appreciate this challenge. Hill wrote to Obregón, "Our colleague Alvarado is dominated by spite and envy, exacerbated by incommensurable vanity." He also reported that Alvarado had made preparations to form a separate liberal party that would support his own candidacy, but the PLC leadership had squashed plans to meet with twenty-two party members for that purpose. According to Hill, "No one takes [Alvarado] seriously anymore around here."[63]

Alvarado also made clear that he did not accept Carranza's authority. In January 1920 he attempted to return to Yucatán against Carranza's orders. On January 14 he was arrested in Tabasco. After his release ten days later, Alvarado moved to exile in New York City.[64] From there, he sent a letter to Carranza urging him to refrain from pushing Bonillas's candidacy. "In this country," he maintained, "no one knows [Bonillas]."[65]

Diéguez sided with Carranza. Over the past five years, he had rediscovered his roots in Jalisco after almost two decades in Sonora. He had become a powerful cacique and controlled a wide swath of western and central Mexico; in contrast, the disastrous failure of the war against the Yaqui had soured him on Sonora. After Obregón's return to Sonora, he had served as *oficial mayor* (chief clerk) of the Secretariat of War. Based on his ongoing association with the president, his biographer has drawn an ideological contrast between his affinity to the supposedly "Juarista" Carrancistas, whom he considers defenders of the constitutional order and national sovereignty, and the "Jacobin" and "pro-Yankee" Obregonistas.[66] Diéguez had become a "pillar of Carrancismo,... the conservative current of the movement" that had emerged victorious in the revolution.[67] At one point, he sent Carranza three bottles of tequila in exchange for extra money from the federal government.[68]

Not coincidentally, Diéguez was front and center in the growing conflict. Carranza had increasingly interfered in Sonora as part of a larger project of repression that aimed at demoralizing Obregón's supporters. In June 1919—ten days after the proclamation of the Nogales Manifesto—the president had federalized the Río Sonora, a stream that did not empty into the ocean. Important because jurisdiction determined taxation, this measure annulled a promise from Madero to leave the stream under state control. Governor de la Huerta decried this attempt to encroach upon his prerogatives and unsuccessfully petitioned the Carranza administration to reconsider.[69] Carranza also opposed de la Huerta's signature success as governor—an agreement that disarmed the Yaqui in exchange for a legal guarantee of their land rights. With good reason, de la Huerta accused Carranza of trying to provoke another armed campaign. Carranza tried to have de la Huerta arrested for refusing to follow "orders of the federal government," with the aim of installing Pesqueira as governor.[70]

In early April 1920 Carranza sent Diéguez to Hermosillo with 250 troops. While this expedition ostensibly aimed to establish his headquarters in another campaign against the Yaqui, de la Huerta and Calles believed that it targeted the state government.[71] Calles warned Diéguez in a telegram, "If troops march on this state, there will be a civil war that will perhaps be the bloodiest ever, and you will be one of those responsible for that war."[72] An Obregonista general chimed in, "You and Mr.

12. Governor de la Huerta takes office, 1919. Fideicomiso Archivos Plutarco Elías Calles y Fernando Torreblanca (FAPECFT), Fototeca, Archivo Fernando Torreblanca, Fondo Plutarco Elías Calles, Oficial, serie *Gobierno de Sonora, 1915–1919*, mfn 101, imagen 10, inventario 184. Used with permission.

Carranza are the only ones who don't understand that the entire army is Obregonista; it is not necessary for them to rise up in arms."[73] Paralyzed by fear, Diéguez watched as his troops mutinied and withdrew from the state. On April 11 Carranza disavowed de la Huerta, named Pesqueira governor, and mobilized eight thousand troops for an invasion. With due reciprocity, de la Huerta and the state legislature withdrew recognition from Carranza. The ominous events of 1913—when the state government defied Victoriano Huerta—appeared to repeat themselves.

Meanwhile, Carranza ordered Obregón to Mexico City as a witness in the trial of an Obregonista general, Roberto F. Cejudo, who was accused of treason. Arriving from a campaign stop in distant Matamoros, he appeared before a judge in Santiago Tlatelolco prison on April 11. The government's principal evidence was a possibly forged letter that suggested a conspiracy with General Guadalupe Sánchez, among others. Because of Obregón's popularity, the presiding judge continued the hearing until the following day. Obregón retired to the house of a friend, Miguel Alessio Robles, where he learned of the escalation of the conflict between de la Huerta and Carranza.[74] Obregón understood that his life was in danger and believed that his Sonoran colleagues had only made things worse. He reportedly exclaimed, "Adolfo and Plutarco must have good reasons for what they are doing, but we're caught here in a mouse trap."[75] Obregón complained that Calles quit his cabinet post to return to Sonora and "stir up trouble there so that the federal government would have sufficient reasons" to send him to prison.[76]

That same evening, two railroad workers took Obregón to the Buenavista train station. He spent the early hours of April 12 in a nearby hiding place behind baskets filled with live chickens while the police questioned Obregón's friend about his whereabouts. Disguised as a railroad worker, he boarded a boxcar bound for Acapulco, disembarking in Iguala, Guerrero. Defying Carranza's order to have Obregón arrested, the governor, General Fortunato Maycotte, gave shelter to the fugitive. As a result, Obregón could make plans to march toward the capital. Located sixty miles south of Cuernavaca, Iguala was Zapatista territory, and the caudillo received the enthusiastic support of Zapatista generals Genovevo de la O. and Gildardo Magaña. The three generals and Hill forged an alliance that cemented Obregón's reliance on agrarian movements as a base of support. On April 20, 1920, Obregón accused Carranza of spending public funds on Bonillas's candidacy and proclaimed his adherence to de la Huerta.[77]

Thus began Obregón's alliance with Antonio Díaz Soto y Gama from San Luis Potosí, who was to wield enduring influence during the 1920s. In contrast to the homespun education of Obregón and many other leaders, Soto y Gama had a law degree. He affiliated with the Partido Liberal Mexicano and spent several months in prison before exile in the United States in 1903. This strident intellectual cofounded the COM in 1912 and joined the Zapata faction the following year. Soto y Gama's speech at the Convention of Aguascalientes that assailed the Mexican flag as a symbol of the "triumph of reaction" earned him a radical reputation. As an intellectual, Soto y Gama was in many ways Morones's counterpoint, and in that capacity he was useful to Obregón. The foundation of the Partido Nacional Agrarista (PNA, or National Agrarian Party) in June

13. Calles reads the Plan de Agua Prieta. Fideicomiso Archivos Plutarco Elías Calles y Fernando Torreblanca (FAPECFT), Fototeca, Archivo Fernando Torreblanca, Fondo Plutarco Elías Calles, Oficial, serie *Plan de Agua Prieta, 1920*, mfn 112, imagen 1, inventario 196. Used with permission.

1920 produced a situation in which two rivaling parties postured as representatives of poor working people: one branding itself "laborista" and the other, "agrarista."[78]

Later in April, 107 Sonoran leaders signed the Plan de Agua Prieta. Published in English on April 22 and in Spanish on April 23, the plan appealed to readers on both sides of the border. It provided "guarantees to nationals and foreigners and . . . very special protection to the development of industry, commerce and all business." The signatories included Calles, de la Huerta, Serrano, Alvarado, and Rodríguez. As de la Huerta's chief of military operations, Calles headlined the list. The plan withdrew recognition from the Carranza government, created a "Liberal Constitutionalist Army" under the interim command of "Supreme Chief" de la Huerta, and disavowed the results of recent state elections.[79]

Rather than an expression of support for Obregón, the Plan de Agua Prieta staked a claim for the Sonorenses as a group. Calles and de la Huerta used the opportunity of Obregón's persecution to assume leadership over the coming rebellion and precipitate action by the caudillo's rivals, and especially González, who commanded more than twenty-two thousand troops. Their choice to draft a Sonoran manifesto rather than an open-ended invitation to other rebels to join their cause—as Carranza had done in the Plan de Guadalupe—staked claims for their own influence in a future government. At Calles's request, the plan's author, Gilberto Valenzuela, had changed the name of this proclamation from Plan de Hermosillo to Plan de Agua Prieta in order to emphasize Calles's regional base over the state capital where Governor de la Huerta ruled.[80] A strong Obregonista, Valenzuela claimed decades later that de la Huerta was indecisive and "wilted" before the decisive moment.[81]

The Sonorenses then set about finding new allies. The governors of Zacatecas and Michoacán expressed support. Magaña and other Zapatistas also signed on to the Plan de Agua Prieta. Gómez initiated contact with Peláez, the strongman of the oil-rich Huasteca region and supposed co-conspirator of Obregón. The "El Águila" oil company had financed Peláez's rise in return for his assistance in staving off revolutionary violence close to the wells. A staunch defender of foreign property rights, Peláez figured among the top military leaders during the Huerta dictatorship and joined forces with the U.S. Marines to protect the oil fields. In 1917 he allied with Félix Díaz. At its height, the Felicistas controlled southern Veracruz and adjacent states. The Sonorenses would not conclude a pact with Díaz but sent Gómez to broker an agreement with Peláez that promised him the position of zone commander in the Huasteca region. Finally, González and Obregón came to an agreement in which both would collaborate in Carranza's removal so that free elections could take place.[82]

The coalition was too much for Carranza. Calles anticipated that "this revolution will be the quickest, the least bloody, and the definitive one."[83] He and de la Huerta gathered an army in Sonora, while González positioned his troops near Mexico City. With Obregón, Hill, and the Zapatistas marching on the capital, Carranza saw the writing on the wall. On May 7 he fled toward Veracruz with his entourage. The trains that whisked the Carrancistas away to the east were a combined eight miles long, including at least eight thousand passengers and the loot of five years in power: the funds in the national treasury totaling 11 million gold pesos as well as hundreds of tons of booty.[84] Two days later, Obregón once again entered the capital at the head of a victorious army: in the words of one historian, "like Caesar returning from Gaul."[85]

A different kind of history replayed itself in the president's death. In the state of Puebla, a military detachment led by none other than Zapata's murderer, Jesús Guajardo, held up some of the trains, and then torn-up track derailed the remainder. Informed that General Guadalupe Sánchez of Veracruz had joined forces with the rebels, Carranza and his aides decided to flee on foot. After a march of several days, General Rodolfo Herrero—who claimed to be a Carranza loyalist—offered the group shelter in the hamlet of Tlaxcalantongo. In the wee hours of May 21, 1920, armed men including Herrero's nephew entered Carranza's abode and killed him in cold blood. The assassination remains shrouded in mystery. Evidence ties Obregón to the crime, including the fact that he made a payment to Herrero, who remained in the army until 1937. In private, Obregón reportedly declared great satisfaction at Carranza's death. Publicly, he harshly criticized the officers in Carranza's company for failing to protect the president's life. Rumors of Obregón's involvement sullied his reputation even as the caudillo was savoring the triumph of the rebellion.[86]

Because the Constitution of 1917 had abolished the office of vice president, Carranza's death required Congress to select an interim president to serve until November 30. On May 24 Congress appointed de la Huerta, the nominal leader of the rebellion, despite the constitutional bar in article 82, section 7, which stipulated that the president "shall not have taken part, directly or indirectly, in any uprising, riot or military coup."[87] The winners of this episode of the revolution once again did as they pleased. After considerable debate, Don Fito received 88 percent of the vote.

De la Huerta entered the capital with Yaqui troops serving as his escort. It was a powerful reminder of his ability to reconcile with the Yori's most intractable enemy, and also the beginning of a short interval when negotiation won out over brute force. With Calles, Hill, and Obregón providing "strong and determined sustenance," the interim president took office in a rare moment of unity.[88]

The de la Huerta Interregnum

Often overlooked as an interlude, de la Huerta's interim presidency (May 24–November 30, 1920) marked an important period of transition. As his first task, de la Huerta oversaw the federal elections. As González had dropped out of the race in May in light of Obregón's superior support, Obregón loomed as the prohibitive favorite and faced only token opposition from the engineer Alfredo Robles Domínguez. Although Robles was no match, Obregón launched a brief campaign tour. On September 5 he won in a landslide. According to official results, he garnered more than 1.1 million votes to Robles's 47,441.[89]

De la Huerta's greatest difficulty lay in coming to terms with the U.S. government. The Wilson administration cited its practice of refusing diplomatic recognition to governments resulting from violent changes of power. The regime change was also an opportunity to exert pressure to resolve outstanding U.S. claims for losses incurred during the revolution and to insulate foreign investors from the economic nationalism in the new constitution. Without recognition, the de la Huerta administration could not obtain loans in the United States, and the Neutrality Act did not apply to exiles using U.S. territory to plot insurrection. During his brief tenure, de la Huerta could not obtain recognition, a personal disappointment to him as he spoke English and had served as consul in New York City.

De la Huerta's initial Council of Ministers (hereafter cabinet), included two Sonorenses: Secretary of Finance Alvarado and Calles, the secretary of war and the navy.[90] As the custodian of the national treasury, Alvarado oversaw the beginning of a period of economic recovery. After a year of revenue shortfalls engendered by the postwar dip in demand for commodities, a rising silver price offered better prospects. Export tax revenues reportedly totaled 42 million pesos in the first half of 1920, an increase of almost 7 million pesos over the second half of 1919. In addition, exports amounted to 424 million pesos, while imports only totaled 265 million pesos: a margin of 159 million pesos (or approximately 60 percent).[91]

Buoyed by the good economic news, Alvarado prepared for negotiations with the Wilson administration regarding new loans. With the presidential elections approaching in the United States, he knew that he only had a

14. De la Huerta, Calles, and Hill celebrate Independence Day. Fideicomiso Archivos Plutarco Elías Calles y Fernando Torreblanca (FAPECFT), Fototeca Colección de Álbumes Fotográficos de los Archivos Plutarco Elías Calles y Fernando Torreblanca, Fondo Fernando Torreblanca, álbum 2, *Historia política de México 1913–1920*, Volumen II, fotografía 575, inventario 72. Used with permission.

small window of opportunity. As he told Obregón, "It is imperative that Mexico utilize every single day between now and the inauguration . . . because the happy circumstance that an idealist who is an enemy of Dollar Diplomacy occupies the White House will not be repeated, at least not in the next term."[92] Alvarado went on several futile missions to the United States to procure new loans.[93] As he told his U.S. audience, "The foreigner who has suffered in his interests on account of this state of affairs, or who owns property in Mexico, . . . will scarcely believe the good news that the situation will soon improve in such a way as to surprise the world."[94] However, the audience was unsympathetic due to Alvarado's undeserved reputation as a "Bolshevik." Investors remembered Alvarado's radical rhetoric as governor of Yucatán rather than his pragmatic rapprochement with the planters, let alone his sensible handling of the national treasury. In response, the secretary of finance characterized Bolshevism thus: "If Bolshevism [means] conflagration and destruction and ruin, . . . I myself

15. President de la Huerta flanked by Hill, Calles, and Alvarado. Fideicomiso Archivos Plutarco Elías Calles y Fernando Torreblanca (FAPECFT), Fototeca, Archivo Fernando Torreblanca, Fondo Plutarco Elías Calles, Oficial, serie *Secretario de Guerra y Marina, 1920*, mfn 117, imagen 6, inventario 207. Used with permission.

am opposed to such a system; but if it is a new form of government, constructed on scientific principles for the amelioration of humanity, and if its application is viable in Mexico, then I believe that the reactionaries themselves will approve my subscription to its doctrines."[95]

After Obregón's election, Alvarado signaled his intention to return to private life. Aware that Obregón had opposed his appointment, he made clear that he would not support the caudillo in the same way that he had aided de la Huerta. Nonetheless, he sent Obregón a cordial letter that praised him as the "chief of a group of honorable and patriotic men" and downplayed their differences as "differences in detail perfectly explicable by ... peculiarities of temperament." As he stated, "to be a member of the national government offends my temperament, as I am sure it does that of Adolfo, Calles, and you, as well as anyone not born as a courtesan."[96]

Secretary of War Calles faced a difficult assignment, as enemies remained at large, including Villa, Félix Díaz, several Carrancista generals, and González. Calles assisted de la Huerta in striking deals with most of these rivals, including Díaz and González.[97] Coming to terms with Villa proved a more vexing challenge. Obregón had never forgiven him for ordering his death during their negotiations in the fall of 1914. Villa had eluded capture and remained a leader of mythical stature in the North. But he had tired of the chase and held de la Huerta in high esteem. Hoping that Villa's surrender might earn him U.S. diplomatic recognition, de la Huerta sent a journalist as his emissary. On July 2, 1920, Villa tendered his surrender in exchange for a guarantee for his personal safety, free elections in Chihuahua, and the grant of a hacienda large enough to feed his family and retinue of approximately five hundred troops. De la Huerta offered Villa the ranch of Canutillo in Durango, land for 250 supporters, and a personal escort of 50 men under arms. However, his emissary derailed the talks by leaking details to the press. The resultant firestorm of protest among the *divisionarios* made de la Huerta declare that he would never agree to Villa's conditions.[98]

Obregón was aghast. He wrote to de la Huerta, "In all sincerity, negotiations would constitute the greatest moral defeat for the present government," conferring "impunity for all the crimes that [Villa] has committed."[99] Another missive added that "morality, justice, and civilization" condemned Villa's past actions and that the U.S. government might not agree with the proposed deal. In his opinion, a U.S. request to extradite Villa would put de la Huerta in a delicate position. Privately, Obregón also worried that Villa would owe de la Huerta political favors in the future. De la Huerta replied that Obregón had gotten his wish with the suspension of negotiations.[100]

Aware that the Sonorenses did not speak with one voice, Villa transferred his operations to Coahuila. Unlike war-torn Chihuahua, Coahuila had prospered since the Constitutionalist victory, and Villa knew well that a move toward that state would scare local elites and U.S. investors. De la Huerta faced the choice of resuming peace talks or risking the embarrassment of a raid on Coahuila. Fortunately for the interim president, both Calles and Hill agreed that the Villista threat needed to end at whatever cost.[101]

On July 26 de la Huerta asked Hill and Serrano to inform Obregón of his decision to accept Villa's surrender on mutually acceptable terms. Hill and Serrano complied, opining that the agreement constituted the "most convenient measure to bring to an end the problem of the north."[102] The caudillo was livid: "I don't know why the president may have decided to ask you to inform me of his treaties with Villa, because he knows my opinion on this subject very well." In an allusion to de la Huerta's civilian status, he continued, "I would like to ask you to inform the president that if Villismo imperils the stability of his government, I will once again become a soldier with the same enthusiasm with which I have served the fatherland."[103] Nonetheless, Obregón grudgingly accepted the agreement, although he refused to sign it, as Calles, Hill and Serrano had done pursuant to Villa's request.[104]

While de la Huerta successfully accommodated a broad spectrum of regional leaders, from the conservative Angel Flores (Sinaloa) and Tiburcio Fernández Ruiz (Chiapas) to the radical Francisco Múgica (Michoacán) and Adalberto Tejeda (Veracruz), intractable rebels required tougher measures. As the most important example, de la Huerta ordered an expedition to subordinate the territory of Baja California to federal rule. Ironically, this expedition resembled the same endeavor the Plan de Agua Prieta had just resisted—but of course, Baja California was a territory, not a state. Strongman Esteban Cantú was a Porfirian military officer dispatched to Tijuana in 1911 to suppress the activity of anarchists. Aided by income from the brothels and casinos that served North Americans fleeing Prohibition-era restrictions, he had become an important player in the Northwest, first backing Villa and then Carranza. With a force estimated at twelve hundred troops, Cantú defied the new order in Mexico City.[105]

To subdue the rebellious warlord, Colonel Abelardo L. Rodríguez—who had earlier spied on Cantú on the government's orders—led several thousand soldiers into Baja California in August 1920. Even though their principal vessel, the warship *Guerrero*, had sunk en route in Mazatlán, Rodríguez's well-equipped troops had little trouble. Cantú delivered his office to a provisional governor and went into exile. Once appointed zone commander, Rodríguez undertook the "moralization" of the territory. Borrowing Calles's and de la Huerta's language, that effort entailed the closure of the brothels in Tijuana and Mexicali by invoking the legal prohibition of prostitution. In reality, however, moralization only went so far, as Baja California depended on revenue from vice tourism. By 1922 the casinos were back, and over time Rodríguez became the territory's most important entrepreneur.[106]

The de la Huerta interregnum prepared not only the transition to the Obregón presidency but also what observers had come to call the "Grupo Sonora." Obregón tapped de la Huerta, Hill, and Calles for the three most critical cabinet positions: finance, war, and interior (the ministry in charge of internal security and relations with the states). Ten percent of the leadership of the anti-Carranza rebellion had hailed from Sonora.[107] Yet the new political arrangement brought about its share of dissension. Alvarado drifted away from the Sonorense coalition. Likewise, Diéguez's service on Carranza's side burned all remaining bridges. Six years after the split between Governor Maytorena on the one side and Alvarado, Calles, and Hill on the other, factional differences loomed at the moment when the Sonorenses had reached the pinnacle of power at the national level, a decade after the beginning of the Mexican Revolution.

Part 3 ❖ The Sonoran Triangle, 1920–1924

5 ❖ The Sonorenses in Power

Obregón was the military caudillo; de la Huerta, the civilian representative; and Calles, . . . a politician. —Ramón Puente

A few weeks before Obregón's inauguration, Calles, Hill, and PLC boss Novelo boarded an elevator in the Palacio Nacional, one of the first in Mexico. On the way down, Calles gravely insulted Novelo, whose intention to limit presidential power had bothered him for a long time. To Calles's surprise, Hill defended Novelo and upbraided Calles for his outburst. On December 1, Obregón's first day in office, the political class gathered for a banquet designed to make peace. Among the guests were President Obregón; Hill, the secretary of war; Calles, the secretary of the interior; and Novelo. Now that the Sonorenses had ascended the pinnacle of power, the crisis required a resolution. Hill, Calles, and de la Huerta were members of the cabinet.

The banquet had a tragic outcome. Hill, dubbed the "missing right arm of Obregón," fell ill shortly after the festivities and died two weeks later. The official cause of death was food poisoning.[1] As Novelo had experienced the same symptoms (but recovered), Hill's demise provoked a storm of rumors. Although food poisoning was not a rare occurrence, and although a report circulated that Hill had died of cancer, many suspected foul play. But by whom? Probably not Obregón. The correspondence between Obregón and Hill's widow after the general's death remained cordial, a sign that Hill's family did not suspect Obregón's involvement. Obregón even acted as legal guardian for two of Hill's sons while they studied at a military academy in New York and at least once directed the Mexican consulate to send them money, as Hill left only a modest fortune.[2] True, in 1938 Miguel Alessio Robles, Obregón's secretary of industry, commerce, and labor, blamed Calles for what he called the "feast of the Borgias." However, Alessio was a partisan witness as one of Calles's most noteworthy political adversaries, and no evidence corroborating his charge has ever surfaced.[3]

Whatever the truth, the incident proved a harbinger of trouble for the new government. Many believed that Hill had held the inside track to succeed Obregón in the 1924 elections, due to his extensive experience, his role in the ruling PLC, and his closeness to the caudillo. Moreover, Obregón faced formidable international adversaries: the U.S. and British governments, which withheld official recognition; and the Holy See, which protested the anticlerical provisions of the constitution. Finally, rival military officers, civilians disaffected with Praetorian rule, regional strongmen, and social unrest challenged the Obregón administration.

The Sonoran Triangle therefore presided over a weak and precarious state. Until 1923 it held together due to the strong and genuine friendship between Calles and de la Huerta, bolstered as well by Obregón's dependence on both of these Sonorenses in his political coalition. Serrano, Obregón's close friend and kin, would also come to play an integral role in the Sonorense regime.

Defending Sovereignty

One of the primary challenges of the Obregón administration was the refusal of the U.S. government to award diplomatic recognition. Because President Wilson had cited the violent overthrow of the Carranza regime as a reason for withholding recognition to de la Huerta, Mexican officials hoped that the election of a new president would change this stance. But the State Department refused to recognize Obregón until he agreed not to apply article 27 to U.S. companies. As the *New York Times* editorialized, "Recognition ... will not be accorded unless Mexico consents to undo the mischief of her construction of Article 27 and to perform those duties required of her by international law which she has disregarded."[4]

The victory of Republican Warren G. Harding in the U.S. election in November 1920 further complicated matters. Even though Harding initially sent encouraging signals, bankers close to the new president advised against diplomatic recognition so long as Mexico did not repay its debt.[5] In addition, Carranza's nemesis, Albert B. Fall, became secretary of the interior. With Fall's ascent, two of his friends, leading U.S. oil magnates Edward L. Doheny and Harry S. Sinclair, obtained influence in the Harding administration. During de la Huerta's tenure, a Senate subcommittee under Fall's direction had issued a scathing report on conditions in

Mexico. Initially, Fall expressed great satisfaction with Obregón's pro-business positions. In his words, Obregón was "a strong, clear-thinking, conscientious type of Mexican executive"; he added, "Recognition of the new Mexican president-elect is the only course open to the United States."[6] According to one of Obregón's subordinates, Fall offered to work for recognition in January 1921 in return for a bribe of US$130,000. One month later, however, he advocated a "rigid policy" and eventually supported uprisings by Peláez and Cantú.[7] Fall's position epitomized the pro-business, antiregulation Republican Party of the 1920s.

The failure to procure immediate diplomatic recognition put Obregón in a bind. He was a president far more amenable to U.S. business interests than Carranza had been: his campaign had even assailed Carranza's economic nationalism. That said, Obregón opposed concessions as the price for diplomatic recognition, which Wilson had accorded to Carranza's unelected, preconstitutional administration. But the end of World War I had left the United States as the world's greatest power, free to take a hard line against economic nationalism. Thus, Obregón pledged "all kinds of guarantees" for capital and also promised to pay the country's foreign debt.[8]

But Obregón recognized that he could at least extract money from the oil industry. Oil had recently emerged as the nation's top export commodity. While the value of silver and copper exports had declined from 158 to 78 million pesos year-over-year, demand for oil grew due to the automobile boom in the United States. Mexico's oil production was second to only that of the United States, and in 1921 the nation took the top spot in global exports, with a share of 26 percent.[9] Thus far, Porfirian-era concessions had allowed the oil companies to pump at low rates of taxation. On May 24, 1921, the administration imposed an ad valorem tax of 10 percent, and two weeks later, it added an export tax. The oil companies responded by threatening a stoppage, but the united front crumbled within weeks as several producers found that they could not afford to halt production. The new taxes provided immediate help to the treasury: according to de la Huerta, the oil companies paid $5 million in gold.[10]

Taxation brought the oilmen to the negotiating table. A delegation of five prominent representatives, including Doheny and Sinclair, traveled to Mexico City in order to meet with Obregón and de la Huerta. This so-called Committee of Five aimed to secure a number of guarantees as well as lower tax rates. The final agreement kept the taxes in place but allowed the oil companies to pay the export tax with Mexican bonds, which reduced its effective cost by approximately 50 percent. The oil companies got further good news in August 1921, when the Mexican Supreme Court ruled that article 27 did not apply retroactively. Nonetheless, the oil companies made moves to prospect in Venezuela and the Middle East in an exit strategy occasioned by concern about further nationalist measures.[11]

De la Huerta and Obregón also tackled the matter of foreign-held debt. The Huerta dictatorship had defaulted on bond payments in 1914. In May 1922 de la Huerta traveled to New York City for negotiations with Thomas W. Lamont, the chair of the International Committee of Bankers on Mexico (ICBM). The talks were difficult, and the finance secretary sent Obregón exasperated missives about what he saw as an impossible mission. In the end, the de la Huerta–Lamont agreement assumed responsibility for $1 billion of debt, including interest. De la Huerta was unable to obtain new loans, which, as Lamont's team argued, required U.S. diplomatic recognition. The agreement severely weakened de la Huerta's standing in the cabinet, especially after he asserted (too optimistically, it turned out) that U.S. recognition would be forthcoming soon. Foreign Secretary Alberto J. Pani, who had emerged as his chief adversary in the government, criticized the agreement as unfavorable for Mexico. Having blessed each of de la Huerta's steps, Obregón agreed with Pani rather than the emissary who had gone to New York City on his behalf.[12] Calles tried to calm the waves, telling Don Fito, "Have absolute confidence and keep working with full conviction."[13] Although the government approved the treaty on September 29, 1922, de la Huerta lost trust in Obregón.

While de la Huerta's strategy of making concessions to bankers in order to weaken oilmen (who opposed taxes that could have helped pay the debt) had not borne fruit in the short term, prospects brightened the following year. An emerging scandal tainted Fall as well as the oil lobby in general. Fall had authorized leases of naval oil reserves in Teapot Dome, Wyoming, and two locations in California without competitive bidding and on excessively favorable terms. During an investigation that ultimately uncovered a bribery scheme involving Doheny's and Sinclair's payment of an interest-free loan and other considerations worth more than US$500,000, the interior secretary left office in March 1923. Later on, he served a prison term. This scandal helped the Obregón administration in negotiations that began on May 15 in a building on Mexico City's Bucareli Street. The talks did not make much progress until Harding's death on August 2, 1923. The new president, Calvin Coolidge, proved more amenable, and on August 13 the two parties signed the Bucareli Agreement, which confirmed the nonretroactive nature of article 27 and left in force the existing concessions. It also created a mixed claims commission and provided guidelines for the compensation for land expropriations. In return, the U.S. government awarded diplomatic recognition. The agreement exacted a steep price for something that many Mexicans felt should have been tendered without conditions, and it took de la Huerta by surprise. He had been left out of the negotiations with the understanding that the emissaries were only conducting informal conversations.[14]

The long campaign for U.S. diplomatic recognition reflected a multilateral approach that also saw Obregón improve relations with the Catholic Church. The Holy See and its episcopate remained opposed to the revolution and its constitution. The church's ability to mobilize its faithful forced the Obregón administration into a difficult balancing act between anticlericalism and accommodation.

On the one hand, the president and many of his collaborators, especially Calles, Morones, and Tejeda, harbored deep-seated anticlerical attitudes that reflected those of a broad segment of the public. Obregón once wrote that religious "fanaticism" made citizens willing accomplices of tyranny. "It atrophies the brain, because it disavows the right to investigation and discussion, and it withers civic mindedness because it establishes the unconditional submission to its priests." Obregón went on to claim that fanaticism "is incapable of generating any noble ambition for improvement, because its realm is not of this world ... nothing is more fruitless than fanaticism."[15] Obregón was not alone in his opposition to the church. In 1921 a bomb exploded near the residence of the Mexico City archbishop, and another detonated underneath the altar of the Virgin of Guadalupe at the basilica. One morning, a black-and-red flag—the symbol of the CROM—adorned the Mexico City cathedral.[16] Radical movements at the state level, and particularly in the Southeast, targeted organized

Catholicism. In the words of one scholar, "revolutionary anticlericalism was not just orchestrated from above."[17]

On the other hand, the church commanded a powerful presence in the homes and hearts of the vast majority of the population and actively promoted an alternate vision via grassroots organizing. Catholic associations included the Gran Confederación Nacional Católica de Trabajo (Great National Catholic Work Confederation), the Unión de Damas Católicas Mexicanas (UDCM, or Union of Catholic Mexican Ladies), and the Asociación Católica de la Juventud Mexicana (ACJM, or Catholic Association of Mexican Youth).[18] Since faith-based parties remained illegal under the constitution, these associations constituted the extent of Catholic political organization. In the contest for hearts and minds, the reliance on grassroots politics allowed the church to be more inclusive than the state. For example, the secular state still limited the franchise to men at a time when the Nineteenth Amendment had already passed in the United States. On the other hand, the church had long relied on lay associations led by women. Within a framework that portrayed women as mothers, wives, and daughters, the statutes of the UDCM endeavored the protection and strengthening of the "religious, moral, and economic interests of the Mexican woman," as well as the promotion of Catholic education and the provision of care for Catholics in need.[19]

Obregón inclined toward pragmatism. He was not likely to win a fight with the church but could take advantage of divisions between the high and low clergy as well as regional and social differences. In 1922 he reached out to the Holy See following the death of Pope Benedict XV. Seeing an opportunity for a tentative understanding in the new pope, Pius XI, Obregón sent him a congratulatory telegram following his selection on February 6, 1922. Soon thereafter, the two sides reestablished diplomatic relations. The new papal delegate, Ernesto Filippi, pointed out that Obregón's government had "never committed an act that might be considered hostile toward the Church."[20] Filippi gauged Obregón's sentiments correctly. Although Obregón had proven his credentials as a redemptive anticlerical in the aftermath of the Huerta dictatorship, when he punished the church due to its support for that dictatorship, he made an attempt to reconcile the differences between church and state as president.

However, the Cubilete affair showed the limits of accommodation. Since the late Porfiriato, Catholics had been planning a "Christ the King" shrine on Cubilete Hill in the state of Guanajuato, at the exact geographic center of the nation. The local governor, Arturo Madrazo, was a devout Catholic and critic of the constitution. On January 11, 1923, Filippi laid the shrine's first stone in the presence of approximately fifty thousand faithful, while the officiating bishop proclaimed Jesus Christ the "king of Mexico." Obregón's response utilized the very anticlerical articles the church opposed. With reference to article 24 of the constitution, which outlawed unauthorized outdoor religious celebrations, Obregón ordered the governor to stop construction. Citing article 33, he expelled the papal delegate, labeling Filippi's actions a provocation.[21] The decision highlighted the difficulty of Obregón's balancing act. His stance won the applause of Calles and Morones, both of whom had opposed the massive public ceremony at Cubilete Hill. But it also provoked widespread protests. For example, a representative of the UDCM called Filippi's expulsion "ignominious."[22]

To manage the fallout, Obregón addressed the church hierarchy, stressing the similarities between the state project and the moral teachings of Roman Catholicism: "Certain members of the high Catholic clergy have not sensed the transformation which has occurred in the minds of the people toward a modern outlook... while effective social programs have gained strength. To these latter the high Catholic clergy has not only denied its measure of cooperation but has actually opposed their development with systematic obstruction, particularly in those very features which are essentially Christian. It is certainly regrettable that the lack of sincerity in certain members of the Catholic clergy causes a continuation of this ancient struggle, when the two programs could so well cooperate." He also called on the clergy not to "calumniate nor injure the progress of that essentially Christian and humanitarian program which the government seeks to develop."[23]

The episcopate would have none of it. In a letter published in the press, they conceded that both church and state sought to address the same ills, albeit by means of radically different solutions: one "Socialist" and the other Catholic. The prelates blamed the liberal laws of the nineteenth century for what they called "social disaggregation." As the letter stated, "so long as there are so many laws in existence that abridge the rights of Catholics, there will be a religious question."[24]

The Cubilete incident therefore tested the equilibrium between anticlericalism and political pragmatism that marked Obregón's approach to the Catholic Church.[25] The church remained on the offensive, determined to shrink the boundaries of laws the clergy considered injurious to the faithful. In September 1923 the episcopate announced its intention to "resolve the so-called social question by reestablishing among the different classes, and especially between ... capital and labor, the lost peace and to settle it solidly." The group issued specific charges to each of the Catholic social organizations. For example, in defiance of secular education, it asked the UDCM to ensure "religious training in childhood."[26] In October 1924 the National Eucharistic Congress in Mexico City again violated the restrictions on outdoor worship and featured the attendance of foreign dignitaries. Obregón referred the matter to the attorney general, which prompted the cancellation of some of the congress's events, including the closing ceremony at the Teatro Olimpia, and the CROM successfully pressured the venue's employees not to cooperate.[27]

Similar pragmatism informed Obregón's stance toward the Soviet Union. The Bolsheviks aimed to eradicate social classes and the capitalist economy. They nationalized land and industry with remarkable speed. Although the capitalist Sonorenses could hardly applaud the triumph of Socialism, faraway Soviet Russia figured as a useful counterpoint to the United States and Britain. Equally importantly, the Constitutionalist triumph had brought into the government a number of radical intellectuals who gazed admiringly at the transformation of the Soviet Union, especially after the Bolsheviks' hard-won victory over the reactionary White Russian forces and their foreign backers. They pushed their own government to engage in meaningful social reform.[28] Eager to co-opt this clientele, Obregón gradually expanded connections with the Soviet Union. However, the two nations did not exchange ministers until his last year in office.

Centralizing Power and Winning Hearts and Minds

Obregón and the other Sonorenses addressed the political landscape in Mexico with the same pragmatism. Obregón continued Carranza's project of strengthening the presidency vis-à-vis the legislative branch, the judiciary, the military, and state governors. The Sonorenses confronted divergent interests in Congress and continued the long-term project to reduce the army in size. At the same time, they harnessed popular movements that demanded the social rights outlined in the constitution.

The legislative branch played an important role despite the constitutional reforms that gave the president additional powers as well as virtual immunity. It fell to Congress to pass implementing laws of the constitution's provisions. The bicameral legislature provided a theater for several political parties, most of them loyal to the executive. In the 1920–22 legislature, the PLC dominated both the Senate and the Chamber of Deputies. The Cooperatistas constituted the PLC's primary rival.[29] While there were parties associated with *agrarians* and workers—the PNA and the PLM, as well as the new Partido Socialista del Sureste (Socialist Party of the Southeast) under the leadership of Yucatán governor Felipe Carrillo Puerto, the PLM had experienced a resounding defeat in the 1920 elections. A party formed out of the remnants of Maderismo, the Partido Nacional Antirreleccionista (National Anti-reelectionist Party) became a counterweight to the pro-government coalition. De la Huerta was an advocate for a strong legislature. In part due to his influence, Obregón made good on a campaign promise to support a constitutional reform designed to strengthen Congress. One amendment made it more difficult for the president to escape legal accountability for his actions. Another enhanced the power of the congressional leadership. As a result, early on, de la Huerta opined, "On the part of Congress, there is no resentment whatsoever regarding the federal executive."[30]

However, the honeymoon did not last. Hill's death robbed the PLC of its most exalted representative, and Obregón and Calles worked to undermine the dominant party. An example of the new dynamic came on May 13, 1921, when a crowd of 150 workers occupied the Chamber of Deputies to the shout of "Long live the Russian Revolution" and placed a red-and-black banner on the rostrum. Immediately afterward, Soto y Gama and his primary PNA ally, Aurelio Manrique, delivered impassioned speeches invoking Zapata's revolutionary memory.[31] Incensed, the chamber's majority approved a memorandum to Obregón that charged Calles with "fomenting [a] radical movement." As evidence, they alleged that

Calles had done nothing to prevent this incident as well as other social conflicts in several states of the republic.[32] Although Obregón condemned the demonstration, he refused to weigh in on a congressional debate. The ultimate result was the resignation of the agriculture secretary, General Antonio J. Villarreal, one of only two PLC members of the cabinet.[33]

The decline of the PLC accelerated when the party unveiled plans for a constitutional reform to build a true parliamentary republic. The reform proposed the creation of the office of prime minister and the right of Congress to appoint the members of the cabinet from a slate nominated by the president. Moreover, the PLC majority also endeavored to assert the legislature's budget-writing authority via an end to the emergency fiscal powers of the executive that had persisted since 1917. Strongly opposed to both projects, the Sonoran Triangle entered into an alliance of convenience with the PNC and leaned on the PLM and PNA, which supported the centralization of power so long as the government made good on its promises to both parties.[34]

The effort to weaken the PLC bore ultimate fruit in 1922. The other parties formed a new bloc that seized control of the powerful Permanent Commission, which oversaw the most important budgetary and personnel processes in the Chamber of Deputies. In a rotation that became a common phenomenon in the 1920s, many PLC deputies defected to the PNC. In the words of one historian, the PNC's growing power "scandalously fomented opportunism in its midst, as many of its adherents only did so ... to capture a public office or cushy job."[35] The PLC then suffered a disastrous defeat in the midterm elections. The outcome was a realignment in favor of the executive. In the twenty-eighth legislature (1920–22), the Chamber of Deputies initiated 74.5 percent of all legislation, as opposed to the executive branch at 21.3 percent. That was the highest percentage since the Constitution of 1917. In the twenty-ninth legislature (1922–24), the executive branch originated 50.8 percent of all legislation, and the Chamber of Deputies only 40.8 percent.[36] Thus, the PNC's ascendancy did not create a stronger or more effective legislature. Soon, the PNC and Obregón clashed over the legislature's authority over judicial appointments.[37]

Amid this ongoing tension with the legislative branch, the Sonoran Triangle ruthlessly suppressed dissent, especially after Serrano became secretary of war in December 1921. Serrano squashed a series of regional uprisings in Michoacán, Puebla, and Tabasco. In August, the army defeated the rebellion led by Francisco Murguía, a veteran of the battles against Villa.[38] The assassination of General Lucio Blanco provided another example of repression. Credited for the first documented agrarian reform undertaken at Félix Díaz's expense in August 1913, Blanco represented the unfulfilled promises of the Constitutionalist coalition. He had gone into exile after the Plan de Agua Prieta, and Obregón considered him an ongoing threat. On June 7, 1922, a group of criminals seized Blanco and one of his associates in Laredo, Texas. The kidnappers drove both men across the border, where they riddled them with bullets and dumped their handcuffed bodies into the Rio Grande. The murders produced an outcry in Texas and led to an investigation by the local district attorney. While authorities never solved the crime, its careful execution suggested government involvement.[39]

Another important project was the downsizing of the revolutionary army, a task begun under de la Huerta. Many officers and enlisted men appeared on the rolls without actually serving in the armed forces. In 1921 the Secretariat of War moved nineteen hundred officers, including ninety-one generals, to reserve status at half pay. On September 1, 1922, Obregón reported the decommissioning of 2,697 officers, including 77 generals over the preceding twelve-month period. One year later, Serrano had shrunk the army to approximately fifty thousand enlisted men commanded by twelve thousand soldiers of rank, including thirty-two divisional generals.[40] Serrano and Obregón also moved to restrict the political activity of officers. They desired to purge the military of disloyal elements, a process that strengthened its role in upholding the status quo, and also increased the number of military zones from twenty to thirty-five in an effort to diminish the power of individual zone commanders.[41] In the words of one historian, "military reform would be crucial to the new regime's power and to its self-image as a progressive, modern regime that had broken with the past."[42] It also made good fiscal sense, as the army's share of the budget declined from 65 to 44 percent in three years.[43]

Balancing out this reliance on repression and a smaller, modern army, the Obregón administration used negotiation in its dealings with agrarian movements and organized labor. Accompanying an ambivalent stance vis-à-vis the constitution, the Sonorense regime assumed a similar position toward the emergent popular movements. During Obregón's tenure, agraristas and workers made slow progress.

Most importantly, Obregón gave new impulse to land reform. At the time he took power, an estimated 71.4 percent of the population worked in agriculture, fishing, forestry, and hunting.[44] Yet the government did not have a clear position on agrarian reform. On one side, Soto y Gama expected an immediate resolution of the "agrarian problem." On the other, Serrano argued that land redistributions would ruin the rich without helping the poor, and that the expropriation of legally acquired land amounted to robbery.[45] In October 1920 Obregón appeared in the Chamber of Deputies to share his thoughts as president-elect. He announced that he would distribute six million hectares to a million smallholders, asserting that the availability of underpaid agricultural labor had encouraged hacendados to retain antiquated methods of cultivation, while also starving their workers. Aware of his own large estate, he also espoused the benefits of modern, privately held commercial agriculture as a creator of wealth. Obregón opposed giving peasants more land than they could farm and demanded due compensation for expropriated land. Although he called for the establishment of *ejidos*, tracts of land designated for communal farming, he warned that expropriating all estates larger than fifty hectares, as the PNA had proposed, would cause famine and ruin. He proclaimed, "Once property and agrarian credit have been destroyed, we will chase away the foreign capital that we need more than ever; we will have created an economic disequilibrium as there will not be anyone from whom to collect taxes, just because there is a law that does not allow anyone to own more than 50 hectares."[46] Significantly, Obregón proposed redistribution by *dotación* (grant) rather than restitution. In contrast to both Zapatista demands and Carranza's Veracruz Decrees, which had promised the return of the land stolen by large landowners, Obregón promised to give out land to campesinos who needed it.[47]

This presentation outlined the direction of land reform. The 1921 Ley de Ejidos set the framework for communal farming and paved the way for some degree of collectivization of agriculture, with an important proviso. As Obregón told Congress, "although the most advanced revolutionary principles have inspired [this law], it is grounded in the concrete knowledge of the necessities of this country."[48] In the end, the administration parceled out 1,100,117 hectares, less than 20 percent of what Obregón had envisioned.[49] Still, the amount was seven times as high as Carranza's redistributions, and Soto y Gama proclaimed Obregón "the executor of the ideas of Emiliano Zapata."[50] Obregón blamed Congress for the slow pace of reform and called for "more ejidos [and] less politics."[51] The criticism was unfair, as landowners could file an *amparo* (injunction) in court against a land distribution order. In addition, his law required presidential approval to turn provisional into definitive land grants.[52]

Obregón's policy obeyed opportunistic dictates. The Zapatista area in Morelos, southwestern Puebla, and northern Guerrero figured prominently in the land distributions, and Yucatán constituted a second regional focus. Governor Carrillo Puerto expropriated 20 percent of arable land but largely spared the henequen export economy. Finally, the administration expropriated the Terrazas's uncultivated land in Chihuahua in exchange for 13.5 million pesos in compensation. Elsewhere, agricultural production trumped land reform. For example, the Yaqui vainly waited for land distribution. Obregón had promised to end the concession of the Compañía Constructora Richardson, which had still not fulfilled its terms. As president, however, he reaffirmed the concession as part of his effort to gain U.S. diplomatic recognition, in exchange for a promise to build new canals and hydraulic plants. As another example of Obregón's emphasis on agricultural production, he allowed Canadian Mennonites to settle in Chihuahua. He not only exempted them from military service but also allowed them to operate religious schools in violation of the constitution. Obregón believed that the Mennonites would serve as a model of productivity for their neighbors. Finally, sometimes the president played favorites. For example, in Puebla, Obregón spared the estate of the Tennessean William O. Jenkins, who would later become one of the country's preeminent magnates, but signed a decree confiscating the hacienda of the British American Rosalie Evans.[53]

Obregón assumed a similarly opportunistic posture toward labor, and particularly the CROM. In January 1921, just over a month after taking office, his government financed the Third Congress of the Pan-American Federation of Labor in Mexico City. Presided over by Samuel Gompers, the congress brought together delegates from the United States, Mexico,

Central America, and the Dominican Republic.[54] The administration also rewarded the CROM for its alliance. In contrast to Carranza's heavy-handed approach, Obregón initially gave free rein to the labor confederation and allowed them to collect mandatory contributions of up to 10 percent of wages to finance CROM and PLM activities. His first year in power witnessed more than three hundred strikes involving more than one hundred thousand workers in total. Obregón named a cobbler chief of the Federal District. During his presidency, the CROM's claimed membership rose from 100,000 to 1.2 million. Through ties with Secretary of the Interior Calles, organized labor got a seat at the table. De la Huerta had appointed Morones head of munitions and army supplies—the first time that someone from the urban working class had been appointed to a national political post. Morones continued in that position under Obregón. Congress began to write implementing legislation of article 123, the provisions concerning labor that Carranza had virtually ignored. This legislation provided a regulatory framework for the workforce in private business that included the right to strike, subject to presidential veto. Obregón also supported the type of social security legislation pioneered by Alvarado, Calles, and de la Huerta during the 1910s, but he was not able to secure congressional approval for this initiative.[55]

Obregón ultimately disappointed the CROM and labor movements more generally. The president never fulfilled the terms of his pact with Morones, which included the creation of a separate labor secretariat and full implementation of article 123.[56] Obregón's relationship with Morones soured as the president favored the PNA over the PLM. But the CROM remained fortunate compared to other labor organizations. Obregón did not tolerate strikes that had not received prior authorization, or the formation of radical unions. Organizations that had resisted CROM incorporation, such as the railroad workers and the Confederación General de Trabajo (General Workers' Confederation [CGT], which had developed connections with de la Huerta during his interim presidency), found themselves targets of repression, as did the Gran Confederación Nacional Católica de Trabajo. When the railroad workers struck without authorization, Obregón reportedly exclaimed, "Either the workers rule, or I rule!"[57] The president also expelled activists from the Industrial Workers of the World. Not surprisingly, a representative from a rival workers' confederation complained, "All of our efforts within legal channels have been useless, because neither the state's executive nor the legislative powers will attend to our demands."⁵⁸ As a consequence, labor leaders took matters into their own hands, and strikes increased in frequency.

The 1922 renters' strike in Veracruz served as a case in point. In protest against squalid living conditions, the city's sex workers coordinated a refusal to pay rent in excess of 2 percent of the value assessed for taxes. Soon thereafter, Herón Proal, an anarchist one-eyed tailor, founded a renter's syndicate that expanded the purview of the strike to the entire city and its surroundings. At the peak of the movement, more than ten thousand renters refused to pay, and Proal emerged as the real local authority in Veracruz, defying both Obregón and Governor Adalberto Tejeda. He set up revolutionary courts and administered his own version of justice, targeting especially landlords and other property owners. Although Tejeda had the strike leader jailed, Proal escaped from prison, remaining on the run until December 1923.⁵⁹

Calles and de la Huerta took advantage of Obregón's difficulties with organized labor. As we have seen, Calles had begun cultivating workers' organizations in 1919 while serving as secretary of industry, commerce, and labor. He met Morones in the Obregonista campaign headquarters. As internal security was the job of the secretary of the interior, it was Calles whom workers credited for allowing the CROM to operate without impediment. De la Huerta was able to burnish his credentials as well due to his well-deserved reputation as a skillful negotiator. Even though dealing with labor movements was not part of the secretary of finance's portfolio, the president asked him to attempt mediation with the radical railroad workers union. Similarly, as someone who had not given up his elected position as governor of Sonora, de la Huerta played a leading role in renewing talks between the Yaqui and the provisional state government under the direction of Calles's first cousin, Francisco S. Elías.⁶⁰

This discussion of Obregón's policies would not be complete without reference to his government's cultural program, and especially its commitment to rural education. Upon de la Huerta's advice, Obregón founded the Secretaría de Educación Pública (SEP, or Secretariat of Public Education). To head the new agency, the president nominated José Vasconcelos, the rector of the National University. De la Huerta had befriended Vasconcelos in April 1913 while visiting Carranza on the occasion of the Monclova Convention. The task: implementing article 3 of the constitution, which prescribed free, secular, and universal education.

A lawyer, philosopher, and writer, Vasconcelos was what one historian has described as Mexico's "cultural caudillo."[61] He was not only a foremost theorist of *mestizaje*, or racial mixing, but also a contrarian within a secular administration dominated by military men. Vasconcelos attended the elite Escuela Nacional Preparatoria with de la Huerta. As a law student, he joined the Ateneo de la Juventud (Youth Atheneum), a circle of radical students critical of the Díaz regime and opposed to U.S. influence. Vasconcelos edited an anti-reelection newspaper and then served Madero's government. The Huertista takeover drove him to exile in Paris. Vasconcelos returned after Huerta's defeat and became minister of education under Conventionist president Eulalio Gutiérrez. In a compromise space between a secular administration and Mexico's Catholic majority, Vasconcelos's belief system focused on Jesus's ethics rather than his divinity or miracles.[62]

Vasconcelos's SEP aimed to raise literacy from a rate of 15 to 20 percent of the adult population. A secondary goal was to inculcate a federally mandated curriculum, including civics classes that promoted allegiance to the nation as well as instruction in public health and hygiene, an important matter given the high death toll of the influenza outbreak in the late 1910s. Helped by a budget second only to that of the army, the SEP built more than one thousand rural schools over the next three years. These schools became a contested site between teachers and the local population and their priests, who often resisted the secular teachings of the strangers who had arrived in their midst. Although the new schools did not suffice to bring universal literacy, they brought the teachers who instructed rural Mexicans in reading, math, writing, hygiene, and social studies into contact with a different world. As the 1920s progressed, many of these teachers were trained in new rural *normales*, or teacher schools, which became sites of radical politics. The teachers found communities that often resisted their curriculum and soon realized the need to negotiate their assigned task with local priorities. Women considered that task rewarding, as it gave them a sense of belonging to the nation even as they remained disfranchised in federal elections.[63] The government's efforts to inculcate secular education in the countryside made for a more active church. In Tlaxcala, for example, priests made regular appearances at Sunday mass in rural areas that they had previously visited only a few times per year.[64]

The education campaign again showed the difficulties of the Sonorenses, and specifically Obregón, in coming to terms with urban intellectuals like Vasconcelos. The president considered his education secretary arrogant in his adherence to "Western" and particularly "classical" education. A story of that time relates an anecdote from a trip through rural Mexico in which Obregón's group, which included Vasconcelos, had lost their way. As the story goes, the president approached a poor Indigenous couple:

"Compadre! ... Can you tell us where we are?"
 The man shook his head.
"But what place is this? What town are we near?"
 Again the man did not know.
"Were you born here?" Obregón asked.
"Yes."
"And your wife also?"
"Yes."
"So you were born here, your wife was born here. You've both lived out your lives on this spot, and yet you don't know where you are?"
"No."
"José," Obregón said to Vasconcelos, "make a note of this man so you can send him a complete edition of the classics you've just edited."[65]

An important part of the education campaign involved showcasing revolutionary art, and especially on murals in government buildings. Three famous muralists, Diego Rivera, José Clemente Orozco, and David Alfaro Siqueiros, painted their work in public spaces. Of these, Rivera was the most significant. This project began in 1922. Rivera painted his most famous murals inside the National Palace and the SEP. Neither the Sonorenses nor Vasconcelos agreed with Rivera's Marxist interpretations, which depicted history as an epic class struggle between capitalists and caudillos on one side and the poor on the other. But they knew that their tolerance of radical public art was a way of co-opting some of their critics on the left.[66]

The Sonorenses in Power 149

This campaign to conquer hearts and minds coincided with a new influx of foreign observers who wanted to study a revolution from up close. During the 1910s only intrepid souls such as John Reed and Ambrose Bierce, both fascinated by Pancho Villa, had dared visit Mexico. The arrivals in the 1920s included the writers D. H. Lawrence and Katherine Anne Porter, the journalists Carleton Beals, Ernest Gruening, and Frank Tannenbaum, and the photographer Tina Modotti. Beals, Gruening, and (initially) Tannenbaum would go on to become propagandists for the Sonorenses. Notable Latin American visitors included the Peruvian politician Víctor Haya de la Torre and the Chilean poet Gabriela Mistral, who worked with Vasconcelos in the SEP. Occasionally, Obregón would play to the stereotypes of his Anglo-American guests. As he once told Gruening, "When I left the country and came into the city, the bandits all came in with me. Confidentially, I have some of them in my Cabinet now!"[67] For her part, Mistral became one of Obregón's most vocal propagandists during her two-year stay that saw her attend a number of official functions as one of the few women present. One of her writings assailed the image of Obregón as a gunslinging and uncultured ruffian, an image cultivated by Spanish novelist Blasco Ibáñez: "The president of Mexico never appears like that general without any culture, full of grotesque vanity" portrayed in Ibáñez's "sensationalist work."[68]

Finally, Obregón grasped the symbolic significance of the centennial of the consummation of independence under Emperor Agustín de Iturbide. In contrast with the celebrations of 1910, which had highlighted the disconnect between Porfirio Díaz and the agrarian rebels that had commenced the Wars of Independence under the leadership of Father Miguel Hidalgo, 1921 offered an occasion to commemorate state-making by compromise. Just as Iturbide had brought together insurgents and loyalists to end eleven years of war, so had Obregón's faction finally tamed a revolution after ten long years. Of course, Obregón was not too eager to have his citizens compare him to Iturbide, a controversial and self-aggrandizing emperor who left office in disgrace. But he visited the national cathedral accompanied by the diplomatic corps and deposited a floral offering at the altar containing Iturbide's remains, thus extending an olive branch to Catholics, who remembered Iturbide as someone who had ensconced Catholicism as the state religion. A committee composed of Calles, de la

Huerta, and Pani organized a great *fiesta patria*, this one less ostentatious than Don Porfirio's event commemorating the centennial of Hidalgo's rebellion and his own eightieth birthday in September 1910. At least in Vasconcelos's opinion, the fiesta was still too expensive for a nation that had just emerged from a decade of revolution.[69]

A Triangle and a Camarilla

Two different networks structured the Sonorense coalition in power: a "triangle" and a *camarilla*. Both these networks included both Calles and Obregón. Defined as Obregón, Calles, and de la Huerta, the Sonoran Triangle controlled the political scene in the powerful executive branch. The triangle included Serrano and Gómez as junior partners and high-ranking officials in the capital (Serrano as secretary of war and Gómez as commander of Mexico City). Composed of Obregón's business partners, the camarilla operated through economic rather than political connections. Aside from Obregón, Calles, and Rodríguez, it also included Obregón's private secretary and Calles's son-in law, the Mexico City native Fernando Torreblanca, fellow Sonorenses José María Tapia and Ignacio Gaxiola, the Nuevo León native Aarón Sáenz, and the Chihuahuense Luis L. León.[70]

The triangle featured a unique dynamic among its primary members. It was asymmetrical in terms of power, with Obregón holding overweening authority. However, according to one observer, the two weaker members were closer friends: "General Obregón, Calles, and de la Huerta ... were good friends, but the latter two loved each other like brothers. The Sonorense caudillo could sometimes show resentment toward them, but Calles and de la Huerta marched to the same beat. They had a frank and loyal friendship."[71]

Calles made up for his lack of charisma via a deep understanding of Obregón's personality. As one observer put it, "In Obregón, one finds a plethora of life, of self-confidence that makes him as powerful as a tidal wave ... Calles exudes less vitality, an energy that one might call passive, and an intimate confidence that results in a quiet character. When Obregón comes with the momentum of an unstoppable wave ... the wave clashes as if it hit a jetty." In that observer's view, Calles was the stronger half of the pair. "Calles fundamentally understands Obregón's soul. He seems to have dedicated all of his ... pedagogical practice to probe this spirit.

He understands it like that of a child; he penetrates and dominates him like a man.... Obregón never comes to understand Calles. Probing souls is not his specialty."[72] As a result of this understanding, Calles often pushed the caudillo to the limits, but he knew when to stop and defer to the primary Sonorense patriarch.

The relationship between de la Huerta and Obregón deteriorated over time. Obregón did not respect civilians the way he did fellow generals—even deficient ones as he believed Calles to be. He was suspicious about the circumstances that led to the Plan de Agua Prieta. He had never forgiven de la Huerta for procuring Villa's surrender under what he saw as exceedingly favorable conditions. De la Huerta's negotiations with bankers and oilmen in New York City had left the secretary of finance and president leery of one another, and the Bucareli Agreement made matters much worse. Don Fito could not help but notice a double standard, as Obregón had harshly criticized him for concessions to Lamont that were much smaller than those to the U.S. negotiators in the Bucareli Agreement.

One crucial imbalance within the triangle came from its overlap with a camarilla that used political leverage to enhance its wealth. This camarilla drew Obregón and Calles closer together, to the exclusion of de la Huerta. While Obregón and Calles portrayed themselves as friends of the agrarians and organized labor in Congress, they followed a different script in Sonora and elsewhere where their own investments were at stake. In Sonora handpicked leaders pursued a developmentalist policy that gave ample facilities to U.S. investors and their Mexican allies. At the same time, a state that had set up a "Cámara Obrera" in 1916 closed its doors to the CROM, let alone more radical workers' organizations. As one historian has argued, in Sonora, Obregón and Calles "applied those economic and political initiatives that they considered a priority, without the concessions and constraints that they allowed at the national level."[73]

Sonora's governors enjoyed close ties first to de la Huerta, then Obregón, and finally, Calles. Until 1923 a series of interim governors ruled along with de la Huerta, who had been elected to a four-year term in 1919 and never formally gave up the position despite holding offices in the national government. During that time, the state government returned to the Yaqui six out of their eight villages. Alejo Bay Valenzuela (1923–27) was related to Obregón by marriage and triumphed over a candidate backed by Calles.

Fausto Topete Almada (1927–29) was a distant relative of Obregón and the former chief of his personal escort. After Topete's participation in the Escobar Rebellion, Francisco S. Elías (1929–31), Calles's first cousin, became interim governor, followed by Calles's eldest son, Rodolfo (1931–35).[74]

The Sonorenses depended on these governors to a varying degree. Obregón held the largest stake, as the lion's share of his investments was located in the state. During the 1920s the holdings of the Calles clan grew more dispersed but remained confined to the north, including a citrus hacienda in Nuevo León, a sugar estate in Tamaulipas, and another one in Sinaloa, in addition to Rodolfo's holdings in Sonora. Rodríguez first invested in Baja California before branching out elsewhere in the republic. These three affluent Sonorenses participated in what one historian has called an "evolving elite-foreign enterprise system" that had commenced in the Porfiriato.[75] Just like the científicos, the Sonorenses camarilla established close business ties with U.S. citizens and corporations.

Rodríguez's burgeoning fortunes deserve special mention. Rodríguez transformed a territory in the process of intense economic development into a sinecure. Unlike the elder members of the group, he made his name as an entrepreneur more so than as a general or politician. As such he put down deep roots in Baja California. In February 1922 he was named zone commander in Nayarit. But after circulating among six different military positions in different regions, Rodríguez returned to Baja California as zone commander in late October 1923. Obregón named him interim governor. Since Baja California had not yet attained statehood, the governorship was a federally appointed position. Thanks to his support of the federal government and a number of shared business ventures with Calles and Obregón, Rodríguez held it for six consecutive years. Despite frequent popular complaints about the growth of vice tourism in the territory, which contradicted the government's commitment to "moralization," Obregón allowed Rodríguez's ventures to grow without any impediments.[76]

Rodríguez became the single most influential Mexican entrepreneur in the state, owning fisheries and pioneering wine production. 1927 saw the opening of the glamorous Agua Caliente hotel and casino, an establishment that one historian has dubbed "America's greatest gaming resort."[77] Funded by Southern California investors such as Baron Long,

Wirt Bowman, and James Crofton and helped along by the diversion of federal building materials toward its construction, Agua Caliente enjoyed the protection of a government officially devoted to "moralization." It enjoyed an ample water supply when Tijuana remained underserviced in terms of its water needs.[78] Not surprisingly, the U.S. trio became derisively known as the "Border Barons," with Rodríguez as an unofficial fourth member.[79] The governor frequently reminded Obregón and Calles that the casinos provided tax revenues and that the barons had "demonstrated their friendship" toward the government. The brisk tourism business in the Prohibition era allowed Tijuana bosses to pay some of the highest wages in the republic: stone masons made 24 pesos a day and even campesinos took home 4 pesos (US$2), or four times as much as in the rest of the country.[80]

Rodríguez was not alone in taking advantage of his military and political position. As U.S. journalist Ernest Gruening later wrote, "Exceptional was the *jefe de operaciones* who did not carry several side lines—usually the exclusive gambling house concession, forbidden by law, the proceeds of a hacienda or two, to which his soldiers would carry the manure of the *jefatura's* horses, or the lucrative task of 'protecting' other hacendados from agrarians. The fault, at least in part, was Obregón's."[81]

The Sonorenses strengthened their camarilla through family and business alliances. In 1922 Calles's eldest daughter, Hortensia, married Fernando Torreblanca, Obregón's private secretary, who henceforth became a crucial intermediary between the two Sonoran patriarchs. Another such intermediary was Soledad "Cholita" González, who served as personal secretary to Madero, Obregón, and Calles. Cholita had typed up Madero's treatise *La Sucesión Presidencial* at the age of thirteen and later, Obregón's lengthy memoir of his revolutionary campaigns. She became Calles's confidante and later married his personal physician. Calles's second-oldest son, Plutarco "Aco" Elías Calles Chacón married the sister of Aarón Sáenz Garza, an Obregón loyalist and distant relative of Monterrey's powerful Garza Sada family. The Calles and Sáenz families later acquired thirty-eight thousand acres in the Huasteca region of Tamaulipas. Established in 1930, the Compañía Azucarera El Mante became one of the largest sugar estates in the country and a symbol of Sonorense corruption.[82] At the same time, Calles and Obregón began to collaborate with Rodríguez in his business ventures. The other Sonorenses remained excluded from these entrepreneurial networks, setting up a distinction between the "core" group of Obregón, Calles, and Rodríguez and the "periphery."

As part of this periphery, Serrano enjoyed entrepreneurial success, in part due to his leverage as secretary of war. While he had participated in Obregón's early ventures, their commercial interests drifted apart in the 1920s. Serrano joined four other partners, including Sáenz, in founding a business dedicated to the repair of railroad engines and cars in the Federal District. Along with Calles and several others, including Manuel Peláez, he also participated in a treasure-hunting venture in La Malinche, a volcano on the border of the states of Puebla and Tlaxcala. Serrano's most important entrepreneurial initiatives involved General Juan Andreu Almazán of Nuevo León, a political chameleon who had affiliated with Madero, Huerta, Félix Díaz, and Zapata before supporting the Sonorenses. The two friends collaborated in banana production in Oaxaca and in a project to convert arid land in Durango into irrigated farmland. Almazán later became one of the wealthiest revolutionary generals—on par with Rodríguez. An opponent of land reform, Serrano was tone-deaf in his ventures in former Zapatista territory. In 1923 he attracted the attention of an agrarista cacique in western Puebla when he and his retinue toured the area in search of haciendas to buy. A few years later, he also bought a large estate and sugar mill in Cuernavaca. What is notable about the Serrano-Almazán combination is its independence from the Calles-Obregón-Rodríguez camarilla. That independence would eventually come at a cost.[83]

Life in the Big City

The Sonorenses residing in Mexico City meshed with the metropolitan elite to varying degrees. As we have seen, Obregón disliked the upper class in the national capital. The high society reciprocated, resenting the revolutionary generals and Obregón in particular as lower-class parvenus. Yet as the old elite took measure of the Sonorenses, they found moderation rather than radicalism. They especially liked de la Huerta's conciliatory measures such as amnesty for political opponents (as president) and negotiations with U.S. bankers (as treasury secretary). It helped that de la Huerta knew the city and its elite well, having earned a high school degree there at the turn of the century and spending time as a senator and then government official under Carranza. Over time, they also warmed to Obregón and the other generals. In 1921 the government drew favorable reviews for the celebrations commemorating the centennial of independence. These celebrations featured the leadership of Pani, an Italian Mexican from a prominent family whom the elite considered one of their own. Pani organized lavish balls and dinners that allowed the *gente alta* to mingle with foreign diplomats as well as government functionaries and their wives. Linked by conspicuous consumption such as the ostentatious use of automobiles, the old elite and the new rulers from the desert frontier came to terms.[84]

Despite Pani's cosmopolitan vision, life in the capital still served up reminders of the decade of violence. Homicide was commonplace. For example, a lieutenant colonel in Calles's service reportedly shot a comedian on stage to impress his girlfriend, a dancer in the show he was attending. León, a member of the Chamber of Deputies, recalled that he never left the house without a firearm. "We took guns to the meetings, we took pistols to the chamber, because we did not know how things would end up."[85]

The private lives of most of the Sonorenses mirrored the macho archetype of the drinking, womanizing, gambling, and violent leader. In the words of one historian, they exemplified "the masculine practices of the new revolutionary elite, consisting largely of uncultured, crude men accustomed to physical violence."[86] On the other hand, de la Huerta and Gómez were known for their sobriety. We will not concern ourselves here with the personal habits of Alvarado, Diéguez, Maytorena, and Pesqueira, sidelined by the Conventionist defeat and Obregón's triumph, respectively.

The excessive drinking among the Sonorenses has been well documented. Although Obregón liked to tell jokes that involved alcohol abuse, he drank in moderation. Not surprisingly given his father's own struggles with alcoholism, Calles drank heavily in his youth and as a young adult. He continued even as he crusaded against the evils of alcohol as governor in Sonora. Despite his doctor's exhortations considering his health problems, which included colitis and other gastrointestinal ailments, Calles consumed hard liquor on a daily basis. However, he stayed sober in public, no doubt mindful of the humiliating memories of his father.[87] Less subject to scrutiny in Mexicali, Rodríguez did not follow this model of public sobriety and private inebriation. He reportedly organized booze parties in the cabarets, and, on one occasion, even in the Palacio de Gobierno that housed the state government. Serrano showed even less compunction about getting drunk in plain view, even in the middle of the day. His excesses rivaled those of Morones, famed for his bacchanals in his residence in Tlalpan.[88]

The Sonoran generals strayed outside the bounds of matrimony. Again, Obregón demonstrated more restraint in this regard than his comrades, although a letter points to at least one casual extramarital affair.[89] Calles reportedly had at least two mistresses during his years in Agua Prieta, including the U.S. proprietress of a hotel. In 1918, aged forty-one, he courted seventeen-year-old Amanda Ruiz, who bore a son the following year. Alone among the children of the revolutionary generals born out of wedlock, Manuel Calles Ruiz received public recognition after the death of Calles's first wife in 1927. Calles also reportedly frequented cabarets while in Europe in the summer of 1924.[90] Rodríguez's and Serrano's penchant for casual sex were well known. Rodríguez was a frequent visitor to Mexicali's infamous brothels. On one occasion, the governor chased a foreign-born sex worker through the hallways of a hotel with a gun in his hand. Serrano might have been the worst in this area. According to his biographer, he seduced at least six underage girls and fathered at least seven children out of wedlock.[91]

A look at their families accentuates this picture of the Sonorenses as flawed patresfamilias who skillfully managed kinship ties in order to advance their interests. The wives of the primary Sonorense leaders were white, part of a larger historical pattern in which leaders often wed women of a complexion lighter than their own. Witness, for example, the *criolla* spouses of Juárez, Díaz, and Huerta. Most of them were from well-to-do families. It was a time when conspicuous consumption had reached elite women, especially after the arrival of the automobile. On the flip side, the Sonorense wives also found unprecedented pressure to perform at public functions. Just like in the United States, the Mexican First Lady was a significant public figure. The wives of the Sonorenses played a role in advancing their husbands' political careers. Many of their children attended U.S. boarding schools, and some, universities.[92]

Obregón was married twice. In 1903, at the age of twenty-one, he wed Refugio Urrea from Álamos. The couple had four children. In 1907 his

16. Alvaro Obregón and María Tapia Monteverde on their wedding day. Library of Congress Prints and Photographs Division, Washington DC, 20540, https://www.loc.gov/pictures/item/2002707928 (accessed July 3, 2022).

wife died giving birth to the youngest of these children. Following the death of the newborn baby and one of its sibling, Obregón left the remaining two children in the care of his older sisters. In 1915 he married the Hermosillo native María Tapia Monteverde. While Urrea had come from humble origins, Tapia descended from a wealthy family whose branches included Italian immigrants and none other than Governor Maytorena,

17. Abelardo L. Rodríguez's family. Fideicomiso Archivos Plutarco Elías Calles y Fernando Torreblanca (FAPECFT), Fototeca, Archivo Abelardo L. Rodríguez, serie *Familia Rodríguez Sullivan, 1932–1961*, mfn 25, imagen 6, inventario 25. Used with permission.

who was locked in battle with Obregón's Constitutionalists at the time of the wedding. She was fluent in English due to her studies in Los Angeles. Tapia's kinship connections helped Obregón with his business ventures. The couple had seven children.[93]

Calles also had children from two marriages. In 1899 he wed Natalia Chacón Amarillas from Mazatlán, Sinaloa, the daughter of a customs inspector. Of the couple's twelve children, nine survived to adulthood. Natalia and their children spent most of the period 1913–20 away from the fighting in Nogales, Arizona, and their eldest sons were educated at U.S. military academies. Rodolfo, a graduate of Columbia University, later served as governor of Sonora and a member of Lázaro Cárdenas's first cabinet. Plutarco served as interim governor of Nuevo León, followed by two terms in the Chamber of Deputies and one as mayor of Monterrey. As we have seen, the marriage of the eldest daughter, Hortensia, to Fernando Torreblanca forged an important connection between the two erstwhile Sonorense clans. The wedding also offered a glimpse into the anticlericalism of the family's patriarch, as Calles did not attend the church wedding of his seventeen-year-old daughter. Plagued by asthma and other health conditions for most of her life, Natalia died in June 1927. Three years later, the *jefe máximo* married a soprano singer, Leonor Llorente of Mérida, Yucatán. The couple had two children before Leonor succumbed to a brain tumor in 1932.[94] In many ways, Hortensia was the most important woman in Calles's life: his confidante and eventually, the custodian of Obregón's and Calles's papers.

For Abelardo L. Rodríguez, the third time was the charm. His first marriage, to Luisa Montijo Hugues, from Guaymas, ended in divorce. In 1921 Abelardo wed Earthyl Vera Meier, the only Sonorense spouse born in the United States. In September 1922 Earthyl committed suicide, unable to adjust to his itinerant life cycling through military posts, which included her own presence during a shooting in Sinaloa. His third wife, Aida Sullivan Coya, was born in Puebla to a U.S. father and a Cuban mother and married Rodríguez in 1924. The couple raised their children in a bilingual household. Rodríguez had four sons: Abelardo Luis, from his marriage to Luisa; and Juan Abelardo, Julio Fernando, and Abelardo, from his union with Aida.[95] (See figure 17.)

Finally, there was Serrano, married since 1912 to Amada Bernal López. Obregón and Calles were concerned about Serrano's public image: when they sent him on a lengthy study tour of Europe in 1925, they attached the requirement that Serrano take his wife with him, as well as a prohibition against visiting Paris (which Don Pancho would ignore). In Obregón's and Calles's minds, his inability to maintain even the pretense of marital harmony constituted a serious political liability, especially at a time when the advent of mass media augmented the spreading of gossip.[96]

De la Huerta defied the pattern of his military counterparts. Clara Oriol Ortiz de la Torre was his partner for life, and he was not known for any extramarital affairs. Like Adolfo, Clara was a native of Guaymas; she was also a great musical talent as an accomplished pianist. The couple had two sons, Arturo and Adolfo. At the outset of Don Fito's interim presidency, the family had planned to remain in faraway Hermosillo, perhaps aware of the short-term nature of de la Huerta's position or repelled by the presidential residency at Chapultepec Castle. On the day of de la Huerta's inauguration, however, an acute appendicitis sidelined the new president, and the family came to live in Mexico City. Nonetheless, Clara stayed out of the limelight during her husband's five months in office, uncomfortable with the pomp and circumstance.[97]

Gambling was an important pastime for a group of men who had personally experienced the whims of chance since the beginning of the revolution. The Sonorenses created the Centro Recreativo Sonora-Sinaloa (Sonora-Sinaloa Recreational Center), also known as "Son-Sin." It was an open secret that "Son-Sin" was a gambling den. One of the most popular stories about Obregón's legendary memory involved his ability to memorize the sequence of an entire deck of cards. So skilled was the general that the proprietor of one casino reportedly banned him from playing. While Obregón relied on his memory, Calles loved poker and saw games of chance as a representation of politics. Although one of his earliest decrees as governor of Sonora had banned such games, as secretary of the interior, Calles invited his friends to evening gatherings that involved poker and heavy drinking. The inhabitants of Baja California knew Rodríguez as a professional gambler.[98] According to the U.S. military attaché, Serrano was an "inveterate gambler and is reputed to be the principal owner of two well-known gambling houses in the capital."[99] As General Gonzalo N. Santos claimed in his memoirs, the Sonorenses and other members of the governing elite embezzled government funds in order to play.[100] Once again, de la Huerta and Gómez appeared the exception from this pattern, showing no interest in games of chance.

The first half of the Obregón administration constituted the apex of the so-called Sonoran Dynasty. Four Sonorenses played prominent roles in the government: Obregón, de la Huerta, Calles, and Serrano who had succeeded a fifth—Benjamín Hill—after his untimely death. This government bore the stamp of the revolution's caudillo, who brought a piecemeal approach to what he saw as a project of national reconstruction, mixing coercion and negotiation to accomplish his goals. Unlike the Porfiriato, however, Sonorense rule did not bring the stable rule of a close-knit faction as the name "Sonoran Dynasty" might imply. As the 1924 presidential election approached, the Sonorenses who had united against Carranza in the Plan de Agua Prieta found themselves at odds with one another.

6 ~:~ The Triangle Broken

For somehow this is tyranny's disease, to trust no friends.—Aeschylus, *Prometheus Bound*

During a car ride through Chapultepec Park, President Obregón, de la Huerta, and Calles once reportedly discussed the presidential succession. Said the caudillo, "You and I, Plutarco, cannot leave politics, because we would die of hunger; on the other hand, Adolfo knows how to sing and give classes in voice and music. Under these circumstances, who do you feel should follow me in the presidency of the Republic?" De la Huerta replied, "Well, after you should come Plutarco."[1] This reported "pact of gentlemen" featured an agreement that might have ensured a continuation of the Sonoran Triangle for the foreseeable future.

Not only did such a pact not exist, but things turned out quite differently. While a significant coalition arrayed behind Calles, most notably the CROM, Soto y Gama's agraristas, and southeastern Socialists, Calles faced significant opposition within the military and among many of the 165 Cooperatistas in the Chamber of Deputies. All other parties combined had only one hundred deputies. Even as de la Huerta repeatedly affirmed his support for Calles, PNC leaders such as Jorge Prieto Laurens and others dissatisfied with the apparent fait accompli pressured Don Fito to declare his candidacy. They believed that de la Huerta would allow Congress to shape government policy. At the same time, de la Huerta increasingly opposed Obregón. The result was a rebellion that once again agreed only on the removal of the current regime. The shattering of the Sonoran Triangle revealed deep fault lines in the Sonorense group and the weak foundations of the revolutionary regime.

The Official Candidate

After Benjamín Hill's untimely death in December 1920, Calles emerged as a top presidential contender. As early as 1922 rumors circulated that

18. Calles, Morones, and CROMistas. Fideicomiso Archivos Plutarco Elías Calles y Fernando Torreblanca (FAPECFT), Fototeca, Archivo Fernando Torreblanca, Fondo Plutarco Elías Calles, Oficial, serie *Secretario de Gobernación, 1920–1923*, mfn 131, imagen 10, inventario 217. Used with permission.

Obregón would anoint Calles in a similar way that Carranza had attempted the imposition of Ignacio Bonillas two years prior. But the parallel was deeply flawed. Unlike Bonillas, Calles had built a network on the national level. He was the powerful secretary of the interior and had held the governorship of his native state and three different cabinet positions. In January 1923 an unnamed politician cited in a U.S. intelligence report identified Calles as his nation's true leader as opposed to Obregón, a "figurehead" and "great disappointment." According to this report, Calles commanded a "Bolshevist" movement, manipulating the popular classes to support his campaign. The informant affirmed that Calles would be the next president.[2] Two months later a *New York Times* article predicted that Obregón would "pass power to Calles."[3] In April more than 100 out of the Chamber of Deputy's 265 members signed the Torregrosa Pact supporting Calles for president. A Bonillas Calles was not.[4]

Calles had indeed managed to create a significant power base. He had solid support from three parties: the PLM, the PNA, and the Partido Socialista del Sureste (PSS, or Socialist Party of the Southeast). The PLM's Morones and the PSS's Carrillo Puerto were Calles's most steadfast allies and helped him craft the image of what one historian has called the "worker-campesino candidate."⁵ Calles could also count on support from two other prominent southeastern radicals, Tomás Garrido Canabal of Tabasco and Carlos Vidal of Chiapas. Prieto Laurens, Emilio Portes Gil, and other PNC leaders initially signaled that they would support Calles as well. A number of PNC deputies signed on to the Torregrosa Pact.⁶

Calles's association with Morones set him apart from Obregón, who had cooled on the labor leader due to his efforts to incorporate rural workers into the CROM. Morones postured as a radical and even a sympathizer of the Soviet Bolsheviks. This rhetoric cloaked his pragmatic approach to social reform, not to mention his personal ambition. Calles found it easy to cultivate a close connection to Morones. In January 1921 at the Mexico City meeting of the Pan-American Workers Confederation, and with Morones and AF of L leader Samuel Gompers in attendance, Calles proclaimed his support for "the struggle of the proletariat of the world."⁷ Later that year, he sent an emissary to the United States as his representative with the AF of L.⁸

Meanwhile, Carrillo Puerto constituted Calles's intermediary with radical agrarians in the Southeast. As early as November 1920, a congressional representative from Yucatán had warned Obregón of a "new caste war" in case Carrillo Puerto and Calles had their way.⁹ Indeed, Carrillo Puerto followed Alvarado's lead in a progressive administration that fostered education, land reform, women's rights, and popular mobilization. The policies of this self-described Socialist resembled those of European social democrats rather than those of the Russian Bolsheviks.

Of middle-class and mestizo origins, Carrillo Puerto hailed from Motul, thirty miles northeast of Mérida. He spoke Yucatec Maya. In 1919 Carranza's attempt to repress the Yucatecan Socialists had aligned Carrillo Puerto with Obregón. The two leaders pledged to support one another's ambitions at the national and regional levels, respectively. Once in power, Carrillo Puerto took Alvarado's program as governor to the next level. He carried out a modest land reform program and reorganized the Ligas de Resistencia. He also introduced new farming technology and expanded the rights of women. As Calles had done in Sonora, Carrillo Puerto tried to prohibit alcohol and promoted elementary education.¹⁰

In February 1921 Obregón sent Calles to Mérida out of concern that Carrillo Puerto would lead his party into the Communist International.

Instead of reminding the governor of the moderate direction of the national government, Calles jumped on his bandwagon and described himself as a Socialist who admired his work. He also portrayed Mexico City as a reactionary capital where he and Obregón alone guaranteed the ongoing success of the revolution.[11] Calles professed "great respect and affection for our primitive races" and announced his support of the campaigns against alcohol and domestic violence.[12] He allowed Carrillo Puerto to organize the PSS in neighboring states, despite the protestations of other regional parties.[13] In response Carrillo Puerto recognized Calles as the "paladin of the working classes."[14]

Tabasco's Tomás Garrido Canabal also factored in Calles's southeastern support. Garrido was born into a wealthy landowning family near Palenque in the neighboring state of Chiapas. After studying law, he served in Alvarado's state government before joining that of Francisco Múgica in Tabasco. In 1919, at just twenty-eight years of age, Garrido became interim governor. He was elected governor in 1920. Well-known for his virulent anticlericalism, he despised alcohol and launched an anti-alcohol campaign without peer in the entire republic. His administration also emulated Alvarado's mobilization of the Resistance Leagues and its use of export revenue to hike wages. Garrido considered himself a Bolshevik but cultivated a partnership with the U.S.-owned Standard Fruit Company. Like Guatemala, Honduras, and Nicaragua, Tabasco developed a thriving export economy based on bananas.[15]

Garrido hitched his wagon to the Sonorenses. During Obregón's ascendance, he cultivated the caudillo as a political ally. In July 1919 one of the party's representatives offered assistance to Obregón.[16] Garrido began working closely with Calles after the secretary of the interior's trip to the Southeast in January 1921. In March of that year, he congratulated Calles on his role in resolving a railroad worker's strike as well as on "the highly beneficial work that you have done on behalf of this state."[17] Garrido's primary loyalty remained with Obregón, but his significance to the Callista machine would increase over time.

Finally, in Chiapas Calles cultivated the opposition. Governor Tiburcio Fernández Ruiz represented the conservative Mapache faction, a coalition of ranchers and planters strenuously opposed to southeastern Socialism. That faction had signed on to the Sonorense Plan de Agua Prieta, and Obregón remained loyal to it. In the 1922 elections two Socialist candidates won election to the federal Chamber of Deputies. In a February 1923 memorandum to Calles, these deputies assailed Fernández for repressing the Socialist Party and violating municipal autonomy.[18] The missive put Calles in a difficult position as it asked him to move against one of Obregón's clients. Given Calles's alliance with Socialists elsewhere in the Southeast, however, he needed to take these complaints seriously. In response to these claims, Obregón sent Calles to Chiapas on a fact-finding mission. Calles reported that the state government violated municipal autonomy via the imposition of local authorities and asked for the use of force, but Obregón demurred.[19]

This dynamic produced another critical ally for Calles. Carlos A. Vidal viewed the secretary of the interior as a partner in the struggle against Fernández. Vidal's middle-class background resembled that of many of the Sonorenses. He grew up on a small farm in northwestern Chiapas, joined the Constitutionalist army in late 1913, and spent most of the next years on various military posts outside his home state. Like Alvarado and Carrillo Puerto, Vidal was a self-described Socialist.[20] In January 1920 he helped found the Partido Socialista Chiapaneco (Chiapanecan Socialist Party). Stymied by Fernández, Vidal received orders from Calles (then secretary of war) to come to Mexico City along with his troops in June 1920. Vidal stayed in the national capital and rose through the ranks until his promotion to brigadier general in August 1923.[21] The case of Chiapas provides further evidence that the two foremost Sonorenses sometimes worked at cross-purposes. The president's support for Fernández cemented Calles's standing with the Socialists.[22]

At the same time that Calles was cultivating southeastern Socialists, he also built support in the United States. As early as February 1921, the *New York Times* published a highly favorable editorial that included a lengthy interview with Calles, which linked him to the United States' own revolutionary tradition. The editorial concluded that Calles, "the strong man of Mexico," represented "liberalism and progress.... [T]o the mind of the young democracy in Mexico, Calles is Alexander Hamilton and Thomas Jefferson combined." After characterizing Calles as an "intrepid leader possessing a power of physical endurance to an extraordinary degree," the editorial represented his primary goals as educational reform and social progress. To impress his U.S. audience, Calles stated, "I can see success only through going to work. We are building. We begin by building schools, roads, irrigation plants. We are settling the unemployed upon land—their own land, otherwise we could not succeed."[23]

Calles had plenty of detractors, however. His somber and austere demeanor precluded victory in any popularity contest. He also found himself caught between civilians opposing his military rank and generals mocking his civilian demeanor. Obregón reportedly called Calles "the least general-like of the generals."[24] One Calles associate recalled that he "did not use military uniform in many years of campaign, and never a pistol or sword. In fact, the only time that we saw him in uniform, his friends needed to get him a uniform of a divisional general in a hurry."[25] A powerful association of generals who had fought with the Maderistas strongly opposed Calles's candidacy: the Unión de Militares de Origen Revolucionario 1910–1913 (Union of Military Leaders of the Origins of the Revolution). This group included Alvarado, Diéguez, Veracruz strongman Guadalupe Sánchez, and Enrique Estrada, the former secretary of war, among many other veterans of the early revolutionary years who considered both Obregón and Calles latecomers to the revolution. Several of these generals harbored presidential ambitions of their own. In addition, Calles—like de la Huerta—was arguably ineligible for the presidency due to his involvement in the Plan de Agua Prieta, an act of insurrection against the government.

On September 5, 1923, Calles announced his candidacy on the hacienda Soledad de la Mota in Nuevo León, the property of his son, Plutarco Jr. The declaration firmly placed Calles within the context of global social democracy: the quest to help the less fortunate within a capitalist framework. Far more progressive than Obregón's program, it reflected on a nation beset by great income equality despite the existence of a constitutional framework designed to remedy this ill. Calles proclaimed his enthusiasm for articles 27 and 123 and styled himself an advocate for the "humble classes."[26] As required by article 82 of the constitution, Calles resigned from his post in the national government so he could figure as a candidate.

In contrast to Obregón's platform, Calles's populist program sought to uplift ordinary Mexicans.[27] It focused on three areas of concern to campesinos and workers: the expansion of public primary education, the division of hacienda land into smallholdings, and the implementation of Article 123. Hedging his bets, Calles cautioned his audience not to expect either "miracles or chimerical transformations.... I only promise to sustain ... our Constitution and its revolutionary postulates."[28] Delivered just weeks after the Bucareli Agreement, one campaign speech advocated economic nationalism and the protection of national sovereignty. In a special gesture to the middle class, Calles said, "In the class struggle of the modern world, there is a third class that should play a great role: the middle class. Always repressed, the middle class has been put down and exploited by those above, without acquiring a sufficient degree of understanding by those below.... I would be very pleased if I could achieve ... that the middle class ... occupy its rightful place."[29]

The Opposition Candidate

While Calles campaigned, de la Huerta remained on the sidelines. He insisted that he had no interest and desired to support his childhood friend. In public, he often referred to himself as the country's premier Callista. De la Huerta's memoirs suggest that he did not seriously consider a candidacy until Obregón impugned his integrity, violated the sovereignty of several states, and injured national sovereignty.[30]

But we do not know that to be true. De la Huerta was extremely careful in his public pronouncements, and his private papers do not yield clarity as to his intentions at that time. In addition, the twenty-six-year-old Prieto Laurens, an erstwhile Calles supporter, was a young man of extraordinary ambition. At the same time that he held a senior position in the PNC and a seat in the Chamber of Deputies, he stood for election as the governor of San Luis Potosí.[31] To Prieto Laurens and several other politicians, de la Huerta was a vehicle to achieve national prominence. One must wonder why Prieto Laurens and others kept insisting despite de la Huerta's public disavowals unless they had reason to hope that he would change his mind. From Calles's and Obregón's vantage point, de la Huerta's words did not appear forthright since Don Fito's friends—many of them their adversaries, such as Villa and Alvarado—kept pushing his candidacy. The most plausible explanation is that de la Huerta, just like Guzmán's protagonist in *La sombra del caudillo*, Ignacio Aguirre, vacillated in private.[32] At the very least, the activities of some of the most fervent Delahuertistas undermined Calles's candidacy, and de la Huerta's relationship with both Obregón and Calles.

For good reason, the possibility remained in everyone's mind. Don Fito was superbly qualified given his experience as governor, diplomat, interim president, and secretary of finance. According to de la Huerta, Obregón encouraged him to announce his candidacy in April 1923, citing Calles's health problems that forced him to seek treatment in a clinic in San Francisco.[33] Such talk probably served to leave all options open. Calles's illness indeed appeared serious until his physician, whom he called "a wise man and not a charlatan," returned him to good health "quickly and successfully."[34] As Obregón reportedly said upon hearing de la Huerta's public denials, "Imagine that Calles fails for any reason. De la Huerta will have nullified himself completely, and we would not be able to make use of him."[35] Obregón also considered his closest Sonorense friend, Ramón Ross, a Constituyente and negotiator for the Bucareli Agreement. Ross was a regular at the "Son-Sin" club, where he reportedly once had a few drinks before attending a session—and then promptly fell asleep.[36] Obregón's exploration of other candidates suggests that Calles's bid was not a foregone conclusion.

Among the Sonorenses, Alvarado supported de la Huerta. He had always been jealous of Obregón. Initially, he had weighed a candidacy of his own. In February 1921 he helped found the Mexican Socialist Party, despite its name, a moderate group. Harassed by the government, Alvarado soon realized the difficulties of a candidacy. As a prolific writer who believed in political rather than military solutions, he believed that Obregón lacked tact, erudition, and convictions. In addition, he resented his late entry into the revolution, calling him a Porfirista or Corralista, with reference to Díaz's vice president, Ramón Corral.[37] Alvarado considered Calles an inferior leader who owed his ascent to Obregón's patronage. He wrote articles critical of Calles's status as the inevitable candidate. By mid-1922 he openly supported de la Huerta, in whose cabinet he had served in 1920. As Carrillo Puerto reported to Calles, two officials in his state government had received letters from Alvarado asking them to work for de la Huerta.[38]

Alvarado's position echoed that of others in the above-mentioned Unión de Militares, composed of Maderista revolutionaries who preferred the civilian de la Huerta over a general whom they regarded as a latecomer to the revolution and mediocre strategist who had won victories over the Villistas due to the help of other Sonorenses, whether Hill during the defense of Naco or Gómez during the Battle of Agua Prieta. These military men also detested Calles's supporters, and most importantly, Morones. Notably, Serrano and Gómez resolutely supported Calles, but they were in the minority. De la Huerta thus became the possible candidate of the anti-Callistas in the military.[39]

The support of the generals accompanied a rightward shift in de la Huerta's political profile. Initially, some had considered him a champion of the Left. Following the CROM's invasion of the Chamber of Deputies in 1921, PLC legislators had charged him with financing socialist propaganda with public funds.[40] Two years later, however, a U.S. diplomat noted, "General Calles continues to lead the ... agrarians, while Mr. de la Huerta appears to be taking a more decided stand in favor of conservative agrarianism and the observance of ordinary economic obligations."[41] It would be a mistake to impute any sort of ideological polarity to the emerging competition between Calles and de la Huerta. But the latter's political supporters—whether civilians in the Chamber of Deputies or generals in the Unión de Militares—favored the social and economic status quo more so than Calles's supporters from the PNA, the CROM/PLM, and the "Socialist" Southeast. As a group, they were also less anticlerical than leaders allied with Calles such as Tejeda, Morones, Carrillo Puerto, or Garrido.

This dynamic added to a deteriorating relationship with Obregón, the beginnings of which the previous chapter has already outlined. In 1921 the president and the secretary of finance sparred over the reserves in the treasury, as Obregón temporarily blocked the sale of gold for silver without the secretary's knowledge. In 1922 Obregón had harshly criticized the outcome of de la Huerta's negotiations with the ICBM.[42] In 1923, de la Huerta came to oppose Obregón in three areas: the assassination of Pancho Villa; the Bucareli Agreements; and federal interference in statewide elections.[43]

On July 20, 1923, gunmen assassinated Villa in the city of Parral when he was on his way home to his hacienda. The killing was an orchestrated event. An accomplice stopped Villa's automobile by stepping into the street and shouting "Viva Villa!" The prompt brought forth a hail of bullets from several strategically positioned assassins. As the person who stood most to gain from this tragedy and also the official in charge of the federal police, Calles faced suspicion. Villa favored de la Huerta as president and had even stated that he would return to the battlefield on de la Huerta's behalf.[44] Speculation grew until Jesús Salas Barraza, a member of the Durango chamber of deputies, confessed to having ordered Villa's assassination. While the confession initially calmed the waves, most Mexicans believed that someone more powerful bore responsibility for the murder. Salas assumed responsibility to exculpate the local zone commander, General Joaquín Amaro, who had commissioned Salas to carry out Villa's assassination.[45] But who had ordered Amaro to do such a thing? A commission established by the Chamber of Deputies concluded that Villa's assassination owed to political motives, and many Cooperatistas blamed Obregón and Calles. One historian suspects that Calles ordered Villa's murder at the behest of Obregón, who had strenuously objected to the 1920 agreement between de la Huerta and Villa.[46] Addressing the possibility that Calles might have ordered Villa's removal, another observer pointed out that Calles did not have authority over the army and that "assassination was more Obregón's than Calles's style."[47] Obregón's and Calles's letters to one another denied complicity.[48]

The Bucareli Agreement amounted to a matter of honor for de la Huerta. As we have seen, Obregón had faulted the secretary of finance for offering too many concessions to U.S. banks, and he had also assured him that the Bucareli meetings were only of an informal nature. However, when de la Huerta studied the minutes of the Bucareli meetings, he learned that the conferences had held an official character, which meant that he should have been included in the negotiations. He also found out that Obregón's negotiators had made a promise not to apply article 27 retroactively. He considered these concessions far more substantial than his own deal with Lamont and regarded the agreements as a frank sellout to the United States.[49]

The conflict over gubernatorial elections in San Luis Potosí and other states involved the future of the PNC as an opposition party. The decade featured numerous contested elections accompanied by violence and federal interference. As one historian has argued, "political violence surrounding elections at the local, state, and national level was the order of the day."⁵⁰ By the time the San Luis Potosí election took place on August 5, 1923, the PNC had already complained about irregularities after losing in Colima, Guerrero, and Tlaxcala. In San Luis Potosí the PNC nominated Prieto Laurens to oppose the PNA's Aurelio Manrique, an ardent Obregonista and ally of the state's preeminent cacique, General Saturnino Cedillo. The contest devolved into chaos. Cedillo unleashed his armed supporters, agricultural colonists whom he and Obregón had rewarded with land in exchange for their allegiance. On Election Day, violence prompted the closing of many voting booths, particularly in areas that supported Prieto Laurens. Afterward, the PNC claimed victory, but the PNA alleged widespread fraud. Both sides set up state governments and legislatures: Prieto Laurens, in the state capital of San Luis Potosí, and Manrique, in Cárdenas. All eyes were on Obregón, authorized under the constitution to declare the "disappearance" of state powers and ask the Senate to name a provisional governor. The president initially declared himself unable to resolve the crisis.⁵¹

As the official inauguration date of a new governor approached, tension bubbled over in Congress. On September 1, 1923, Obregón prepared to give his customary address to the legislature. According to tradition, Obregón and Prieto Laurens, the incoming president of the Chamber of Deputies, were to exchange their messages before the event. But Prieto Laurens never sent his text to the president. His response to the presidential address was the final item in an agenda that also included presentations by all the government secretaries, including Calles and de la Huerta. Prieto Laurens's speech praised de la Huerta's work as secretary of finance and criticized federal interference in elections. Unexpectedly, he addressed the issue of Obregón's succession. "In the presidential election campaign that has already begun, it is clear that there are elements that use their official power and stain the prestige of the administration, abusing the trust that you have placed in them." Referring to Calles, Prieto Laurens clarified that these elements included the heads of "most important government agencies" whose actions aroused "popular indignation."⁵² Three days later, PNC president Emilio Portes Gil, a Calles supporter, resigned due to his opposition to this speech.⁵³

On September 21, four days before a new governor was to take office, Obregón denied recognition to both Prieto Laurens and Manrique as well as their legislatures. When Prieto Laurens nonetheless assumed duties as the state's duly elected governor, Obregón declared the governor's power null and void and ordered the Senate to organize new elections. Along with similar strife in Nuevo León, this incident demonstrated that the government would put obstacles in the PNC's path. On the floor of the Chamber of Deputies, a livid Prieto Laurens loudly accused both Obregón and Calles of obstructing the work of Mexico's first genuine opposition party.[54]

The spat over state elections became what Obregón called "the straw that broke the camel's back"[55]—the precipitating event for the breakup of the Sonoran Triangle. On the day before Obregón was set to ask the Senate to declare the disappearance of powers in San Luis Potosí and Nuevo León, Don Fito came for a visit to try to settle their differences. He told him that he did not agree with federal interference. When Obregón sternly rebuffed him, de la Huerta announced that he would resign his post as secretary of finance. Without his permission, Guzmán's newspaper, *El Mundo*, published the draft resignation letter that de la Huerta had shared with him and the president. This premature publication achieved Guzmán's aim as a member of the PNC leadership: an exacerbation of the disagreements.[56]

Calles found himself in the difficult position of having to choose sides between his foremost ally and his best friend. In a letter to Calles, de la Huerta lambasted Obregón's flagrant violations of state sovereignty—actions that resembled Carranza's in Sonora. He expressed the wish that Calles, his "old and loyal friend," shared his opinion.[57] Calles defended Obregón's decisions and blamed de la Huerta's state of mind on frail health and work-related stress. He asked him to "reflect serenely" upon his decision, to no avail.[58] The following week, de la Huerta wrote a letter faulting Calles for not encouraging Obregón to strike a more conciliatory tone. As a result of the president's uncompromising position, "there has been a considerable cooling off in the enthusiasm with which the people have applauded our regime, and it is logical that the effects reflect principally upon your candidacy."[59] Calles reportedly lamented "the loss of a brother, for so I considered Adolfo."[60] Obregón claimed that de la Huerta's resignation resulted from his "excessive goodness," which allowed the PNC to take advantage of him.[61]

Once outside the government, de la Huerta again faced pressure to run. He initially continued to refuse to enter the presidential contest. As he stated in a press release, "Let others contribute their energies to giving new life to the work of reconstruction that the nation needs."[62] But he changed his tune when the press published a scathing report authored by Pani, the new secretary of finance. Citing defamatory comments from Obregón, the report charged that Pani found a treasury in a "state of material and ... moral bankruptcy," and that de la Huerta had diverted funds earmarked to the payment of the foreign debt. According to Pani, Obregón had to request that all public servants, including soldiers and officers in the army, forgo 10 percent of their salary as a "sacrifice."[63] Pani was not altogether wrong in criticizing de la Huerta's tenure for accounting mistakes and other errors, but the allegations of corruption and mismanagement were far beyond the pale. Therefore, de la Huerta declared his candidacy on October 19, 1923.[64]

The conflict soon escalated. Accusations flew between the two camps. The Senate opened an official investigation into de la Huerta's tenure as secretary of finance. The PNA endorsed Calles, while the PNC (sans the Callistas who had left the party) threw its weight behind de la Huerta. Even though de la Huerta was a civilian, he also got support from the Unión de Militares. Guadalupe Sánchez, a prominent member of that group, invited Prieto Laurens to move the legislature to Veracruz, hopeful that its presence would help him in his long-running feud with Governor Tejeda, a staunch supporter of the federal government. When Sánchez found out that de la Huerta feared for his life, he offered him sanctuary. On December 4, after learning that Mexico City commander Arnulfo R. Gómez had ordered his arrest, Don Fito shook off the government agents who were keeping him under surveillance and boarded a train to the port city that had served Carranza so well in the middle of the 1910s. On board was Prieto Laurens.[65]

Obregón remained undaunted in the face of the brewing storm. On December 6 he told the Associated Press in apparent disregard of the injury that he had suffered in 1915, "The lion of Celaya is not dead yet, nor even disabled. . . . I firmly believe that Mexico will display the proper spirit and pacific transmission of the Presidency will become a reality. The revolution cannot prosper without the sympathy of the rural classes."[66]

The De la Huerta Rebellion

On December 5, 1923, de la Huerta and Prieto Laurens arrived in Veracruz. Ignoring Don Fito's wishes for the least possible fanfare, Sánchez welcomed the group with music and a gun salute. De la Huerta told Sánchez that he opposed a rebellion, but Sánchez and Prieto Laurens had already begun plans for an uprising. Prieto Laurens sent a declaration to the Veracruz newspaper *El Dictamen*. On December 6 the newspaper proclaimed that "the revolution has broken out here: General Guadalupe Sánchez withdraws recognition from Obregón, and Don Adolfo de la Huerta is named Supreme Chief of the Revolutionary Movement."[67] De la Huerta expressed shock that a rebellion had begun without his authorization, but Sánchez's and Prieto Laurens's actions left him no choice but to go along with their plans.[68]

On December 7 de la Huerta issued the Plan de Veracruz. The manifesto claimed the provisional leadership of the movement for de la Huerta and lambasted the "rascal" Obregón for his imposition of Calles. According to the plan, Calles's presidency would pave the way for the return of the caudillo in the next elections. The document also cited a litany of transgressions ranging from the violation of state sovereignty to the kidnappings of federal senators. Just like many other political plans, this program stated more clearly what it opposed than what it desired. Striking a balance between landowners and peasants, and between bosses and workers, the plan favored the social and economic status quo. In contrast to the economic nationalism enshrined in the Constitution of 1917, the Plan de Veracruz promised equal guarantees to foreign and Mexican capital. It was the first major political program that supported women's suffrage.[69]

What posterity would remember as the De la Huerta Rebellion was a set of disparate movements without common leadership. These movements were as diverse as those that had aligned under Madero in 1910 or against Huerta in 1913. These separate rebellions featured four major theaters in Veracruz, Jalisco, the South (Guerrero and Oaxaca), and the Southeast. The common theme was the "imposition" of Calles. A conciliator rather than a warlord, de la Huerta was ill suited to streamline this diverse coalition. He called himself "Jefe Supremo de la Revolución" (Supreme Chief of the Revolution) but never attempted to unify the rebellions by means of a common organization or strategy. Maintained General Raúl Madero, the brother of the slain ex-president, "He is not a man who will come out and say how he stands on certain questions. . . . He is a good man, in fact too good to succeed as a Mexican president."[70]

The movement most closely associated with de la Huerta was that of Sánchez, his chief military commander. Sánchez was a staunch ally of hacendados, oil companies, and the Catholic Church; the opposite of Tejeda, the anticlerical agrarista governor. In May 1920 he had supported President Carranza against the Plan de Agua Prieta, only to betray him in the eleventh hour. Sánchez enjoyed the good fortune that the Gulf section of the navy had deserted, which supplied him with thousands of experienced troops. Jalisco's Enrique Estrada came from Obregón's inner circle, having served as secretary of war.[71] While large landowners helped fund the rebellion of a general who had emerged as a prominent critic of Obregón's ejido program, Estrada enjoyed the support of former Michoacán governor Francisco J. Múgica, a preeminent Jacobin at the Constituyente. In addition, he counted on the loyalty of Diéguez and his retainers. General Fortunato Maycotte, who had rescued Obregón when Carranza sought his arrest in April 1920, led a rebellion in the South, and in Yucatán, the henequen planters sought Governor Carrillo Puerto's ouster.[72]

These disorganized revolts posed a stern challenge. According to official estimates, 102 out of 509 generals, 2,417 out of 8,583 officers, and 23,224 out of 59,030 troops defected from the federal army to join the uprisings. These numbers did not include more than twenty thousand rebels not on the army's rolls as of December 7, including veterans who had served until they lost their commission as a result of the downsizing of the military. In total, an army of 44,518 confronted rebel forces totaling over 56,000.[73] In addition, the revolts caught the government in a two-front war. Despite Serrano's assertions that the federal army would attack on both fronts, the government took defensive positions, leaving Sánchez to take undefended Puebla, a mere ninety miles east of the capital. When the rebels overthrew Carrillo Puerto on December 21, the situation of the government appeared bleak.[74] On January 3, 1924, the rebels court-martialed and executed Carrillo Puerto along with three of his brothers and nine of his friends. One week later, they took Villahermosa and ousted Garrido, the government's principal remaining ally in the Southeast.[75]

However, Carrillo Puerto's execution had created a rallying point for supporters of the government.[76] Calles wrote a letter to a pro-government newspaper that exhorted the editor to "let the Mexican proletariat know that the true assassin of Felipe Carrillo Puerto was Adolfo de la Huerta," who had ordered the execution and rewarded the officer in charge with a promotion in rank. These deeds demonstrated "the eminently reactionary nature of the Delahuertista movement and revealed to the naked eye the hypocrisy, evil, and perversity of de la Huerta."[77]

Although there is no evidence that de la Huerta had indeed ordered the court-martial and execution, those responsible had done the rebellion no favors. In a letter, Calles called Carrillo Puerto an "apostle devoted to the improvement of the ignored masses." And he continued, "More so than a military one, this revolution is class-based, and for the Yucatecan reaction, Felipe was … the only one who could save the poor people from the fangs of … the rich.… They have only stoked the fire with this horrendous crime. All of the worker and campesino organizations have sounded the alert. Now, more than ever, they will … show that the Mexican working people are no longer the herd of sheep that they were twelve years ago."[78]

Carrillo Puerto's death helped the government claim the mantle of defenders of southeastern Socialism. A few months after the end of the rebellion, Calles visited Carrillo Puerto's hometown of Motul, where he paid enthusiastic homage to the legacy of the fallen Yucatecan leader and granted an ejido to local villagers.[79]

The government responded with repression and mobilization. Obregón sent two bills to Congress asking for a suspension of individual rights and special financial powers for the executive. The legislature (now purged of all PNC members loyal to de la Huerta) stopped the first measure but granted him great latitude in allocating federal spending, which Obregón used to beef up security in the capital. Fearing a further spread of the rebellion, the government arrested the governors of Coahuila, Querétaro, San Luis Potosí, and Tamaulipas under the pretense of disloyalty.[80] Calles—who had suspended his campaign and rejoined the army—recruited new detachments from among the CROM, which remained a steadfast ally and even defended the government internationally through its ties to the AF of L. To that end, the government helped spread an apocryphal report purporting the execution of the popular Veracruz strike leader, Herón Proal, at the hands of rebel forces. In San Luis Potosí Calles enlisted the help of Cedillo, who reportedly told the recipients of provisional land grants that refusal to serve in the army would lead to the forfeiture of their land. Calles promised sharecroppers that military service would allow them to keep their entire 1924 crop.[81]

The government also painted the opposition as the harbingers of reaction. Obregón blamed "three military chiefs, drunk with ambition and forgetful of loyalty, to make the Mexican people a herd of cattle tamed to the service of their ambitions."[82] Calles accused hacendados in the cotton-rich Laguna area in the Northeast of "open hostility" and even of buying the services of campesinos to cause difficulties for the government. As Calles told Obregón, those who did not comply faced arrest by a complicit judge who had received payoffs from the hacendados.[83]

Nonetheless, the problems of the Obregón administration kept multiplying, even within the circle that ostensibly remained loyal. General Ángel Flores of Sinaloa called upon Obregón to resign to pave the way for an interim president and clean elections.[84] "Do you think the people will stand for what you, Calles, and Serrano are doing: ... playing poker all night and losing 160,000 pesos and then paying the debt ... from the National Treasury? ... What happened to other presidents ... wishing to impose a candidate on the people will happen to you."[85] The charge had substance, although the only one of the three to play cards in public was Serrano, noted for his debauchery since his appointment as secretary of war.

In confronting numerically superior rebel armies, the Obregón administration could count on the U.S. government. Having just conferred recognition, President Coolidge opposed a rebellion that sought to abrogate the Bucareli Agreement. Thus he lifted the embargo on arms exports. In December, the U.S. government shipped more than ten thousand Springfield rifles, ten million cartridges, and ten military planes to Mexico. Even more significantly, it blocked the rebels from making arms purchases. As Secretary of State Charles Evans Hughes explained, "A Government that has made a zealous attempt to meet its obligations at home and abroad has been assailed, and an attempt is being made to overthrow it by violence. It has appealed to this government for aid to the end that order may be restored.... This government ... has responded with its support for stability and orderly constitutional procedure in the best interest of all concerned."[86] Gompers also lent his support, especially after Carrillo Puerto's assassination. As he stated in a letter to Obregón, "So long as the leaders of the revolt continue their traitorous movement, they can expect nothing but contempt from us."[87]

U.S. assistance made a significant difference. A U.S. warship foiled the Delahuertista blockade of Tampico, which would have prevented exports from the oil-producing Huasteca region. The boycott of the rebels foreclosed the sale of henequen, their other principal source of export revenue. Obregón also secured the assistance of the oil companies, which preferred the status quo to the possible victory of a group of rebels that had disavowed the Bucareli Agreement. For example, the Huasteca Petroleum Company made a loan of 10 million pesos to the government. Reportedly, U.S. fighter pilots also bombed the rebels in their Jalisco stronghold, and the War Department stationed warships close to Veracruz to monitor the movement of ships and blockade that port if necessary. In vain, conservative Mexican business leaders beseeched the U.S. government to condition aid to Obregón upon Calles's withdrawal from the presidential race.[88]

Frustrated in his endeavors to access arms and credit, the Jefe Supremo assailed Obregón's government as a lackey of the United States. He represented his own movement as opposing "the one that has sold Mexican sovereignty to the most powerful foreign government in exchange for gunboats, airplanes, rifles, ammunition, and money."[89] A de la Huerta supporter lamented later on, "the Department of State does not want to hear anything other than the voice of Obregón."[90] Still, de la Huerta could count on the British government, which had never recognized Obregón and considered the rebellion a magnificent opportunity to regain influence.[91]

With new recruits and weapons, the government went on the offensive. On January 28, 1924, the federal army routed Sánchez's forces at Esperanza, Veracruz. Two weeks later, they occupied Veracruz against minimal resistance, as de la Huerta and his shadow cabinet had fled eastward to Tabasco. In the West, Obregón led troops into battle against Estrada in Jalisco. The denouement came February 1–11, during the decisive Battle of Ocotlán, where Obregón's troops confronted Alvarado's.[92] Alvarado coordinated the defense of four bridges across the Río Lerma separating government and rebel troops. But the government's fighter planes softened his defenses, and Obregón improvised a river crossing by means of floating wooden platforms, buoyed by tires and other rubber objects. The federal army then moved on Guadalajara, which it occupied on February 12. Obregón later called the Battle of Ocotlán his hardest-won victory.[93] The battle also revealed a new military star: General Joaquín Amaro, who would lead the Secretariat of War by the end of the year.

Captured and sentenced to death during the battle, Alvarado escaped his fate thanks to the efforts of Lázaro Cárdenas, a Calles protégé who had fallen into his enemies' hands during the first few weeks of the rebellion. A letter from Calles to his half-brother, Arturo M. Elías, consul general in New Orleans, reported that Cárdenas escaped his captors.[94] According to one historian, however, he owed his life to none other than Alvarado, who ensured that the injured general received appropriate medical care.[95] To repay the favor, Cárdenas allowed Alvarado to board a boat en route to exile rather than face certain death by court-martial.[96]

As the rebels lost decisive battles, de la Huerta tried to revive their spirits by means of a new manifesto that shifted the rhetoric from political reform to nationalism. He repeated his charge that Obregón and Calles had violated the sovereignty of several states by means of the Secretariat of the Interior, the "laboratory of immoral elections." He also accused the U.S. government of supporting his enemies against the "unanimous" opinion of the U.S. public and that of all foreign nationals living in Mexico. As de la Huerta argued, his movement had morphed into a defense of the nation's sovereignty.[97]

Nonetheless, the rebels continued to lose ground. By March a series of defeats had reduced their territory to the Yucatán Peninsula, Chiapas, and Tabasco. In April Garrido reassumed control over the state government of Tabasco. With Garrido's participation, the army went on a prolonged offensive but met dogged resistance.[98] De la Huerta went to Yucatán, then Cuba, and finally to the United States. From there, he attempted to buy arms and obtain loans from Europe. De la Huerta could count on the help of El Águila Mexican Petroleum Co., an oil company owned by Royal Dutch and Shell Transport. Delahuertista agents worked through the offices of Dr. Arnold Krumm-Heller, Madero's private physician who had gone on to serve Obregón as chief of artillery while working for the German secret service. But Krumm-Heller's pleas fell on deaf ears. His government blocked his efforts to send arms to Mexico, leaving the agent to launch futile attacks against Obregón and Calles in German newspapers.[99]

De la Huerta could also not expect help from the Holy See, which was still chafing from the expulsion of papal delegate Filippi. Although de la Huerta was a liberal anticlerical more tolerant of organized religion than Calles, he did not make a good impression with Tito Crespi, the papacy's chargé d'affaires, who appreciated de la Huerta's alliance with "conservative elements" but stated that "he is ... more hypocritical than Calles."[100] Wrote Crespi, "Without character or principles, he is a man from which nothing good should be expected.... He does not know how to do either good or bad, but he will let both good and bad things happen."[101] As he noted, Calles's discourses "have not contained any aggressive note against the Church or the clergy."[102] Crespi struggled to reconcile evidence for Calles's anticlericalism—such as the fact that he had not attended his daughter's Catholic wedding—with his reasoned and pragmatic tone, which suggested the possibility of a working relationship.[103]

For all intents and purposes, the rebellion ended on July 26, 1924, with the execution of the former Villista general Manuel Chao in Chihuahua. The war had claimed more than seven thousand casualties and cost the government an estimated 70 million pesos. The rebellion's three primary leaders were in exile: de la Huerta and Estrada, in the United States, and Sánchez, in Cuba.[104]

The Fallout

The De la Huerta Rebellion shrank and reorganized the Sonorense coalition. It represented the final act for Diéguez and Alvarado, Sonorense revolutionaries of the first hour who had not followed Obregón into power. Ever since his decision to side with Carranza against his former allies, Diéguez had belonged to the political "outs," although he had belatedly declared his adherence to the Plan de Agua Prieta. Estrada's rebellion offered him a chance for redemption. But troops loyal to Obregón captured Diéguez. After a perfunctory court-martial, a firing squad executed him on April 21, 1924.[105] Alvarado, too, paid the ultimate price. De la Huerta named him interim supreme chief and smuggled Alvarado into Yucatán aboard a steamship chartered to transport the henequen crop. On June 9, 1924, one of his subordinates betrayed and murdered him in El Hormiguero, Tabasco, possibly with Garrido's help.[106]

Compared to Alvarado and Diéguez, de la Huerta and his family were lucky. On Obregón's orders, the federal Monetary Commission, which had impounded the family's bank account, released the funds to de la Huerta's wife, Clara, before she left for the United States in January 1924, a time when the outcome of the rebellion remained very much in doubt.[107] One might see this gesture as a sign that Obregón perhaps retained some appreciation for his former civilian ally. More likely, the funds were modest indeed. Certainly, if the de la Huertas had enriched themselves, the Obregón administration would have advertised that fact to the public—just as it had promoted Pani's charge that de la Huerta had misused public funds. In Los Angeles de la Huerta gave lessons to prominent singers who had lost their voice as well as to novices, among them Enrico Caruso Jr.[108]

On the other hand, the De la Huerta Rebellion showcased three Sonorense generals loyal to the government: Serrano, Gómez, and Rodríguez. Serrano had received accolades for orchestrating the victorious campaign against the rebels. He liked de la Huerta better than Calles, and he also felt pangs of conscience when his role included liquidating Diéguez, but his loyalty to Obregón trumped any other considerations. His decision to assume an initially defensive position until the government could overcome its numerical disadvantage had proven prudent.[109] Serrano had reason to believe he was set up for a presidential run in the 1928 elections.

Gómez provided invaluable help to the government in his capacity as the commander of Mexico City. This position was important because of the continuing role of Congress, located in the national capital. Working closely with Morones, Gómez intimidated PNC members in the Chamber of Deputies. In response, twenty-three deputies signed a manifesto on December 23 that charged Gómez with planning the assassination of PNC representatives.[110] On January 16 Morones upped the ante. Blaming the PNC for Carrillo Puerto's murder, he thundered, "The Cooperatistas ... will meet punishment for their crimes. They are greatly mistaken in believing that their immunity will be respected, as labor takes no heed

19. Obregón, Serrano, and Calles confront the rebellion. Fideicomiso Archivos Plutarco Elías Calles y Fernando Torreblanca (FAPECFT), Fototeca Colección de Álbumes Fotográficos de los Archivos Plutarco Elías Calles y Fernando Torreblanca, Fondo Álvaro Obregón, álbum 5, *Campaña militar contra la rebelión delahuertista, Volumen III, Tabasco, Jalisco. 1923–1924*, fotografía 201, inventario 67. Used with permission.

of it."[111] On January 23 the assassination of PNC senator and CROM critic Francisco Field Jurado drove home this threat. Many—including Obregón—blamed Morones for his murder.[112] There were rumors that the police would raid the Chamber to punish the remaining Delahuertista deputies for their association with a treasonous movement. After the kidnapping of two additional legislators, several deputies and senators went into hiding, and others switched over to the Calles camp.[113] In January 1924 Gómez's garrison also played a leading role in the crackdown on the crime wave engendered by the rebellion. He announced with reference to criminals that his forces would "meet 'em with lead."[114] His men also eliminated several radio transmission stations controlled by the rebels and positioned on rooftops of private residences. Gómez called radio "the principal enemy of the government."[115] These efforts earned him the coveted rank of divisional general. For its part, the PNC ceased to exist after de la Huerta's defeat.

Finally, the government could count upon Rodríguez, the military governor of Baja California. Rodríguez appreciated the latitude that Obregón had given him in the remote territory. His state government needed federal assistance for his infrastructure projects.[116] The day before the outbreak of the rebellion, Rodríguez had urged Obregón to support the construction of a railroad from landlocked Mexicali to the coast at the cost of almost US$10 million. He was aware of the need to have friends in the federal government.[117] He provided MX$500,000 (approximately US$250,000) for the purpose of fighting the rebellion and helped the Obregón administration purchase two airplanes. Obregón rewarded these acts of loyalty. Rodríguez, too, became a divisional general. Ignoring one of his prior decrees, the president also allowed the operation of casinos in Baja California. Because the president designated the governors of the nation's two remaining territories, Baja California and Quintana Roo, Obregón could permit Rodríguez to remain both governor and zone commander. Making an exception from the policy of rotating the zone commanders, Obregón and Calles kept Rodríguez in Baja California until 1929 as the nation's longest-serving governor of his time.[118]

The De la Huerta Rebellion represented the embers of the Maderista military movement. Many of its generals were among the longest-serving veterans of the revolution, having taken up arms against Porfirio Díaz at the outset of the fighting. Likewise, de la Huerta's coalition, like Madero, largely focused on political rather than social change. They feared lower-class radicalism and sought to slow down drives to redistribute land or to unionize workers. Finally, de la Huerta (just like Madero) never provided any effective leadership. And perhaps no such leadership was even feasible. Although it would be unfair to label the rebellion as "conservative," "reactionary," or even "counterrevolutionary," its ranks included leaders who wished to roll back the reforms made under Carranza and Obregón or even to rescind the radical articles of the Constitution of 1917. Nonetheless, the opinion of one historian that the rebellion was "a struggle for power in which ideological questions were almost absent" is not far from the mark.[119] It was, first and foremost, a rebellion against Obregón and Calles.

The De la Huerta Rebellion pruned the Sonorense group to just five members: Obregón, Calles, Serrano, Rodríguez, and Gómez. What remained of the alliance augured future rivalries. Calles had built up a power base independent from Obregón's, and Serrano, Gómez, and Rodríguez all desired an opportunity to reach the presidency. More than any of the previous conflicts that had divided the group, this rebellion showed the limits of friendship and the deadly penalty for defying the group's patriarch. It also further enhanced Obregón's reputation as an "undefeated" general who would continue to assert enduring influence after the end of his term. Finally, the war focused what remained of the "Grupo Sonora" to make sure that a large-scale revolt would not happen again. That meant an end to Obregón's efforts to triangulate opposing interests, especially as regarded the church, which had supported Sánchez and de la Huerta in Veracruz.[120] The Calles administration would feature more reform, but also more repression.

In March 1924 Calles resumed his campaign, albeit with a heavy liability. The war had highlighted Obregón's role in Calles's candidacy. Many observers believed that Calles owed his opportunity to become president to Obregón, and that he had promised the caudillo that he would support him for another term after his own tenure ended. To offset this impression, Calles positioned himself on the left. At the outset of the rebellion, Calles had characterized the Delahuertistas, and particularly Sánchez, as "redoubts of reaction" while he fought for the "true" revolution.[121] This theme also served in his campaign against the only opposition candidate, General Ángel Flores, a leader who counted on the support of many de la Huerta supporters and claimed to enjoy the backing of the Catholic Church.[122]

Sizing up Flores's challenge, Calles got out his worker-campesino playbook. On April 10, 1924, Calles gave an address at Zapata's tomb on the fifth anniversary of his murder. Accompanied by Soto y Gama and other agrarista leaders, he announced that Zapata's program was his own. Calles proclaimed, "I will always stand on the side of the most advanced principles of humankind.... The revolutionary program of Zapata, the agrarista program, is my own." Speaking for the Zapatistas, he went on, "The hero rests in peace, and his work is done."[123]

As a crucial aspect in his image as the worker-campesino candidate, Calles enjoyed the support of Mexico's tiny Partido Comunista Mexicano (PCM, or Mexican Communist Party). Founded in 1919 as one of the first such parties outside the Soviet Union, the PCM had thus far refrained from electoral politics. Declining to interfere in what it viewed as a struggle among capitalist caudillos, the party had made its presence felt informally in the rent strikes in Veracruz and Mexico City; in labor unions independent from the CROM; and among the Mexico City intelligentsia, including the famous muralists of the era. In advance of the 1924 presidential elections, however, the Comintern instructed the PCM to support non-Communist candidates friendly to the interests of the proletariat. Following this directive, the PCM endorsed Calles.[124]

On the issues of women's rights and religion, Calles portrayed himself as a moderate politician for his time. One speech appealed to women, calling them "half of the fatherland," yet did not propose to award them the franchise, which would not be granted at the national level until 1953.[125] As another example, Calles took an equivocal approach toward religion. As he declared in Morelia, Michoacán, "I . . . understand and approve all religious beliefs because I consider them beneficial for the moral program they encompass. I am an enemy of the priest caste that sees in its position a privilege rather than an evangelical mission. I am the enemy of the political priest, the scheming priest, the priest as exploiter, the priest who intends to keep our people in ignorance, the priest who allies with the hacendado to exploit the campesino, and the priest allied with the industrialist to exploit the worker."[126] The Holy See's chargé interpreted these remarks favorably. As Crespi reported, Calles's "last few discourses have been very moderate."[127]

Like Crespi, the U.S. government considered Calles the lesser of two evils. As the anthropologist Manuel Gamio recalled his conversations with Hughes and other high-ranking government officials in the United States, "even the most reactionary [politicians] consider him an honorable person and, principally, as a strong man who will know how to control all of the elements, whether conservative or radical. Of course, they would prefer to see power in the hands of a pro-capitalist ruler, but if that is impossible, they will prefer the strength of Calles over the weak mediocrity of a de la Huerta."[128]

Calles may have defined his candidacy best with the following lines, written privately to Obregón almost one year before the election: "I am an enemy of great promises and great programs. In most cases, the parties

20. Gómez and other generals at Calles's inauguration. Fideicomiso Archivos Plutarco Elías Calles y Fernando Torreblanca (FAPECFT), Fototeca, Archivo Fernando Torreblanca, Fondo Plutarco Elías Calles, Oficial, serie *Presidencia de la República, 1924–1928*, mfn 171, imagen 4, inventario 269. Used with permission.

and candidates know in advance that they will not become reality, and that they deceive the people."[129] As the elections approached, Calles postured as a pragmatic problem solver. During the first-ever radio address by a Mexican leader, he announced that his efforts to lift the proletariat out of its misery and ignorance did not imply an effort to destroy the propertied classes.[130] According to official results, he garnered 1,340,634 votes, compared with 250,500 for Flores.[131]

After his victory, Calles decided to spend a few months abroad in Europe and the United States. Most of this sojourn found him in a Berlin suburb receiving treatment for an array of health problems. While in the German capital, Calles took careful notes on a country that he had long admired. He learned that the fallen German Empire had built an enduring social safety net that sheltered the sick, retirees, and workers. His stay also allowed him to study European social democracy as a possible model for a capitalist government emanating from a social revolution. Weimar

Germany had such a party in the Social Democratic Party. Closely aligned with trade unionism, the party called for Socialism but played within the capitalist system, pushing for enhancements to the social safety net, public education, and the wellbeing of workers. Calles felt drawn to President Friedrich Ebert, a leader from a working-class family who promoted the rebirth of industry after the war despite the French and Belgian occupation of the Rhineland. Finally, he assiduously studied the German model of cooperative agriculture, the *Genossenschaften*. Calles concluded that he could learn a lot from this example.[132]

Part 4 ~:· The Duarchy, 1924–1928

7 ∵ On Trial before the World

Deep is the cleft that divides Mexico.—Ernest Gruening

On November 30, 1924, Calles was sworn in at the new Estadio Nacional, the first time the ceremony was held outdoors. The ceremony marked only the fifth instance in Mexican history that a president handed over power after a full term in office, and the third since the Juárez era. Porfirio Díaz had seized power in 1876 and stepped aside in favor of his protégé, Manuel González, in 1880. González handed power back to Díaz in 1884. Would Obregón be the new Díaz, and Calles, the new González? While the *New York Times* concluded that Calles could "by no means of the imagination ... [be] compared to Díaz's puppet," it also acknowledged that Mexicans were "wondering if history [would] repeat itself."[1] As *Foreign Affairs* opined, "The real authority in Mexico will still remain in the hands of Obregón."[2]

Indeed, the Obregonistas occupied important posts in the executive branch, the federal legislature, and state governments. Calles's first cabinet included Secretary of Finance Pani, Secretary of the Interior Gilberto Valenzuela, and Foreign Secretary Sáenz, although the latter was an "Obrecallista" with close ties to both Sonorenses. The primary loyalty of PNA leader Soto y Gama was to Obregón. At the state level, Obregón's allies included San Luis Potosí's Saturnino Cedillo and Tabasco's Tomás Garrido Canabal, among many others. The caudillo's sway over caciques secured the support of many of the estimated eight thousand regional and local parties.[3] But the notion of an overweening caudillo sells Calles's agency short. Callistas played important roles, and most significantly, Morones, the new secretary of industry, commerce, and labor, who had reportedly just signed a secret pact with Calles.[4] Another ally was Communication and Public Works Secretary Adalberto Tejeda, whose party formed part of a pro-Calles bloc in Congress.

President Calles was the other half of the duarchy.[5] Boasting a more favorable scenario than Obregón four years prior, he charged out of the gate with an assertive reform program. As he had done as governor of Sonora, Calles focused on government revenue and economic production, imposing regulations on foreign investments, and centralizing power. This program also promoted agrarian reform, public health, literacy, and social welfare—the items on which the "worker-campesino" candidate had staked his candidacy. Calles found a series of adversaries arrayed against his administration, including the Catholic Church and the U.S. government, and his uncompromising stance toward the former contributed to a popular uprising that undid many of his administration's achievements. This chapter will examine the Calles years from the vantage point of the president's agency; the next will focus on Obregón's.

An Auspicious Beginning

Calles enjoyed a honeymoon of sorts during his first year in office. According to a U.S. military intelligence agent who had once portrayed him as an extremely unpopular politician, Calles worked a "miracle" in his first two months. He seemed "to enjoy the confidence of all classes. All are supporting him enthusiastically in the hope that, at last, there has begun a period of peace and economic stability. Even the reactionaries are hopeful." The agent expressed his opinion that Calles would "keep within the law."[6] Adding to his popularity was his intention to reduce administrative and military bloat. On December 24 Calles announced budget cuts totaling 79 million pesos, almost half of them at the expense of the military.[7]

Calles's alliance with Morones yielded advances for workers, impelling wage increases in businesses where the CROM dominated the labor force. In the textile industry wages for male workers increased by 34 percent over the next four years.[8] Implementing article 123, the government decreed a reduction of the workday from twelve to eight hours (local practice, of course, was another matter). Calles backed a strike of streetcar drivers, threatening to expel the foreign owner of the Mexico City streetcar company under article 33 of the constitution.[9]

Calles and Morones also took on the powerful oil industry for deliberately suppressing production in order to gain leverage for a reform of article 27. Oil production had plummeted since 1921, as the companies diverted new exploration to countries like Venezuela where laissez-faire capitalism still prevailed. In response Calles disavowed the Bucareli Agreement and asked Morones to lead the effort to craft an implementing law of article 27 in the specific area of oil. Beginning on December 30, 1924, Congress debated what would become the Petroleum Law.[10] Progress was slow as Morones's "radicals" clashed with Pani's "moderates." As Calles vented to Obregón, "The antiquated and slow-moving administrative machine holds up and muddles everything. One loses one's time in miserable details, and days go by without definitive resolution.... It seems that the only thing the revolution has done is to get rid of don Porfirio Díaz ... and the other mummies. The procedures ... and even the lower-ranked personnel have stayed the same."[11]

U.S. Ambassador James R. Sheffield insisted on property rights. A wealthy corporate attorney with close connections to oil lobbyists, Sheffield hated Mexico. He spent as little time there as possible, taking lengthy leaves of absence. Sheffield saw his role as helping to "uplift ... this backward people."[12] He claimed that there was "very little white blood in the cabinet ... Calles is Armenian and Indian; ... Saenz [sic] the Foreign Minister is Jew and Indian; Morones more white blood but not the better for it."[13] The ambassador vigorously opposed the Petroleum Law and demanded guarantees to foreign property owners. Influenced by Sheffield, Secretary of State Frank B. Kellogg adopted a ham-fisted policy. According to his June 12, 1925, press release, Obregón had depended on U.S. assistance to defeat de la Huerta, and future support was contingent upon the Mexican government meeting its obligations. Kellogg declared that Mexico was "on trial before the world."[14]

This tough talk backfired. Calles defended his "patriotic and humanitarian" efforts on behalf of ordinary Mexicans against Kellogg's blackmail and "selfish" agenda.[15] In the tradition of Juárez and Carranza, he posed as a patriot standing up to a foreign threat. He thundered, "If the Government of Mexico, as affirmed, is now on trial before the world, such is the case with the Government of the United States as well as those of other countries."[16] Kellogg's rhetoric also elicited opposition within the U.S. government. An agent of the War Department General Staff asserted that the diatribe appeared like "an attempt to dictate to and coerce the present Mexican administration toward the selfish ends of American interests." He pointed out that Calles was opportunistic and eager to promote economic development but depended on the organizations that had helped him gain power, and most notably, the CROM. In a surprisingly blunt formulation, the agent blamed the trouble on Sheffield and Kellogg's "very marked change in public policy." Although he charged Calles with "flagrant neglect . . . of diplomatic procedures," he believed that a patient stance would cause a swing back to moderate policies.[17] Calles and Morones emerged strengthened from their first confrontation with the U.S. government. Meanwhile, relations with Great Britain thawed to the point that the two nations exchanged ministers.[18]

While Calles and Morones's nationalist agenda won accolades, their alliance created an authoritarian arrangement. Calles allowed Morones to try and force independent unions and rural workers into the CROM. Although the CROM claimed two million members, or 12 percent of the entire population, its real membership was much smaller. Independent organizations persisted; for example, the more radical CGT, the railroad workers' union, and the Catholic CNCT.[19] The CROM represented the type of cooptation that had also characterized Sonora's Cámara Obrera under Governor de la Huerta. The number of strikes declined from 136 in 1924 to 7 in 1928, in large part because of CROM and government repression. One particular strike—the national railroad strike of 1927—crippled transportation. Arbitration decisions disfavored workers. In 1925 arbitration boards issued 195 decisions favorable to employers (3.5 percent of the total); and in 1927, in a full economic crisis, they issued 643 in their favor (17.2 percent).[20]

Morones's critics considered him a corrupt leader whose forced levies on public-sector wages enriched him rather than promoted the wellbeing of workers. The labor leader reportedly entertained extravagant orgies at his private residence. Diamond rings adorned his fingers. Critics translated the CROM acronym as "cómo roba oro Morones," or "how Morones steals gold."[21] Not for nothing did the U.S. writer Katherine Anne Porter caricature Morones in her short story "Flowering Judas."[22]

Calles's financial reform program addressed the mounting government debt that included US$1.6 billion in obligations to the United States. The federal budget deficit exceeded US$40 million on a yearly basis—a figure already far lower than in 1922 (US$100 million). Pani further decreased it by means of a national income tax ranging from 2 to 8 percent. Helped by a growing economy, fiscal year 1925 ended with a surplus of 24 million pesos, the first such surplus since the beginning of the revolution.[23]

On better fiscal footing, the administration sought a stronger financial system. The most significant tool was the creation of the Banco de México (Banxico), the nation's first official bank of issue since 1842. On August 31, 1925, the bank began operations with a government stake of 55.7 million pesos. It guaranteed its paper money for up to half of its value in gold and initially operated as a commercial lending institution. In that capacity, Banxico became a source of cheap credit for the entrepreneurial activities of the Sonorenses and other selected members of the national elite more so than an engine of economic development in general. Nonetheless, it aimed to inspire confidence in domestic lenders that new debts would be repaid.[24] With an initial investment of 18 million pesos, the new Banco Nacional de Crédito Agrícola (BNCA, or National Agricultural Credit Bank) expanded rural access to loans. The BNCA backed local banks that provided credit for the purchase of equipment or seeds, or for building irrigation systems, dams, or warehouses. As in the case of Banxico, the BNCA lent to the Sonorenses.[25]

The government also addressed the foreign debt. In October Pani met with the ICBM in New York City to amend the De la Huerta–Lamont Treaty. The resultant agreement almost cut the debt in half and set lower interest rates in exchange for a resumption of debt payments and the privatization of the railroads.[26] However, the trip featured a rumored affair with a young Catalan dancer, Gloria Faure. On October 14 the front page of the *New York Daily Mirror* quoted Faure as exclaiming, "Mr. Pani is a wonderful lover." In response to the scandal, Pani offered his resignation, which Calles rejected with the comment that he did not want a cabinet of "eunuchs."[27] At the same time, the scandal inclined the ongoing discussions about the Petroleum Law in Morones's favor.

An important component in improving government finances lay in the continuation of Obregón's program to shrink and modernize the army. In comparative terms, the army still featured six times as many generals as the U.S. armed forces. There were twenty-one divisional generals, and the army had not become the politically neutral entity the Sonorenses desired. Calles put this project into the hands of General Joaquín Amaro, the new undersecretary of war. Over the next decade, Amaro reduced the army's share of the budget from 44 to 25 percent, mostly by decommissioning troops and lower-ranking officers. Legislation scheduled inspections of army units, regularized promotions, set penalties for corruption, and created a pension system as well as a mandatory retirement age. Aware of the limits of anticorruption measures, Amaro delegated enforcement to the divisional generals, which meant that these generals now received bribes from lower-ranking officers in exchange for overlooking their abuses. Finally, Amaro reopened the Colegio Militar, hoping to train a patriotic and honest officer corps.[28]

The Calles administration placed great emphasis on infrastructure improvements, and particularly road building. In the age of the automobile, roads played a crucial role in economic development. Following an unsuccessful road building effort under Obregón, Calles and several governors created a national commission of roadways tasked with the construction of ten thousand kilometers of new roads, funded by a gasoline tax. Progress was slow: only 10 percent of this goal was completed or under construction by the end of 1927. The project nevertheless led to notable improvements; for example, a road from Mexico City to Acapulco and work on the Pan-American Highway that would ultimately connect Texas with Guatemala. In railroad construction, a new track connected the Northwest with Guadalajara and Mexico City.[29]

The government also supported efforts to increase industrial production in order to meet consumer demand and reduce dependence on manufactured imports. During the Porfiriato, Monterrey had emerged as an industrial hub that produced steel, beer, and glass. The Puebla and Veracruz border region saw the growth of textile mills. Revolutionary violence had interrupted industrial development, and the Sonorenses aimed to restore the momentum with the help of tax incentives. In 1925 Ford Motor Company invested in an assembly plant, and other corporations such as DuPont, Bayer, Hoechst, and Palmolive followed suit. Often, industrialization involved joint ventures involving the state and Mexican and foreign entrepreneurs; witness, for example, the San Rafael paper mill and CIDOSA, a textile conglomerate. A significant figure in these endeavors was Foreign Secretary Sáenz, a distant relative of Monterrey's Garza-Sada clan.[30]

With more than 65 percent of the population living in the countryside, the Calles administration accelerated agrarian reform. His government parceled out 2,972,876 hectares (almost three times as much as its predecessor), benefiting 297,428 recipients.[31] These redistributions focused on areas controlled by allies such as Cedillo and Tejeda and spared estates producing export commodities or food for urban consumption. Like Obregón, Calles preferred the *pequeña propiedad* to the *ejido* and prioritized production over social justice.[32] As he argued, large landowners "will gain by conceding lands to the villages" so that they "shall become real agriculturalists . . . and they will cease to be exploiters of men." Hence, he also focused on infrastructure, including hydroelectric dams and irrigation projects.[33] One of the seven new dams would provide water to El Mante, the sugar estate in Tamaulipas owned by the Calles and Sáenz families.[34]

Calles furthered the ambitious rural education project begun by Vasconcelos. At the outset of his term, the overall literacy rate stood at less than 25 percent. After one thousand rural schools had opened during Vasconcelos's tenure, the SEP added two thousand more. As Calles declared, "the happiness, the glory, and the greatness of the fatherland depend on the preparation given to [future] generations."[35] In 1928, 46 percent of primary school–aged children attended school—a number that had tripled since 1920. Secondary and preparatory school remained the preserve of the wealthy, with only 16,024 students, plus another 9,763 in professional schools.[36] In addition to this quantitative improvement, Calles also enhanced the authority of the SEP in determining the location of rural schools at the expense of state governments.[37] Under the direction of Undersecretary Moisés Sáenz, a Presbyterian minister and former student of the U.S. educational reformer John Dewey, the focus shifted from classical education to action pedagogy, or learning by doing. Sáenz, the brother of Foreign Secretary Aarón Sáenz, argued that "it is as important to rear chickens as to read poetry."[38] Like Vasconcelos's, Sáenz's program aimed at the assimilation of Indigenous people and a nationalist ideology that would lead rural citizens to abandon allegiance to their *patrias chicas* in favor of the *patria grande*. However, theory greatly differed from practice. A recalcitrant population often resisted the official curriculum as well as the radical and secular teachers trained in the *normales*.[39] In these settings, teachers were the face of the government and became targets during the church-state conflict.[40]

A public health campaign complemented the education effort. Revolutionary violence and the Spanish flu had highlighted the importance of halting the spread of disease, whether through beverages, food, open sewers, or airborne vectors. The vehicle to carry out this effort was the new department of public health that issued hygiene guidelines and carried out regular inspections of butcher shops, canteens, markets, and restaurants. The agency also required the registration of sex workers and inoculated against smallpox. It regulated the lives of ordinary citizens, and especially women workers. The department did not have enough money to do its work, corruption hampered its effectiveness, and one initiative important to Calles—the prohibition of alcohol—remained unaddressed.[41]

Like Obregón, Calles grasped the symbolic aspect of nation building. For example, his administration transformed the famed Porfirian-era Angel of Independence located on the capital's posh Paseo de la Reforma into a monument to secular nationalism. On Independence Day 1925 the government unveiled a mausoleum containing the remains of the independence heroes, to date preserved in the National Cathedral. The bones of Miguel Hidalgo, José María Morelos, Vicente Guerrero, and many others came to repose beneath the column supporting the majestic gold-covered angel. Calles refused to include Emperor Iturbide. He explained to U.S. journalist Ernest Gruening, "I left Iturbide [at the cathedral], among his kind, where he belongs." According to Gruening, "To the Mexican conservatives and clergy . . . , Iturbide is *the* liberator, the others a shabby lot, and the issue is thoroughly alive. It has been presented to me with as much heat as if it dealt with contemporary figures. Deep is the cleft that divides Mexico."[42]

Calles's position on the anticlerical side of this cleft became clear in his response to an effort to found a schismatic church. On February 21, 1925, a crowd of one hundred entered the Iglesia Soledad de Santa Cruz, a sixteenth-century church in a working-class eastern Mexico City neighborhood, and drove out the priests under the threat of violence. The crowd included several CROM-affiliated Knights of Guadalupe—a group established as competition to the U.S.-based Knights of Columbus. Subsequently, a former priest, Joaquín Pérez Budar, installed himself as patriarch of the Iglesia Católica Apostólica Mexicana (ICAM, or Mexican Catholic Apostolic Church). A few days later, more than one thousand protesters interrupted the church's first Eucharist. Calles ordered that Soledad be turned into a public library and awarded to the ICAM the unoccupied Corpus Christi church, centrally located at Alameda Park.[43]

This incident had widespread repercussions. From the prelates' perspective, the president had supported a schismatic church. Eighty petitioners (more than sixty of them females) asked for the Holy See's intervention in order to foil "the satanic cry that calls for rebellion and arrogance."[44] Catholics organized the Liga Nacional de la Defensa Religiosa (LNDR, or National League for Religious Defense), an umbrella organization for the Catholic associations that had burgeoned since the beginning of the decade. Though decidedly prorevolutionary, the ICAM was not merely a tool of Calles and Morones. It might have started as such, but it soon took on a life of its own. At its peak, the ICAM was a popular, reformist church loyal to the state, imbued with "Mexicanized" religious practices and reliant on a heavily Indigenous constituency. It boasted hundreds of congregations, especially in the eastern half of Mexico and therefore became a dissenting voice within the Catholic tradition.[45] Obregón recognized this potential and even worried that this "pseudo-Catholic" movement might sap the "Liberal" consensus among the ruling revolutionary group.[46] The emergence of the ICAM showed that anticlericalism was a more deeply rooted phenomenon than the whim of a president.

Broadly speaking, the first year of the Calles presidency witnessed a steady drift toward conflict with the church. State legislatures passed laws limiting the number of priests or imposing strict limits on their activities. For example, the legislature in Tabasco reserved religious practice to married priests, which gave the clergy a choice between breaking canonical and secular law. This law forced the local bishop, Pascual Díaz, to move to Mexico City. Meanwhile, the LNDR claimed a membership of thirty-six thousand, most of them in central and western Mexico. A new apostolic delegate arrived on April 1 but left for the United States six weeks later. When he tried to return to Mexico, an embassy official in Washington DC told him that Calles wanted him to stay away.[47] The president did not give any indication that tensions would soon escalate. He told an Argentine anticlerical visitor who recommended a firm position that "clericalism now signifies no danger at all" and added that his government would instead focus on social and economic reconstruction.[48] But trouble was on the horizon. In December 1925, a papal encyclical, *Quas primas*, introduced the Feast of Christ the King, a direct challenge to secular nationalism in its celebration of Jesus Christ as the king of humanity.

Calles's reform drive illustrated commonalities and differences with the other two Sonorense presidents. It shared with its predecessor an effort to centralize political authority, increase government revenue, and mix social reform with a paternalistic effort to incorporate social movements under the aegis of the president. Blessed with U.S. diplomatic recognition, Calles had taken on the powerful oil industry: in the words of Banxico chief Manuel Gómez Morín, foreign capital "should be the servant rather than a master of the Mexican economy."[49] Calles had also leaned on the CROM and PLM rather than the agraristas. In all, the Calles administration was off to a good start.

However, as the Calles administration entered its second year, it confronted significant headwinds. The disagreements with the Catholic Church erupted in open conflict. At the same time, the Petroleum Law and the new Alien Land Law exacerbated a growing controversy with the U.S. State Department; and rebels used U.S. territory to plot to overthrow the government.

Conflict with the Church

While older scholarship counted devout Catholics among the adversaries of the revolution, recent research has produced a more nuanced view. Some historians have presented the picture of a bifurcated revolution featuring Jacobin and Catholic variants. According to one scholar, the Catholic vision—informed by the 1891 encyclical, *Rerum novarum*—was "on the way to creating a system of Christian democracy before the term had been invented." The government considered it a competitor in its quest for control over the masses.[50]

What one historian has called a "Catholic alternative to the revolution" was not monolithic.[51] An older generation such as the philosopher Antonio Caso embraced the social Catholicism that emerged after *Rerum novarum*, including the emergence of faith-based parties, youth and women's organizations, and trade unions. They sought a third path between "savage capitalism" and Socialism—an economy dominated by small and midsized family properties. Social Catholicism was in the PCN's program during the Madero period. Its basic tenets informed Catholic associations as the church's presence in the public sphere, in the absence of faith-based parties.[52] Younger Catholics in the ACJM took a more radical view. They rejected the revolution as antinational, equated Mexican nationalism with Catholicism, and opposed consumer culture, which they viewed as debasing to the soul.[53] Finally, much of the Catholic hierarchy remained opposed to the revolution, and especially the primate archbishop, Mora y del Río, and his colleague from Guadalajara, José Francisco Orozco y Jiménez. Members of aristocratic families and products of the Porfirian-era church, they viewed the revolution as a nefarious "Socialist" attack on power, privilege, and property. They preferred the poor to be meek. In a memorandum to his superiors, Ernest Lagarde, the French chargé d'affaires, called the episcopate "indiscreet, restricted in vision, intransigent, vain, and thoroughly disunited" and Mora y del Río "a decrepit old man, an opportunist without willpower, a believer in political intrigue." Lagarde also had choice words for the "coarse, ignorant, greedy, and dissolute" lower clergy, which, as he thought, regarded the church "not as an apostolate but as a lucrative and easy profession."[54] The notion of a separate Catholic revolution that pursued "political and democratic modernity" therefore needs some nuance.[55]

The modus vivendi between the church and the revolutionary regime implied restraint from overt criticism of the constitution in exchange for toleration of activities that defied the anticlerical articles. As the central political document of the revolution, the constitution was a "public transcript": "the self portrait of dominant elites as they themselves would be seen."[56] This public transcript structured discourse. In 1917 the archbishops had enjoined their flock to disobey the anticlerical articles.[57] But since then, and even during the Cubilete affair in January 1923, both sides had stayed within the bounds of this modus vivendi, which resembled Porfirio Díaz's long-standing arrangement with the church despite the existence of anticlerical provisions in the Constitution of 1857.

But the modus vivendi fell apart in early 1926, when a newspaper article dredged up the archbishop's initial reaction to the constitution. On February 4, *El Universal* quoted Mora y del Río as follows: "The Episcopate, Clergy, and Catholics do not recognize and will combat Articles 3, 5, 27, and 130." Published on the eve of the ninth anniversary of the constitution, the newspaper article had quoted a long-forgotten statement. But it was clear that Mora y del Río had not changed his position. The archbishop had released a similar pronouncement regarding state-level policies on January 19, and when given the chance to distance himself from his old statements, he declined to do so.[58] On February 8 *El Universal* published another article that quoted the episcopate as opposing the constitution for violating "the most sacred rights of the Catholic Church, Mexican society, and Christian individuals."[59] The Holy See's chargé d'affaires characterized Mora y del Río's impolitic personality thus: "Mgr. Mora y del Río has an irreducible tendency to pose as a *homo politicus* even though he does not know how to act like one."[60] Upon his arrival in March, the new apostolic delegate, George Caruana, also criticized the archbishop's stance. As this native of Malta and naturalized U.S. citizen explained to his counterpart in the United States, the Holy See "ought to use the utmost caution" with regard to the revolutionary program, "praising what there is to praise and repudiating the rest."[61]

The affair brought forth the wrath of Secretary of the Interior Tejeda, a rabid anticlerical. In August, Tejeda had replaced Gilberto Valenzuela, an Obregonista and a voice of moderation on religious matters. Valenzuela's departure had removed a conciliatory voice in favor of "one of the most implacable and terrible enemies of the Catholic Religion."[62] Tejeda referred the archbishop's statement to the attorney general as a criminal matter and explained, "The state . . . cannot permit the church to ignore or combat the constitutional laws."[63] The archbishop denied having used the word "combat" and clarified the fact that his remarks were nine years old—a statement that ended the criminal proceeding.[64] Still, on February 17 Tejeda ordered foreign-born clergy to cease ministry and closed all monasteries and convents. Six days later, Calles asked all governors to enforce the anticlerical provisions of the constitution, since the tolerant attitude under the modus vivendi had created the recent difficulties in the first place. By mid-March, the federal and state governments had expelled two hundred foreign-born priests and closed one hundred religious schools as well as eighty-three monasteries and convents.[65]

Tejeda's role demonstrated the fact that the escalating conflict between church and state followed a larger political context more so than Calles's dictum (not to mention Obregón's unquestionable continuing influence).

A second major wave of anticlericalism originated in the South and center rather than the North and had significant popular support, even as a minority position. This second wave was as diverse as its adherents, including agraristas, workers, students, and teachers. Its regional leadership included committed atheists such as Tabasco's Garrido Canabal. While some historians have blamed Calles for the upsurge of state-level anticlerical measures, such assertions overstate his reach.[66] Instead, anticlericalism percolated up from the states before it received reinforcement from the federal level.

Tejeda's position also highlighted the prominent place of anticlericals within Calles's cabinet, constructed to balance Calles's desire for an independent presidency with Obregón's continuing influence in national politics. The most influential cabinet member in this regard was Morones, followed by Tejeda. The secretary of war, General Joaquín Amaro, had a reputation as a ruthless opponent of the Catholic Church. His enemies also feared Amaro, nicknamed "the whip of God" for his uncompromising methods.[67] This trio not only held the key to the enforcement of central government authority but also to the control over Mexico's largest labor organizations. Of these, Morones's CROM and its political wing, the PLM, were most influential, as they suggested a wide popular reach of anticlerical policies.

Catholics resisted the new strictures. When Tejeda required a permit from the clergy of Sagrada Familia in Guadalajara for the purpose of worship, they carried on as usual. In response, Tejeda ordered the church closed, which occasioned a fight in the streets between two thousand protesters and the police that left at least seven protesters dead and another sixteen injured. A similar street battle took place in San Luis Potosí over a statewide measure to reduce the number of priests. As a result, the government backed down from wholesale enforcement of Tejeda's and Calles's orders.[68]

In this atmosphere, the new apostolic delegate did not last long. The anticlericals portrayed Caruana as a U.S. citizen who meddled in Mexican affairs, while Catholics saw him as too willing to compromise. Caruana established an episcopal committee composed of the archbishops of Mexico City, Guadalajara, Morelia, and Puebla, in addition to bishops sojourning in the capital. Upon his initiative, the LNDR became the Liga

Nacional Defensora de la Libertad Religiosa (LNDLR, or National League for the Defense of Religious Liberty). In response, Calles expelled Caruana, charging him with having entered the country with forged immigration documents as well as illegal religious practice.[69] Mora y del Río pointed to Caruana's diplomatic status in arguing that the administration should have asked for his recall rather than expel him. A collective letter accompanying his note warned, "If the goal of the repeated expulsions of Apostolic delegates is to relax and sever . . . the traditional links of the Mexican Church with Rome, Mr. President, know that every new instance of pain is a new connection of love and union" with the Holy See. Calles responded that his government would "use all necessary energy to ensure" compliance with the law.[70] In a subsequent exchange, Calles used yet a harsher tone: "Any act of rebellion . . . and lack of respect to the authorities will be punished without considerations of any kind."[71]

The ultimate confrontation with the church came with the so-called Calles Law, published on July 2, 1926. This reform to the penal code obligated all priests to register with local authorities before exercising ministry. The episcopate interpreted this measure as an attempt to take away their power of appointing clergy. The law restricted ministry to native-born Mexicans, proscribed clergy from wearing vestments in public, barred religious organizations from operating educational institutions, prohibited all political activity by the clergy, and ordered the closing of all monasteries, convents, and religious schools.[72] Catholics noted that the zeal with which the law criminalized violations of the constitution's anticlerical provisions contrasted with the insufficient or nonexistent implementation of many of the social rights provisions.

The church mounted an immediate counterattack. The LNDLR called for an economic boycott, and on July 24, the Episcopal Committee announced the suspension of religious ceremonies on July 31, the effective date of the new law. They did so with the full support of the Holy See, which had thus far attempted to stay above the fray. According to Cardinal Pietro Gasparri, the pope's top diplomat, "The Holy See condemns the law and also any act that might be interpreted by the faithful as compliance with or acceptance of that law."[73] On Sunday, August 1, there was no public mass for the first time since the Spanish conquest.

At first, Calles was sanguine about the church strike. He reportedly boasted that "each week without religious services would make the Catholic religion lose about 2 percent of its adherents."[74] But the LNDLR boycott soon buffeted the economy, especially in Jalisco. The Calles Law had gathered the faithful, the episcopate, the Holy See, and the LNDLR in opposition. The conflict quickly escalated. The government intimidated the press and arrested LNDLR activists, and sporadic violence began in different parts of the country. On August 3, four hundred armed Catholics ensconced themselves in a Guadalajara church and exchanged gunfire with federal soldiers.[75]

Why did Calles pick this fight with the Catholic Church? Most historians would argue that Calles had always hated the clergy. As Lagarde put it, the president was "a malignant and implacable enemy . . . who has resolved to exterminate the Catholic faith from Mexico."[76] One historian has called Calles Mexico's "arch-clerophobe."[77] There was truth in that sentiment, and Calles confronted a more muscular church than either Carranza or Obregón due to the rapid growth of the LNDNR, which claimed more than thirty thousand members. But how much influence could Calles wield, as a single person, amid a wave of anticlericalism that had deep regional and social origins, especially in a political system in which Obregón still loomed as a powerful individual? As we have seen, the makeup of Calles's cabinet influenced the formulation of policy. The Tejeda/Morones/Amaro coalition reflected significant popular support for anticlericalism in at least some regions of the country. Some of the most strident anticlerical measures took place at the state level, and not always under Callista clients.

This analysis suggests a more contingent explanation. Until 1926 Calles had not stood out for his anticlericalism. In the 1910s other Constitutionalist governors had joined him in expelling the Catholic priests from their states, and until 1926, Calles had not issued the shrill anticlerical tones that came from leaders such as Garrido. As a result, even the papal delegate had believed that the church could work with Calles. It appears that Calles identified the Catholic hierarchy as a primary enemy as a direct result of the crisis of 1926; in Lagarde's words, the church had "here more than elsewhere to form a state within the state and not to accept from the civil power any regulation, any law."[78] Less willing than Obregón to sacrifice priorities for expediency, Calles saw himself as the guardian of the constitution that he had sworn to protect. In his words, "As long as I am President of the Republic, the Constitution of 1917 will be obeyed."[79] The transnational activities of the church, which included the mobilization of Mexican rebels north of the border, also factored in his opposition. Finally, even though Mexican and U.S. intelligence services kept him well informed about his adversaries, including the church, Calles underestimated the ability of Catholics to undercut his government via mass action.

As a result, Calles made a major mistake in passing up the chance to resolve the crisis through negotiations that reflected the existing divisions within the church. Worried that the church strike might alienate the lower clergy, which depended on religious services for their income, the episcopate attempted a negotiated solution. Mora y del Río and Pascual Díaz, the bishop of Tabasco and secretary general of the Episcopal Committee, asked Calles for a reform of the anticlerical articles, the suspension of all criminal charges, and the immediate resumption of religious education and welfare. In response, Calles warned that clergy engaged in "open revolts ... to the end of abolishing or reforming the constitution," "illegal resistance to ... the laws. ... or crimes against the public order," and "provoking rebellion through their attitude or sermon." He pointed to Congress as the proper channel to address concerns with the constitution.[80] On August 21 Calles met with Díaz and Archbishop Leopoldo Ruiz y Flores of Morelia, a moderate who had openly criticized Huerta's seizure of power in 1913. The president again insisted on enforcing the new law and reiterated his recommendation to ask Congress to reform the constitution. He starkly warned that the church could choose between Congress or armed rebellion. That said, Calles gave the prelates an opening by stating that his government only desired the registration of priests for statistical purposes.[81] Encouraged, the Episcopal Committee voted to recommend the resumption of church services if Calles publicly clarified that the registration requirement only served statistical purposes. However, a newspaper article that quoted the president as denying any progress led the committee to hold off. Calles responded with exasperation, telling Lagarde that he would never again accept a papal delegate.[82]

Despite the failure of negotiations, the episcopate brought to Congress a request for reform of the offending articles, along with what they represented as one million signatures. The Chamber of Deputies rejected this request on the basis that the bishops had lost the right to petition by conspiring with a foreign power, the Holy See.[83] In response, Pius XI issued an encyclical, *Iniquis afflictisque* ("sad and unjust") that condemned religious persecution in Mexico, and particularly the Calles Law.

The conflict escalated into war. On November 26, 1926, LNDLR leader René Capistrán Garza issued a manifesto that called for the overthrow of the government. Campesinos in Colima, Guanajuato, Jalisco, Michoacán, and Zacatecas rose up to the cry of "Viva Cristo Rey" ("Long Live Christ the King"). Thus began La Cristiada, or the Cristero Rebellion.[84] Explaining the regional appeal of the Cristeros, one historian has cited three important characteristics of these states: (1) a relatively intact pattern of smallholding, which limited the appeal of agraristas; (2) widespread opposition to federal land reform as an effort to centralize political power; and (3) a strong network of Catholic organizations.[85] The Cristiada combined religious fervor with political grievances and the defense of private property. In rural communities such as San José de Gracia, Michoacán, it drew upon more generalized opposition to the government and local oppressors.[86] Without blessing by the episcopate or the Holy See, the rebellion resembled the spontaneous popular uprisings of the early years of the revolution: Orozco's in Chihuahua and Zapata's in Morelos. On March 15, 1927, the Cristeros dealt the army an embarrassing defeat at the Battle of San Julián (Jalisco), after federal troops had mistaken an approaching Cristero contingent as men under Amaro's command.[87]

The government responded with more repression. In April 1927 Tejeda ordered the arrest and expulsion of Mora y del Río, Ruiz y Flores, and four other prelates on charges of sedition. By the end of May, most of the episcopate was in exile in San Antonio. Preserved in intelligence records, emigration documents reveal interesting insights. For example, all of them claimed mestizo ethnicity, even Mora y del Río and Orozco y Jiménez. Only two of the archbishops, Mora y del Río and Ruiz y Flores, professed knowledge of living foreign languages such as English, French, and Italian.[88]

Meanwhile, after suffering heavy early losses due to the inexperience of its military leaders, the rebellion became a serious threat. In July the

21. Fallen Cristeros in Colima. Fideicomiso Archivos Plutarco Elías Calles y Fernando Torreblanca (FAPECFT), Fototeca, Archivo Fernando Torreblanca, Fondo Plutarco Elías Calles, Oficial, serie *Presidencia de la República, 1924–1928*, mfn 272, imagen 42, inventario 307. Used with permission.

Cristeros secured the services of General Enrique Gorostieta Velarde. Born in 1889 and raised in a secular family, Gorostieta trained at the Colegio Militar and became a prominent figure in Victoriano Huerta's army as its youngest general. He agreed to lead the Cristeros for political ambition, a desire to make money, and a chance to defeat the revolutionary regime that he hated. Yet over time, he embraced the cause, wearing a cross and professing allegiance to the faith.[89] Gorostieta brought much-needed discipline to the Cristeros, who reached a strength of fifty thousand—a size similar to that of the Constitutionalist army in 1915. The war claimed more than ninety thousand lives and devastated an area known as the country's breadbasket: national grain production dropped by almost 40 percent.[90] One year into his campaign, Gorostieta formulated the Plan de Los Altos. The plan postulated him as president and demanded a return to the 1857 constitution minus the anticlerical reform laws.[91] Gorostieta's platform demanded women's participation in plebiscites, reflecting the role of the Feminine Brigades of St. Joan of Arc, which provided logistics support to Cristero soldiers, including the smuggling of guns and ammunition.[92]

While the Cristiada posed the most serious challenge to Sonorense rule since the De la Huerta Rebellion, it ultimately failed to achieve its objective. The Cristeros could no more overthrow the government than the government had been able to vanquish the Catholic Church. As Calles's term approached its final year, the two sides lurched toward an exhausted stalemate. The fight with the church had proven a tragic mistake, one that undid much of the work of Calles's first year and a half as president.

Threats from the North

The church-state conflict coincided with an equally serious crisis with the U.S. government and highlighted the dangers posed by Mexican exiles in the United States. As much as Kellogg and Sheffield had fought Calles's nationalist policies in his first year in office, their opposition intensified when the Petroleum Law became reality on December 31, 1925. The law was not as bad for the oil companies as it could have been, requiring foreign companies to apply for confirmatory concessions valid for fifty years, long after the projected depletion of the wells. But it shredded the Bucareli Agreement, and oil companies opposed the precedent as well as the fact that the law made them liable for the environmental impact of their activities.[93]

Worse yet from the standpoint of the State Department, the Mexican Congress also passed an Alien Land Law. Promulgated on December 23, 1925, it implemented another set of provisions in article 27, outlawing foreign ownership of land within fifty kilometers of the coast or one hundred kilometers of the border. A large percentage of U.S.-held property (for example, most of the copper mines and oilfields) lay inside that zone. The law also barred foreigners from holding a majority interest in any agricultural development company. It alarmed the State Department in part because Mexico had nationalized almost two hundred thousand hectares of U.S.-held land since 1917—approximately 8 percent of all expropriations.[94]

In response, Sheffield portrayed the Calles administration as a Soviet-style "Bolshevik" regime. He charged that the tiny PCM and the Soviet legation enjoyed virtually free rein and called the strongly anti-Communist Morones a "Bolshevist" [sic].[95] Few within the government agreed with this assessment. An internal memorandum in the State Department conceded:

"There is little tangible evidence... that the Mexican Government is... bolshevist [sic]. The word 'bolshevist' has become an epithet rather than a useful definition."[96] As one agent in the War Department put it, "The policies of the State Department... are... being watched with careful interest by the Military Intelligence Division, with the object only of safeguarding the national interest of the whole American people, and not for the benefit of any group or groups of priviledged [sic] and selfish organized interests."[97]

Calles's appetite for antagonizing the State Department peaked in summer 1926 when his conflict with the church escalated. Both conflicts were interrelated. Indeed, the Knights of Columbus had pressured the U.S. government to lift its embargo on supplying arms to Mexican rebels. In addition, Sheffield railed against anticlericalism, especially after Caruana's expulsion. While Kellogg would not remove the arms embargo, he asked Sheffield to deliver an official note of protest for violating the freedom of worship, a cornerstone value of the U.S. political system.[98] In addition, Pani resigned from his post as secretary of finance in September 1926. An opponent of the Petroleum and Alien Land Laws, he viewed Morones and Tejeda as responsible for the deterioration of relations with the United States. His resignation reflected the apex of Morones's and Tejeda's influence.[99]

Evidencing this political constellation, Calles challenged the United States on another front by means of an adventure in Central America. He threw his support behind Nicaragua's former vice president, Juan Bautista Sacasa, who sought to unseat President Emiliano Chamorro, an unpopular U.S. ally who had overthrown the elected government via a coup d'état. Sacasa obtained Calles's support for an insurrection in a country that had just recently featured a thirteen-year U.S. occupation designed to keep leaders like Chamorro in power. Calles supported Sacasa because he sympathized with his nationalist and social reformist aspirations. Several Mexican commercial vessels took rifles, ammunition, and exiles to Nicaragua. Calles took personal interest in the rebellion and transferred 2 million pesos from his presidential discretionary account to the ambassador in Guatemala. The Nicaragua affair backfired, as it suggested to U.S. policymakers a revolutionary contagion. As a result, Marines landed in Nicaragua on Christmas Eve, 1926. On January 12,

1927, Kellogg gave a statement that portrayed Mexico as a host that spread Bolshevism in Latin America.[100]

Kellogg attacked the Calles administration at what he believed to be a propitious moment. A few weeks before, the U.S. military attaché had summarized the situation thus: "Mexico has been ... a vast proving-ground on which fantastic experiments have been conducted ... by ... men ... unacquainted with the nature and the effect of the forces with which they have been dealing. The unfortunate feature of this proving-ground is that it is inhabited by some fifteen million people who ... must continue in a state of misery, suffering, and helplessness resulting from experiments conceived in the laboratories of ignorance, vanity and vicious caprice." As the attaché concluded, "The Calles administration ... finds the great majority of the people against it and its tenure of office [is] apparently dependent upon the sufferance of ... Obregón and the unknown policy of the United States."[101] The report overstated the threat to the government. A memorandum by the British minister focused on the consolidation of political authority under Calles and recommended coming to terms with a pesky economic nationalism that the minister considered constitutive of the political order.[102]

In response, Calles once again emphasized the right of a sovereign nation to make and enforce its own laws. But he also did not penalize the oil companies that had defied the Petroleum Law and offered to submit the dispute to international mediation. In this endeavor, Calles could count on the help of progressive intellectuals such as Carleton Beals and Ernest Gruening, who knew that Kellogg faced harsh criticism in the U.S. Senate at a time when the Teapot Dome scandal had discredited the oil industry. Sheffield bitterly lashed out at these critics for caring "more for the interests of other countries and other peoples than their own."[103]

The weeks following Kellogg's statements saw rampant speculation regarding a U.S. invasion, especially after Morones announced that his office would not issue further drilling permits to companies that had not applied for confirmatory concessions. Calles expressed concern that Marines would land in Veracruz to secure the nearby U.S.-owned oil fields. In the event of such an intervention, he ordered Cárdenas, the zone commander in the Gulf region, to set the oil fields ablaze so that, as the president commented, the flames could be seen as far away as New

Orleans. Fortunately, neither Coolidge nor the Senate had any interest in a military conflict, despite Sheffield's advocacy for the use of force.[104]

While the Calles administration played up these fears in part to gin up domestic support, it did have reason to worry. It had managed to place a spy within the embassy close enough to the military attaché to steal copies of sensitive documents. These documents highlighted Sheffield's animus toward the government to which he was accredited, including a desire to achieve the fall of the Calles administration. In February 1927 the Calles administration saw to it that three hundred documents reached the U.S. government in a play for leverage, as the aggressive, demeaning, and racist comments constituted a source of embarrassment.[105]

Another important use of the stolen documents was in tracking the activities of rebels who used the United States as sanctuary even though the embargo prevented them from acquiring weapons. The files as well as information from Mexican consuls in the United States as well as the Dirección General de Investigaciones Políticas y Sociales (DGIPS, or General Directorate of Political and Social Investigations) traced plots from several different groups. Among others, these potential rebel movements included Catholics and adherents of Adolfo de la Huerta, Félix Díaz, and Pablo González.[106]

De la Huerta was a particularly prominent opponent. Don Fito still saw himself as the true champion of the Mexican people, as the "Supreme Chief of the Revolution." He and his brother, Alfonso, appointed supporters to military ranks in their "Ejército Libertador" (Liberating Army).[107] De la Huerta planted himself to the right within the political spectrum. He called himself "a staunch supporter of respect to private property" and demanded the "exact fulfillment of legitimate international obligations" as well as "liberty of conscience."[108]

In August 1925 intelligence agents observed a plan to organize a Delahuertista rebellion from New York City. As one of the leading conspirators told a U.S. informant, "You would be surprised at the large number of supporters that we have who are yet in the employ of the Mexican government. De la Huerta was and is a very popular man in Mexico still. Only the ring leaders of the Sonora crowd were against de la Huerta ... Calles and his whole damn crowd of Bolsheviks are a bunch of cutthroats ... who are holding on to office not through the will of the people, but through ... murder and plunder of innocent citizens."[109]

DGIPS agents dug up worrisome details about de la Huerta's connections to other rebels. In 1925 they discovered discussions between de la Huerta and representatives of the oil companies to find money and allies for an insurgency, and they traced efforts by representatives of Pablo González, Félix Díaz, and Catholic representatives to ally with de la Huerta. The Felicistas and Gonzalistas reached out to former interim president León de la Barra in Paris, only to earn a summary rebuke: "I am still a patriot and as such will not conspire ... with any faction having as its object the purpose of inflicting further suffering upon the Mexican people." The man who had replaced Porfirio Díaz went on, "There is only one remedy to be applied to those who ... bring about bloodshed, starvation, and ruin in the ranks of the peace-loving people of Mexico: the firing squad. That was the only and most effective method of Don Porfirio."[110] In the end, the plot did not gain traction. De la Huerta attended only a few of the meetings and rebuffed González's overtures for a united front.[111]

Instead, de la Huerta preferred to act on his own. For example, in October 1925 a Delahuertista rebel arrived in San Antonio seeking materials to make bombs. U.S. agents arrested the rebel on the charge of violating immigration law. Prieto Laurens and other exiles saved him from extradition by securing the intervention of James J. Davis, the U.S. Secretary of Labor.[112] In December 1926 de la Huerta named personal representatives in several states to aid an "Army of Liberation that shall save the Republic from the tyranny imposed ... by the despot, Obregón."[113] In late 1926 and early 1927, he also supported the Yaqui in their final large-scale military conflict with the federal government.

But de la Huerta's fear of the DGIPS and U.S. law enforcement made him cautious. Because the U.S. government never ceased its collaboration despite Kellogg's warning to the contrary, what one historian has called "transnational projects of repression" hampered the activity of all political exiles.[114] Indeed, de la Huerta never felt safe. Two agents watched his comings and goings, and more observed the movements of his allies. According to the testimony of one of his friends, de la Huerta once received two men who offered him money, weapons, and ammunition in order to start another rebellion. During the visit, one of the visitors took off his coat, which slid off the back of the chair and fell to the floor, revealing a note with Obregón's signature that promised a large sum of money upon delivery of the "agreed-upon merchandise" in Mexico.[115] U.S. law enforcement posed another challenge. The U.S. Justice Department charged de la Huerta, his brother, Prieto Laurens, and ten others with violations of U.S. neutrality laws. Fortunately for de la Huerta, intercepted letters did not bear his name, as he had signed them with the letter "M" or the pseudonym "Melquíades."[116] In the end the de la Huertas and Prieto Laurens did not face any punishment, although eight collaborators had to pay a fine of $2,500 each.

Meanwhile, General Enrique Estrada attempted the rebellion that Don Fito hesitated to lead. Estrada found an accomplice in Félix Díaz, with whom he coincided in their rejection of revolutionary anticlericalism. In August 1926 the U.S. Department of Justice observed efforts in Tucson, Arizona, to unify the opposition in a rebellion. On August 16 a caravan of military vehicles, including Estrada's brother, crossed the Imperial Valley in Southern California on its way to the border, but agents apprehended 136 men before they could cross over into Mexico. Estrada had funding from a California investor whom he had promised access to the casino sector in Baja California dominated by Abelardo Rodríguez and his associates. In San Diego, a federal court sentenced him to one year and nine months' imprisonment.[117]

The same indecision that had plagued de la Huerta during the rebellion affected him in exile. According to one historian, he "continued to represent vacillating, contradictory leadership, incapable of functioning for what he was chosen to do: to bring together an opposition movement."[118] A quarrelsome bunch, the chiefs in exile needed someone to coordinate a "revolt of the losers."[119] The publication of a former ally's disparaging book titled *La rebelión sin cabeza* (The Headless Rebellion) might have further discouraged him.[120] As González asked Maytorena, "Do we have to lose all hope in don Adolfo?"[121] It appeared so, as the opposition remained hopelessly divided. According to the Consul General in San Francisco, "There is a division between de la Huerta and Estrada, and consequently, their supporters are also divided, to the extent that, as I am told, they insult each other."[122]

Mirroring the controversy with the Catholic Church, the Calles administration had dialed up the challenge to the U.S. State Department. It did so both in the area of property rights and in trying to help overthrow a government headed by a U.S. client in Nicaragua. The U.S. government retaliated but had thus far not succeeded in thwarting the Calles government. As this crisis reached its peak, Calles was fortunate that his various opponents exiled in the United States had not managed to coordinate a rebellion. He needed a solution that allowed him to save face.

The Retrenchment

By the summer of 1927 both sides had reasons to compromise. Kellogg faced mounting criticism in the Senate, especially after the revelation concerning the stolen documents. Sheffield resigned in June, in part as a result of the document scandal. Following a reassuring telephone conversation between Calles and Coolidge—the first-ever such talk between the U.S. and Mexican heads of state—a new ambassador, Dwight W. Morrow, arrived in October. Unlike Sheffield, Morrow was a career diplomat. While Sheffield had often followed the advice of his friends in the oil industry, Morrow was a partner at J. P. Morgan and in close contact with the ICBM, a group more amenable to compromise. He looked for pragmatic solutions and to deescalate tensions with the Mexican government.[123] That approach meant letting Mexico set its own laws while working to accommodate U.S. businesses in the application of these laws.

Calles had good reasons to seek reconciliation as well. His government battled on too many fronts: to mention a few, the Cristeros, the Yaqui, and a major railroad worker strike. The latter conflict spawned the Junta Federal de Conciliación y Arbitraje (JFCA, or Federal Board of Conciliation and Arbitration), an institution empowered with mediating national labor conflicts. The upheaval weighed on a deteriorating economy at a time of favorable economic conditions worldwide. While purchase-parity adjusted GDP had grown by 14 percent between 1924 and 1926, it declined 4.5 percent in 1927.[124] Government revenue had decreased almost 10 percent year-over-year. The causes for this crisis included the Cristiada, falling oil production, a prolonged drought in the North, and declining prices for silver, copper, lead, and zinc. The U.S.-Mexican standoff had contributed to capital flight. As oil reserves depleted, production declined to one-third of its 1925 level, contributing to a 15 percent drop in the value of exports between 1925 and 1928. Industrial production fared better, including cement, steel, and textiles.[125]

Especially important, Obregón decided to run for a second term (of which more in the next chapter). Calles increasingly turned to his counsel. Obregón initially supported Calles's policies regarding U.S. influence and the church but advocated for rapprochement when both of these conflicts heated up. In this capacity, Obregón consumed more and more of the oxygen in the political system. Said one of his former cabinet members who had joined the De la Huerta Rebellion in 1923, "Calles is not the problem ... It is Obregón. You cannot imagine the ambition there is in that man! Don Porfirio was a joke in comparison!"[126]

Obregón's foreign-policy posture changed as the crisis evolved. At first, he supported an uncompromising stance. One missive warned that the religious conflict gave the State Department greater incentive to push Calles to resolve disputes in Wall Street's favor, especially as it viewed Mexican Catholics as its "allies." Obregón enjoined Calles to refuse the U.S. demands, playing for time until the end of the religious conflict gave him more leverage. Referenced in a U.S. intelligence report, another letter (hand-delivered with instructions to destroy it immediately) recommended pursuing the goodwill of Great Britain as well as "develop a policy in Central America, then go into Venezuela" and threaten U.S. dominance over the Panama Canal. This strident letter might not be authentic.[127] Perhaps in part because he had decided to return to the presidential chair, Obregón's position softened as 1926 came to a close. After Kellogg's aggressive January 1927 statement, the caudillo counseled Calles to avoid arbitration and work out a solution with the oil companies.[128]

Obregón's position toward the church also changed in the same timeframe. He initially applauded the Calles Law and recommended firmness with an enemy whom he believed to be coordinating an attack on national sovereignty with the United States.[129] But he also helped arrange the August meeting of Calles, Ruiz y Flores, and Díaz through the services of Eduardo Mestre Ghigliazza, an industrialist from Puebla who enjoyed contacts to U.S. Catholic leaders, including the former editor of the *Catholic World*, John J. Burke. In March 1927, with the Cristiada in full swing, Obregón offered his mediation. In July, Mestre and a Foreign Secretariat official negotiated with the prelates exiled in San Antonio. The two sides hammered out an agreement, but its premature publication in the press (induced by journalists close to Morones) forced Calles to deny that any progress had been made. Nonetheless, Obregón had established a channel of communication that would help end the church strike two years later.[130]

Obregón's role accompanied a close collaboration with Morrow after the antagonistic Sheffield years. Morrow and Calles conferred on a regular basis during a series of breakfast meetings. The two found a face-saving way out of the oil controversy. With Calles's encouragement, the Supreme Court granted relief to the oil companies, reiterating its 1921 verdict. This decision helped lead to a revision of the Petroleum Law in 1928. Morrow also induced Calles to address Mexico's foreign debt in arrears. In exchange for a moratorium on debt payments, Calles agreed to have an U.S. accounting firm examine the books of the government. In the process, Morrow tutored Secretary of Finance Luis Montes de Oca, who adopted an austerity program that reduced spending and curtailed the money supply. Morrow started new efforts toward a resolution of the church strike, joined by Calles, who suddenly displayed flexibility that he had lacked during his August 1926 negotiations with the archbishops.[131] Morrow took Spanish lessons, displayed Mexican crafts in his residence, and invited the famed aviator, Charles Lindbergh, who flew nonstop from New York to Mexico City. At his destination, Lindbergh met the ambassador's daughter, Anne Morrow, whom he later married. Morrow was a gringo whom Mexicans could admire.

One should not overstate Morrow's influence, however. Multiple factors contributed to the retrenchment from the reform drive, including an economic crisis and the mounting cost of the Cristiada.[132] What the ambassador called the "radical rampage" of the previous two years had burned itself out. Morrow might have put it best when he told Sheffield, "Time, responsibility and fiscal pressure ... have doubtless had their effect.... The adamantine stubbornness at Chapultepec may become an asset if ... converted into something approximating steady pursuit of the right line of policy."[133] In April 1928 he claimed that British residents considered Calles the best president since Díaz.[134]

On April 30, 1928, Morones delivered a fiery speech at the Hidalgo Theater. A day before May Day, the secretary praised Calles as a friend of organized labor. Morones exclaimed, "Let our enemies take away from us the congressional seats ... and two or three governorships that have been controlled by the Labor Party. Let them take our positions, ... but we shall never permit them to attack the right of the worker to organize and to protect his interests."[135] Morones also lambasted Obregón, whose allies in the legislature had approved a series of laws directed at weakening the CROM's influence, as a traitor to the revolution on account of his attempt to have himself elected to another term.

Morones's words also indicated a sense of loss. The first two years of the Calles administration had witnessed the most radical phase in the Sonorense era. Calles had allied with representatives of labor and agrarian movements who shared his commitment to state-sponsored social reforms. Nonetheless, Calles and his allies sought these reforms within a capitalist framework, as evidenced in the government's banking and infrastructure projects. The last two years of the Calles presidency witnessed the failure of his challenges to the Catholic Church and the United States. Both challenges had been too ambitious. His failure forced him to rely on Obregón, who appeared even more powerful at the end of Calles's term than at the beginning.

8 ∻ Almost Porfirio

Power is not a means; it is an end. One does not establish a dictatorship in order to safeguard a revolution; one makes the revolution in order to establish the dictatorship.—George Orwell, *1984*

Obregón's campaign for a second presidential term remains one of the great tragedies in Mexican history. The caudillo's legendary lack of political convictions left observers to joke that "Obregón is a man of the left ... someone with only a left arm."[1] This void became clear when he sacrificed the revolution's central principle—effective suffrage, no reelection—for his own ambitions. Indeed, Obregón saw his project as an updated version of the Old Regime. As he had once allegedly told a confidant, "Don Porfirio's only sin ... was to grow old."[2]

Obregón's campaign for a second term was not as inevitable as it is often portrayed in historical scholarship. As one historian has argued, Obregón considered himself indispensable on the national political scene: "The presidential chair attracted him not for the power it would give him ... but for the aura of duty and sacrifice surrounding the position."[3] But Obregón's actions early in Calles's presidency indicated less certainty of his political future. For a while, other candidates—and specifically Serrano—had reason to hope that they were well positioned to succeed Calles.

A Struggling Emporium

Obregón gave the appearance that he had tired of the spotlight and life in the big city. According to a close friend, the president had spent much time in Chapultepec Park during his last year in office. There, he mused about his properties in Sonora and made plans to return after Calles's inauguration.[4] Shortly after Obregón's arrival in Sonora, the Japanese minister visited him on his way back to his home country. Stunned to see Obregón in farmer's clothes, he asked him whether he was wearing a disguise. The former president replied, "No, Your Excellency, I am not in disguise. This is my normal state. You saw the one wearing a disguise in the National Palace."⁵ He was also rumored to be in poor health.

Indeed, the caudillo focused on his agribusinesses, which had not fared as well during his presidency as he would have liked. According to a U.S. military intelligence report, he had "failed ... to enrich himself during his four years as president."⁶ Obregón moved to a new ranch, Náinari, in the village of Cajeme (present-day Ciudad Obregón). The name evoked erroneous visions of smallness in what was in fact a four-thousand-hectare estate: *náinari* is the Yaqui word for "louse." Yet it appropriately described Obregón's role in the economy. Using his leverage, he fed upon the allies who sustained him. Obregón's first birthday celebration at Náinari in February 1925 serves as an example. The caudillo invited his primary allies in the Northwest, including Rodríguez and Sonora governor Alejo Bay. Before the event, one of Obregón's minions asked each attendee for the princely sum of 3,000 pesos for the purchase of a residence for the caudillo. Eighteen people agreed to pay up.⁷

Obregón's business vision involved the type of intraelite cooperation that recalled the Porfirian *científicos*. Obregón proposed the purchase of land in Sinaloa and the Yaqui Valley to Calles, Rodríguez, and their longtime associate Fernando Torreblanca. He dreamed of a network of irrigation canals—the long-term goal of the Compañía Constructora Richardson. The nexus among these political leaders was Ignacio P. Gaxiola, Obregón's partner at the Oficina Comercial de Álvaro Obregón and Rodríguez's private secretary. In 1925 Obregón and Gaxiola founded a holding company named Álvaro Obregón y Compañía, Sociedad Civil. In the next two years, Obregón and Gaxiola started a number of new businesses, including a flourmill.⁸

This investment spree marked a sharp departure from Obregón's cautious approach. According to one of his descendants,

> Not being the conservative or frugal businessman he once was in his youth, Obregón, the consummate risk-taker with good credit, continued to borrow extensively..., allowing him to tinker in a myriad of expensive agricultural experiments in his big garden in Náinari: planting henequen, fig trees, Spanish melons, and orange trees, and even Californian orange and apple trees. Aside from the customary garbanzo

crop, he was also planting parcels of tomatoes, corn, rice, wheat, peas, and beans. He was no doubt a horticulturalist *par excellence*, but he was now listening to the beat of a different drummer.[9]

The different drummer was Obregón's political weight backing up his investments. Obregón refused to pay his old debts and required significant new loans.[10] His allies stood ready to help. As Calles told the caudillo, "I would appreciate it if you told me your true financial situation in confidence but with total frankness. If you will need funds to conclude the agricultural projects you have been undertaking, I would like to know the grand total, so that we can see if there is a way to get them to you."[11] In July 1925 Calles and Torreblanca obtained 150,000 pesos on his behalf, and Rodríguez gave Obregón 6,000 pesos. In October 1925 the Calles administration lent the caudillo another 150,000 pesos. Obregón also borrowed from the BNCA to purchase land from the Richardson and procured several loans from the Banco de México.[12] True, government officials professed unease at helping Obregón with public funds. An anecdote that Torreblanca related to one of Calles's grandsons reveals some of the emotions surrounding these transactions. Reportedly, the president's request to send a payment to Obregón prompted a nervous question from an official: "To whom do we make this out, officially?" Replied Calles, "To the balls of General Obregón!"[13]

Obregón was aware of the optics. A 1925 letter warned:

> With generosity and plausible opportunity, General Calles has decided that the [national] treasury should help us with large sums: not only for various needs of the business, but also to cover very great debts, which were overdue and which we had to pay with a large part of those sums. Now, we do not have the right to seek more help, and I would not ask for further help, either, because doing so would mean accepting amounts the payment of which would not be sufficiently guaranteed. I do not want to give others any reason to consider the general too generous, and even careless in giving loans by way of an official institution.[14]

He also knew that Calles did not consider himself his subordinate. The caudillo had no such compunction pressuring other officials like Rodríguez and Secretary of Finance Pani, whom he once beseeched to forgo a costly inspection of an oil tank.[15]

Obregón's expensive schemes also led to an increasing reliance on his U.S. business partners. During his visits to the United States, he portrayed himself as a friend of free trade. He once told his audience that California and the Mexican northwest constituted "one of the greatest centers of production in the entire world." If the government sought to "impose new taxes in order to wage a commercial boxing match, we would commit not only a crime, but also an error that would hurt our own interests."[16] However, on another occasion, Obregón opposed "filibuster capital" that came with strings attached.[17]

Obregón's extensive political capital did not save him when the bill for his audacious ventures became due. In 1926 drought cost him 60 percent of his wheat harvest, and his garbanzo export business incurred greater expenses than expected. To compensate, the caudillo embraced even higher risk, and Obregón y Cía. bought a majority stake in the heavily indebted Richardson. Under the terms of the agreement, Obregón and Gaxiola assumed its liabilities. They hoped that modern methods of irrigation could render the company's lands more valuable than their purchase price. But they had overextended themselves, and the BNCA ultimately bought out Obregón's and Gaxiola's shares. Most likely, Calles orchestrated the deal to save Obregón from insolvency, but it also constituted part of a larger plan to shore up the financing of irrigation projects on the Yaqui, Mayo, and Fuerte Rivers.[18] The following year fluctuations in commodity prices and a natural disaster left Obregón scrambling for loans. The chickpea price continued to decline, and Obregón struggled to turn a profit from the crop that had once made him rich.[19] In late September 1927 a tropical cyclone led to widespread flooding in the Yaqui Valley. Devout Catholics called this cyclone *el cordonazo de San Francisco* (the lashing of St. Francis), in reference to their belief that the severe storm, which almost coincided with the saint's name day on October 4, constituted punishment for their sins.[20] Indeed, Obregón was by no means alone in his calamitous encounter with the elements. Rodolfo Elías Calles's nearby agribusiness also ran aground. When Calles's eldest son asked Obregón if he could approach his father for help, the caudillo reportedly replied, "Listen to me, Rodolfito! You are the son of the president!"[21]

Obregón's aggressive land schemes also contributed to the final Yaqui war. The Yaqui had favorable memories of de la Huerta's governorship, when they had managed to recover six of their eight communities. While Calles had persecuted the Yaqui at every opportunity, the grandson of a Yaqui woman had proven much more amenable to their interests.[22] Now, prompted by Obregón, the Richardson allowed colonization near the two remaining occupied communities and diverted water toward Náinari and the properties of Rodolfo Calles. The Yaqui opposed the schemes of a caudillo who had asked them to shed their blood for his cause.[23] Noted one exiled Delahuertista, "In the case of Obregón, I know that the Yaqui tribes really hated him."[24]

On September 12, 1926, Yaqui commander Luis Matus held up a train in which Obregón was a passenger, in an effort to secure the release of Yaqui prisoners in Hermosillo. At first, rumors flew that Obregón had lost his life during this attack. While the outside world believed that the caudillo had been killed, Matus hoped to negotiate the terms of his release. But Obregón would not take the bait, arguing that he was just a private passenger in no position to make a deal. He refused to leave his compartment until federal troops had dispersed the Yaqui forces.[25] Once freed Obregón took charge of the final large-scale campaign against the Yaqui. By December, 13,425 troops served in this war, diverting one-fifth of the federal army while much of the rest was fighting the Cristeros and smaller rebellions elsewhere in the republic.[26] Despite this numerical disparity, defeating what a Delahuertista agent called "our brave and active friends" proved no easy task.[27] The war had Catholic overtones, as Yaqui fighters displayed emblems of the Virgin of Guadalupe and distributed handbills demanding religious liberty.

De la Huerta provided inspiration and support. Aware that Don Fito still considered himself the "Supreme Chief," Matus recognized him as the chief of his movement. For his part, de la Huerta promised to assist the Yaqui so long as they were able to seize a border town so he could legally cross into rebel-held territory—an unrealistic prospect. He held a series of meetings with Yaqui leaders in Tucson and Nogales and helped them obtain weapons and ammunition. In November, de la Huerta also declared his intention to direct the insurgency. But the Mexican consul in Tucson notified the U.S. authorities of these plans, and nothing came of them. Beginning in the second half of 1927, poison gas and air raids helped federal troops overwhelm the Yaqui.[28]

By then, Obregón had refocused on his businesses. The caudillo's last will indicated the scale of his financial worries. It stipulated, "All of the assets of our marital union legally belong to my creditors, and they shall be liquidated in order to repay their respective loans." Any remaining assets would be divided equally among his wife, his eight children, and his three sisters who had helped educate him when he was a child.[29]

The caudillo faced a dilemma. As president, he had enjoyed access to the treasury but lost direct control of his faraway enterprises. As ex-president, he struggled to recover his commercial network even though the state's political leadership—and particularly the governors, members of his extended family—remained at his beck and call. This analysis qualifies one scholar's claim that Obregón owned "large canning and soap plants, an important company selling cars, construction materials, machinery, and agricultural tools, a bank, a cereal mill, a warehouse, and chain of gasoline stations."[30] Obregón's friends and relatives owned some of these enterprises; others were in his name, but heavily leveraged. Obregón's wealth had turned into a paper tiger. His struggles as an entrepreneur reminded the caudillo that he had encountered greater success as general and politician and influenced his decision to reenter the fray of national politics.

An Encore for Obregón

On March 31, 1926, Obregón came to Mexico City for the first time since leaving office. He and Calles had not met in person since then. The trip ostensibly served "business" purposes, as the caudillo needed funds from the national treasury.[31] However, it also had political ends. The visit took place just a few months before midterm elections that would shape Congress in the two years leading up to the next presidential elections. Concerned with Morones's consolidation of power, Obregón sought to shore up his coalition.

Equally importantly, Obregón desired to test the waters for a second term. Article 83 of the constitution stated that a president "could not be reelected." This ambiguous phrase did not rule out a second term that followed that of another president. But Mexicans remembered the example of Porfirio Díaz. Eligibility for nonconsecutive terms raised the specter of the two Sonoran patriarchs alternating in the presidency. In 1925 a reform that would have allowed nonconsecutive reelection had failed in Congress. Decades later Soto y Gama explained, "On the one hand, we were [Obregón's] personal friends. On the other hand, we did not think he could legally be elected to the presidency again."[32]

During Obregón's visit, he told the press that article 83 only meant that a president could not succeed himself. In the assessment of the U.S. consul general, the caudillo's statement amounted to a "practical declaration of his intention to become a candidate for the presidency."[33] Obregón said on the same occasion that he did not anticipate a candidacy unless the nation found itself in a crisis, but those words left all options open.[34] It is not apparent, however, whether the caudillo had already decided to do so. For one thing, he was in poor health. A month prior, he had suffered what first appeared to him as a stroke en route to San Francisco.[35] For another, Obregón's eligibility remained a question mark.

After his trip Obregón thus worked to clarify this question. In April 1926 he proposed a reform to the effect that a president could never serve another term, knowing that this reform would not clear the two-thirds threshold. The gambit worked to perfection and allowed his supporters to claim that Congress did not desire to outlaw nonconsecutive terms. The midterm elections improved his math in the legislature. Backed by a larger majority, the PNA once again introduced a reform that also lengthened the presidential term to six years. In the Chamber of Deputies, only seven voted against the legislation, and the Senate approved it unanimously. Once again, Soto y Gama explained the moment: "Political means are simple means. If they are useful to us, we accept them, and if they are not, we reject them . . . when reelection helps us by bringing to power a man who has demonstrated that he is an Agrarista, we [favor it]."[36]

Soto y Gama's words reflected his awareness of the fact that the constitutional reform constituted a blatant power play. Chiapas governor Carlos A. Vidal ordered his state legislature not to ratify the reform.[37] According to Vidal, the federal legislature served Obregón's ambitions: "The great national scandal was the composition of the Chamber of Deputies. Obregón was clandestinely working in the shadow, cold and calculating. Aware that he could not realize his ambitions with a chamber constituted from real and legitimate representatives of the people, he instructed his lackeys and minions to . . . staff a Chamber of Deputies with individuals dedicated . . . to robbing the Mexican Constitution of one of the basic postulates of the revolution."[38]

The PNA's participation in this scheme may have played a role in its subsequent demise. In November 158 representatives founded the Liga Nacional Campesina (LNC, or National Campesino League). The inaugural leadership of this organization included Luis G. Monzón, one of the few Marxists at the Constituyente of 1917 and a Sonorense to boot, as well as the muralist Diego Rivera. By 1927 the LNC had displaced the PNA as the most important *agrarian* organization in the nation.[39]

Obregón then sized up the ambitions of potential rivals. First, there was Morones, a civilian whom most *generals* considered unacceptable. Two *divisionarios*, Serrano and Gómez, had significant following (General Ángel Flores, the loser of the preceding election, had died from food poisoning in March 1926, with ominous parallels to Hill's death in 1920).[40] Serrano in particular enjoyed widespread support. Not surprisingly, Obregón's rivals expressed their disagreement with the constitutional reform. Morones tried to block the measure, and Serrano voiced his displeasure to General Gonzalo N. Santos, the author of the motion.[41]

Next, Obregón needed to consider the stance of the president. De la Huerta's Plan de Veracruz had charged that Calles had agreed to support Obregón's candidacy in 1928 as the price for the caudillo's endorsement for the presidential election in 1924.[42] But no documentary proof of this assertion has surfaced. Valenzuela (who knew both patriarchs well) stated later on that such a pact probably did not exist.[43] Indeed, the caudillo could not take the support of his fellow Sonorense for granted. He knew that Calles considered the reform that allowed nonconsecutive reelection a violation of a sacrosanct revolutionary principle. Furthermore, the president had publicly opposed the first effort in 1925.[44] He had reasons not to support Obregón. In 1923 Calles had unsuccessfully backed his cousin, Francisco S. Elías, for the governorship of Sonora, while Obregón supported Alejo Bay Valenzuela.[45] With good reason, the U.S. consul general judged Calles's friendship with Obregón of "questionable quality."[46] It was in this context that the president gave each of Gómez, Morones, and Serrano the impression that they were viable candidates.[47]

22. Serrano and Fernando Torreblanca. Fideicomiso Archivos Plutarco Elías Calles y Fernando Torreblanca (FAPECFT), Fototeca, Archivo Fernando Torreblanca, Fondo Plutarco Elías Calles, Oficial, serie *Presidencia de la República, 1924–1928*, mfn 204, imagen 39, inventario 304. Used with permission.

Many observers considered Serrano the frontrunner. According to one eyewitness, Obregón at least initially encouraged his candidacy.[48] One document suggests that the caudillo may have signed a pact with a Morones representative in February 1926 by means of which both renounced presidential bids in Serrano's favor. According to this document, considered a forgery by the U.S. consul general, Serrano pledged to support the CROM in its quest to control agricultural labor.[49] While Obregón and a Morones spokesperson denied the existence of this pact, Serrano had reasons to hope for Obregón's support.[50] He had played a crucial role in the caudillo's success, as manifested in his intervention to save Obregón's life in Villa's den, his leadership in the great battles of the Bajío, and his service in defeating the De la Huerta Rebellion. Reportedly, the caudillo had once said to Serrano's mother, "Pancho is my brain. Without Pancho, I am worth nothing."[51] However, in October 1926, the death of Lamberto Obregón, Serrano's brother-in-law, severed an important connection between the two generals.[52]

But the Sonoran patriarchs undermined Serrano. In 1925 Calles sent him on a study tour to Europe with the charge of buying armament to restock the weapons depots of the army. Lasting more than a year, the tour approximated exile more so than a preparation for the presidency. Serrano spent most of his time shuttling between Berlin and Liège, a Belgian city located 450 miles from the German capital. He received orders to place a requisition with one of the leading suppliers there, only to then receive contradictory and temporizing instructions. Forced to idleness, Serrano visited churches such as the Cologne Cathedral, the tallest cathedral in the world. His favorable references to churches showed that he did not share Calles's anticlericalism. Serrano's efforts did procure a shipment of fifty-four thousand machine guns.[53]

One factor hurting Serrano's ambitions was a lifestyle of dissipation even by the standards of the military patriarchy of 1920s Mexico. Although Obregón and Calles had wisely insisted that his wife accompany Serrano on his trip, the general frequented brothels and casinos, and he reportedly developed a new drug addiction.[54] His predilections continued after his return. According to a U.S. military intelligence report, one of his mistresses lived in his house along with her mother, while his wife lived in Los Angeles. The report also described Serrano as an "inveterate gambler."[55] In the words of one of Obregón's allies, General Antonio Ríos Zertuche, "This valiant and meritorious military leader ... persisted in living a dissipated and merry lifestyle" despite the caudillo's exhortations. "He could never impose on himself any discipline or reserve that would prevent the adverse notoriety that gave his personality a Bohemian aura of abandon . . . inappropriate for his destiny and his future." Ríos considered Serrano an honest person who did not disguise his excesses, to his own detriment.[56]

Serrano lost more ground when he refused Calles's offer of the post of secretary of the interior in May 1926. This powerful position would have obliged Serrano to enforce Calles's anticlerical policies that he characterized as religious persecution. Thus, Tejeda, a sworn enemy of the church, remained in the position. Serrano subsequently accepted an appointment as chief of the Federal District (Mexico City), a job useful for cultivating political connections and advancing his entrepreneurial ambitions. However, Calles read Serrano's refusal to take the portfolio of secretary of the interior as an act of resistance.[57]

Serrano persisted, nonetheless. His political vehicle was the Partido Nacional Revolucionario (National Revolutionary Party), not to be confused with the new ruling party founded eighteen months later. The party demanded an end to the anticlerical measures of the past three years and advocated for immediate implementation of women's suffrage. On April 27, 1927, the party nominated him for president, although Serrano did not accept this nomination until two months later.[58] Several regional parties supported his candidacy as well.

General Arnulfo R. Gómez was the other major opposition candidate. A U.S. report considered Gómez far superior to Serrano in terms of his "honesty, ability, or intelligence," but not as well positioned politically. A "well-mannered" man of handsome appearance who did not smoke or drink and avoided scandalous behavior, Gómez did not have much political experience. His reputation as a repressive zone commander loomed as a liability.[59] Still, although Gómez faced long odds, he believed in his opportunity, claiming that a pact with Obregón and Calles promised him their support. However, in April 1926 Calles reportedly informed Gómez that he would not support his candidacy.[60] Thereafter, Gómez declared that he was a "simple soldier, eager only to serve his country in his profession."[61]

The Partido Nacional Antirreeleccionista advanced Gómez's political ambitions and formally nominated him for president on June 23, 1927. Based primarily in Puebla and Veracruz, this party constituted a smaller power base than Serrano's organization. According to Mexican intelligence agents, Gómez's campaign events only drew several hundred people, mostly from the railroad workers' union, one of the principal rivals of the CROM. The oil companies allegedly supported his bid, a plausible rumor given his opposition to the CROM.[62]

Gómez's similarities to Serrano were limited to their anti-reelectionist principles. Mindful of his party's Maderista past, Gómez demanded "the absolute respect for the principles of no reelection and effective suffrage to avoid *continuismo* and caudillo rule." Unlike Serrano, however, he did not criticize anticlericalism. His party called for strict separation of church and state, even as Gómez stated that he was "respectful of religions and creeds." In a further difference from the Serranista program, his party did not call for women's suffrage.[63]

Meanwhile, Obregón increasingly gravitated toward a candidacy. He roundly resented Morones's influence, not only because of his status as a civilian but also because of his anticlerical stance. At least in part, the caudillo viewed his own candidacy as a way to forestall the triumph of the labor leader.[64] Obregón knew that Serrano enjoyed the support of much of the military, but he also believed that most of the *divisionarios* and Congress would back his own presidential bid if he were to run again. He also felt that both Serrano and Calles owed their careers to him. In the words of one historian, he was "the caudillo of Mexico, the last of the greats."[65]

Meanwhile, Serrano tendered his resignation as chief of the Federal District effective June 19, 1927, so that he would be eligible to run for president. Calles sent him to Sonora to meet with Obregón. There are different recollections of the ensuing meeting, and indeed, whether it ever happened. Two observers maintained that Obregón refused to see Serrano; and one of them blamed the refusal on the latter's inebriation. Another claimed that Obregón and Serrano's meeting turned "extremely glacial" after the caudillo declared that he had not ruled out another presidential run. When Serrano rattled off a list of officers ready to support him, Obregón replied that these same chiefs had offered him their backing as well.[66] In yet another version, Serrano bade the caudillo farewell with the words: "Well, General, you know that we will have a contest of gentlemen." Obregón replied, "I thought you were smart, Serrano. In Mexico, there are no battles of gentlemen: one goes to the presidency and the other, to the firing squad."[67]

Within days of Serrano's resignation, Obregón was officially in the race. On June 23 Soto y Gama offered Obregón the PNA's nomination, and two days later, the caudillo accepted it via an address in Mexico City. After praising Calles's work, and especially his firm stance toward the church and the U.S. government, Obregón pandered to his audience by promising more land reform, blaming Congress for the slow pace in this and other areas in which the constitution had not been fully implemented.[68]

Obregón announced a program for a second term more radical than the first. On July 1 he returned to Nogales, the site of his first campaign declaration. On the same plaza on which he had declared his intention to improve U.S.-Mexican relations eight years before, Obregón referred to "false tutors" (read: Wall Street bankers) who attempted to goad the government into abandoning the social principles outlined in the constitution. Without mentioning his opponents by name, the caudillo implied that these false tutors financed their campaigns and would force a change in laws if either candidate won the election.[69] Two weeks later a speech in Guadalajara cast Obregón as a populist father of the poor, and particularly campesinos and the urban working class. In rhetoric more strident than Calles's cultivation of the image of a worker-campesino candidate in 1924, Obregón used crude class language that divided Mexico into two great camps: those who hired and those who worked. Obregón labeled his opponents "reactionary" and portrayed himself as the only hope for the survival of "the revolution."[70]

This populist rhetoric reflected an effort to win over a broad segment of the population that had tired of the duarchy. Citizens targeted Obregón and Calles by means of acerbic wit, always an important political weapon of the oppressed. As the Serranistas mocked the caudillo,

> El manco latifundista
> Es traidor no es agrarista
>
> Is a traitor, not an agrarista[71]
> The one-armed large landowner

Opponents also invented anagrams of the two patriarchs: "vengo a robarlo" (I have come to rob you) for Álvaro Obregón; and "el turco pescó la silla" (the Turk nabbed the presidential chair) for Plutarco Elías Calles.[72] Because both Serrano and Gómez came from the army, his own mainstay of support, the caudillo could not afford to take their challenge lightly. One of de la Huerta's agents believed that Obregón's "ill-concealed spitefulness indicates clearly that he does not see his position as very firm. The military regards him, who considers himself their idol, with a degree of indifference that indicates withdrawal."[73]

However, Obregón held the advantage in several areas. Most significantly, Calles came around. He needed his help to address his administration's multiple crises. In the opinion of Amaro's private secretary, Ignacio A. Richkarday, Calles personally opposed Obregón's reelection, but "his loyalty to his friend, the commitments made to the political sectors around [the caudillo], and many other issues that only he could perceive and calculate, obligated him to accept ... the historical responsibility that the politics of his time and the ambitions of the moment loaded upon his shoulders."[74] Rodríguez made his loyalties clear in a letter to a business associate who also cooperated closely with Calles and Obregón. Characterizing Serrano's action as "treason," Rodríguez continued, "Most likely, his vices have induced ... [Serrano's] lack of gratitude and disloyalty."[75] Rodríguez sent Obregón a personal contribution of US$50,000.[76] The caudillo could also count on his loyalists in the federal legislature. The Obregonistas mobilized regional parties at the state level, and Vidal's valiant effort to build a grassroots-based network for Serrano fell short.[77] Finally, Obregón confronted two competitors rather than one. Not until September did Serrano and Gómez agree on a single campaign, and the question of a unified candidate remained unresolved.[78]

A Sonorense Bloodbath

The campaign rhetoric of the three former allies soon heated up. Obregón asserted that Serrano's career owed to the caudillo's patronage and mocked Gómez for lacking both vice and virtue.[79] On July 23, 1927, Serrano declared that the caudillo would never give up power once elected to another term. His manifesto lambasted the reform of article 83 as the demise of Madero's hallowed principle. As Serrano reminded his audience, Obregón had not fought in Madero's rebellion: "It was the blood and sacrifice of others that conquered this principle [of no reelection], which needs to be restored ...

as a sacred and untouchable jewel." This manifesto also posited Serrano as a moderate alternative to a government embroiled in the church-state conflict and a diplomatic standoff with the United States. Serrano criticized the government's agrarian reform measures as acts designed to reward allies and punish enemies. He reaffirmed religious liberty. Serrano vowed to protect domestic entrepreneurs while opening doors for foreign investors: "Without careful protection of capital, it does not make sense to expect foreigners to come or to abandon his hideouts, and, without that factor, our so-called wealth will continue being a myth." He pledged the nonretroactivity of article 27 before concluding with a call for "Mexico for all of the Mexicans," a motto that contrasted with the economic nationalist credo, "Mexico for the Mexicans."[80]

Both opposition campaigns warned of violence. According to Vidal, "the only way to consolidate peace is to make sure that the succession in power occurs through institutional means."[81] A press release denounced "those who shred and falsify our institutions [and] those who have betrayed the revolution. In contrast, we are ready to defend the integrity and purity of our principles."[82] Gómez stated that "we do not want war, but if it is necessary, we will fight it with a smile on our face" and called upon his audience to join him in fighting "Álvaro Santa Anna" if the conflict ended in violence.[83] He reminded his audience of Obregón's oft-cited remark that "no general can resist a cannon shot of 50,000 pesos."[84] In a letter to *Excélsior*, Obregón denied ever having made such a remark.[85] Meanwhile, the government arrested and harassed hundreds of anti-reelectionists, especially after a Serrano appearance in Puebla brought out more than thirty thousand supporters.

As the campaign gained in intensity, two crucial Obregón opponents remained on the sidelines. For the Delahuertistas, Obregón, Serrano, and Gómez were all part of the same gang that caused Mexico's ills, but the fight among them served the larger aim of overthrowing the government.[86] Morones saw no shot at winning, and the field officially winnowed to three when the PLM endorsed Obregón.[87]

In August Calles grew concerned about reports about an uprising. For the past three months, the spy in the U.S. embassy had extracted military intelligence documents suggesting that Gómez angled for U.S. assistance in planning an uprising.[88] An agent within the army, General Eulogio

Ortiz, reported that the cotton-rich Comarca Lagunera area was a hub of Gomista activity. Earlier that month, Ortiz himself had received an invitation from the Serrano campaign to join forces. Rumors flew that Serrano would launch a coup against the legislature on September 1, the day of the presidential *informe* and the opening of the sessions of Congress. According to these rumors, Calles supported the plot.[89]

However, September 1 came and went without any trouble. Gómez declared at a banquet in Vidal's honor that he continued to trust Calles "because we have fought together for many years." As he claimed, "General Calles has always listened to me."[90] Serrano and Vidal both believed that Calles did not support Obregón's reelection. In a private meeting, Serrano asked Calles to disband the legislature, the "nest of Obregonismo," which had devolved into "political clubs designed to ensure at all costs the victory ... of General Obregón." Calles listened impassively to Serrano's astounding proposal, which was asking for complicity in a coup. The president then asked his interlocutor which generals supported him. Naively, Serrano named, among others, one of his drinking partners, General Eugenio Martínez, who had trained Obregón's battalion in the 1912 campaign against Orozco.[91] Calles later claimed that he had attempted to dissuade Serrano, and that he had not arrested the officers Serrano had named in order to salvage their "military decorum."[92]

Serrano's revelations proved a tragic mistake. The president immediately summoned Obregón from faraway Náinari. Both Sonorenses interrogated a trembling Martínez, who told the two leaders that he and General Ignacio Almada held a commission from Serrano to assassinate them and Amaro during a flight show at Balbuena airfield on October 2. Calles and Obregón's deaths would pave the way for Vidal's selection as interim president. Vidal would immediately lead a campaign to defeat a concomitant insurgency spearheaded by Gómez while Serrano would await the result of this coup in Cuernavaca. After this meeting, Calles sent Martínez on a "study mission" to Spain, from which he would not return alive.[93]

Aside from Martínez's testimony, the government received other reports that suggested a possible coup attempt. An unsigned memorandum informed of the movement of former army officers loyal to Gómez and Serrano into various states, including Coahuila, Puebla, and Veracruz. One report claimed nationwide preparations for an insurrection, including Vidal's plans to march toward Tabasco and Veracruz with ten thousand troops, and yet another related plans to assassinate Calles, radio stations distributed throughout the republic to disseminate pro-rebel propaganda, and a conspiracy involving high-ranking officers.[94] On September 27 the U.S. chargé d'affaires reported on one of Obregón's lackluster campaign appearances and ominously remarked, "It is doubtful whether the federal government would so thoroughly protect the lives of Generals Gómez and Serrano as it is attempting to do in the case of General Obregón."[95]

Martínez's testimony provided the pretext for a bloody climax. On the day that Martínez had indicated, Almada abandoned Mexico City without authorization, moving his troops first to Texcoco and then to Veracruz. Interpreting this movement as evidence of the plot, Calles ordered Gómez's and Serrano's arrest. On October 3 federal forces arrested Serrano, Vidal, and twelve of their allies in Cuernavaca. A few hours later, General Claudio Fox took possession of the prisoners. Near Huitzilac, Morelos, Fox's men lined them up and executed them. The day after, Calles spoke of a general "military insurgency" and reassured the nation that the government had decisively defeated the rebels.[96] The roadside executions indicated the weakness of the government's evidence. In the words of the one historian, "The Sonorans' mistake in 1927 was answering potential violence with preemptive violence."[97]

Indeed, the testimony of an accomplice exonerated Serrano while implicating Gómez. Juan Barragán, Carranza's former chief of staff, had managed to flee to Cuba, where he recounted his version of the events to a U.S. embassy official. Barragán had met with Almada, Gómez, and Serrano on September 30 to discuss an antireelectionist coalition. During this meeting, Gómez suggested a preemptive coup d'état in order to forestall the government's plans to execute them. As evidence for his worries, Gómez cited Martínez's sudden overseas commission, which suggested that he had informed the government of the conspiracy. Gómez proposed to gather his forces in Veracruz; meanwhile, Serrano would remain in Mexico City, ready to take over the garrison once Almada's men had arrested Amaro, Calles, and Obregón. In Gómez's opinion, 80 percent of the military would support the rebels. Skeptical, Serrano insisted that he would celebrate his saint's day at his hacienda near Cuernavaca. According to Barragán,

Serrano's refusal to go along with Gómez's plans, as well as his "childish confidence" in the honor of his former comrades, doomed the rebellion.[98]

Did Calles or Obregón bear responsibility for the killings? Probably both of them, with Calles giving the orders in his official capacity. As related by Barragán, Calles and Obregón were meeting at Chapultepec when General Roberto Cruz informed them of Serrano's capture. Rather than awaiting the convoy of prisoners, Calles ordered Cruz to drive back toward Cuernavaca to shoot them. When Cruz refused, citing his friendship with Serrano, Obregón flew into a rage, and Calles tasked Fox with the gruesome job.[99] Richkarday, who attended that same meeting, reported that the caudillo questioned the need to bring the prisoners to the capital, taking their execution as a given: "Why bring them to Mexico if we have to get rid of them anyway? It's better to execute them en route."[100] According to Richkarday, Calles drew up the order to execute the prisoners. As Fox told a court ten years later, he discarded these instructions in a cuspidor after the arrival of the bodies.[101] Based on indirect evidence, a cabinet member insisted on Obregón's innocence. Tasked with informing Obregón of Serrano's death, he recalled that the caudillo showed "a shade of wrath on his noble face," implying that the news came as a surprise.[102] Finally, according to one journalist, Obregón conspired with Calles's chief of staff to assassinate the prisoners against the president's wishes.[103]

The massacre at Huitzilac began a wholesale purge as thorough as the one following the De la Huerta Rebellion. Just two days after, the U.S. military attaché estimated the total number of casualties at more than five hundred.[104] In Nogales, government agents murdered General Alfonso de la Huerta, the brother of the former president. Amaro dismissed Brigadier General José J. Obregón, the caudillo's brother and Calles's former opponent for the governorship of Sonora.[105] The Chamber of Deputies ousted twenty-eight members believed to be linked to Serrano or Gómez. The next wave of violence came soon thereafter, when Gómez called for a general insurrection and moved to Veracruz. Only the commanders of five isolated federal garrisons agreed to support him.[106] Under the leadership of General José Gonzalo Escobar, two thousand soldiers pursued the rebels, and Gómez fled into the mountains. On November 4, 1927, they found him hiding in a mountain cave. After a trial on the spot, Escobar oversaw his execution in the graveyard of Coatepec, Veracruz.[107] According to an eyewitness, he told Gómez, "I have orders from [Obregón] to finish you, as you know. You have twenty minutes to write to your family; do what you want until the notary gets here."[108]

In the case of the Coatepec killings, Obregón overrode Calles's objections to eliminating one of his *compadres*: someone who had counted among the president's closest allies until the presidential campaign of 1927. Yet once the order was in place, Calles denied Gómez his last chance. According to José Vasconcelos, Gómez's last request before his execution was to phone Calles, who, as he told Escobar, had been the one encouraging him to run for president in order to avoid Obregón's return. The president would not take the call.[109]

The Huitzilac and Coatepec killings marked such a cynical highlight of the duarchy that even those responsible expressed mixed feelings about what they had done. As Fox quoted Obregón upon seeing Serrano's mutilated body, which had suffered twenty bullet wounds, skull fractures and a bayonet strike in the back: "Pancho! They sure left you pretty ugly! But don't say that I didn't give you your present: in a few minutes it will be the day of San Francisco."[110] If this story is authentic, this cruel attempt at humor revealed Obregón's reaction at seeing the body of his former *compadre*. The comment also masked deep sadness about the course of his life, as well as the careers of the Sonorenses more generally. The caudillo might have avoided what Luis Cabrera labeled a "second Agua Prieta," but at what price?[111]

The shadows of Huitzilac and Coatepec lingered for decades. In 1930 the exiled former Delahuertista Martín Luis Guzmán published the premier novel depicting the Sonoran era, *La sombra del caudillo* (The shadow of the caudillo). Based on both the De la Huerta Rebellion and the events of 1927, the novel fictionalized the tragic disintegration of the Sonorense alliance. The government banned its sale in Mexico. Thirty years later, in 1960, the novel was made into a movie, but the government again blocked the story from reaching its audience. The film was not cleared for distribution until 1990. As recently as 1997, Serrano's descendants unsuccessfully petitioned the government to release the files pertaining to the Huitzilac murders.[112]

With Serrano and Gómez out of the way, Obregón ran unopposed. The caudillo placed his campaign on autopilot. He spent long periods of time at his ranch in Sonora, and he no longer attempted to appeal to the political base. "No more promises," Obregón exclaimed during a campaign rally in April. "The nation already knows our points of view."[113]

One reason for the less intense campaign was the fact that the caudillo feared for his own life after the massacre of his opponents. As one of his old Delahuertista adversaries warned him from exile: "Serrano's glorious ghost will follow you like Macbeth [followed] Banquo. His blood will choke you forever."[114] In November, a Catholic rebel threw three bombs at his car. In response, the Calles administration did not only execute the would-be assassin, but also Father Miguel Pro, a prominent priest. Pro's wrongful death made him into a martyr: forty thousand faithful lined the streets where the funeral procession passed, and another twenty thousand awaited at the cemetery. In the spring Obregón suffered a second attempt in Orizaba, Veracruz.[115]

On July 2, 1928, Obregón won a hollow triumph purchased with the blood of his former allies. Unlike 1920 there was little public excitement, but rather, a sense of resignation. The assassination of Obregón's adversaries only added to the cynicism that increasingly enveloped political life. The caudillo knew that his own life was in danger as a result of his reckless gamble. He reportedly told Calles's eldest daughter, Hortensia, "I will live until someone trades his life for mine."[116]

These words were prophetic. On July 17, 1928, Obregón attended a luncheon in his honor in the restaurant La Bombilla in the suburb of San Angel. While the orchestra was playing Obregón's favorite piece, "El limoncito," a young man posing as an artist worked his way around the table. José de León Toral approached Obregón and showed him his portrait. Obregón saw the sketch and began to laugh. When the caudillo returned his attention to the food, León Toral took out his pistol and fired six shots in Obregón's direction. Five found their target. Dead instantly, Obregón fell face forward into a plate of roasted goat and then to the ground. While scholars have long portrayed the assassin as a Catholic fanatic who had mistakenly identified Obregón as the church's primary enemy, a recent study persuasively argues that León Toral killed Obregón in the belief that tyrannicide would confer martyrdom upon him.[117] Although Obregón did not match Calles in his anticlericalism, he died in unbelief, having stipulated in his last will that his burial "not be desecrated by any religious ceremony."[118]

The murder ended a life spiraling into the abyss at the age of forty-eight. Ten years later, a chronicler of the Sonorenses would observe "formidable contradictions" in the caudillo. On the one hand, he noted Obregón's "valor, recklessness [and] audacity," all qualities associated with macho authoritarian leadership. On the other hand, he described "egotism to the point of narcissism," "greed," and cold indifference toward human lives.[119] Obregón's second presidential bid had manifested a dark side. As one of his opponents noted, "He was only a grotesque caricature of Bonaparte; the Bonaparte of the 18th Brumaire who seizes power by force, and not the Bonaparte of Montenote and Arcola who conquers unfading laurels for his fatherland."[120]

Obregón's assassination left Calles and Rodríguez as the only remaining Sonorense leaders. Pesqueira had retired to private life, and two other opponents of the government—Maytorena and de la Huerta—lived in exile in the United States. The other six had all died in the last eight years. At least five of them (Alvarado, Diéguez, Serrano, Gómez, and Obregón) had been murdered, and Hill had fallen victim to a mysterious illness in 1920. One might view Obregón's death as the final retribution for the murders that had felled the caudillo's rivals one by one. As one historian has stated, "The blood spilled in Huitzilac demanded more blood because it was spilled among relatives and comrades, which called forth the Furies, the Greek divinities, avengers of fratricides."[121] Obregón's death amounted to the ultimate culling of the group, to the point that it ceased to exist as such.

The Aftermath

According to eyewitnesses, Calles expressed conflicting emotions about the caudillo's death. A leader close to both primary Sonorenses, Luis L. León, recalled Calles as exclaiming, "This time they really screwed us! We will need to unite to resist the force of reaction."[122] Another eyewitness, however, remembered the president's visit to Obregón's deathbed as the occasion for a highly cynical remark that supports the idea that he had opposed the caudillo's return to power. Calles reportedly entered the room with a look of disgust and sneered, "So you wanted to be president? For some reason, you did not make it!"[123]

Not surprisingly, some Obregonistas blamed Calles and Morones for the assassination. Morones had never reconciled with Obregón's second candidacy. As his firebrand speech at the Teatro Hidalgo in April had indicated, he had also opposed the Obregonistas' maneuvers in Congress to weaken the CROM and the PLM. Two weeks prior to the assassination, Soto y Gama had claimed to have learned that Morones was planning Obregón's and his own deaths.[124] To reassure the Obregonistas, Calles replaced the police chief in charge of the investigation with Ríos Zertuche, an Obregón loyalist. He also accepted the resignations of Morones and other Laboristas.[125] Although the police investigation left no doubt in León Toral's culpability, many Obregonistas alleged that Calles and Morones had masterminded the assassination. This refusal to accept the official "lone wolf" theory owed to political considerations, credible reports of thirteen to nineteen entry and exit wounds in Obregón's body (when the five bullets out of León Toral's pistol would have left a maximum of ten) as well as incredulity that a fanatical Catholic would assassinate the wrong leader. In 1963 Ríos Zertuche painted the murder as part of a conspiracy to construct a Socialist state even though his own investigation had not found any evidence implicating Calles and Morones. As late as 1985 an opinion piece in the newspaper *La Prensa* claimed that Calles had ordered Obregón's assassination.[126]

Obregón's murder opened up the succession question only four months before the end of the presidential term. One option was for Calles to remain in office for two more years by means of a retroactive application of the revised article 83. Although both Morones and Ambassador Morrow endorsed this option, the president never seriously considered it because such an action would have only confirmed the suspicions of his enemies.[127] Resolving the issue of succession required three interrelated efforts: a public statement about the assassination and its political consequences; an endeavor to rein in the ambitions of military leaders; and the selection of an interim president acceptable to the Obregonistas who could take office following the completion of his term.

Calles showed that he was up to this task. His greatest moment as a national political leader came six weeks after Obregón's assassination.

On the occasion of his last annual address to Congress on September 1—the first-ever such address broadcast via radio—he announced that he would never serve as president again. In his words, Mexico found itself in transition from a "country of one man" to a "nation of institutions and laws." Calles enjoined all citizens in helping to create democratic institutions. He asked the army to act in the country's best interest and Congress, to choose an interim president according to the law. This reference to institutions and laws disarmed Obregón's supporters, setting the stage for the creation of the official revolutionary party the following year. Calles's unequivocal refusal to stay in power also brought him applause from many who had expected him to exploit the crisis in order to prolong his term in office.[128]

Calles then used this gambit to tackle the ambitions of the military. He knew that a group of generals held regular meetings at the Hotel Regis with the objective of uniting behind a military candidate. The meetings had produced three frontrunners: the Obregonista José Gonzalo Escobar; the Callista Manuel Pérez Treviño; and Juan Andreu Almazán, a wealthy general with excellent connections with the Monterrey industrialists. Aware that many officers remained in the field fighting the Cristeros, Calles summoned thirty powerful generals to a meeting on September 5, 1928. Almost all of them held commissions as zone commanders, and ten were divisional generals. One notable absence was Rodríguez, who resided at a great distance and enjoyed Calles's complete trust.[129] During this meeting, Calles informed the generals that the army should act as a unified entity, and that the candidacy of any one of them would sow division. He asked all of the generals to remain in active military service, which barred them from the presidency. Finally, he requested that those present tell him "if they thought that I am not correct in saying that a military candidate ... would bring the division of our army." One by one, all of the generals signaled their assent.[130] They saw their role as assured due to the army's status as what a newspaper editorial called "the only strongly disciplined group ... [and] the only organized party" in national political life.[131]

With the military on the sidelines, Congress tabbed a civilian as interim president, just as it had after Carranza's death. On September 25, 1928, the Chamber of Deputies designated Secretary of the Interior Emilio Portes

Gil, a civilian with impeccable agrarista credentials who had parceled out almost two hundred thousand hectares as the governor of Tamaulipas. Another act scheduled elections for November 20, 1929, and the end of Portes Gil's term, for March 1, 1930. The constitution stipulated that the interim president would not be able to run, nor would anyone serving in the army, as governor, or as secretary or undersecretary in the national government one year prior to the elections. The timeline hence gave prospective candidates an opportunity to relinquish their positions to preserve their eligibility.[132] From Calles's vantage point, Portes Gil was a perfect candidate—a strong Obregón ally who enjoyed close ties to Calles critics Soto y Gama and Manrique.[133] He had shown his loyalty to the two primary Sonorenses in 1923 when he left the PNC due to its Delahuertista drift. Although Calles likely played an unofficial role, the congressional action constituted an astute reading of the tea leaves rather than the president's fiat. As Portes Gil put it, "I was the unanimous choice. It is not true that General Calles had suggested my candidacy. However, he was quite satisfied with my election because I had been his best collaborator."[134]

Calles also cleared the table for Portes Gil's successor. Ostensibly to preserve the unity of the revolutionary groups, the president ordered all zone commanders and members of the national government to remain in their positions through November 21, 1928. This action rendered them ineligible to run for president in the elections one year later. Meanwhile, Calles and Portes Gil summoned the ambassador in Rio de Janeiro, General Pascual Ortiz Rubio, back to Mexico. Observers could not but wonder if the former Michoacán governor, a supporter of the Sonorenses since the Plan de Agua Prieta, might be under consideration as a candidate.[135]

Calles had handled the crisis with great aplomb. Most of the Obregonistas rallied around Calles after his speech to Congress. He won applause for his determination to curb the ambition of military leaders, and especially his ability to get prominent generals to respect the right of Congress to select an interim president without considering anyone with a military background. Calles therefore prepared to hand over power with the greatest cachet that he had ever enjoyed.

Obregón's quest for a second term destroyed what was left of the Sonorense alliance. Occurring against the backdrop of the Cristero and Yaqui wars, the campaign and its bloody denouement also demonstrated the weakness of the political order. Calles and Obregón could only stop an opposition movement with the use of extreme violence, and the regime was also not able to protect Obregón from the bullets of an assassin. The image of bodyguards ushering Calles out of the Chamber of Deputies after the president had delivered the speech of his life served as a powerful demonstration of the fact that Mexico remained at war eight years after the last violent change of government.[136]

Part 5 ❖ The Maximato, 1928–1934

9 ∴ From Caudillos to Institutions

Every revolution evaporates and leaves behind only the slime of a new bureaucracy.—Franz Kafka

Obregón's assassination marked the most decisive moment in the history of the political system that emerged in the revolution.[1] Just when it appeared that the violence would never end, the elite took a seminal step toward political stability. The following year featured the improvised nomination of Emilio Portes Gil as interim president; the creation of a national ruling party that would keep power for seventy-one years in three different iterations; and the negotiated end of the church strike in June 1929. It also included the Escobar Rebellion, the last installment of the internecine Sonorense conflicts. Afterward, conflict among the Sonorenses no longer served as a disorganizing factor in Mexican politics. As evidenced with the suppression of the independent candidacy of José Vasconcelos, this new order continued to perpetrate violence against its adversaries, and specifically, enemies of Calles, the sole remaining Sonorense patriarch. Between 1928 and 1934, Calles filled the vacuum left by Obregón's death as the so-called *jefe máximo* of the Mexican Revolution.

The twin transitions from caudillo to party rule and from intermittent war to fragile peace accelerated the process of institutionalization that had begun with the Constitutionalist victory in 1915. They also presaged the coming end of the Sonorense era. Within a context of ideological polarization not only in Mexico but worldwide, the framework established in the first four years of the Maximato (1928–32) opened the door to new groups and actors.

A Party, a Patriarch, and a Myth

In his last months in office, Calles helped forge a "country of institutions" by means of a new national ruling party. For better or for worse, the new party constituted one of his most lasting achievements even as it underwent two significant transformations during its first seventeen years of existence. Although Luis L. León would later claim that Obregón had envisioned such a party just prior to his assassination, the caudillo had always undermined parties that demanded a significant slice of power. Whether or not Obregón experienced a sudden political epiphany before his death, his role in life had been precisely to forestall a national ruling party.[2]

The endeavor to create such a party followed two other such attempts: the PLC (1916–22), and the PNC (1922–24). Those parties rose and fell at the whim of Obregón and his faction. A plethora of regional and local parties also functioned as political machines for ambitious leaders, but some of them were organized at the grassroots and made larger claims for their significance. Witness, for example, the Socialist parties in the Southeast and Tamaulipas. Calles and his allies endeavored to create a national party that would subsume those regional entities as well as the national political elite, including agrarian and labor representatives. This project would not come to fruition until the late 1930s. While the new party would not transcend the shadow of boss rule that had plagued the PLC and PNC, it ultimately achieved the highest degree of permanence and dominance of any party in Mexico, and indeed, in Latin America in general.[3]

The first task was to form an organizing committee. The PNR was an elite creation: the meeting took place at León's Mexico City home on November 21, 1928, with only a handful of people present, one day after the date by which candidates for the 1929 presidential election needed to have withdrawn from their posts. Calles and Portes Gil attended, along with veterans of the national cabinet such as Sáenz and Tejeda as well as up-and-coming politicians such as Bartolomé García Correa of Yucatán and Manuel Pérez Treviño of Coahuila. In light of the rumors blaming Morones for Obregón's death, the meeting did not include any Laboristas. The attendees decided that Calles would chair the organizing committee. On December 2, two days after the end of Calles's term, the Mexico City press published an announcement about the formation of the PNR, an invitation to all loyal revolutionaries to join the new party.[4]

On December 8 a conflict between the organizing committee and the Laboristas drove Calles to extricate himself from further direct involvement with the planning effort. In an effort to assuage Morones, who was still smarting from his fall from grace, he attended the annual convention of the CROM and gave an optimistic speech that sought to reassure a confederation restive about its loss of influence.[5] Morones followed with a spirited attack against Portes Gil for permitting the public performance of a skit titled *El desmoronamiento de Morones* (The falling apart of Morones). Rather than take sides in the disagreement, Calles resigned from the organizing committee and announced his intention to "retire absolutely and definitively from political life and return ... to the condition of the most obscure citizen who no longer intends to be—nor ever will be again—a political factor."[6]

The organizing committee planned the first party convention in Querétaro in March 1929. Once again, there was no grassroots involvement; instead, the leaders of the regional parties selected for inclusion in the PNR chose the delegates. Calles helped incorporate some of the most important parties, such as the PSS, Portes Gil's own Partido Socialista Fronterizo (Socialist Party of the Frontier), and Garrido's Partido Radical Tabasqueño (Radical Tabascan Party). Because the PNR saw itself as transcending class differences, it excluded the PLM as a class-based organization. Organized top-down and financed by public funds, the party became a parallel power structure to the executive branch.[7]

The populist rhetoric of the party's founding documents rooted itself in the appeal of the revolutionary constitution to campesinos and workers. As one historian has demonstrated, it borrowed from the political theory and practice of the Socialist parties of the Southeast that became vital cogs in the PNR.[8] The party's declaration of principles pledged the improvement "of the popular masses by enforcing articles 123 and 27 of the constitution, as the party considers the working and campesino classes the most important elements of Mexican society."[9] The draft program announced, "The PNR is the instrument of political action by means of which Mexico's great campesino and worker masses fight to keep the control of the public power in their hands; control wrested from the landowning and privileged oligarchies through the great armed movement that began in 1910."[10] Yet the party also made clear its opposition to radical ideologies. As an editorial in the party newspaper put it, "The Revolution in Mexico was not Communist."[11]

On March 1, 1929, the PNR met for its first convention and to select a nominee for the presidential elections. The frontrunner was Aarón Sáenz, someone who had worked hard to bring the Callistas and Obregonistas together. The owner of numerous sugar mills, Sáenz was one of the wealthiest members of the governing elite and one of its wealthiest members; he and his brother, Moisés, were also the most prominent Protestants in national politics. Aarón Sáenz was a longtime Obregón associate who had joined Calles's extended family through his sister Elisa's marriage to the former president's second-oldest son, Plutarco "Aco" Elías Calles Chacón. He was also a business partner of the Calles family.[12]

However, Sáenz's bid came with drawbacks. In the view of a Mexican intelligence agent, the candidate's Protestant faith constituted a serious liability.[13] In addition, Sáenz enjoyed little support beyond the upper echelons of business and government and represented the industrialists in the new party. As governor of Nuevo León, he had approved tax cuts and business deregulation. He was also regarded as corrupt: together with General Almazán, Sáenz tightly controlled access to government contracts for infrastructure improvements. Portes Gil and his agrarista supporters manifested their opposition, as did Veracruz governor Tejeda and San Luis Potosí strongman Cedillo.[14] Finally, Sáenz did not have support in the army. As Amaro scoffed, he was a "general among *licenciados* and a *licenciado* among generals."[15]

Having promised Sáenz his support, Calles informed the PNR leadership that it should present two candidates, so long as one of them was Sáenz. The second candidate was a dark horse: General Pascual Ortiz Rubio from Michoacán. Due to his long absence as a diplomat in Germany and Brazil, Ortiz Rubio had no political base of his own, but as he later reported in his memoirs, precisely that feature made him attractive to the jefe máximo, who aimed to rein in regional strongmen. Calles's personal role in the decision remains open to question, and his kinship ties to Sáenz precluded an overt advocacy of Ortiz Rubio. But some of his closest allies supported Ortiz Rubio, who emerged as the choice before the convention opened; Sáenz arrived in Querétaro only to find out the fait accompli.[16]

While Sáenz reconciled with this decision despite considerable bitterness, Tejeda left the PNR. At the time, this crucial power broker was

23. The jefe máximo. Fideicomiso Archivos Plutarco Elías Calles y Fernando Torreblanca (FAPECFT), Fototeca, Archivo Fernando Torreblanca, Fondo Plutarco Elías Calles, Oficial, serie *Caricaturas, 1927*, mfn 1561, imagen 4, inventario 1318. Used with permission.

engaging in an experiment too radical for the PNR leadership. Tejeda's second governorship relied on the Liga Nacional Campesina (LCN, or National Peasant League). Led by the famed Socialist Úrsulo Galván, the LNC seized power in over one hundred municipalities throughout Veracruz. At the height of its power, it held twelve out of the twenty-one seats in the state legislature. The LNC used a militia of armed campesinos for the double purpose of seizing private land and serving as Tejeda's security force. However, the governor did not similarly ally with a labor organization despite his state's large textile manufacturing sector. Tejeda considered the CROM too closely tied to Calles and deemed the CGT untrustworthy. His departure contributed to the party's drift away from its commitment to land reform.[17] In the absence of Morones and Tejeda, Calles increasingly relied on allies close to the Monterrey industrialists such as Pérez Treviño.

The presidential candidate selection process revealed the persistence of clientelist connections inside the nascent party. With good reason, one scholar has called the PNR a "confederation of caciques" that encompassed regional and local election clubs rather than mass-based organizations.[18] The greatest cacique was Calles himself, whose shifting allegiance—first to Sáenz and then, Ortiz Rubio—demonstrated his opportunism.

How significant was Calles's influence in the PNR? Referring to what he calls the "presidential Minimato," one historian insinuated that the party's primary purpose was to serve as "an instrument of political imposition on the president to facilitate the power of the jefe máximo."[19] But Calles was not a universally domineering strongman who exerted his will on the party or the national state at every juncture. Rather, he picked his spots carefully and often spent months away from the national capital: during Portes Gil's presidency in Paris, and during Rodríguez's in the remote North. His symbolic power in the party was even more important than his manifest influence.

This symbolic power rested in part on the construct of the "revolutionary family." The idea entailed both a historical and a contemporary dimension. The historical revolutionary family consisted of the great, fallen icons of the revolutionary past: Madero, Zapata, Carranza, Villa, and Obregón. The contemporary family included all those leaders and ordinary people who supported the revolution in the present, and especially in the PNR. Like traditional families, this revolutionary family was hierarchical in structure.

Calles was the patriarch of the contemporary revolutionary family. Although not a great hero like the five leaders who had been assassinated—and especially Villa and Zapata, the epitomes of the agrarian struggle—he was the most significant revolutionary still alive. As Cárdenas wrote with reference to Calles's role in the revolutionary family, "Your noble attitude in declaring your definitive retirement from national politics constitutes . . . a new act of true patriotism and selflessness. . . . Your great work is far above any intrigue, and your strong personality lives in the hearts of the majority of the Mexican people."[20]

The moniker *jefe máximo de la Revolución Mexicana* encapsulated this symbolic role. Both de la Huerta and Obregón had borne similarly honorific titles. As we have seen, the Delahuertista rebels referred to their leader as *jefe supremo de la revolución*. On the first anniversary of Obregón's death, Aarón Sáenz had called his slain friend the *caudillo invicto de la Revolución Mexicana* (undefeated caudillo of the Mexican Revolution).[21] Ironically, the moniker *jefe máximo* originated in a speech by Soto y Gama in September 1928 that argued against Portes Gil's selection. León, the editor of the PNR newspaper, *El Nacional Revolucionario*, appropriated the term to describe Calles's significance.[22] Although Calles himself never used the term, he was one-half of a dualist power structure in which he represented "the Revolution" and the source of unity—the president was the other half. He saw himself as grappling with the big questions of the nation, leaving the messy business of governance to the executive branch. The jefe máximo gave political direction via informal advice rather than overt intervention; nonetheless, this "advice" was powerful, and his interlocutors ignored it at their peril.

Over the next several years, the government moved to cement the public image of the revolutionary family via architecture and art, including two bombastic monuments: the Monumento a la Revolución and the Monumento al General Álvaro Obregón. These monuments portrayed an idealized view of the revolution and assisted the government in laying claim to its legacy.[23] A smaller monument opened in Navojoa close to Obregón's birthplace.[24] These years also coincided with the greatest production of the muralists, and particularly the completion of Diego Rivera's magnificent triptych of Mexican history inside the stairwell of the Palacio Nacional (1929–35).

One particular aspect of this symbolic project was the creation of an Obregón cult. The government used the anniversaries of the caudillo's death, on July 17, as opportunities to reflect upon the revolution and Obregón's symbolic significance. Forgotten was the sanguinary, Machiavellian caudillo complicit in cold-blooded assassinations. In his place stood the image of a revolutionary martyr alongside Pancho Villa and Emiliano Zapata. On the fourth anniversary of the caudillo's death in 1932, Ortiz Rubio eulogized Obregón thus: "Warrior, reformer, politician, statesman, and victorious on the battlefield as well as in the social and political struggle, Obregón is the recent history of Mexico. He is the full and complete realization of the Mexican Revolution."[25] Although it is impossible to measure the popular reception of the Obregón cult, the government's promotion of it is beyond question.

Vanquishing Enemies

Calles and the PNR did not get to claim the mantle of the official representatives of the Revolution without a fight. On March 3, 1929, the delegates learned that Sonora governor Fausto Topete and General José Gonzalo Escobar, zone commander in Torreón, had risen up under the banner of the Plan de Hermosillo. This plan disavowed Portes Gil, whom the signatories considered a Calles puppet, and proclaimed Escobar as the supreme chief of the movement. It lambasted Calles for his authoritarian schemes to exert power after his term as president had ended. The plan used anti-Semitic language in referring to Calles as the "Jew of the Mexican Revolution." It also appealed to Catholic support, mourning the "killing of brothers in the states of Jalisco, Colima, and Michoacán only because they claimed the sacred right of liberty of conscience."[26] Topete's disavowal of the central government marked the third such repudiation in sixteen years (1913, 1920, and 1929)—a unique feature in Mexican history that demonstrated the strength of Sonoran particularism noted in earlier chapters.

Rallying Obregón's allies marginalized after the assassination, the Escobar Rebellion marked the final chapter in the fratricidal conflict that pitted Sonorans against Sonorans. A native of Sinaloa who had earned his first military experience in the Sonoran theater just like Alvarado, Hill, and Serrano, Escobar galvanized opposition to Calles, including the unlikely pair of Yaqui General Francisco Urbalejo and Yori General Francisco Manzo, a major figure in the Yaqui War. The rebellion also showed once again the rift between Callistas and Obregonistas that had existed openly since Calles's election, and covertly at least since the gubernatorial election of 1917 pitted Calles against Obregón's brother.

The Escobar Rebellion spread rapidly across the northern states and Veracruz. At its peak, it included thirty thousand insurgents, including 28 percent of the army. The rebels' greatest success was the seizure of Monterrey on March 3, the first day of the fighting. Five days later, they captured Ciudad Juárez, the most important crossing on the northern border. The rebellion posed a significant threat at a time when a third of the army remained tied up fighting Cristero rebels.[27] The government was fortunate that the Yaqui War was then approaching its conclusion.

Nonetheless, the federal government handled the rebellion with relative ease. Because War Secretary Amaro had suffered an accident while playing polo that resulted in the loss of one of his eyes, Calles replaced him and personally commanded the campaign. The rebels had blundered by including Rodríguez in their communications before the uprising. Rodríguez's warning gave the government advance notice. A communiqué to the Sonora-based army units who supported the rebellion lambasted the Escobaristas as "blind instruments of conscienceless professional politicians" and reminded the soldiers that participation in the rebellion amounted to "treason."[28] Rodríguez also bribed would-be rebels in Nogales to lay down their weapons with money borrowed from a local bank.[29] Other northern power brokers such as Almazán and Pérez Treviño remained loyal as well, as did two significant strongmen with agrarian support, Cárdenas and Cedillo.[30] Sáenz was quick to distance himself from his former allies, criticizing them for their "antipatriotic attitude."[31]

The rebels also vainly sought help from de la Huerta. Back in 1925 Don Fito had written a letter to Escobar assailing the "spurious" and "hated" Calles administration and "the farcical liar" Obregón for their dependence on the United States, their repressive governance, and the incompetence of Morones and other cabinet members.[32] But he refused to help the rebels, whom he found no more palatable than the national government, especially since the uprising pitted military leaders against a civilian interim president. De la Huerta used the occasion to try to patch up relations with Calles. Ten days before the beginning of the rebellion, he left a phone message to apprise the jefe máximo of the Escobarista activities. He closed his message by asserting, "The past is the past, and rest assured that I am the first to recognize the marvelous work of your administration."[33] A few months later, when Calles had not replied, de la Huerta explained his past actions thus: "I had no other choice than to defend my honor tainted by the false accusation that I had caused the economic and moral bankruptcy of my fatherland." He expressed the hope that "when you know the truth about my situation in Mexico and the roots of my estrangement from Obregón, you will once again be the friend you once were."[34] Calles never responded.

As in the De la Huerta Rebellion, the government could once again count on the help of the U.S. government. Escobar had hoped that a quick triumph would garner him the support of the incoming administration of the Republican Herbert Hoover. Instead, Hoover backed Portes Gil's constitutionally formed government, alarmed by the recent dynamiting of a train in which the president had been a passenger. The U.S. government considered political stability paramount. U.S. and Mexican intelligence agencies cooperated in ferreting out Escobarista supporters in the United States and cutting off the flow of money and arms across the border.[35] The use of airplanes constituted a new dimension, especially in the Battle of Jiménez (March 30 to April 3), the first large-scale aerial engagement in the Americas. Both sides hired U.S. pilots to fly rented aircraft. The government, which had only begun to use airplanes two years before as part of the Yaqui campaign, employed a World War I combat veteran to command its airborne squadron. Unable to afford the services of war heroes, the rebels hired U.S. pilots at a weekly rate of US$1,000. The battle ended in a decisive victory for the government. On April 30 federal airplanes dropped twelve bombs on Escobar's last stronghold in Nogales. After his defeat, Escobar left Mexico and lived in Canada until 1942.[36]

The following month Almazán and Cárdenas mopped up the remains of the rebellion in the North and East. The Chamber of Deputies ousted forty-nine of its members rumored to be affiliated with the rebels, including the old Obregonistas Soto y Gama and Manrique. Thus ended the third major revolt since 1920, which once again winnowed the number of divisional generals and severely damaged the prospects of future military coups. In the words of one scholar, it was the "first time that a significant number of subunits under regional command preferred loyalty to the national government over a personal loyalty to their rebel generals."[37]

His work done, Calles resigned as secretary of war and lambasted the actions of the "bad chiefs" who had led good soldiers into rebellion. He demanded the elimination of the military from political life. Calles's words betrayed deep frustration and impatience with the rebellions that had wracked Mexico in the last six years. The uprising had crystalized the role of four prominent generals, or *generalazos*: Almazán, Cárdenas, Rodríguez, and Cedillo. They saw themselves as indispensable to their country's political future, and army officers occupied one-third of government posts.

Calles assailed boss rule, albeit without accepting the ultimate conclusion, which would have necessitated his own removal from the scene.[38] The jefe máximo also did not spare the political system from criticism. As he stated, "in the ... political terrain, in the democratic terrain; regarding the respect for the vote, and in the purity of origin of the people or electoral group, the revolution has failed."[39]

As if to heed Calles's advice, Portes Gil did not reward Rodríguez for his loyalty. After six long years, the governor left his place in Mexicali. On October 1, 1929, Rodríguez sent two letters to Portes Gil: a formal one resigning as of December 1929, and another that explained his thinking in detail. The formal letter cited a need to go abroad for an extended period of time in order to study matters related to construction, a sector on which he intended to focus his future business efforts. The informal one complained about the interference of officials from the Attorney General's office with his businesses in Baja California, and especially "the mode of functioning of the casinos established in the border towns." Rodríguez asserted that the office had sent these agents as spies. "I am really disconcerted, and I do not know how anyone could order proceedings like these against an official like myself, who has shown his loyalty to the government in so many ways ... I am being treated as a vulgar and venal functionary rather than a true servant to the nation."[40]

Portes Gil's stance featured an interim president putting his own stamp on the political system. His ability to constrain one of Calles's closest allies challenges the prevailing view that Portes Gil was the first of three *peleles*, or puppet presidents.[41] His memoirs would even insist that Calles "never intervened in the decisions that I made."[42] While one must view such claims with great caution, Calles's six-month sojourn in France after the Escobar Rebellion showed the jefe máximo taking a breather. In addition, the CROM—his erstwhile ally—lost much of its remaining influence under Portes Gil, who, as governor, had battled the organization for the allegiance of Tamaulipas's workers.

While Calles was in Paris, negotiations took place to end the church strike. Portes Gil paired an effort to bring the church to the negotiating table with a renewed offensive in Jalisco, the theater of operations of five thousand rebels, or about 80 percent of the Cristeros.[43] After Obregón's assassin perished before a firing squad on February 9, 1929, the federal government did not interfere with the thousands of mourners who accompanied his casket to the funeral. The following day, there was a bomb attack on the presidential train. In an attempt to exert pressure on the church while continuing the negotiations, Portes Gil blamed a few "frankly subversive" prelates but stopped short of blaming the church as an institution.[44] The president believed that the church would resume religious services so long as the government offered restraint in the application of the anticlerical laws. Portes Gil made clear that the Calles Law would remain but that he had no interest in enforcing the registration requirement as a means of limiting the priesthood. In May 1929 Portes Gil and Ruiz y Flores (the archbishop of Morelia who had been named apostolic delegate for this purpose) began negotiations, assisted by Ambassador Morrow, who inserted himself into the process to the point that he drafted position papers for both sides.[45] Meanwhile, the army dealt the Cristeros a serious blow in killing General Gorostieta on June 2.

On June 21, 1929, Portes Gil and Ruiz y Flores promulgated an agreement that ended the church strike. The church obtained several concessions, including the right to petition Congress, amnesty for Cristeros laying down their arms, and the use of real property that had converted to state ownership consonant with the Constitution of 1917. On June 30 church bells rang out for the first time in three years.[46] The ambassador told his wife, "I have opened the churches of Mexico."[47] The agreement at last brought a respite to the battered Bajío, a battleground in the War of the Winners, the De la Huerta Rebellion, and the Cristiada. It also allowed Portes Gil to reduce a military budget that once again consumed a third of expenditures.[48]

The agreement amounted to a ceasefire rather than a genuine solution. It excluded the LNDLR and the Cristeros and did not address the issues that had set off the church-state conflict in the first place. In addition, the government did not keep its promises: its troops executed hundreds of Cristeros who laid down their arms, and it failed to return all former church buildings to the use of the clergy as it had pledged. Not surprisingly, some Cristeros stayed in the field, and PNR president Pérez Treviño reported to Calles that the Catholic clergy continued to engage in political activities. In Pérez Treviño's view, campesinos and workers remained the only elements of society not "contaminated" by the enemies of the revolution. From Paris, Calles replied, "We will beat them in whatever terrain they may appear to us."[49]

Portes Gil also accelerated land reform. Under his tenure, distributions spiked at 1,707,750 hectares, or double the pace under Calles on a monthly basis.[50] Michoacán governor Cárdenas proved especially adept at using land reform as a political weapon. To encourage Cristero campesinos to lay down their arms, Cárdenas counseled Amaro to treat them as Obregón had treated the Zapatistas: by offering them land and a cash payout in exchange for the weapons. Although this method did not work well in light of the fact that many Cristeros opposed land distributions by government fiat, Cárdenas persuaded at least one cacique and his men to take the deal.[51]

In the meantime, the administration prepared for the presidential elections. For the purpose of legitimacy, a contested election appeared crucial, especially in the aftermath of Obregón's unopposed triumph the prior year. In that regard, Ortiz Rubio—dubbed *nopalito* (dummy) in popular diction—invited competition. When Calles asked Pani his opinion, he received a caustic answer from someone who had known the candidate since their days as engineering students: "If you had ... searched among the sixteen million Mexicans for the least appropriate president, you would surely have found either Ortiz Rubio or ... me."[52]

To support this unexciting candidate, the PNR juiced turnout at the rallies by offering a warm meal to attendees in a preview of the *acarreado* strategy perfected in the party's later incarnations. Pérez Treviño estimated the crowds as twice the size as those of Obregón's election rallies.[53] Ortiz Rubio showed unflinching loyalty to Calles. At one stop, the candidate announced that "Calles and [Portes Gil] are consolidating the conquests of the revolution," and at another, he praised Calles as a "good, sincere man dedicated to the people."[54] More so than Portes Gil, Ortiz Rubio embraced the jefe máximo's opinions as his own.[55]

The elimination of candidates linked to the Escobar Rebellion left two competitors in the Communist Party and José Vasconcelos. The PCM, which had endorsed Calles in 1924 and Obregón in 1928, fielded its own candidate in association with the LNC and radical labor groups: General Pedro Rodríguez Triana, who had coordinated Calles's presidential campaign in 1923. Rodríguez had scant prospects of victory, and the Portes Gil administration ruthlessly repressed Communists in a year culminating with the rupture of relations with the Soviet Union.[56] Vasconcelos's candidacy mounted a much more serious challenge, as it unified the opposition under a nationalist, civilian, and democratic banner. His political platform resembled Madero's in calling for the removal of the military from politics as well as the full autonomy of state and local elections. Vasconcelos also targeted official anticlericalism; in his mind, the campaign against the church emulated the Protestant-led United States and assailed Mexico's Catholic and Spanish heritage. Finally, the platform called for women's suffrage, the use of referenda, and elected judgeships.[57]

The Vasconcelista coalition was a big tent, just like Madero's and de la Huerta's. The educated urban middle class constituted its primary wellspring, but it also included Maderistas disaffected with the revolution's authoritarian turn; Catholics opposed to anticlericalism; university students and faculty disappointed with the slow pace of reform; and the civilian remnants of the old Delahuertista group who resented the role of the military in national politics. Vasconcelos appealed to all of these groups as a former rector of the National University (UNAM) who had supported Madero and de la Huerta and considered Catholicism an essential part of "Western" cultural heritage. The Vasconcelista challenge even included some Huertistas, científicos, Porfirian army officers, and landowners.[58] In addition, intelligence reports identified a majority of Mexicans in the United States as Vasconcelos supporters.[59]

Vasconcelos presented himself as an alternative to the violent and authoritarian political culture under Calles. He pointedly critiqued the land reform of the past five years, arguing that land expropriations had primarily benefited government supporters. Instead, he proposed to target the land of the Sonorenses and their associates.[60] Vasconcelos also campaigned on his legendary dislike of Calles, referring to him as "Don Nadie" (Mr. Nobody).[61] Finally, he assailed Sonorense corruption: "Obregón and Calles became millionaires and hacendados at the same time that they preyed upon the ... landholdings of their political enemies."[62]

Vasconcelos's primary weakness was his hubris. His autobiography referred to him as a "genius." Vasconcelos also called Greek philosophy his "true spiritual home."[63] Similarly, he mistakenly assumed that he could exploit Rodríguez's growing resentment toward Portes Gil. In his memoirs, Rodríguez claimed that a Vasconcelos agent approached him with an offer to join forces. When he refused, Vasconcelos—who did not know Rodríguez personally—declared himself his "most bitter enemy."[64] It was the second time within a year that Calles's opponents had erred in believing that they could attract one of his most devoted friends to their cause.

The Vasconcelistas found their vessel in the Partido Nacional Antirreeleccionista, Madero's old party repurposed in 1927 to underwrite Gómez's presidential ambitions. After Gómez's assassination, the party had remained under the leadership of Vito Alessio Robles, who had been spared from reprisals given the close friendship between his and one of Calles's daughters. The party's commitment to representative democracy made it a suitable vehicle for Vasconcelos, and its name recalled Maderismo. Vasconcelos brought the party much-needed visibility; as a gifted orator, the candidate attracted large crowds in the cities.[65]

Although Calles had announced the end of caudillo rule, Vasconcelos found out that machine politics remained very much alive. The government used voter intimidation and repression, including the jailing and shooting of Vasconcelista campaign workers and armed displays by public officials supporting Ortiz Rubio. On November 17, 1929, Ortiz Rubio triumphed in an apparent landslide, earning 94 percent of the vote to 5 percent for Vasconcelos and 1 percent for Rodríguez. Some locales announced tallies so lopsided as to defy credulity: Tampico, for example, reported just one vote for Vasconcelos.[66] The election was clearly fraudulent.

Vasconcelos did not accept these results. He traveled to Guaymas to meet with Escobarista officers in order to foment a rebellion. There, he received a telegram from Morrow that asked him to accept the outcome in exchange for Morrow's good offices to procure a cabinet position or a return to the rectorship of the UNAM. Indignantly, Vasconcelos refused. As he related in his memoirs, "I was not going to betray my cause in exchange for public office."[67] Dated December 10, his Plan de Guaymas proclaimed him as the duly elected president who had the election stolen from him. Channeling Madero's 1910 proclamation, the plan anticipated Vasconcelos's exile and predicated his return on an armed rebellion creating suitable conditions for him to assume office. This rebellion never came, however, signaling the reluctance of the government's enemies to take up arms yet again. Vasconcelos spent nine long years in the United States, France, Spain, Cuba, Colombia, Ecuador, and Argentina and did not return until 1938.[68] The call to arms nonetheless gave the government a pretext to crack down on Vasconcelistas over the next several months.

A Presidency in Crisis

On the afternoon of February 5, 1930, a Cadillac whisked Ortiz Rubio away from the Palacio Nacional, where he and several new cabinet members had enjoyed some champagne after an uplifting inauguration ceremony at the Estadio Nacional. As the automobile exited the National Palace, a lone gunman fired six shots at Ortiz Rubio and his wife. Five shots missed, but one hit the president's wife above the right ear. The bullet ricocheted into Ortiz Rubio's right jawbone. Security forces immediately apprehended the gunman, a twenty-three-year-old named Daniel Flores. Flores never divulged his motives even under torture, but a police investigation concluded that he was a Vasconcelos supporter. Under the constitution, Secretary of the Interior Portes Gil was the next in line for the presidency, and some—including Morones—wondered whether Portes Gil had perhaps wanted to reclaim his old job. Other rumors implicated Calles. The uncertainty regarding Flores's motives added to the psychological impact of the experience.[69] Fortunately, Ortiz Rubio and his wife soon thereafter recovered from their injuries.

Whatever Flores's motives, the assassination attempt spurred a fresh round of violence. General Maximino Ávila Camacho ordered the imprisonment of almost a hundred Vasconcelistas. On February 14, 1930, an army lieutenant took a dozen suspects out of confinement, drove them out of town in his truck, and ordered them out near Topilejo, on the road to Cuernavaca. There, his men forced the suspects to dig their own graves and then killed them. Brought to light when hungry dogs dug up the bodies a few weeks later, the massacre marked yet more proof of the authoritarian state that the Sonorenses had created. The bodies reminded observers of the nearby Huitzilac massacre only two years before.[70]

Like Portes Gil, Ortiz Rubio made efforts to build a power base. Unlike his predecessor, the new president confronted a hostile majority in Congress and a jefe máximo who had returned from his long sojourn in France in December 1929. Congress devolved into a battlefield between

Portesgilistas, also known as "reds," and Ortizrubistas, also known as "whites." This conflict highlighted Calles's importance as a unifying figure. The elections of 1930 brought in a Callista legislative majority, a feat that Calles had not been able to achieve while Obregón was still alive.[71]

The Ortiz Rubio administration revealed the Maximato in its ideal type. The inaugural cabinet included Callistas like Almazán, Pérez Treviño, and Puig Casauranc, in addition to Amaro, León, Sáenz and Portes Gil as holdovers from the Calles-Obregón era. Ortiz Rubio had little input except the exclusion of Pani, whom he loathed. The jefe máximo's allies at the regional level included his cousin and governor of Sonora, Francisco S. Elías, before Rodolfo Elías Calles succeeded him in 1931. Approximately two weeks after the assassination attempt, visitors to Chapultepec Castle could read a verse painted in red letters on one of the walls:

Aquí vive el presidente
Y él que manda vive enfrente

Here lives the president
He who rules lives across the way

Downhill, Calles's residence gleamed in the sunlight.[72]

The younger Calles displayed Ortiz Rubio's plight by demonstrating a greater degree of independence from his father than the president. He reportedly declared his candidacy for governor against his father's wishes. As governor, Rodolfo undertook reforms that made him a national political figure. He focused on building up the financial and technological infrastructure for small and midsized farms. A passionate agriculturalist, he operated an experimental farm in the Yaqui Valley, where he grew rice and many other products in an effort to diversify Sonora's agricultural economy. He maintained close ties to the local Yaqui population, and one of his grandsons even learned their language. Rodolfo founded two agricultural credit banks in Ciudad Obregón as well as a center for agricultural research. He also promulgated a small-scale land reform program and expanded access to irrigation. On the negative side of the ledger, he intensified the persecution of the church and expelled the Chinese community from Sonora.[73]

Ortiz Rubio found his government in a constant crisis that forced him to rely upon the jefe máximo. In October 1930 Cárdenas wrote to Calles that "no other personality has ascendancy over [both] politicians and army officers."⁷⁴ The president's collaborative leadership style—which might have been a strength in another time and place—accentuated Calles's influence. Ortiz Rubio conducted frequent meetings with the entire cabinet as well as other high-level officials in *acuerdos colectivos* (collective agreements). These meetings gave the jefe máximo the opportunity to weigh in, either in person or through consultation behind the scenes. The result was chaos. Six secretaries of the interior succeeded each other, as well as eight chiefs of the Federal District. An executive-branch appointment approximating that of an elected mayor, the chief of the D.F. was one of the most coveted positions due to its oversight of petty commerce and the lottery-financed Beneficencia Pública (Public Welfare), which provided lucrative opportunities to collect bribes.⁷⁵

Calles also undermined Ortiz Rubio in symbolic ways. On October 4, 1930, he gave a speech inaugurating an industrial school in Monterrey standing in for the president, who was ill. Citing the need to rally around Ortiz Rubio, he called for the removal of the "bad elements" (read: local and regional caciques, and ambitious national leaders) from the party.⁷⁶ By March 1931 joint appearances of Calles and Ortiz Rubio had become so uncommon that a sighting of the two chatting amicably on Cinco de Mayo Street made national headlines.⁷⁷

Nonetheless, Ortiz Rubio mounted a challenge to the jefe máximo. In May the cabinet resolved to limit Calles's influence by forbidding its members from consulting with him except on the initiative of the president. This decision reflected the influence of the aforementioned four powerful divisional generals in the cabinet—Almazán (communications), Amaro (war), Cedillo (agriculture), and Cárdenas (interior). Institutionalists who respected the power of the office, these generals desired a president with authority.⁷⁸ Ortiz Rubio also began to reward his supporters with benefits, just as the Sonorenses had. For example, he granted a concession for a new casino near Agua Caliente to a syndicate in which his cousin was a partner. The move was one of several directed at Rodríguez and his close ally, Baja California governor José María Tapia, whom Ortiz Rubio dislodged from his position in August.⁷⁹ Thus, the characterization of one scholar that Ortiz Rubio was "one of the most plaintive and pathetic figures in our contemporary history" and "inept at politics" is an exaggeration.[80]

However, these efforts made enemies out of Calles and Rodríguez. None of the four generals would confront Calles openly, and the Callistas kept Amaro under close surveillance. Both Amaro and Calles believed that the other planned a plot. Sensing a chance to get rid of a crucial ally who had gained too much power for his liking, the jefe máximo twice met with the rest of the cabinet in the president's absence to discuss this crisis. The second of those meetings in October 1931 led to the resignation of the entire cabinet and the departure of the four powerful *divisionarios*.[81] The shuffle undercut both Ortiz Rubio and Amaro. Calles served a third term as secretary of war, giving him a direct voice in the acuerdos colectivos. He brought in Rodríguez as Undersecretary and continued playing his game of musical chairs. In December the attendance of several cabinet members at a commemoration of the four hundredth anniversary of the Virgin of Guadalupe's apparition angered the jefe máximo and the "reds" in Congress, now frankly Callista and anticlerical. A final shakeup that brought in five new secretaries the next month, including Rodríguez as secretary of industry, commerce, and labor.[82] "Daily, the office of President became more meaningless with everyone reporting to Calles," one of Portes Gil's associates explained years later.[83]

Ortiz Rubio presided over a country in the throes of the Great Depression. The depression exacerbated Mexico's existing economic crisis and devastated the export sector. Widespread unemployment and anti-immigrant measures drove more than five hundred thousand Mexicans and one hundred thousand U.S. citizens of Mexican descent to cross the border from the United States to Mexico. These arrivals flooded an already crowded labor market. In 1930 Mexico's economy shrank by 4 percent even though the country was at peace for the first time in four years, and government revenue decreased by 25 percent. The depression added to the woes of the oil industry: in 1932 Mexico only produced thirty-three million barrels, less than one-fifth of its 1922 total. Purchase-parity adjusted GDP decreased by 12 percent between 1930 and 1932, adding to the 16 percent decline between 1926 and 1929.[84]

Like the Hoover administration in the United States, the Mexican government confronted the depression by procyclical policies, including the maintenance of a balanced budget. Two years before the publication of John Maynard Keynes's recommendations to use deficit spending to stimulate consumption in times of economic decline, the government worsened the crisis by lowering the pay of government employees and raising tariffs and taxes.[85] A strict monetary policy hurt more than helped. As the new president of the Banco de México's governing board, Calles pegged the silver peso at a permanent exchange rate of 0.75 gold pesos—a price higher than the one on the world market. His Calles Plan demonetarized gold and also prohibited the issuance of new one-peso silver coins. Accompanied by shouts of "long live silver" and "death to gold," Congress approved the Calles Plan on July 25, 1931.[86] In addition, Congress set protectionist tariffs similar to the recent Smoot-Hawley Tariff Act in the United States. When these measures deepened the pain, Ortiz Rubio reluctantly agreed to allow Pani's return as secretary of finance on February 14, 1932. Pani immediately reversed course via a resumption of silver coinage and the issuance of paper currency. He also let the peso float against the gold-based U.S. dollar, and the currency declined 35 percent in value over the next two years.[87]

Calles and Rodríguez and their associates felt the crisis in their export-dependent agribusinesses. The revenues of the Compañía Azucarera Almada, managed by one of Calles's sons-in-law (a distant relative of Obregón) as majority partner, declined by 43 percent compared to the previous year. Most of this decline owed to lower commodity prices. The company reduced production of sugar cane by 12 percent, raw sugar, 14 percent, and alcohol, 22 percent.[88] On August 10, 1930, *Excélsior* quoted Rodríguez as saying that he planned to request an indefinite leave of absence from the military so that he could "serve the country better." In translation, Rodríguez desired to focus on his business affairs, investing in new sectors that he considered less vulnerable. Among other plans, he announced his intention to build factories for automobiles, airplanes, and engines, as well as a new fish packing plant.[89] Without a doubt, Rodríguez's decision also owed to Ortiz Rubio's challenge to his existing business interests, and especially the Agua Caliente casino.

The depression contributed to Calles's drift away from social reform. No longer could the jefe máximo afford to alienate oil companies and foreign landowners. He depended on their goodwill, especially after Ambassador

Morrow departed in September 1930 to fill a vacancy in the U.S. Senate. Gone were the days of the worker-campesino candidate who promised to fulfill Zapata's dreams and implement the social rights in the constitution, or even the nationalist president who had confronted the United States over oil and Nicaragua. Years later, Portes Gil correctly identified anticlericalism and public education as the only two areas in which the jefe máximo had not mellowed.[90]

The issue of agrarian reform particularly stands out. Since the Constitutionalist triumph, land redistribution had faced serious obstacles: the ability of landowners to resist expropriation via *amparo*, or legal injunction; the Sonorense preference for commercial over subsistence agriculture; their tendency to employ expropriations for political purposes; and the need to feed the growing cities. Between 1928 and 1929, the production of corn had declined 35 percent, and the production of beans had diminished more than 40 percent, largely as an effect of the Cristiada in the Bajío and other food-producing areas. This reduction became a pretext for slowing down awards of new *ejidos*, especially since commercial agriculture fared far better. Based primarily in Sinaloa and Sonora, tomato production increased 6 percent despite the ravages of the Escobar Rebellion.[91] Looking at a longer time span, one historian estimates that agricultural production quintupled in the North between 1907 and 1929 but shrank by a third in the center and South.[92] To northern landowners such as Calles and Rodríguez, commercial agriculture appeared more efficient than the ejido.

After the annual distribution of land had grown under each administration since 1917, Calles announced that he favored an end to the granting of new ejidos. In his words, the government had "mostly consummated" the task of redistribution. Fully aware that the national treasury was empty, Calles added that new distributions required immediate cash payments.[93] A series of acuerdos colectivos of the Ortiz Rubio administration prioritized food production. In April, Secretary of Agriculture Pérez Treviño announced that future grants would indeed require cash payments. Two months later, a newspaper reporter quoted the jefe máximo as stating that the agrarian reform program had failed.[94] The government parceled out 548,000 hectares in 1930, but less than half that amount two years later (249,000 hectares) and even less in 1933 (196,000 hectares). Governors with agrarian support such as Cárdenas and Tejeda accelerated land reform at the state level, but the federal government did not ratify most of these grants.[95]

With good reason, Carleton Beals wondered whether Mexico had "betrayed her revolution." Recalling Napoleon's remark in 1801 that the French Revolution had ended and that it was back where it began, Beals wrote in the *New Republic*, "If [Calles] were to utter the same about his own country,... the statement could hardly be denied by anyone who has watched the country slowly revert to those days which preceded Porfirio Díaz's exile. Mexico has washed her hands of the revolution, however altered the social structure of Mexico may be,... the country is repudiating Indianism, communal landholding and doctrine in favor of the old economic doctrines of Europe and Díaz."[96] Beals went even further in an article published in the *Nation*, charging that the PNR sought to keep "the government in power by destroying all opposition" and even likening the government's strategies to "Fascist tactics."[97]

Beals's view of a powerful PNR presents a distorted perspective. Just as the Sonorense-led state initially remained weak, so did the new party. The above-referenced characterization of the PNR as a confederation of caciques defies the idea of a powerful institution. Similarly, some historians have asserted that Calles and his associates created the PNR as a means to route favors to their loyal supporters as a way to illustrate, in teleological fashion, its character as a precursor of the PRI. This notion overstates the ability of the jefe máximo and his loyalists to control a loosely organized party that could not assert effective control over its components.[98]

In addition, the Ortiz Rubio administration registered some successes that qualify Beals's perspective. On August 28, 1931, Congress passed the Ley Federal de Trabajo (Federal labor law). After a similar endeavor under Portes Gil had failed, this law implemented article 123 and strengthened the bargaining position of workers. Most importantly, it legalized national industrial unions as well as the closed shop, a union security agreement requiring all employees of a business to join a union. The law expanded JFCA arbitration of labor disputes; it required mid-sized companies to permit the formation of unions; and, incorporating the Calvo Clause, it also required foreign entrepreneurs to renounce diplomatic protection. However, there were new trammels on collective bargaining. The law superseded regulations at the state level that were often friendlier to labor than the new federal law. It also empowered the government to certify the formation of labor unions, thus handing it a tool to deny registration to those it opposed. Article 234 of the new law gave employers the right to organize as well.[99] The JFCA disallowed most strikes because of the economic crisis. Finally, and most importantly, as one contemporary observer noted, the code found arbitrary interpretation and enforcement at the whim of "personalism, favoritism, and bribery."[100] With good reason, working-class leader Vicente Lombardo Toledano—who had admired Calles in earlier years—criticized the law for seeking a balance between capital and labor, which meant business as usual.[101]

The Ortiz Rubio administration also found success in foreign policy. Continuing the pattern since Morrow's arrival, it favored negotiation in its dealings with the United States. On July 25, 1930, Treasury Secretary Montes de Oca came to an agreement with Thomas Lamont and the ICBM, which forgave most interest on the debt dating back to 1914 in exchange for the resumption of payments on the principal (in dollars). Due to the inability of the government to make repayments, the deal was formally suspended in January 1932, but the absence of interest on this debt had improved the Treasury's balance sheet in the meantime.[102]

The relative political stability and the existence of cordial relations with the United States allowed the Mexican government to define its position in world affairs. On September 27, 1930, Foreign Secretary Genaro Estrada disavowed the practice of awarding or withdrawing diplomatic recognition, especially in the case of de facto regimes. This Estrada Doctrine challenged the 1907 Tobar Doctrine that denied recognition to regimes that had come to power by force. It became a cornerstone of Mexican diplomacy until the early 2000s and one of the nation's primary contributions to international law. The Estrada Doctrine challenged the right of more powerful countries to influence a nation's internal affairs via the awarding, denial, or withdrawal of diplomatic recognition. But it also committed Mexico to maintaining diplomatic relations with any government possessing effective control.[103] As an escape clause, Mexico could recall its diplomatic personnel to break relations de facto. In January Portes Gil had done just that by recalling his minister from Moscow over the supposedly seditious activity of the Soviet legation. The two nations did not again exchange representatives until Mexico's entry into World War II in 1942. Nonetheless, the timing of the Estrada Doctrine was worth noting.[104]

Finally, Mexico joined the League of Nations in September 1931, twelve years after its founding members had snubbed Carranza's nationalist government. Carranza had considered the organization an instrument of imperialism, especially as the league charter recognized the Monroe Doctrine, which he considered injurious to national sovereignty. Even though the United States did not join the league, the Sonorense governments of the 1920s had reiterated Carranza's position. They had also used the Conferences of American States in Santiago (1923) and Havana (1928) to build international mechanisms that discouraged foreign intervention and vindicated each nation's right to make its own laws. No doubt made with Calles's approval, Ortiz Rubio's decision to join the league recognized the role of multilateral diplomacy in fighting for non-intervention and national economic sovereignty.[105] At a time when the depression fueled the rise of both Fascist and Communist movements globally, the League of Nations appeared to Mexican politicians an appropriate forum to advertise their country's membership in an international organization devoted to cooperation.

In September 1932 a scandal involving Ortiz Rubio's brother led the jefe máximo to pull the plug on the president. Francisco Ortiz Rubio served as the head of the Beneficencia Pública. The prior month, doctors working in the agency's hospitals had gone on strike, accusing him of abuse of power, fraud, and corruption for his own benefit. One particular scheme featured a gambling den inside a mental hospital, complete with "nurses" ready for paid sex with guests.[106] Pascual Ortiz Rubio initially acceded to his brother's removal, but then decided to stand by his kin. Aware that enough of Ortiz Rubio's term had passed that his resignation would trigger the selection of a substitute president rather than another election, Calles considered the scandal the perfect pretext. On August 22 the jefe máximo gathered his allies at his home to request that none of them serve in the administration, rendering the president unable to fill the vacant post of chief of the Federal District—his brother's superior. Seeing no way out, Ortiz Rubio tendered his resignation on September 2.[107] The popular story that the president learned of his own resignation via a newspaper story is apocryphal yet seemed all too believable given the events of the last two years.[108] As Ortiz Rubio put it, he "had arrived at the presidency by the aid and will of the General and not through my own popularity or personal strength, even in the Party."[109]

The same day, the PNR bloc in Congress met to consider Ortiz Rubio's replacement. Calles had already mentioned Pani, Rodríguez, and Sáenz as possible options, and those assembled also considered a fourth candidate, General Juan José Ríos of Veracruz. In the end, the majority designated Rodríguez—the fourth Sonoran to serve in just over twelve years—as substitute president. Calles commented on these happenings with "satisfaction and optimism, because [they] show that Mexico has fully entered institutional life, which is what I have so wished for our country. I believe that the resignation of President Ortiz Rubio was an act of spontaneous will, which did not follow anyone's suggestion to do so, much less pressure to resign."[110] On September 4 the change of power became official.

Like Ortiz Rubio, Rodríguez was a newcomer on the national scene. He was far less experienced in the national government than Pani or Sáenz. He had bided his time as the long-term governor of Baja California, a regional strongman with close political and business connections to the jefe máximo. It was not until 1931 that Rodríguez got his first post in the federal government. His first assignment came following the massive shakeup in the cabinet on October 16, 1931, as Calles's undersecretary of war. On January 21, 1932, Rodríguez was named secretary of industry, commerce, and labor, and on August 1—just five weeks before his designation as substitute president—he became secretary of war.[111]

Unlike Portes Gil and Ortiz Rubio, Rodríguez brought a significant economic power base to his position, as well as a reputation for corruption. In the words of a U.S. intelligence officer, he was "one of the biggest grafters in Mexico" who "used to steal pocket knives and other small articles from his brother's hardware store in Nogales, Arizona, to trade for tequila across the line."[112] His business empire had grown along with a burgeoning regional economy. Aided by a Prohibition-era influx of U.S. tourists, his administration had turned the state from a beneficiary of the federal government into a net contributor. When Rodríguez took office in 1923, Baja California received an annual federal subsidy of nine hundred thousand pesos. The next year, he asked for half of this amount; and the following year, the state did not receive any subsidy at all.[113] Tijuana and Ensenada fishers benefited from modernized port facilities and exported thousands of tons of fish and shrimp. Rodríguez and Calles teamed up to develop the region's first vineyard in cooperation with U.S. investors and an Italian vintner. Later on, Calles would spend many months at Rodríguez's country estate assisting in the growth of this vineyard. The governor also had ordered the planting of olive trees in the hills east of the coast, and the region emerged as one of the nation's leading olive oil producers. In the middle of the Great Depression, Baja California was an economic showcase.[114]

The first four years after Obregón's assassination had ushered in a new political system. Instead of the caudillo's formidable informal power, a ruling party and a jefe máximo contested the authority of the president, whether Portes Gil or Ortiz Rubio. Following the blueprint laid out by Calles, power had indeed passed from a caudillo to an institution. Nine years of intermittent warfare and rebellion had given way to a measure of political stability. But the new system retained features of the old. Jefe máximo Calles wielded informal authority, and especially during the presidency of Ortiz Rubio, when Calles shuffled the cabinet at will. Far from a unifying figure, Calles was a disruptor during the Ortiz Rubio administration, just as Obregón had been during the Calles presidency. The bloody repression of the Vasconcelos campaign also highlighted the continuation of authoritarian and violent practices.

Just when Sonorismo appeared to have become an affair of one, however, Rodríguez's emergence highlighted the arrival of a new dyad. With a significant regional power base and substantial personal wealth, Rodríguez stood poised to hold his own vis-à-vis the jefe máximo to a far greater extent than Ortiz Rubio. Hurt by the Great Depression, campesinos and workers were clamoring for a resumption for social reform after years of retrenchment, and they wondered what the presidency of the wealthiest Sonorense would bring.

10 ❖ The End of an Era

> We are not a democracy of individuals, but rather a democracy of
> masses, of multitudes—but organized, disciplined, compact multitudes.
> —Ezequiel Padilla (1932)

Most Mexicans expected the Rodríguez presidency to be more of the same. After Ortiz Rubio's struggles to assert independence, the selection of the fourth Sonorense to serve as president appeared to augur an even greater role for Calles. It also appeared likely that the retrenchment from reform would continue under Rodríguez, a wealthy friend and business associate of the jefe máximo who had reached the top due to his unswerving loyalty. Even as social unrest increased as the Great Depression wore on, the ruling PNR remained a confederation of caciques rather than the mass-based organization that Calles had originally envisioned in looking at Europe's social democratic parties as a model.

However, Rodríguez's term (September 4, 1932, to November 30, 1934) turned to be out more dynamic than expected. Far from being a "completely obedient lackey" as one historian has suggested,[1] the fourth Sonorense president carved out a greater role for himself than Ortiz Rubio, taking advantage of an improving economy and the failing health of the jefe máximo. His administration featured a number of important initiatives, including the implementation of a minimum wage and the formulation of an agrarian code. In addition, it accompanied an upsurge of reforms at the state level, highlighting the role of progressive governors such as Cárdenas, Tejeda, and Hidalgo's Bartolomé Vargas Lugo in pushing for changes at the national level. Rodríguez's tenure constituted a bridge from the Sonorense to the Cardenista era.

The Maximato on Autopilot?

Rodríguez's first day in office on September 4, 1932, reflected a balancing act. First, he sent the nation a resolute message in which he called for "unity of action," a veiled reference to the chaos of the Ortiz Rubio years, and particularly the unchecked influence of the jefe máximo. In the afternoon, he traveled to Cuernavaca to pay Calles his respects, a visit duly covered by the press as a deferential ritual.[2] This first day illustrated President Rodríguez's central paradox. He considered himself an administrator rather than a politician and would have gladly left the big political decisions to Calles, his friend and business associate. But his government faced more political than administrative issues: intensifying labor and campesino unrest, conflicts with the Catholic Church, and the legacy of the Great Depression. Someone who, in his own words, "had never aspired to nor considered reaching the presidency" and who detested "politicking... intrigue, whispers, and treason" had his work cut out for him.[3]

However, the final Sonorense to sit in the presidential chair put his own stamp on the federal government during his twenty-seven months in office. Rodríguez was Calles's trusted friend and ally. While one work has dubbed his presidential period the "Maximato on autopilot," another has referred to it as the "apogee" of the Maximato, arguing that the Calles-Rodríguez dyad was so perfectly constructed that it did not require the kind of constant crisis management that had marked the Ortiz Rubio years.[4] Neither description gives Rodríguez's agency nearly enough credit.

The new officeholder took advantage of developments conducive to a stronger presidency. For one thing, ill health increasingly limited the jefe máximo's influence. In 1924 and 1929, he had twice attended to European clinics to treat gastrointestinal, cardiac, and musculoskeletal problems. In 1932 Calles was diagnosed with arthritis, atherosclerosis, and chronic intestinal disease. Despite warnings from his doctors, he kept up an unhealthy lifestyle reliant on alcohol, coffee, cigarettes, and meat. In November 1932 the unexpected death of his wife, Leonor Llorente, plunged him into a deep depression and left him with two small children.[5]

For another, Calles's poor health contributed to his decision to spend more time away from Mexico City. He owned the nearby hacienda Santa Bárbara, complete with a school featuring one student from each state of the republic. Because life on the *altiplano* worsened his symptoms, the jefe máximo spent much more time at his Cuernavaca estate in the subtropics, where he occasionally hosted cabinet meetings under Rodríguez's supervision. Whenever Calles tired of the hustle of national politics, he journeyed back to the Northwest. One of his favorite spots was his daughter Alicia's beach house in El Tambor, Sinaloa, and another one was a ranch in El Sauzal, Baja California, owned by none other than the president himself.[6]

Calles's sojourns to the Northwest offered up opportunities for the performance of deferential rituals. On one occasion, Rodríguez, the entire cabinet and a throng of legislative leaders, business partners, friends, and relatives gathered at the Buenavista train station to see the jefe máximo and three of his children depart for Sinaloa on the presidential train. Five officials accompanied the family to Guadalajara.[7] Without a doubt, Calles entertained many visitors in El Tambor, more reachable than ever before by train and by air. But he did so with some reluctance. According to one of his daughters, Calles tired of his solicitous visitors, who sought to advance their own ambitions. Brusque and austere, the jefe máximo had never craved adulation, and he increasingly yearned for distance.[8]

A third factor in Rodríguez's ability to carve out a greater degree of independence lay in an improving economy. Between 1932 and 1934 purchase-parity adjusted GDP increased by 18 percent. Secretary of Finance Pani's decision to adopt anticyclical monetary policies had contributed to the improved outlook, and the rising price of silver and other export commodities also played an important role. As Calles stated, "Since the world lacks the amount of gold that it needs for the industrial and commercial lives of all nations, those nations will need to endeavor to revalorize silver as currency."[9] In 1934 exports increased by 68 percent in dollar value, with most of the growth due to commodity exports.[10]

As a final component in a more assertive presidency, Rodríguez also confronted the radicalization of campesino and worker movements, in part as a result of the depression. Responding to popular pressure, several governors carried out land reform by fait accompli. In addition, the CROM began to disintegrate. While it had comprised 1,172 labor organizations in 1928, only 349 remained in 1932.[11] That year, Lombardo and other radical members formed a new bloc within the CROM, which they named the "purified" CROM. The following year, they led the majority of labor unions into a new group, the Confederación General de Obreros y Campesinos Mexicanos (CGOCM, or General Confederation of Mexican Workers and Campesinos), which grew to claim 890,000 members by the end of 1934. Unlike the CROM, the CGOCM forswore state tutelage and encouraged strikes as a preferred means of labor action. Between 1932 and 1934 registered strikes increased from 12 to 202.[12] In addition, students struck at the Universidad Nacional Autónoma de México, the nation's largest and oldest university.

Rodríguez took steps to assert his authority within this context. Much of Calles's power rested on informal conversations during which he offered his "opinions," usually at the request of his interlocutors. In November 1932 Rodríguez reminded the cabinet that they reported to him. He emphasized the fact that the constitution had established a presidential regime and empowered him to "name and freely remove his ministers." In his words, this system made the president "implicitly responsible for each and all of the acts which the different dependencies of the executive power develop."[13] This message not only aimed to limit Calles's interference but also implied the end of the acuerdos colectivos. Instead, Rodríguez discussed most matters only with relevant officials, a tactic that also minimized conflict in the cabinet. In January 1933 the U.S. military attaché reported that Rodríguez was "assuming more and more the responsibilities and decisions, which were formerly left to . . . Calles during the Ortiz Rubio administration."[14] Two months later U.S. President Franklin D. Roosevelt named a new ambassador, Josephus Daniels, a seventy-year-old North Carolinian who had served as secretary of the navy during the 1914 invasion of Veracruz. Although some Mexicans resented Daniels's nomination, the new ambassador proved to be as adept at reading the landscape as Morrow had been—with one exception. In 1934 he prepared a luncheon in Calles's honor in Cuernavaca, at which he planned to read a letter by Roosevelt. Incensed that Daniels had invited the diplomatic corps, which made the event appear like official state business, Rodríguez asked his cabinet not to attend, and the luncheon was canceled under the guise of Calles's poor health.[15]

Calles retreated to the big picture. In May 1933 he suggested that the PNR formulate a *plan sexenal* (six-year plan) as a guide for the next presidential administration. Calles hoped that crafting such a plan long before the PNR convention scheduled for December would bind the party's next presidential candidate to the wishes of its leadership. In an interview with the former secretary of public education, Ezequiel Padilla, the jefe máximo expressed his opinion that "we have seen our strongest constructive aims frustrated and delayed. For one thing, we lacked the human material. The men charged with putting into practice these enormous tasks failed at their jobs." He also outlined some ideas for future policies. For example, Calles blamed Mexico's economic malaise on the drawn-out process of land distributions and criticized the poor productivity of the ejidos. He once again called for an end of land reform so that "trust, the indispensable base of credit and the entrepreneurial spirit," might once again lead to prosperity, warning also that "it is a crime to undertake social experiments at the cost of hunger." He envisioned instead the fully compensated parceling out of great estates that would create *pequeñas propiedades* and agricultural cooperatives modernized enough to meet the cities' need for food. The jefe máximo also blasted workers for seeking unreasonable wage increases and asked them to see their bosses as their allies rather than their enemies.[16] Often cited as evidence of Calles's rightward turn, this interview may not have represented his views quite accurately. In Rodríguez's opinion, Padilla desired to "make [him] look like a dictator."[17]

In any event, the *Plan Sexenal* ended up more ambitious than Calles had envisioned. In July 1933, with Cárdenas already the front-runner for the 1934 elections, Rodríguez chimed in with a priority list, including public education, labor, agrarian reform, as well as infrastructure and communications. He asked all of the cabinet to provide input on the plan. Concerned about the plan becoming an expensive wish list, he specifically asked Secretary of Finance Pani for his commentary. Already weakened by a running feud with Education Secretary Narciso Bassols, Pani overstepped the bounds that Rodríguez had set his associates by lobbying Calles against the minimum-wage legislation then before Congress. Once apprised of this meeting, Rodríguez asked for Pani's resignation. As he told Daniels, he was "no Ortiz Rubio."[18] In what turned out to be his final political post, the jefe máximo replaced Pani. To make sure everyone understood his message, Rodríguez reminded his associates that the executive power was vested in him and asked them not to approach Calles regarding matters within the president's purview, even though he considered the jefe máximo one of his best friends and the man "most knowledgeable about the country's problems."[19]

After some revisions at the PNR convention, the final version of the *Plan Sexenal* presented the state as an "active agent" of economic and social development rather than the "mere custodian" of political stability and peace. Evidencing the influence of Cárdenas and other progressives in the PNR—but also that of Franklin D. Roosevelt's New Deal in the United States—the plan also conditioned private property to serve the greatest number. It called for twelve thousand rural schools, Socialist education, a ban on the hiring of nonunion employees in collective bargaining contracts, further land distribution, government subsidies for Mexican-owned production of minerals, metals, oil, and power, and further road building.[20] The plan guided Rodríguez's last year in office and smoothed a transition to Cardenismo more gradual than the supposed "rupture" proposed by decades of historical scholarship. It also structured public discourse over the issues that Rodríguez had identified as crucial for the next six years. These issues included the role of church and state in education, labor, agrarian reform, and national economic development.

Like the Calles one, the Rodríguez administration found itself defined by controversy over religion. During the Ortiz Rubio administration, states had adopted strict limits on the number of priests: Michoacán, one priest for every thirty-three thousand inhabitants; Chiapas, one for every sixty thousand, and Veracruz, one for every hundred thousand. Catholic place names disappeared; for instance, in December 1931, the government changed the name of San Ángel to Villa Álvaro Obregón.[21] In Tabasco, Garrido's "Red Shirts" burned religious images. Both Garrido and Sonora governor Rodolfo Elías Calles launched "defanaticization" campaigns. In Sonora, Calles's men destroyed figures of Mayo saints on the altars of their churches.[22] On the other side, violence began once more in a Second Cristiada, although the violence was sporadic and paled compared to the original event. Pius XI weighed in with a new encyclical, *Acerba animi* (Sorrow of souls). The encyclical lashed out at state governments for their numerical restrictions on priests and the federal government for breaking the promises that it had made in 1929: "Bishops, priests, and faithful Catholics continued to be penalized and imprisoned, contrary to the spirit in which the *modus vivendi* had been established." It condemned

24. Rodríguez and Cárdenas pay homage to the jefe máximo. Fideicomiso Archivos Plutarco Elías Calles y Fernando Torreblanca (FAPECFT), Fototeca, Archivo Fernando Torreblanca, Fondo Plutarco Elías Calles, Oficial, serie *Maximato, 1929–1934*, mfn 875, imagen 83, inventario 1314. Used with permission.

violence but endorsed "recourse to the Sacraments, sources of grace and strength, and instruction in the truth of the faith."[23]

Although not a committed anticlerical himself, Rodríguez followed the lead of the jefe máximo on religious issues. The president energetically protested the pope's missive, which "openly incites the Mexican clergy to disobey regulations that are in force today and to bring about social upheaval, as part of the eternal work of the clergy." The clergy, Rodríguez continued, "cannot resign itself to losing the dominion over the souls and land possessions through which it kept the proletarian classes, which were exploited impiously, in complete lethargy." As a country marked by institutions and stable government, Rodríguez stated, his nation would not permit foreign interference into its own affairs. "If the arrogant and confrontational attitude manifested by the recent encyclical continues, we will convert the churches into schools and workshops for the benefit of the

The End of an Era 281

proletarian classes of the nation."²⁴ Rodríguez also expelled the papal delegate, Leopoldo Ruiz y Flores, a skillful negotiator and a voice of moderation as archbishop of Morelia during the height of the church-state conflict.²⁵

Adding fuel to the fire, the Rodríguez administration introduced "Socialist education" under the aegis of Narciso Bassols, the secretary of public education first appointed by Ortiz Rubio. A professed Marxist, Bassols represented one political pole of Rodríguez's cabinet, while Secretary of Finance Pani formed the other. Closely hewing to Calles's views on the subject, he conceptualized Socialist education as a secular, scientific approach that rejected religious dogma. Hence, it resembled nineteenth-century French Positivism much more so than Marxist dialectical materialism as taught in schools in the Soviet Union. Bassols's concept of Socialist education also included eugenics and promoted sex education as a strategy to address the high number of teenage pregnancies. In May 1934 Bassols withdrew his sex education proposal in the face of strong opposition and swapped posts with Secretary of the Interior Eduardo Vasconcelos. He only lasted a few weeks in his new capacity, but the government's push for Socialist education continued after his departure.²⁶

Calles chimed in with a message that fanned the flames. As he announced in Guadalajara in July 1934,

> The revolution is not over. . . . It is necessary to enter into a new period, one I would call the period of the psychological revolution. We have to . . . take possession of the conscience of children and youths, because they belong . . . to the revolution. . . . We cannot let the future of the country and the revolution fall into the hands of the enemies. With great deception, the reactionaries declare that the child belongs to the home and the youth belongs to the community. [The revolution must] uproot the prejudices and form the new national soul.²⁷

This speech showed Calles's ongoing commitment to defeating the church in the battle for the hearts and minds of ordinary Mexicans. In October Congress tightened the anticlerical provisions of article 3 and added a requirement of Socialist education.²⁸

The Rodríguez administration prioritized reforms designed to benefit urban labor. Aware that the Secretariat of Industry, Commerce, and Labor served both entrepreneurs and workers—and familiar with that institution after a stint as secretary under Ortiz Rubio—he split it into two separate agencies and tasked the new Secretariat of Labor with addressing matters before the newly empowered conciliation and arbitration boards. In this capacity, the government sought to resolve labor stoppages such as the one at El Águila Mexican Petroleum Co. The strike ultimately required Rodríguez's arbitration. In May 1934 he issued an award in favor of the workers, surprising those who had heard the president call strikes "unpatriotic" early in his term.[29] In October the president made a similar decision in favor of the workers of the Huasteca Petroleum Company, a subsidiary of Standard Oil.[30]

Rodríguez also asked the Mexico City government to build affordable housing in the capital, a city marked by a sharp divide between the rich and the poor. In September 1934, the same month the posh Palacio de Bellas Artes finally opened its doors, the completion of the first of these buildings gave the government the opportunity to exalt its commitment to the "betterment of the working classes." In a similar ceremony, Sáenz, as head of the Federal District, lauded Calles, "one of the most distinguished citizens of our revolutionary movement" and an "enthusiastic defender of proletarian aspirations."[31]

Rodríguez's most important contribution to social policy came in his commitment to a minimum wage. As governor of Baja California, Rodríguez had convinced local authorities in Tijuana and Mexicali to set a minimum wage of 4 pesos at a time when campesinos in southern Mexico earned a mere 75 centavos per day. Five pesos approximated minimum pay on the U.S. side of the border. He unsuccessfully attempted to set a similar wage floor in his tenure as secretary of industry, commerce, and labor. As president, he lost Pani's services in part over his insistence to establish minimums of 1 to 1.50 pesos per day, depending on cost of living. In September 1933 Congress revised the Ley Federal de Trabajo to include minimum wages, and in November a reform of article 123 empowered local arbitration boards to set amounts that exceeded 1 to 1.50 pesos in many cases.[32] It was far from sufficient, but a start nonetheless. The following month, Rodríguez decreed the formation of a national minimum-wage commission that still exists today. On August 17, 1934, the president announced in a radio address, "While one has the obligation to work, one also has the undeniable right to a wage sufficient to cover one's needs, and not only the most pressing ones, but also those that allow cultural growth and to progressively develop one's existence."[33]

The Rodríguez administration gave a modest boost to land reform. A new agrarian code combined dispersed legislation since 1917 and provided a framework for future distributions. The agrarian code contradicted the jefe máximo's 1930 statement and formalized the removal of the amparo, by means of which many landowners had managed to stop expropriation. The Rodríguez administration parceled out 790,694 hectares, 15 percent less than Ortiz Rubio but in three fewer months.[34] This land reform was almost a perfect mirror image of its predecessor: while distributions decreased during Ortiz Rubio's term, Rodríguez could boast an accelerating tendency in his final *informe* of September 1, 1934.[35]

Rodríguez paired these steps with strengthening the system of credit that facilitated loans to farmers and other businesses. True to form, these reforms particularly helped the commercial agricultural economy of the North. In its first year, the Rodríguez administration seeded the establishment of several regional credit institutions.[36] In his second year, the government overhauled the BNCA and created the Nacional Financiera, a national credit institution empowered with making loans to distressed banks and other credit institutions. Congress wrote a new Law of Agrarian Credit, which Cárdenas would later use to help beneficiaries of agrarian expropriations.[37]

Finally, the Rodríguez administration revived the economic nationalism that had marked the first half of the Calles era and paired it with more restrictive immigration rules. In 1933, Rodríguez launched an attempt to federalize the foreign-owned electrical industry, which had charged high rates for electricity throughout the years of economic crisis. He also expressed concern about the slumping oil production—a decrease his government attributed to disinvestment and disinterest on the part of the foreign capitalists who held concessions to exploit the subsoil. In response Congress authorized the administration to establish the first petroleum company with a public stake. With shared financing from the government and private investors, Petromex served as the precursor to the iconic Pemex founded after Cárdenas's expropriation of the foreign oil companies in March 1938.[38] In April 1934 an executive order echoed nativist legislation elsewhere in the Americas and barred the admission of indigent immigrants as well as those from Asia, Africa, and the Middle East. This order also closed the door to Jewish immigration more than one year after the Nazi seizure of power in Germany. Building on a series of increasingly xenophobic laws beginning with the promulgation of the constitution, Rodríguez made it clear that only white, propertied immigrants without Jewish background were welcome in Mexico.

Just like Calles and Obregón, Rodríguez found that being president was not necessarily good for his business. During his presidency, he moved beyond his base in Baja California to build a national entrepreneurial presence. For example, he invested in spas, and particularly the famous Garci-Crespo of Tehuacán in the state of Puebla. Not coincidentally, Calles often frequented that very spa.[39] But his absence from faraway Baja California forced him to rely on speculators such as Wirt Bowman, one of the associates in the Agua Caliente casino. Bowman felt so comfortable with the president that his correspondence crossed the lines of professional propriety. In October 1932 he sent Rodríguez a letter recommending the appointment of the president's brother, Fernando, as governor of Baja California. As part of his characterization of Fernando, Bowman admitted that "possibly he may take a few extra drinks like you and I do."[40] In the end, the inability of the president to tend to his investments cost him. With some exaggeration, a *La Prensa* article from 1938 quoted one of his friends, "He left the presidency in worse shape than if he had been assassinated."[41]

Despite Rodríguez's status as a wealthy entrepreneur, this analysis questions the assertion of one historian that he put reforms "on hold" and that "emphasis shifted to promoting economic development, protecting private enterprise, and attracting foreign capital."[42] For certain, he presided over the most activist administration to date in terms of constitutional reforms. During Rodríguez's twenty-seven months in office, Congress passed nine bills that reformed the constitution, compared to two under Obregón (four years), five under Calles (four years), one under Portes Gil (fourteen months), two under Ortiz Rubio (thirty-one months), and ten under Cárdenas (six years). This high number suggests that the Rodríguez administration witnessed dynamic reform in many areas.[43] Of particular importance was a reform to article 83 that finally outlawed presidential reelection of any kind. No matter whether these reforms were the result of popular pressure, the ascendant Cardenista wing in the PNR, or Rodríguez's own convictions, the fact remains that the final Sonorense presidency constituted a bridge to what came next.

The Rise of Cárdenas

Amid the turn back toward reform, Lázaro Cárdenas emerged as the PNR nominee for the presidential election in July 1934. The jockeying for the nomination began as early as April 1933, when Calles left the capital to spend several months at El Sauzal. With good reason, the jefe máximo worried that presidential hopefuls would hound him at this distant locale. When politicians journeyed to what Portes Gil called the "Mecca" of those in need of advice and assent, Calles labeled efforts to lobby him for presidential ambitions "unpatriotic."[44] At the same time, Rodríguez announced his strict neutrality in the matter of the presidential succession.[45]

Despite the official silence, three military officers close to the jefe máximo shared the inside track. One was PNR president Manuel Pérez Treviño, someone with excellent connections to the Monterrey industrialists and with ample support within the army. Another was Colonel Carlos Riva Palacio, a former governor of Mexico state, close friend of Calles, and secretary of the interior. The third was Secretary of War Lázaro Cárdenas. Of the group, he could point to the greatest military accomplishments in combating the de la Huerta and Escobar Rebellions. Cárdenas had served stints as governor of Michoacán, president of the PNR, secretary of the interior, and zone commander of Puebla. As governor, he had built a reputation as a champion of land reform, yet also as someone nimble enough to get along with the jefe máximo. Though anticlerical, he also had an abiding respect for those who supported the Cristeros.[46]

Even more importantly, Cárdenas commanded the support of many of those disaffected with the Maximato. Ten years later, the transnational intellectual Anita Brenner summarized the case for Cárdenas in stating that the party needed a candidate "friendly enough to ensure continuity for the 'ins,' yet make the irritated 80 percent believe that the [PNR] meant something more than the way people read its initials—Plutarco Needs to Rob." As Brenner continued, "He must be a man with a good revolutionary record who had not gotten rich by it, must be acceptable to the army and liked by the peasants and labor and, above all, not identified with Callismo."[47] In contrast to the other two candidates, Cárdenas fit the bill.

Agrarian leaders helped drive popular excitement that buoyed the viability of a candidate like Cárdenas. Witness, for example, the group surrounding Tejeda, which had radicalized with the upsurge of grassroots activism in Veracruz, and particularly the Liga Nacional Campesina "Úrsulo Galván." The league had added the name of its former leader after his untimely death in 1930. With Tejeda's assent, it carried out de facto expropriations. In May 1932 the governor signed a decree that nationalized all private property in Veracruz. Similar dynamics operated in San Luis Potosí and Tamaulipas as well as in Cárdenas's home state of Michoacán. Ironically, first as zone commander in Puebla and then as secretary of war, Cárdenas played a role in repressing radicalism in Veracruz—a role that increased his stature among the moderate majority in the PNR leadership. Federal and state authorities crushed the Liga Nacional Campesina "Úrsulo Galván" and other agrarian defense leagues. Cárdenas's participation in repressing these movements constituted a loyalty test that he passed with flying colors.[48]

This building momentum for Cárdenas drowned out Calles's exhortation to hit the pause button on the process. By late April, Cedillo and the Tamaulipas faction within the PNR (headed by Portes Gil and his agriculture secretary, Marte R. Gómez), had signaled their support. On May 1, Portes Gil presented a pro-Cárdenas manifesto to Rodríguez bearing signatures from agrarian leagues in several different states. The president recognized Cárdenas's appeal among the agraristas and his loyalty toward the government. A letter to Calles dated May 3 enumerated Cárdenas's significant qualities but cautioned that he enjoyed "adulation" as well as *chismes*, or rumors. Rodríguez reported that Cárdenas had denied any interest in running, but that he had asked him about the opinions of the two remaining Sonoran patriarchs in case he would take such a step. On May 15 Cárdenas asked for a leave of absence to explore a presidential run, and three weeks later, he expressed his interest in being a "precandidate:" one of the leaders whom the PNR would consider as its nominee.[49]

Things swiftly inclined toward Cárdenas from that point on. On May 30 Rodríguez told Calles that the candidate counted on majority support within the party.[50] On June 5 Calles sent a missive to Rodríguez asking Pérez Treviño to stand aside if "the balance of the precandidatures inclined toward Cárdenas." Pérez Treviño complied, and Riva Palacio never made any moves.[51] Long before the PNR convention, the jefe máximo endorsed Cárdenas's candidacy at a joint appearance on July 24. In his words, "General Cárdenas is a son of the Revolution. He has fought for it, he has defended it, and he has suffered for it; he cares for it and has faith in its destiny."[52] When PNR delegates gathered in Querétaro in December, Cárdenas's nomination was a foregone conclusion.

Calles's role in Cárdenas's selection remains a subject of debate. In interviews conducted in the 1950s, most eyewitnesses downplayed it. Plutarco Elías Calles Jr. stated that his father wished to let the party decide among the three "possibilities, all of whom would be a guarantee for the continuation of the Revolution ... Gen. Calles made no 'indication' of favoring any one of the three and furthermore wished it to be left that the most favored one win." According to Calles Jr., his father gave his sons "complete liberty" to support whomever they pleased.[53] Unlike 1929, when Rodolfo had supported Ortiz Rubio and Plutarco Jr., his brother-in-law, Sáenz, both backed Cárdenas this time around. Rodríguez's private secretary and business partner, Francisco Javier Gaxiola, also stressed the independence of the two sons. Riva Palacio asserted that the "official revolutionary machinery decided to back Cárdenas in 1933 as it did Ortiz Rubio in 1929."[54] Finally, Padilla insisted that Calles chose Cárdenas as a *candidate* because he wanted "new blood" in the government, aware that his failing health would not allow him to control the political scene to the extent that he had thus far. However, Padilla was not saying that the jefe máximo anointed Cárdenas as the *nominee*, since Calles had always supported putting multiple candidates forward.[55] As had been the case in 1928 and 1929, Calles's reading of the political environment trumped whatever personal preference he might have had.[56]

After the convention, Cárdenas paid the jefe máximo a visit at the beach cottage in El Tambor. This visit was pleasant, as both leaders recapped the convention. Before it was time to say goodbye, Calles invited Cárdenas to go for a swim, as many of his other guests had done over the years. But instead of accompanying Calles into the water at his favorite spot, Cárdenas dipped in several hundred meters away in the company of one of his friends. While the incident in itself did not seem important, it was an early indication that Cárdenas would not operate within Calles's boundaries as his predecessors had done.⁵⁷

Like Ortiz Rubio, Cárdenas confronted opposition. The Partido Nacional Antirreeleccionista, which had nominated Vasconcelos in 1929, considered Luis Cabrera and Antonio Villarreal this time around. More challenges came from the Left. With the backing of a new Socialist party, Tejeda critiqued Cárdenas as an establishment candidate and portrayed himself as the true choice of the working people. The Communist Party nominated Hernán Laborde. Cabrera withdrew, and Villarreal, Tejeda, and Laborde appeared on the ballot along with Cárdenas.⁵⁸

Although the PNR's backing assured Cárdenas's triumph, the candidate embarked on the longest campaign tour the country had ever seen. Eager to expand his base and learn more about the social reality, he visited every state and territory in the seven months preceding the elections, making sure to include stops in cities, towns, and rural areas. Unlike the jefe máximo, Cárdenas genuinely enjoyed his interactions with ordinary people. Building upon a more robust party and economy in addition to his considerable political gifts, Cárdenas would not become another Ortiz Rubio. The election itself was anticlimactic. Cárdenas won by an enormous margin, gathering more than 2.2 million votes, while Villarreal, Tejeda, and Laborde received fewer than fifty thousand votes combined.⁵⁹

On November 30, 1934, Cárdenas took the oath of office in the Estadio Nacional before a crowd estimated at more than thirty thousand people. His inaugural speech highlighted his country's social inequalities, especially among Indigenous people, as the chief lesson that he had learned during his campaign travels. Solving these problems required the help of the state, in his opinion, the only entity acting in the common interest and the only one with a comprehensive vision. Cárdenas blasted mining as a pursuit that benefited the few rather than the many. He promised to revive the agrarian reform program while also increasing agricultural output by means of providing greater financial and technological support. In veiled references to the Sonorense objections to the ejido, he reminded the audience that most *ejidatarios* had received land unsuitable for intensive cultivation. He announced future redistributions, stating that "whatever [the campesinos] had done as serfs, they would do much better as free men." Cárdenas also pledged to fight for workers who confronted not only their bosses but also rivalry between worker groups. Finally, he pledged his commitment to Socialist education, strict adherence to international law, and the building of a civil service in alignment with the ideology of the government.[60] The civil service built on Rodríguez's law of April 9, 1934, which had deferred its creation until the next administration.[61]

Cárdenas also established greater rapport with ordinary Mexicans. Citizens could send free telegrams to the president. Cárdenas refused half of his salary and did not wear a coat and tie on most days. He refused to live in Chapultepec Castle—the presidential residence since Emperor Maximilian—and instead lived in a nearby ranch that had also served as Calles's home when he was Obregón's secretary of the interior. Expanded into a sprawling compound in later years, "Los Pinos" remained the presidential residence until 2018, when President Andrés Manuel López Obrador (who styled himself in Cárdenas's image) opted to remain in his modest home in southern Mexico City and turned Los Pinos into a museum, many decades after Cárdenas had done the same with Chapultepec Castle.[62]

Cárdenas assembled a youthful and largely civilian cabinet. While this cabinet contained a number of Callistas, including Rodolfo Elías Calles, Sáenz, and Garrido, Cárdenas assiduously cultivated new leaders in both Congress and the army—leaders who would be loyal to his administration and not to the jefe máximo. Below the Callista cabinet members and on his own staff, Cárdenas placed many of his own loyalists.[63]

The new president showed right away that he was striking out into new directions. Within his first year, the government distributed more than 2.5 million hectares to one hundred thousand families—almost as much land as during the six-year Maximato. It also facilitated the provision of credit, water, seeds, and other supplies to the ejidatarios who benefited from the redistributions. Cárdenas also unleashed organized labor. The increase in the number of strikes in Rodríguez's last year had illustrated the rise of more radical labor activism under the purview of the CGOCM. In Cárdenas's first year, oil and railroad workers—two marginalized groups in the CROM era—drove an increase in strike activity from an official count of 202 to 642, not counting wildcat strikes. Labor action targeted the Huasteca and El Águila oil companies, Mexico City streetcars, railroads, and telecommunications. Cárdenas showed his support: "It is urgent that opportunity be given to the laboring classes to incorporate themselves into civilization, for they have always suffered injustices, disregard, and privations."[64]

The End of Sonorismo

The Cardenista reform drive did not please Calles in the least. In early 1935 U.S. consular reports alleged that the jefe máximo pondered support for a rebellion.[65] This specter appeared particularly daunting because of the resurgence of political unrest. On one side stood the "Camisas Rojas" (Red Shirts) affiliated with Garrido, a Callista who had treated Tabasco as his personal fief ever since the De la Huerta Rebellion. In his capacity as secretary of agriculture, Garrido organized the Red Shirts in the national capital. According to one of his critics, Red Shirts offered Garrido a martial greeting upon his arrival at work, followed by the secretary asking, "Does God exist?" only to hear the drilled reply, "He has never existed!"[66] On December 30, 1934, Red Shirts fired on worshippers at a church on the outskirts of the capital, killing five and injuring many more. On the other side arose a right-wing paramilitary organization known as the "Dorados" or "Gold Shirts." Founded by a former Villista who broke with his leader during the Convention of Aguascalientes, the Gold Shirts copied their style from Nazi Germany's Sturmabteilung (SA), demonizing Communists, Jews, and the Cárdenas administration. Yet their moniker also sought a connection to the Villista legacy.[67]

Aware of the tenuous political situation, Cárdenas tried to keep a good relationship with someone whom he had always considered a mentor. In April 1935 the president sent Secretary of Finance Bassols to El Tambor to discuss monetary policy. Calles gave his visitor very little attention before sending him on the long journey back to the capital.[68] When word reached Cárdenas that Calles had continued with his time-tested private reunions during which he offered "advice" to prominent politicians, the president asked him to stop these meetings. As per a May 3 diary entry, "In the course of two conversations with the general, I have suggested . . . withdrawing from the politicians, not only for the good of the government but also for his own." Calles, who had recently recovered from gall bladder removal, reportedly replied, "I am already tired of telling them to leave me alone."[69] In early June Calles returned to Mexico City. According to one historian, Cárdenas picked him up from the airport and took him to his daughter Hortensia's home in the Colonia Roma, not far from Chapultepec. On the way, Calles vowed that he would stop interfering.[70]

But he did the opposite. On June 12, 1935, the Mexico City newspapers published "sensational declarations of General Calles." These articles quoted the jefe máximo's comments to a group of senators at his country estate in Cuernavaca. The remarks criticized the "constant strikes that have rocked the nation for six months" and blasted Lombardo and other labor organizers for a "lack of gratitude" for the endeavors of Cárdenas's government. Ominously, Calles invoked the time of Ortiz Rubio as an example of political divisions that tore apart the nation, and he called upon Congress to end the struggle between Callistas and Cardenistas. His words carried an implicit threat—what had happened to Ortiz Rubio could happen to Cárdenas.[71] It is not clear whether Calles intended his remarks for publication, but the damage was done. Notably, the strike that had upset the jefe máximo the most was one affecting him as a stockholder in the Mexican Telephone and Telegraph Company.

Cárdenas immediately counterattacked. He denied fomenting political divisions and defended the labor organizations for advancing their interests via strikes. The president pointed out that his political opponents had worked incessantly and "with full fury" against his reform program.[72] He then obtained the resignation of his entire cabinet and assembled one of his own choosing. This shakeup eliminated Secretary of Communications Rodolfo Elías Calles, Agriculture Secretary Garrido, and Sáenz, the head of the Federal District, among others.[73]

Callista hegemony collapsed rapidly after that. Anti-Garridistas took over in Tabasco; the new state government aligned less with Cárdenas on questions of ideology, but more in its loyalty to his administration. Plutarco Elías Calles Jr. lost his chance in Nuevo León, where the PNR had already announced his victory in a likely fraudulent election.[74] Most Callistas in the legislature pledged support to Cárdenas, and those who did not received heavy pressure to abandon their positions. The end of Calles's influence in the Chamber of Deputies came on September 11, 1935. That afternoon, tempers flared over a proposal to increase the compensation of legislators until gunfire rang out in the venerable building, killing two Cardenista deputies. In response, the chamber's leadership expelled seventeen

Callistas. The ease with which former Callistas rebranded themselves has led one historian to call them "skin-deep and tactical" Cardenistas.[75]

Amid the crumbling of his political edifice, Calles decided to let emotions cool off. One week after the newspaper reports, Calles and his family flew to Sinaloa, and in early August, they continued on to Hawaii. Before his departure, the jefe máximo informed Portes Gil, the new PNR president, of his intention to retire definitively from political activity. According to Portes Gil, Calles wished Cárdenas well and enjoined his friends to support the president.[76] Despite this pledge, he issued scathing critiques. A letter to Pérez Treviño alleged that the Cardenistas "clearly and openly attempt to transform our constitutional government into communism."[77] In response to a number of critical Calles statements to the press, Cárdenas asked him to remain in the United States until further notice. Calles agreed, citing poor health and concern that the government would seize his property if he refused.[78]

With Calles out of the way, the Cardenistas revisited the 1927 Huitzilac murders in a symbolic gesture. Beginning in August 1935, a series of articles in the Mexico City press rendered the versions of eyewitnesses regarding the events that had claimed the lives of Serrano and his allies eight years prior. Most worrying to Calles was the account of General Claudio Fox, who had overseen the executions. Although Fox had not publicly spoken of these events since then, newspapers repeated his assertion that Calles had ordered the murders. To be sure, Fox was a damaged witness as an Escobarista with a reputation as a bloodthirsty assassin. But his allegations nonetheless prompted two of Serrano's siblings to ask the Senate to investigate the case. The Senate ratified the petition, which ended up in the hands of the attorney general of military justice because Calles remained an army officer. In 1936 that office agreed to investigate the murders. The inquiry proceeded the following year. Without the testimonies of Calles and Torreblanca, the investigation amounted to a showcase. Several witnesses, including Fox, blamed Calles for the assassinations. Although the investigation was useful to the Cárdenas administration in strengthening its authority, it did not lead to any punishment.[79] Because Obregón was dead, the public focused on Calles's role.

The last gasp of the Sonoran era came on December 13, 1935, when Calles and Morones returned to Mexico City against Rodríguez's and Cárdenas's advice. The timing appeared propitious as Cárdenas was ill, and the strikes had spread to the national university, where protesting students had occupied several buildings. A crowd of loyal supporters estimated at one thousand greeted Calles and Morones at the airport, including Amaro, León, and more than twenty congressional deputies and senators. This reception made Calles feel that he still enjoyed widespread support. As he told the throng, he had returned to counter the slander leveled at him since his remarks in June. Calles also used the occasion to claim complete responsibility for the policies of his administration and emphasized that Obregón never played any role in his government. On December 17 he hinted at the foundation of an opposition political party.[80] This allusion delivered Cárdenas the pretext to strike another blow. The PNR expelled Calles and several of his prominent associates, and Congress ousted all of those members who had met Calles at the airport. Only two days after his arrival, the Senate ordered Morones's arrest upon the discovery of a large stash of arms and ammunition in his house.[81]

On December 22 Cárdenas addressed a demonstration of some eighty thousand workers. His speech referred to an "impassioned group" attempting to "agitate a country with personalist aims" using "intrigue and lie" as its "only weapon." After reminding his audience that his government had addressed the needs of campesinos and workers after two decades of limited progress, Cárdenas asserted that the country was stable and that both campesino and labor organizations supported rather than subverted the state over which he presided. He concluded, "We do not need to decree the expulsion of anyone from this country, and we do not need to ask for his imprisonment on foreign territory. General Calles and his friends are not a problem for the government or the working classes. Let those classes agree that these elements should stay here, in our national territory, even if they are delinquents or deserters of the Revolution, so that they will feel the shame and the weight of their historical responsibility."[82] Despite Cárdenas's words, his supporters expressed outrage. A few weeks later, the electrical workers union announced a nationwide strike lest the president expel Calles. That same month, 250 campesina women attempted to occupy Santa Bárbara.[83]

The Cardenistas did not stop at the national level. They took a page out of the Sonorense playbook by threatening nullify the governors' power in four states ruled by Callista governors. There had been twenty-one of these governors in December, but seventeen switched to Cárdenas after Calles's return. In 1937 a Mayo general and veteran of the Escobarista Rebellion, Román Yocupicio Valenzuela, became governor of Sonora. A devout Catholic opposed to Socialist education and organized labor, Yocupicio differed from Cárdenas in many ways. But he strongly disliked the Callistas and favored land reform. With his collaboration, the national government transferred five hundred thousand hectares of farmland to the Yaqui and thus finally fulfilled Obregón's promise to that community. In 1938 the Yaqui signed a peace agreement with the Cárdenas administration. Yocupicio's tenure demonstrated the pragmatic nature of Cardenismo and would contribute to a turn toward moderation in the last half of the Cárdenas *sexenio*.[84]

In April 1936 the dynamiting of a passenger train, which claimed thirteen lives, changed Cárdenas's mind regarding Calles's presence. Because a prominent critic of Calles had been aboard the train, several senators accused Calles of masterminding the attack.[85] Late at night on April 9, ten officers called at Santa Bárbara and gave the inhabitant the choice between arrest and exile. By the next morning, Calles had boarded a plane bound for Brownsville, Texas, along with León, Morones, and Melchor Ortega. Cárdenas justified the expulsions with reference to "criminal work" that impeded the development of the nation's institutions. He asserted that his government was "anxious not to follow the lamentable precedents existing in the history of our cruel political struggles, in which the principle of respect for human life has frequently been underrated," a reference to the violent ends of many leading revolutionaries since Madero's assassination in 1913.[86] On April 11 Calles arrived in Los Angeles, and a short while later, he moved to San Diego. He initially lived with Hortensia, whose daughter attended a Catholic school there, before moving into a house on the edge of Balboa Park that a son-in-law had won at the San Diego World Fair. Many praised Cárdenas's decision to send Calles into exile. Twenty thousand workers, headed by a group that carried the ashes of the three railroad workers who lost their lives in the dynamiting, marched to the National Palace to express their support.[87]

The Cardenistas also eroded the former jefe máximo's economic base, expropriating the thirty-eight-thousand-acre Compañía Azucarera El

Mante owned by the Calles and Sáenz families, Santa Bárbara, and Rodolfo's lands in the Yaqui Valley. Of the major holdings of the Calles family, only the Nuevo León hacienda of Plutarco Jr. and Jorge Almada's sugar estate in Sinaloa escaped wholesale expropriation. Calles's own net worth declined dramatically. In 1945 his last will listed just over 2.5 million pesos in assets, no more than US$515,000.[88]

At the time of his exile, Calles's contemporaries remembered the autocrat more so than the reformer. As the *New York Times* summarized, "Calles has been described as ruthless and thirsty for power. There are ... characteristics that recall Porfirio Díaz, Huerta, and other dictators of his country, but he enjoyed a good deal of popularity in certain circles, notably among the military and some industrialists. A man of iron will, he has shown himself extremely intolerant on meeting opposition, but even his worst enemies admit that he has been able and energetic."[89]

The Cardenistas consolidated their control by means of a program of social reform far more ambitious than that of the Sonorenses. A key to this effort was the formation of a new national labor union, the Confederación de Trabajadores Mexicanos (CTM, or Mexican Workers' Confederation) in February 1936. A fusion of the CGOCM and several smaller organizations, the CTM grew to one million members by 1937 under the leadership of Lombardo, by then a professed Stalinist. The first CTM program called for the expropriation of private property and the end of capitalism. Cárdenas's patronage of the CTM resembled Calles's of the CROM, but the similarities ended there. Most significantly, new industrial unions such as those representing workers in mining and metalworking, railroads, the sugar industry, and petroleum served as the backbone of the CTM. Meanwhile, the Cárdenas administration carried out a sweeping land reform. Using the agrarian code approved during the Rodríguez administration, it redistributed 18,786,131 hectares, more than twice the amount of the period 1917–34.[90] Unlike the Sonorenses, Cárdenas took aim at large commercial estates. Notable expropriations targeted the Comarca Lagunera in Coahuila and the Yaqui Valley. The Cardenistas favored the *ejido* over the *pequeña propiedad* and awarded communal *ejidos* in order to facilitate the collective farming that indigenous villages had undertaken for centuries before losing their lands to haciendas. However, a lot of land remained in private hands.[91]

Thus encouraged, Lombardo and other Cardenistas resolved to bury Callismo. In June, Lombardo accused Calles of stirring up trouble by his accusations that the administration was Communist, and he drew parallels between nineteenth-century caudillo Antonio López de Santa Anna and Calles, whom he called a "creole Fascist."[92] Meanwhile, the newspaper *La Prensa* printed excerpts from a Calles biography by one of his Porfirian teachers—a biography best characterized as a Catholic diatribe. Following the last installment of this work, the newspaper ran an editorial with the headline "The Demonic Fangs of the Black Machiavelli."[93]

Faced with this atmosphere, Calles rejected Cárdenas's invitation to return under amnesty terms, pointing out that doing so would justify his expulsion.[94] As a 1938 newspaper article quoted an eyewitness as saying, "General Calles has entered full decrepitude. The man ... seems exhausted. He is no longer the supercilious old man with a profound, sagacious, ... and dominant gaze. Rather, the old man brings forth the commiseration of the people who have had the opportunity to see him."[95] In truth, Calles was only sixty-one, but he was in failing health.

Behind the facade of retirement, Calles aided the political opposition—just as dozens of other exiles had done. He backed the right-wing Partido Revolucionario Anti-Comunista (PRAC) under the leadership of Pérez Treviño, which emerged as a reaction to Cárdenas's 1938 transformation of the PNR into the corporatist and mass-based Partido de la Revolución Mexicana (PRM). With the reported support of León, Morones, and Rodríguez, the PRAC unsuccessfully advanced the presidential ambitions of General Joaquín Amaro. Calles's investment in this party was small but symbolic ($150 per month).[96] In a turnaround from 1931, when he had procured material assistance to the Spanish Republic, Calles also supported Francisco Franco's Falangist government and sought its help in preventing the victory of PRM candidate Manuel Ávila Camacho in the 1940 elections. In part, this shift was due to the arrival of thousands of Republican exiles who ardently supported the Cárdenas administration.[97] But Calles now favored the extreme Right. He admired the "magnificent" organization of the German armies and justified the *Blitzkrieg* as a series of preemptive strikes.[98]

Calles's ouster gave two surviving Sonorense leaders vanquished by the Callistas and Obregonistas an opportunity to return to Mexico. On

November 28, 1935, de la Huerta arrived in the capital after eleven years of exile. He expressed support for the government's left turn, stating that he desired to "fight, here or elsewhere, for the cause of the proletariat." True to his Maderista commitment to democracy, Don Fito cautioned that "instead of talking about the dictatorship of the proletariat, one should express an aspiration toward the public power being in the hands of the proletarian classes, because dictatorships always restrict liberty."[99] Although de la Huerta disavowed any intention of resuming political life, he took charge of the visitation of Mexican consulates in the United States. In 1938 Pepe Maytorena also returned. Unlike de la Huerta, who had become accustomed to the capital during his career in the national government, Maytorena moved back to Sonora, where he split his time between Hermosillo and Guaymas.[100] Both de la Huerta and Maytorena thus found closure, as did many other Calles opponents invited back to Mexico, including José Vasconcelos, Enrique Estrada, and Gilberto Valenzuela.

Sonorismo fell fast and furious because its demise was overdue. It only persisted as long as it did because of what social psychologists refer to as "pluralistic ignorance."[101] In this case, pluralistic ignorance involved a shared belief among most of the elite in the existing political system, and, in particular, the ongoing hegemony of the jefe máximo. Once Cárdenas had built a powerful base, a precipitating crisis tested this consensus and unleashed what one political scientist has called a "preference cascade"[102]—a rapid change in political allegiance.

This dynamic becomes apparent in Rodríguez's March 1936 letter to Juan de Dios Bojórquez, Cárdenas's first secretary of the interior. This letter offers the author's perspective about the last months before Calles's exile. Rodríguez told Calles that "it was the opportune moment for him to retire completely..., disregarding the adulation of servile politicians and human parasites, who would abandon him the moment they found better accommodation." When Calles objected, claiming that "he intervened only in those matters when he was consulted," Rodríguez conceded that the jefe máximo had never said anything "that I could interpret as the slightest indication that such and such a thing be done" when he was president. "It was the politicians ... who grovelingly requested his orders and are responsible for the present situation of the General." Rodríguez also blasted León—the quintessential Callista—for propagating the "jefe máximo" moniker that had defined Calles's public persona since 1928.[103]

While Rodríguez had ample reason to deemphasize Calles's role in his administration, his letter makes the larger point that the Maximato relied on hegemony. For every instance in which Calles intervened directly, there were many others when his associates did what they believed Calles would have wanted, amplifying the mythical power of the patriarch of the revolutionary family. Once Cárdenas wrested that role from Calles, most of these associates quickly followed suit. Those who did not adapt to the new political reality pushed Calles into a confrontational direction, thus forcing the dramatic rupture between December 1935 and April 1936.

The Cardenistas followed in the footsteps of Sonorismo rather than built an entirely new system. The belief in the state united Sonorenses and Cardenistas. They had built a corporatist system that finally extinguished the flames that had been burning since November 1910. Although some historians have compared Cardenismo to Peronismo in 1940s Argentina, it was also an end rather than the beginning; in the words of one scholar, it was "the last kick of the old revolutionary cause before a new leadership, espousing a new project, took control of the country in the 1940s."[104]

Epilogue

The fatal result of our previous revolutions [was] not to allow the nation to liberate itself from its liberators. —Álvaro Obregón

What was the legacy of the Sonorenses? Were they the great reformers, rebuilders, and institutional architects who paved the way from revolution to evolution in Mexico? Were they a gang of thieving bandits who reprised the worst sins of the Porfiriato even as "the methods of their plunder became more sophisticated," as one historian stated with reference to the generals as a whole?[1] Must we emphasize above all their Jacobinism—their opposition to Catholic Mexico and their determination to educate citizens primarily loyal to the Mexican nation rather than their *patrias chicas* or the church? Or do we most remember the group's authoritarianism and their internecine conflicts that left most of them dead or exiled by the time Cárdenas ended the Sonoran era? Or finally, should we conclude that reality is complicated?

Asking questions about the legacy of the Sonorenses means inquiring about the nature of Mexico's revolutionary project. And perhaps, even more broadly, it means asking questions about political culture since independence. During the decades of PNR/PRM/PRI rule, it appeared that the state and party apparatuses that the Sonorenses had inaugurated had turned the page from personalism to machine politics. PRI rule produced predictable six-year tenures in the presidential chair and a remarkable degree of political stability, compared to other Latin American countries, even as recent scholarship has demolished the notion of a *pax priista*. However, democratization and the 2000 triumph of the opposition candidate Vicente Fox Quesada highlighted the fact that nothing lasts forever, and that the PRI's claim on the legacy of the revolution could not keep the party in power indefinitely. After Fox, the rise of Andrés Manuel López Obrador (also known as AMLO) recalled in some ways the decades analyzed in this study. Once again, violence consumes much of Mexico, in the form of the drug war. Like the presidential hopefuls of the revolutionary regime, AMLO and his supporters founded a party in 2012 in the hopes that it would help him win the presidency: the Morena party (Movimiento de Regeneración Nacional, or Movement of National Regeneration). Six years later, AMLO won in a landslide. And like Obregón and Cárdenas, a personality cult surrounds AMLO. This project started more than thirty years ago as an effort to understand the legacy of a violent and chaotic past; today, it appears relevant for comprehending the present as well.

※ ※ ※

An understanding of this legacy begins with a brief analysis of the Sonorenses after Sonorismo. Calles lived on until 1945; de la Huerta, until 1955; and Rodríguez, until 1967. All three would meet as part of a show of national unity months after Mexico had joined World War II on the side of the Allies. Meanwhile, Maytorena lived a quiet life in Sonora. In 1943 President Manuel Ávila Camacho, Cárdenas's successor and a leader who—like de la Huerta—aimed to reconcile political differences, awarded him the rank of divisional general. Maytorena died on January 18, 1948, at the age of eighty.

Ávila Camacho also invited Calles to return to Mexico. Upon his arrival in May 1941, only a few relatives and friends greeted the former jefe máximo. A newspaper article referred to the prevailing atmosphere as "Siberian indifference" compared to the "interminable court of lackeys who dented the roads with the tires of their vehicles on the way to Cuernavaca, where they would go down on their knees before him and beseech him just as the fanatics do before their saints of their devotion, in favor of a 'miracle.'"[2] A year later, another article opined, "This is no longer the arrogant and dry Calles, with the gaze of a lynx. He is . . . a friend of the tranquility of the home."[3] Indeed, Calles lived a private life, highlighted by sunbathing and time with family and friends. He no longer gave any political commentary of any kind and pursued a newfound fascination with spiritism after a life lived as an atheist. At his birthday in 1944, only eight guests attended aside from members of his family.[4]

Calles assisted Ávila Camacho in portraying an image of national unity. In a press interview he stressed that he remained a soldier on active duty and that he would be pleased to serve his country again in battle.[5] On the occasion of the independence celebration on September 15, 1942, Ávila Camacho joined all six living ex-presidents (de la Huerta, Calles, Portes Gil, Ortiz Rubio, Rodríguez, and Cárdenas) on the Zócalo. Organized by Rodríguez, the event sought to display a united revolutionary family. Accounts of Calles's encounters with the other ex-presidents diverge. According to a newspaper article, Calles did not speak with either Cárdenas or de la Huerta. However, Alicia Elías Calles remembered that her father and Cárdenas treated each other courteously.[6] As Cárdenas recorded in his diary, "When the former presidents gathered . . . , we cordially greeted each other and conversed as if some of us had not factored in the political events that ended up dividing one from another." He added, "This meeting served to showcase . . . six soldiers united on the national team who have wholly offered their services to the fatherland."[7]

On October 13, 1945, Calles underwent surgery for abdominal adhesions at the Hospital Inglés. He took a sudden turn for the worse on the morning of October 19, spitting up blood after suffering an internal hemorrhage.[8] Calles's last words were, "Do not do anything . . . it is useless."[9] At 2:40 p.m., the former jefe máximo took his last breath. The funeral at the secular Panteón Civil de Dolores featured Ávila Camacho and several cabinet members. León read the eulogy, recalling a man of "unbreakable energy and [a] character of steel."[10] Cárdenas wrote in his diary, "He leaves a favorable balance in his life as a teacher, revolutionary, and statesman. Once the political passions have calmed down, one will be able to judge him better."[11]

De la Huerta teetered between favorable regard and oblivion. Ávila Camacho appointed him director of pensions in 1946. In Don Fito's final years, he became a witness to the Cold War. In a 1954 letter to John W. F. Dulles written two months after a CIA-sponsored coup d'état overthrew the democratically elected president of Guatemala, Jacobo Arbenz, de la Huerta revealed his opposition to Arbenz's policies, which included the nationalization of lands of the United Fruit Company. Knowing full well his addressee's relation to Secretary of State John Foster Dulles, and his brother, CIA director Allan Dulles, he lambasted Arbenz for abridging civil liberties and using the death penalty in the months leading up to the coup. De la Huerta wrote, "I do not think that the government had popular support."[12] However, an earlier letter had criticized the State Department narrative of Arbenz as a Communist leader and Soviet puppet.[13] De la Huerta's exchange with Dulles confirmed his lifelong stances in favor of civilian rule and against the use of violence but also a penchant for supporting the economic and social status quo.

On July 8, 1955, de la Huerta suffered a massive heart attack just hours after a meeting with President Adolfo Ruiz Cortines, with whom he had developed a close friendship. He died early the following day.[14] After de la Huerta's death, the anniversaries of his passing became public opportunities to commemorate an honest politician. On the fourteenth anniversary, *El Nacional* devoted an editorial to de la Huerta's memory entitled "humane and clean." As the editorial put it, de la Huerta had never stolen a single centavo in his government positions.[15]

Abelardo L. Rodríguez found a modus vivendi with the Cárdenas administration. He privately groused about Cardenista radicalism, especially after the government expropriated the Agua Caliente in Tijuana, the Foreign Club in Mexico City, and the Casino de la Selva in Cuernavaca in the name of "moralization." Seeing the sign of the times, Rodríguez had drastically reduced his stake in this sector before the nationalization. But he reconciled himself to the new order and even congratulated the president on his rousing *informe* of September 1, 1937, which took stock of three years of social reforms. Rodríguez also applauded Cárdenas's oil expropriation decree of March 18, 1938.[16] Nonetheless, die-hard Cardenistas criticized Rodríguez, especially when rumors surfaced that he considered running for president in 1940. Citing Rodríguez's scathing attacks on Soviet Russia following a visit there, a senator from Sinaloa called him a "fascist" and claimed that he was no longer a revolutionary. Seeking to allay the rumors, Rodríguez ruled out a return to politics the following month.[17]

Despite this announcement, Rodríguez once again played a significant role after 1940, thanks in part to his close ties with Manuel Ávila Camacho's brother, Maximino, the strongman of Puebla and one of his own business associates. On July 1, 1941, the president named him commander of the Gulf Coast military region, a sensitive area at a time when Mexico's entry into the war was drawing near. In October 1942 he appointed him supervisor of national production. Rodríguez had sought the governorship of Sonora, but the local branch of the Confederación Nacional Campesina

(National Campesino Confederation) refused to support his candidacy. In 1943, he nevertheless mounted a successful bid for governor. His campaign confronted rumors about the origins of his considerable wealth.[18] Rodríguez pledged that the governorship would be his last political post. He stayed true to that pledge although he served as the president of the national commission of fisheries from 1961 to 1964.[19]

Rodríguez also became a mouthpiece for the Right. In February 1941 a speech at a Senate banquet implored Mexicans to let go of "experiments based on exotic theories" as well as "demagoguery," in clear reference to Lombardo Toledano and his left-leaning group in the CTM. With great irony, Rodríguez attacked the CTM leadership for its corruption.[20] He supported the nomination of the Sonorense Ernesto P. Uruchurtu for the presidential elections in 1958, a nomination that went to Adolfo López Mateos, the favorite of the Cardenista wing within the PRI.[21] In the 1960s Rodríguez gained notoriety with his scathing attacks on the Cuban Revolution.[22] Not surprisingly, he was a darling of the political class in the Cold War United States, where he earned the Legion of Merit as well as an honorary doctorate at Berkeley.[23]

Meanwhile, Don Abelardo became an even more crucial cog in the national economy. According to his autobiography he founded between seventy and eighty businesses—more than half of them in the 1940s. Beginning in his own presidency, Rodríguez had shifted gears from his primary emphasis on the regional economy to invest nationally in new sectors. For example, Rodríguez moved into cinema during Mexico's "golden age" of film. Through his continuing association with Southern California investors, he acquired dozens of movie theaters in northern, western, and central Mexico, as well as the concession stands that sold snacks and soft drinks to the audience.[24] Rodríguez eventually owned several hundred theaters as well as stakes in movie production and at least one studio. In doing so, he confronted the U.S. entrepreneur William O. Jenkins, whose Compañía Operadora de Teatros S.A. controlled 80 percent of the movie theaters in the republic. Jenkins had never forgotten that President Rodríguez—eager to build progressive credentials and divert attention from his own riches—had ordered his imprisonment in August 1934. In 1951 Rodríguez and his business associates founded the rival Impulsora de Cines Independientes. He could not compete with Jenkins and, in

1957, sold out to his rival.[25] Toward the end of his life, Rodríguez moved his investments into bank accounts and the stock market.

※ ※ ※

Mexican historical memory primarily remembers two Sonorenses: Obregón and Calles. In general, it has been harsh with respect to Calles and kinder to Obregón. The primary reason for this imbalanced view is that Obregón's murder decisively colored historical memory. As the jefe máximo retrenched from reform after the caudillo's death, in the late 1920s and 1930s, it was easy to forget the caudillo's offenses. The Calles-Cárdenas split also made Calles persona non grata while Cárdenas emerged as the new patriarch of the revolution.

In fact, Obregón best represented the Machiavellian opportunism represented in negative views of the Sonorense era. Once again, we turn to Martín Luis Guzmán for an illustration: Obregón "did not live on the ground of everyday sincerities, but on a tableau: he was not a person ... but an actor. His ideas, his beliefs, his sentiments were those of the ... theater, to shine before an audience. They lacked all ... internal reality with attributes of their own. He was, in the direct sense of the word, a fraud."[26] This work has highlighted Obregón's ability to impose his will on a society in upheaval. These qualities served him well in the revolution but also amounted to a lack of political direction.

The slain caudillo had a significant afterlife in public memory that recalled his malleable opportunism. The Obregonistas first reimagined him as a precursor to Cardenismo. Beginning in 1935 speakers at the new Monumento Obregón depicted him as a friend of campesinos and the proletariat in general. In his dedication speech, Sáenz—himself a wealthy member of the governing elite—called Obregón a "protector of the working-class movement" who "laid the groundwork for new justice in the distribution of land."[27] In the same vein, the inveterate Obregonista Juan de Dios Bojórquez manufactured a decisive role for his hero in championing the cause of the Jacobins at the Constituyente.[28]

The pendulum swung back after Ávila Camacho's inauguration in 1940, allowing Obregón's friends to forgo the contortions required to fit into the Cardenista framework. At a time when Mexico prepared for war alongside the United States, it was no longer convenient to celebrate a slain leader for his ostensible support of the proletariat, especially someone who had promoted capitalist development throughout his career.[29] The Asociación Cívica General Álvaro Obregón reinvented the caudillo as a liberal capitalist who rejected totalitarian ideologies such as Communism and Fascism as well as Cardenista populism. On July 17, 1941, a speaker represented Obregón as Cárdenas's antithesis, and as someone who had focused on agricultural production rather than collective ownership.[30] In 1943 the transfer of Obregón's severed arm into the monument reinforced the narrative of his martyrdom.

As Obregón's client and then strongman in his own right, Calles fits the paradigm of Sonorismo less conveniently. Whatever his flaws, he saw political rule as serving a set of ideas. Unlike Obregón, Calles needed justifications for his actions, some of which were not in the least pragmatic. For example, his unwavering opposition to the Catholic Church earned him many enemies and weakened his position as president. Without a doubt, a "pragmatic" president would have displayed a more flexible attitude once the church-state conflict escalated to war at a time of crisis in the economy and U.S.-Mexican relations. While both Obregón and Calles advanced the restoration of an authoritarian state, Calles believed that his policies contributed to the material and moral progress of the Mexican people. Obregón, by contrast, viewed all political ideas with great suspicion, if not cynicism. This study has revised the conventional wisdom that favors Obregón's role over Calles's.

What to make of the relationship between Calles and Obregón? These pages have suggested a utilitarian partnership rather than a close and trusted alliance. When asked about the relationship, Gilberto Valenzuela mused, "Trust? Who knows—in those days there was little of it around."[31] Obregón and Calles needed each other, but neither would concede ground. Although Obregón dominated this asymmetrical relationship—as he demonstrated in his successful return to the national spotlight during Calles's presidency—he could never control Calles, who had built a power base of his own in the CROM and Southeast. The preceding chapters have also laid out a pattern of conflict between the two that belies the traditional understanding of them as close allies.

Compared to the two Sonorense titans, the other members of the group have received much less attention. Hill might well have succeeded

Obregón if he had survived the December 1920 banquet, and he would certainly have continued to figure as an important leader, perhaps as an exponent of parliamentary rule and an opponent of land and labor reform. Maytorena, Alvarado, and Diéguez represent Maderista and Carrancista governorships during the 1910s, and the latter two lost their lives during the De la Huerta Rebellion. Gómez and Pesqueira have slipped into historiographical and public oblivion.

De la Huerta was a civilian alternative to the generals. An honest politician who respected democratic rule and the separation of powers, Don Fito presided over a brief interregnum that brokered peace deals with some of the most obstreperous adversaries of the Sonorense coalition. He, Alvarado, and Hill imagined a more democratic Mexico, an independent role for the legislature and judiciary, the subordination of the military to civic authority, and greater local and regional autonomy. One may call their perspective "civic liberalism,"[32] or an updated Maderismo attuned to social change. De la Huerta was too decent to make the deals needed to survive in a political world dominated by divisional generals, but also too naive and timid to assemble a winning coalition. His decision to publicly disavow interest in the presidency while privately cultivating connections to Prieto Laurens and others was a mistake, as these connections ultimately swept him up in an opposition movement that he could not control. Once in exile, de la Huerta was unable to coordinate a rebellion against a vulnerable Calles government.

Rodríguez's contributions as substitute president were significant indeed. While most existing scholarship has portrayed Rodríguez as the final puppet of the Maximato, he oversaw a bridge to Cardenismo by means of a progressive six-year plan, legislation to establish a minimum wage, and an agrarian code of use to the Cárdenas administration in elevating land reform to a national priority. More so than any other Sonorense, Rodríguez took advantage of the entrepreneurial opportunities that his position in the revolution provided him in the form of longtime service as a military commander and governor of a distant border state. Unlike his colleagues, Rodríguez fluidly moved in U.S. culture as he did in Mexican culture, and the generalization introduced in the anecdote that opened this book—that the Sonorenses were the "North Americans" of Mexico—applied much more to him than to the others.

Serrano's importance transcends his role as a presidential candidate and in the resistance to Obregón's second presidential campaign in 1927. He was a pro-Catholic alternative to the anticlerical Calles, as well as a victim of the Huitzilac massacre, the culminating event in the long history of Sonorense authoritarianism. Until then, he had been a loyal ally of the Obregonistas, and particularly the caudillo himself. He had stood by Obregón's and Calles's side during the revolutionary wars of the 1910s, in the overthrow of Carranza, in the suppression of several minor rebellions during Obregón's rule, and in the victory over General Enrique Estrada during the De la Huerta Rebellion. But he had not joined the camarilla that tied together the business interests of Rodríguez, Calles, and Obregón (as well as Aarón Sáenz), instead building a different network. Even in the rough macho world of the Sonorense patriarchs, Serrano stood out for a dissipated lifestyle. And finally, the Cristiada and Obregón's efforts to win a second term irrevocably turned Serrano against his former allies.

※ ※ ※

An article published in the Mexico City newspaper *El Universal* on July 17, 1980, on the occasion of the anniversary of Obregón's death defined Sonorismo as "modernity, a presence, ... a set of ideas and political practices, the common institutions of the revolutionary regimes." The article defined the legacy of Sonorismo thus: "Since we now live in the anti-imperialist era ... it serves us well to see that Carrancismo, on the one hand, and Obregonismo, on the other, with Callismo as its bloody appendage, exhibit and patent the invading currents of imperialism."[33]

Indeed, it is tempting to identify Sonorismo with many of Mexico's long-standing ills. The Sonorense era played a significant role in rebuilding the national state after the fiesta of bullets. Like both the Porfirian dictatorship and the PRI regime, the Sonorans used coercion to achieve their ends. They also disdained much of traditional Mexican culture in favor of a "modern," that is, Anglo-Saxon-inspired world. Their internecine wars showcased the worst aspects of craven and unbridled personal ambition, and the merciless killing of their adversaries highlighted political assassination as one of the defining characteristics of Mexican history during the first two decades of the revolution.[34] And finally, the Sonorans did not keep their promises to make a better, more socially just Mexico.

This study has suggested a more nuanced view. Mexico is the only Latin American nation without a successful coup attempt in the last century. One reason for the survival of the Sonoran regime was its ability to change with the times and show different images of itself to different people. Obregón managed to accommodate the needs of landowners and foreign capitalists despite his alliance with agrarista representatives in Congress. Calles turned from a self-styled worker-campesino president to a repressive jefe máximo. And the fratricidal conflicts that consumed the Sonoran Dynasty showed the willingness of its members to hitch themselves to different causes and groups. The Sonorans captured separate currents time and again. For example, in 1923 liberal democracy (de la Huerta) faced off with authoritarianism (Calles and Obregón). In 1927 anti-reelectionism (Gómez and Serrano, who had both played significant roles in defeating de la Huerta four years prior) stood against a second term for Obregón (Calles and Obregón). The 1920s Sonorenses represented overlapping circles, including a ruling triangle and a business-based camarilla. Spearheaded by Obregón until his assassination and thereafter, Calles and Rodríguez, the camarilla won out.

As a second important argument, the Maximato overshadows the rest of the Sonoran era in teleological fashion. The Maximato featured social unrest, economic stagnation, and an increasing authoritarian jefe máximo who turned his back on land reform and alienated organized labor once his client, CROM boss Morones, faded from the scene. In the aftermath of the murders of Huitzilac and Coatepec (1927) and the assassination of Obregón (1928), the two Sonorenses who remained in power found themselves increasingly isolated. Calles, in particular, faced the wrath of a population that believed the Maximato had betrayed the promises of the revolution. This perspective, however, overlooks the Sonorenses as nationalists and reformers in the period 1914 to 1926.

This dynamic leads to a final observation regarding the role of the Sonorenses in "the revolution." Unlike other twentieth-century social revolutions such as the ones in Russia, China, Cuba, and Iran, the Mexican Revolution did not have a unifying ideology. Instead, the Constitution of 1917 provided a novel commitment to social rights and economic nationalism. The Sonorenses realized the need to defend this constitution but favored different parts within it: de la Huerta, the articles guaranteeing parliamentary rule; Serrano and Gómez, the anti-reelectionist article 83; and Calles, the anticlerical provisions. They also knew that the new constitution set goals rather than a framework. For one thing, Mexico lacked strong democratic traditions and had just emerged from a decade-long destructive war. With the exception of de la Huerta, the Sonorenses favored executive authority over the purview of Congress and individual states, although they cited relevant passages of the constitution when it suited them. For another, powerful enemies aligned against the government: for example, much of the Porfirian oligarchy, the U.S. government, foreign investors, and the Catholic Church. Finally, the Constitution of 1917 was radical because everyone in Querétaro knew that the path from constitutional theory to political practice passed through congressional implementing legislation and the judicial redress in the amparo.

While historians can and should criticize the Sonorenses for their political methods and their failure to implement "revolutionary" reforms, these protagonists pragmatically practiced the art of the possible. The Sonorenses—and particularly the two primary patriarchs, Obregón and Calles—struck a balancing act between the Constitution of 1917 as radical prescription, and a set of political practices that required accommodation of propertied interests, including their own.[35] The Sonorenses fully deserve blame for their role in creating an authoritarian state apparatus, but they did not betray the revolution. They lived its contradictions, and these contradictions remain relevant today.

Notes

Preface

1. Guzmán, *Eagle and the Serpent*, 163.
2. Buchenau, *Calles and Last Caudillo*.

Introduction

1. Ramírez Plancarte, *La ciudad de México*, 61–64.
2. For state formation in Mexico as a negotiated process, see Joseph and Nugent, *Everyday Forms of State Formation*.
3. Fowler, *Grammar of Civil War*, 9.
4. E. Simpson, *Ejido*, 315.
5. Hamilton, *Limits of State Autonomy*, 80–103.
6. For the reference to U.S. Progressivism, see J. Castro, *Apostle of Progress*.
7. Aguilar Camín, *La frontera nómada*, 303–49.
8. P. Smith, *Labyrinths of Power*, 70–72.
9. Levitsky and Way, "Durability of Revolutionary Regimes," 5.
10. Middlebrook, *Paradox of Revolution*, 6–8.
11. Hobsbawm, "Revolution," 25.
12. Hobbes, *Leviathan*, 592.
13. On the multiple meanings of the word *campesinos*, see Boyer, *Becoming Campesinos*, 1–12. For a particularly good study of these transformations in Mexico's Southeast, see Osten, *Mexican Revolution's Wake*.
14. Gramsci, *Prison Notebooks*, 276.
15. Wakild, *Revolutionary Parks*, 1.
16. Knight, "End of the Mexican Revolution," 47–50.
17. For example, Alexander, *Sons of the Revolution*.
18. Gillingham, *Unrevolutionary Mexico*.
19. Many other Sonorenses played important roles in the early revolutionary years such as Pedro Bracamontes, Juan Cabral, Esteban Baca Calderón, Lázaro Gutiérrez de Lara, Severiano Talamante, and Yaqui leaders Francisco Urbalejo, José María Acosta, and Luis Matus. Others, such as Gilberto Valenzuela, helped negotiate the new order after Carranza's and Obregón's victory in 1915. Yet others, including General José Gonzalo Escobar and the Topete brothers, figured in the fractious politics of the 1920s.

20. Aguilar Camín, *La frontera nómada*, 20–21. In his work on Jalisco in the revolution, Robert Curley calls Diéguez a "Sonoran." Curley, *Citizens and Believers*, 146.
21. Castro Martínez, *De la Huerta y la Revolución*, 173.
22. The most important favorable contemporary interpretation of the Sonorense years is Gruening, *Mexico and Its Heritage*.
23. Quoted in Almada Bay, "De regidores porfiristas," 729.
24. Guzmán, *Shadow of the Strongman*, 47.
25. Vasconcelos, *Tormenta*, 57.
26. Daniels, *Shirt-Sleeve Diplomat*, 60.
27. Tannenbaum, *Mexico*, 69–70.
28. Womack, *Zapata*; Brunk, *Emiliano Zapata!*; Hart, *Zapata*; Katz, *Pancho Villa*.
29. Biographies include Hall, *Obregón*; P. Castro, *Obregón*; Buchenau, *Last Caudillo*; Buchenau, *Calles*; Macías Richard, *Vida y temperamento*; Castro Martínez, *De la Huerta y la Revolución*; Alarcón Menchaca, *Maytorena*; Aldana Rendón, *Diéguez*; and P. Castro, *A la sombra*. For studies of specific topics, see Gómez Estrada, *Lealtades divididas*; Almada, "De regidores porfiristas," 729–89; and N. Cárdenas, *La reconstrucción del estado mexicano*.
30. Dulles, *Yesterday in Mexico*.
31. Dulles to Edward Wallace, June 4, 1956, JWFD, box 4, folder 7.
32. Gilly, *La revolución interrumpida*.
33. Aguilar, *La frontera nómada*.
34. Almada Bay, *La conexión Yocupicio*, especially 133–52.
35. Córdova, *La revolución en crisis*.
36. Aguilar Camín, "Antes del reino," 68.
37. Wasserman, "You Can Teach," 262.
38. Meyer, Sherman, and Deeds, *Course of Mexican History*, 442.
39. For sympathetic studies of Cardenismo, see Gilly, *El cardenismo*, and Pérez Montford, *Cárdenas*. For a revisionist view, consult Córdova, *La política de masas*.
40. Córdova, *La ideología de la Revolución Mexicana*, 307.
41. For the case for a gradual transition from Callismo to Cardenismo, see also L. Brown, "Calles-Cárdenas Connection," 158.
42. Osten, *Mexican Revolution's Wake*.
43. Bailey, "Revisionism," 62–79; Córdova, *La política de masas*; Hamilton, *State Autonomy*; and Kiddle and Muñoz, *Populism in Twentieth Century Mexico*. One historian has gone so far as to argue that "millions of Mexican peasants despised Cárdenas, and the broader goals of the Cardenista project . . . did not endure." Sherman, *Mexican Right*, xvii.
44. Benjamin, "Leviathan on the Zócalo," 195–217.
45. Knight, *Mexican Revolution*, 1:559. See also N. Cárdenas, *La reconstrucción*, 7–18.
46. For example, see Vaughan, "Cultural Approaches," 269–305.
47. Quoted in Joseph and Nugent, *Everyday Forms of State Formation*, 19.

48. Knight, "Corruption in Twentieth-Century Mexico," 220.
49. For these terms, see Olson, *Power and Prosperity*, 6–10.
50. Tobler, "La burguesía revolucionaria," 213.
51. Morris, "Continuity and Change in Mexican Politics," 193.
52. Knight, "Corruption in Twentieth-Century Mexico," 227. Some of the analysis was published as Jürgen Buchenau, "'La Bola.'" I appreciate the permission from the journal to reuse this material.
53. Quoted in Lieuwen, *Mexican Militarism*, 64–65.
54. Quoted in Valadés, *Las memorias*, 58.
55. Aguilar Camín, "Regreso a la frontera nómada," *Nexos*, January 2, 1997.
56. Almada, "De regidores porfiristas," 729–89; Castro Martínez, *De la Huerta y la Revolución* and *A la sombra*.
57. Vaughan, "Rural Women's Literacy," 106–24. See also Rath, "Modernizing Military Patriarchy," 807–30.
58. Quoted in Ramírez Plancarte, *La Ciudad de México*, 65–66.

1. The Making of a Faction

1. Almada, *Breve historia de Sonora*, 19.
2. Carr, "Las peculiaridades del norte mexicano," 320–46.
3. Kirchhoff, *Mesoamérica*.
4. Romero, "Mexico a Central American State," 32–37.
5. Quoted in Aguilar, *La frontera nómada*, 9.
6. Almada, *Breve historia de Sonora*, 27–37.
7. Reff, *Disease, Depopulation, and Cultural Change*.
8. Spicer, *Cycles of Conquest*, 12.
9. Evelyn Hu-DeHart, *Missionaries, Miners, and Indians*; Folsom, *Yaquis and the Empire*, 71–95.
10. Voss, *On the Periphery*, 7.
11. Almada, *Breve historia de Sonora*, 97.
12. Almada Bay, "De regidores porfiristas," 765.
13. INEGI, *Estadísticas históricas de México*, 13; Gerhard, *North Frontier*, 24.
14. Humboldt, *Political Essay*, 64.
15. Voss, *On the Periphery*, 34–40.
16. González de Reufels, *Siedler und Filibuster*, 60–253; Almada Bay, "De regidores porfiristas," 731–32.
17. Quoted in Estupiñán Munguía, *Los sonorenses*, 11.
18. Dillon, *President Obregón*, 32–33.
19. INEGI, *Estadísticas históricas*, 13; González de Reufels, *Siedler und Filibuster*, 55–56.
20. Spicer, *Cycles of Conquest*, 67–68; Hu-DeHart, *Yaqui Resistance and Survival*, 18–93.
21. Folsom, *Yaquis and the Empire*, 1.

22. González de Reufels, *Siedler und Filibuster*, 57.
23. Almada Bay, "¿Cuál triángulo sonorense?," 204–5.
24. Martínez, *Intimate Frontier*, 6.
25. Almada Bay, "¿Cuál triángulo sonorense?," 199–205.
26. Departamento de la Estadística Nacional, *Resumen del censo general de habitantes*, 62.
27. Departamento de la Estadística Nacional, *Censo general de habitantes*, 26.
28. Ibáñez, *Mexico in Revolution*, 52–53.
29. Quoted in P. Castro, *Obregón*, 35–36.
30. Buchenau, *Calles*, 8; Bojórquez, *Forjadores de la Revolución Mexicana*, 65.
31. Almada Bay, "De regidores porfiristas," 736–52.
32. Katz, *Secret War in Mexico*, 9.
33. Garner, *Porfirio Díaz*.
34. Schell, *Integral Outsiders*.
35. Tinker Salas, *In the Shadow*, 79–100.
36. Acuña, *Sonoran Strongman*, 121–34.
37. Voss, *On the Periphery*, 277–87; Tinker Salas, *In the Shadow*, 14–16.
38. For a history of the Terrazas clan, see Wasserman, *Capitalists, Caciques, and Revolution*.
39. Mecham, "Jefe Político in Mexico," 333–52.
40. Mijangos Díaz, *La dictadura enana*.
41. Almada Bay, *Breve historia de Sonora*, 130–31.
42. Figueroa Valenzuela, "Los indios de Sonora," 185–87.
43. These categories remained fluid and were an overgeneralization.
44. Aguilar, *La frontera nómada*, 74.
45. Vaughan, *State, Education, and Social Class*, 42; Okada, "El impacto de la Revolución Mexicana," 91–143.
46. Hall, *Obregón*, 13–15.
47. INEGI, *Estadísticas históricas*, 13.
48. Chao Romero, *Chinese in Mexico*, 1; Hu-DeHart, "La comunidad china," 4:197.
49. Beezley, *Judas at the Jockey Club*, 6.
50. INEGI, *Estadísticas históricas*, 100 and 110. Vaughan presents a lower estimate (33.52 percent overall) in *State, Education, and Social Class*, 44.
51. Jiménez Ornelas and Figueroa Acuña, "Colegio de Sonora," 2:152–53.
52. Castro Martínez, *De la Huerta y la Revolución*, 14; Buchenau, *Calles*, 19–21.
53. Mora, "Sonora al filo de la tormenta," 61–70.
54. Wasserman, *Capitalists, Caciques, and Revolution*, 94.
55. Turner, *Barbarous Mexico*, 37–49; Hu-DeHart, *Yaqui Resistance and Survival*, 163–96; N. Cárdenas, "'Lo que queremos,'" 1870.
56. Gonzales, "United States Copper Companies," 655–59.

57. Rivera, *La revolución en Sonora*, 111–16; Deeds, "Maytorena (Part 1)," 24–25.
58. Rodolfo Reyes to Maytorena, October 27, 1908, Maytorena to Rodolfo Reyes, April 10, 1909, and Bernardo Reyes to Maytorena, July 16, 1909; JMMP, box 1, vols. 3 and 4.
59. Madero, *La sucesión presidencial*.
60. Rodolfo Reyes to Maytorena, February 5 and June 11, 1910, JMMP, box 1, vol. 4; Maytorena to Bernardo Reyes, May 19, 1910; Madero to Maytorena, October 26, 1910, JMMP, box 1, vol. 3.
61. Quoted in M. Meyer, *Mexican Rebel*, 24.
62. "Plan de Caborca," April 11, 1911, DHS, reel 9; Deeds, "Maytorena (Part 1)," 26–27.
63. Aguilar Camín, *La frontera nómada*, 123–24.
64. Aguilar Camín, *La frontera nómada*, 22–23, 29.
65. Quoted in Aguilar Camín, "Relevant Tradition," 118.
66. Quoted in Aguilar Camín, *La frontera nómada*, 29.
67. Obregón to de la Huerta, May 23, 1921, P-OC, 101-S-12.
68. Castro Martínez, *De la Huerta y la Revolución*, 13–21; Aguilar Camín, *La frontera nómada*, 85–86.
69. Rivera, *Revolución en Sonora*, 165–66. There is no good biography, but see the hagiographical Flores Vizcarra and Granados Roldán, *Salvador Alvarado*; and Hernández Enríquez, *El genio de la raza*.
70. Aldana, *Diéguez*, 23–75; enclosure in Josephus Daniels to Secretary of State, November 22, 1915, DS, 812.00/16843, 31.
71. P. Castro, *A la sombra*, 21–26.
72. Castro Martínez, "La campaña presidencial de 1927–1928," 123–26.
73. P. Henderson, *In the Absence of Don Porfirio*.
74. Rivera, *Revolución en Sonora*, 238–40.
75. Almada Bay, *Maytorena*, 6.
76. Beezley, "Madero," 1–24.
77. Simpich to Secretary, December 23, 1912, DS, 812.00/5751; "Informe presentado por el C. José María Maytorena, gobernador constitucional del estado de Sonora, ante la XXIII legislatura de la misma," September 23, 1912, DHS, reel 9.
78. P. Henderson, "Un gobernador maderista," 173–81; N. Cárdenas, "Lo que queremos," 1879–80.
79. P. Henderson, "Un gobernador maderista," 177.
80. Almada Bay, *Maytorena*, 7.
81. M. Meyer, *Mexican Rebel*, 52–93. A copy of the plan can be found in Garciadiego, *La Revolución Mexicana*, 151–58.
82. Almada Bay, *Maytorena*, 6.
83. Hall, *Obregón*, 20–24.
84. P. Castro, *A la sombra*, 22.

85. Hall, *Obregón*, 24–25; Guzmán Esparza, *Memorias*, 28.
86. For the civilian origins of the revolutionary armies, see Camp, *Generals in the Palacio*, 7.
87. Obregón, *Ocho mil kilómetros*, 8–10; Dillon, *President Obregón*, 65.
88. Obregón, *Ocho mil kilómetros*, 10–25; Hall, *Obregón*, 31–34.
89. Macías Richard, *Vida y temperamento*, 43–44.
90. Eugenia Meyer, interview with Alicia Calles Chacón de Almada, June 4, 1975, PHO.
91. "Acusaciones contra autoridades," Calles et al. to Prefecto, Distrito de Arizpe, October 18, 1909, AHGES, vol. 2418.
92. Buchenau, *Calles*, 23–24; Valadés, *Las memorias*, 6.
93. Guzmán Esparza, *Memorias*, 24–26; Valadés, *Las memorias*, 9.
94. Calles to Maytorena, May 22, 1912, AHGES, vol. 2886, Distrito de Arizpe, "Tranquilidad pública (1912)."
95. Macías Richard, *Vida y temperamento*, 151–54. On the significance of electrification in modern Mexico, with a focus on Mexico City, see Montaño, *Electrifying Mexico*.
96. A. Rodríguez, *Autobiografía*, 7.
97. A. Rodríguez, *Autobiografía*, 31–55.
98. Cruz Rivas, Remigio Marcial, and Lizárraga Cano, *Rodríguez*, 3.
99. A. Rodríguez, *Autobiografía*, 10.
100. "¿Quién es quién en la revolución? Abelardo L. Rodríguez, el progresista," *La Prensa*, May 11, 1939.
101. A. Rodríguez, *Autobiografía*, 58.
102. Castro Martínez, *De la Huerta y la Revolución*, 22; Almada, *La revolución*, 64–65; Almada Bay, *La conexión Yocupicio*, 92; Aguilar Camín, *La frontera nómada*, 346.

2. The School of War

1. Azuela, *Underdogs*, 58–59.
2. Knight, *Mexican Revolution*, 2:26.
3. Guzmán Esparza, *Memorias*, 44–46.
4. For a revisionist case, see M. Meyer, *Huerta*.
5. Knight, *Mexican Revolution*, 1:297–300, 2:5.
6. Knight, *Mexican Revolution*, 2:13–16.
7. Beezley, *Insurgent Governor*, 156–62.
8. Guzmán Esparza, *Memorias*, 55.
9. Maytorena, "Informe del gobernador de Sonora sobre el golpe de estado de febrero de 1913 y hechos posteriores," October 30, 1913, DHS, reel 9; Hostetter to Secretary, February 22, 1913, DS, 812.00/6434.
10. Maytorena, "Informe," October 30, 1913, DHS, reel 9.
11. Hostetter to Secretary, March 7 and March 15, 1913, DS, 812.00/6726, 6820; Knight, *Mexican Revolution*, 2:17.

12. Deeds, "Maytorena (Part 2)," 128–29.
13. "XXIII Congreso de Sonora," March 4, 1913; "Ley que autoriza al ejecutivo para desconocer al c. general Victoriano Huerta como presidente de México," March 5, 1913, DHS, reel 9.
14. "Manifiesto del gobernador interino del estado de Sonora," March 7, 1913, DHS, reel 9.
15. Obregón, *Ocho mil kilómetros*, 34.
16. "Mexico's Latest Man of the Hour," *New York Times*, March 14, 1915.
17. Valadés, *Las memorias*, 19–20.
18. "Manifiesto a los habitantes de Sonora," March 12, 1913, in Calles, *Pensamiento político*, 28–31.
19. "Datos biográficos del general Abelardo L. Rodríguez," AALR, ser. 01.01.03.
20. Guzmán Esparza, *Memorias*, 61.
21. Ryan to Southern Department, April 19, 1915, MID, box 1940, 8534-67.
22. Serrano to Maytorena, March 17, 1913, JMMP, box 3, folder 18.
23. Richmond, *Carranza's Nationalist Struggle*, 1–44.
24. Richmond, *Carranza's Nationalist Struggle*, 77.
25. Katz, *Pancho Villa*, 64–206.
26. Quoted in Guzmán Esparza, *Memorias*, 56.
27. Womack, *Zapata*, 3–128.
28. "Convención de Monclova," DHS, reel 9.
29. Guzmán Esparza, *Memorias*, 66–67; Valadés, *Las memorias*, 21.
30. Knight, *Mexican Revolution*, 2:28–29.
31. Obregón, *Ocho mil kilómetros*, 36–45.
32. Aguilar, *La frontera nómada*, 327. In the original, "broker fronterizo."
33. Deeds, "Maytorena (Part 2)," 133; Bliss, "Border Report," May 31, 1913, DS, 812.00/7760.
34. Knight, *Mexican Revolution*, 2:26–27.
35. N. Cárdenas, "Lo que queremos," 1888–89.
36. Quoted in Padilla Ramos and Ramírez Zavala, "Los yaquis en la revolución carrancista," 194.
37. Bojórquez, *Forjadores*, 131–32.
38. Aguilar Camín, *La frontera nómada*, 363.
39. Hall, *Obregón*, 48–49.
40. Hall, *Obregón*, 47; Richmond, *Carranza*, 45–46.
41. Breceda, *México revolucionario, 1913–1917*, 2:196.
42. Slattery, *Felipe Ángeles*, 60–63.
43. Maytorena to Obregón, September 13, 1913, and Maytorena to Carranza, September 13, 1913, DHS, reel 9.
44. Hall, *Obregón*, 51.
45. Quoted in Breceda, *México revolucionario*, 2:195.

46. Quoted in Katz, *Secret War*, 129–30 and 133–34.
47. Quirk, *Mexican Revolution and the Catholic Church*, 45–50, Valvo, *La Cristiada*, 14.
48. Aldana, *Diéguez*, 119–24; Hall, *Obregón*, 60.
49. Richmond, *Carranza*, 48–49.
50. Katz, *Pancho Villa*, 354–56.
51. Obregón, *Ocho mil kilómetros*, 132–34.
52. Aldana, *Diéguez*, 129–44.
53. Quoted in Aldana, *Diéguez*, 132.
54. Obregón to Carranza, August 15, 1914, FFT, ser. 010201, exp. 47/55, inv. 80 "Serrano, Francisco (Gral.) Álvaro Obregón (Gral.)."
55. Breceda, *México revolucionario*, 2:93–94; Hall, *Obregón*, 56–57.
56. Lear, *Workers, Neighbors, and Citizens*, 246.
57. Knight, *Mexican Revolution*, 2:26.
58. Katz, *Pancho Villa*, 361–62.
59. Calles to Carranza, May 29, 1914, DHS, reel 9.
60. Maytorena to Acosta and Urbalejo, May 30, 1914, JMMP, box 4, vol. 4.
61. Calles to Carranza, June 7, 1914, DHS, reel 9.
62. Alvarado to Carranza, June 17 and 29, 1914, DHS, reel 9.
63. Francisco S. Elías to Secretario, July 4 and 13, 1914, AHSRE, L-E-776, vol. 27.
64. Hall, *Obregón*, 62; "Orden de suspensión de hostilidades," August 20, 1914, DHS, reel 9; Hostetter to Secretary, August 20, 1914, DS, 812.00/13142.
65. Almada Bay, *Maytorena*, 11.
66. Obregón, *Ocho mil kilómetros*, 169.
67. Obregón, *Ocho mil kilómetros*, 169–79; Katz, *Pancho Villa*, 364–67.
68. Obregón, *Ocho mil kilómetros*, 185–86; Katz, *Pancho Villa*, 367.
69. Obregón, *Ocho mil kilómetros*, 203.
70. Villa to Maytorena, August 24, 1914, JMMP, box 4, folder 9; Leon Canova to William J. Bryan, September 25, 1914, DS, 812.00/13326; Obregón, *Ocho mil kilómetros*, 199–210; Katz, *Pancho Villa*, 367–72; P. Castro, *A la sombra*, 34–36; "Manifiesto de don José María Maytorena," September 23, 1914, DHS, reel 9.
71. Hall, *Obregón*, 78; Katz, *Pancho Villa*, 373–74.
72. Barrera Fuentes, *Crónicas y debates*, 234–35.
73. Quoted in P. Castro, *Obregón*, 44.
74. See also Katz, *Pancho Villa*, 376–81.
75. Quirk, *Convention of Aguascalientes*; Katz, *Pancho Villa*, 382–85; Hall, *Obregón*, 85–89.
76. Ávila Espinosa, *Las corrientes revolucionarias*; Alessio Robles, *Historia política de la revolución*, 175–77.
77. "Manifiesto a la nación," in *DHRM*, I.1, 396–97.
78. Quoted in Quirk, *Convention of Aguascalientes*, 135.

79. Quoted in Aguilar Camín, "Antes del reino," 61.
80. Quoted in Aguilar Camín, "Antes del reino," 63.
81. Calles, "Informe relativo al sitio de Naco," January 20, 1915, DHS, reel 9; Simpich to Secretary, September 28, 1914, DS, 812.00/13318; Mumme, "Battle of Naco," 157–86.
82. Knight, *Mexican Revolution*, 2:302–3.
83. Calles, *Partes oficiales*, 1–62; "Acuerdo," January 1, 1915, enclosed in Hill to Carranza, March 17, 1915, AVC, carpeta 111, vol. 12750; Calles to Carranza, January 20, 1915, and Carranza to Calles, February 2, 1915, FP, ser. 0201, gav. 83, exp. 3, inv. 712 "Elías Calles, Plutarco (Gral.) 1915."
84. Almada Bay, *Maytorena*, 12.
85. L. Cárdenas, *Apuntes*, 1:66.
86. Joseph and Buchenau, *Mexico's Once and Future Revolution*, 65–73.
87. Cabrera, "La revolución es revolución," 274.
88. Hall, *Obregón*, 141–42.
89. Carranza, "Adiciones al Plan de Guadalupe."
90. Hall, "Alvaro Obregón and the Agrarian Movement," 127–30.
91. Quoted in P. Castro, *Obregón*, 47.
92. Richmond, *Carranza*, 71–74; Hall, *Obregón*, 114.
93. Obregón, *Ocho mil kilómetros*, 270.
94. Lear, *Workers, Neighbors, and Citizens*, 271–73; Aguilar Camín, *La frontera nómada*, 413; Hohler to Foreign Office, February 25 and 26, 1915, FO, 371/2396, file 15003, and 371/2398, file 40183; "Declaraciones del General Álvaro Obregón," February 25, 1915, AHSRE, L-E 1573.
95. Hall, *Obregón*, 116–17.
96. Obregón, *Ocho mil kilómetros*, 299–385; Katz, *Pancho Villa*, 487–98.
97. Obregón, *Ocho mil kilómetros*, 370–72.
98. Elías L. Torres, "Cómo perdió el brazo Obregón," in Archivo Histórico General y Licenciado Aarón Sáenz, Mexico City, exp. 183/1641.
99. Obregón, *Ocho mil kilómetros*, 372.
100. Quoted in Knight, *Mexican Revolution*, 2:328.
101. Calles to Obregón, February 15, 1915, JMMP, box 5, vol. 2; Katz, *Pancho Villa*, 387; Flores and Granados, *Alvarado*, 67.
102. Aguilar Camín, *La frontera nómada*, 415.
103. Calles, *Partes oficiales*, 1–62; Hostetter to Department of State, August 9, 1915, DS, 812.00/15822.
104. Gómez, *Lealtades divididas*, 63–65.
105. Calles, *Decretos 1915*, 3–9.
106. Maytorena, "Al noble pueblo de Sonora," August 30, 1915, JMMP, box 5, folder 15.
107. Calles, "Al valiente pueblo de Sonora," September 24, 1915, AHGES, vol. 3046.

108. Alarcón, *Maytorena*, 458.
109. "Weekly Report of General Conditions along the Mexican Border," November 13, 1915, DS, 812.00/16842; Naylor, "Massacre at San Pedro de la Cueva," 125–50; Katz, *Pancho Villa*, 520–26.
110. Garner, "Autoritarismo revolucionario," 238–99.

3. Inside the Revolutionary Regime

1. Richmond, *Carranza's Nationalist Struggle*, 83–101.
2. Richmond, *Carranza's Nationalist Struggle*, 121–24.
3. Haber, *Industry and Underdevelopment*, 132–38.
4. Radding de Murrieta, "El triunfo constitucionalista," 4:265–66; Aguilar Camín, "Antes del reino," 71. The term "laboratories of the revolution" is attributed to President Lázaro Cárdenas by Martínez Assad, *Laboratorio de la revolución*, 14. Cárdenas referred to the state of Tabasco in the 1920s, and not the state-level experiments during the Carranza era that preceded that case.
5. Calles, *Decretos 1915*, 15.
6. AHGES, vol. 3072; Calles, *Decretos 1915*, 17.
7. Calles, *Decretos 1915*, 34–41.
8. Farmer, "Plutarco Elías Calles," 238–41; Calles, *Decretos 1915*, 54.
9. Calles, *Decretos 1916*, 68–69; Farmer, "Plutarco Elías Calles," 242–43.
10. Calles, *Decretos 1916*, 51–57 and 86–87.
11. Farmer, "Plutarco Elías Calles," 182; Hall, *Obregón*, 108.
12. L. Cárdenas, *Apuntes*, 1:67.
13. Calles, *Decretos 1915*, 19–21, 41–45, 47–48; Farmer, "Plutarco Elías Calles," 339.
14. Calles, *Decretos 1916*, 59–61.
15. Calles to Moreno, March 19, 1916, AHGES, vol. 3129.
16. Quoted in Almada Bay, "De regidores porfiristas," 770–71.
17. Bantjes, "Regional Dynamics of Anticlericalism," 112.
18. Knight, "Revolutionary Anticlericalism," 28.
19. Obregón, *Ocho mil kilómetros*, 471.
20. Obregón, *Ocho mil kilómetros*, 471; Dabdoub, *Historia del Valle del Yaqui*, 198–99.
21. Calles, *Decretos 1916*, 62–64.
22. "Weekly Report of General Conditions along the Mexican Border," March 11, 1915, DS, 812.00/17592; Katz, *Pancho Villa*, 560–614.
23. Obregón to Enrique Estrada, March 28, 1916, ASDN, Archivo de Cancelados, exp. XI/III/1–44, vol. 1, 69.
24. "Weekly Report of General Conditions along the Mexican Border," January 15, 1916, DS, 812.00/17152; Bigelow to Hetrick, May 19, 1916; Commanding Officer to Commanding General, May 20, 1916, and Bigelow to Commanding General, September 12, 1916, MID, box 1940, 8534/80, 84, and 134; Cándido Aguilar to

Obregón, July 28, 1916, and Calles to Obregón, August 3, 1916, ASDN, Archivo de Cancelados, exp. XI/III/1–44, vol. 1, 93 and 96.
25. Guzmán Esparza, *Memorias*, 109–13; Carranza, "Decreto," n.d. [1916], AVC, carpeta 145, vol. 16751; Bigelow to Commanding Officer, April 4, 1916, MID, box 1940, 8534-50.
26. De la Huerta, "Informe," May 19, 1917, AHGES, vol. 3132.
27. Commanding Officer to Southern Department, May 20, 1916, MID, box 1940, 8534-84.
28. Buchenau, *Calles*, 65–70.
29. Calles to de la Huerta, August 9, 1918, FP, ser. 0202, gav. 83, exp. 2, inv. 719 "Elías Calles, Plutarco (Gral.) 1918."
30. Calles to Obregón, October 21, 1916, and Obregón to Calles, October 24, 1916, ASDN, Archivo de Cancelados, XI/III/1–44, vol. 1, 105–7.
31. Commanding General to Chief of Staff, October 30, 1916, MID, box 2163, 9700-42.
32. Aguilar, "Antes del reino," 75.
33. P. Castro, *A la sombra*, 42–43.
34. De la Huerta, "Informe," May 19, 1917, AHGES, vol. 3132; Guzmán Esparza, *Memorias*, 93–98.
35. Aguilar, "Antes del reino," 81–83; Castro Martínez, *De la Huerta y la Revolución*, 31–32.
36. Quoted in Hall, *Obregón*, 198.
37. Hostetter to Secretary, June 2 and 7, 1916, DS, 812.00/18409 and 18420.
38. Calles to de la Huerta, January 17, 1920, in Calles, *Correspondencia personal*, 1:36.
39. Figueroa, "La Revolución Mexicana y los indios de Sonora," 4:373.
40. Plutarco Elías Calles, "Aviso," August 30, 1916, AHGES, vol. 3063.
41. Guzmán Esparza, *Memorias*, 76–77.
42. Quoted in Dabdoub, *Valle del Yaqui*, 203.
43. "Weekly Border Report," March 31, 1917, MID, box 1943, 8536-207.
44. "Weekly Border Report," June 9, 1917, MID, box 1943, 8536-246.
45. "Weekly Report of General Conditions along the Mexico Border," February 3, 1917, DS, 812.00/20536.
46. "Weekly Border Report," January 20, 1917, MID, box 1943, 8536-156.
47. "Weekly Report of General Conditions along the Mexico Border," February 9, 1917, DS, 812.00/20512.
48. "Weekly Border Report," May 19, 1917, MID, box 1943, 8536-241.
49. "Manifiesto," AADH, ser. 01.02, exp. 3, inv. 20 "Decreto 71, Manifiesto Electoral y Artículo 123."
50. Obregón to Calles, June 5, 1917, FAO, ser. 020100, exp. 14, inv. 99 "Elías Calles, Plutarco (Gral.)."

51. Bantjes, *As If Jesus Walked on Earth*, 3. For a more nuanced view, see Almada Bay, *La conexión Yocupicio*.
52. Aguilar, *Saldos de la revolución*, 18.
53. Curley, *Citizens and Believers*, 100; "Informe rendido el día 10 de febrero de 1919 a la XXVIa legislature del Estado por el C. Gobernador Constitucional Gral. Manuel M. Diéguez," in *Jalisco y sus gobernantes*, 204; Aldana, *Diéguez*, 124–25.
54. Aldana, *Diéguez*, 165–71; Davis to Secretary, November 4, 1914, DS, 812.50/3.
55. Aguirre y Santiago, *Mis memorias de campaña*, 64; Knight, *Mexican Revolution*, 2:272.
56. Aldana, *Diéguez*, 138.
57. Curley, *Citizens and Believers*, 112–18.
58. Quoted in Aldana, *Diéguez*, 140.
59. Knight, *Mexican Revolution*, 2:272–88; Davis to Secretary, February 2 and 15, 1915, DS, 812.00/14486 and 14492.
60. Quoted in Knight, *Mexican Revolution*, 2:306; Curley, *Citizens and Believers*, 128.
61. Knight, *Mexican Revolution*, 2:211.
62. Enclosure in Daniels to Secretary, November 22, 1915, DS, 812.00/16843.
63. "Weekly Report of General Conditions along the Mexican Border," March 11, 1915, DS, 812.00/17592.
64. Quoted in Figueroa, "La Revolución Mexicana y los indios de Sonora," 372.
65. Davis to Secretary, May 17, 1916, DS, 812.00/18185.
66. Secretary of War to Secretary of State, September 29, 1917, DS, 812.00/21312.
67. Knight, *Mexican Revolution*, 2:305.
68. Curley, *Citizens and Believers*, 141–68.
69. Joseph, *Revolution from Without*, 93–96.
70. Alvarado's own account can be found in *Pensamiento revolucionario*.
71. Alvarado, *Pensamiento revolucionario*, 308.
72. Flores and Granados, *Alvarado*, 91.
73. Quoted in Bantjes, "Saints, Sinners, and State Formation," 139.
74. Alvarado to Carranza, January 25, 1916, in Buchenau and Henderson, *Mexican Revolution*, 125–27.
75. Osten, *Mexican Revolution's Wake*, 25.
76. S. Smith, *Gender and the Mexican Revolution*.
77. Joseph, *Revolution from Without*, 105.
78. Flores and Granados, *Alvarado*, 80–90; "Report on Conditions in Mexico," November 8, 1917, MID, box 2168, 9700-495; Hernández Chávez, "Militares y negocios," 187; Guyant to Secretary, May 15, 1916, DS, 812.00/18239.
79. Joseph, *Revolution from Without*, 141–42.
80. Joseph, *Revolution from Without*, 103–5.
81. Alvarado, *Pensamiento Revolucionario*, 1.
82. Joseph, *Revolution from Without*, 93–121.

83. Quoted in Flores and Granados, *Alvarado*, 14.
84. Quoted in Hernández Enríquez, *El genio de la raza*, ix.
85. Alvarado to Calles, August 12, 1917, and October 23, 1917, Calles to Alvarado, September 25, 1917, FEC, ser. 0202, exp. 19, inv. 874 "Alvarado, Salvador (Gral.)."
86. Hall, *Oil, Banks, and Politics*, 3.
87. Garcíadiego, "Constitución de 1917," 1183–270.
88. Niemeyer, *Revolution at Querétaro*, 31–42.
89. Richmond, *Carranza's Nationalist Struggle*, 108.
90. Sánchez Aguilar, "La integración del Congreso Constituyente," 1271–322.
91. P. Smith, "La política dentro de la revolución," 395.
92. Buchenau, *Last Caudillo*, 90.
93. Lieuwen, *Mexican Militarism*, 57–58.
94. Hall, *Obregón*, 143–44.
95. Bórquez, *Crónica del constituyente*; see also Hall, *Obregón*, 167–68.
96. Garciadiego, "Constitución de 1917," 1238; Knight, "Forjar constitución," 11–38.
97. *Diario de los debates del Congreso Constituyente*, 1:596.
98. De la Huerta, "Informe," May 19, 1917, AHGES, vol. 3132.
99. Bórquez, *Crónica del constituyente*, 66.
100. Niemeyer, *Revolution at Querétaro*, 64–65, 263–67.
101. Niemeyer, *Revolution at Querétaro*, 101–210. An English translation of the constitution is in Parker to Secretary, February 7, 1917, DS 812.011/31.
102. Archbishops to Carranza, September 10, 1917, AHAM, Mora y del Río, box 160, exp. 70.
103. Blancarte, "Personal Enemies of God," 589–90.
104. Spenser, *Impossible Triangle*, 51–58.
105. Quoted in P. Castro, *Obregón*, 57.
106. Quoted in Buchenau, *Last Caudillo*, 85.
107. Hall, *Obregón*, 200–201; memorandum, Col. Harry O. Williard, April 29, 1918, MID, box 1936, 8532-736/1; Hernández Chávez, "Militares y negocios," 192.
108. Enclosure in Hanna to Secretary, January 4, 1918, DS, 812.00/21636.
109. Memorandum, Col. Harry O. Williard, April 29, 1918, MID, box 1936, 8532-736/1.
110. Obregón to Francisco V. Bay, February 2, 1919, CDFVB, exp. 1, inv. 1 "Correspondencia con el general Álvaro Obregón," vol. 1.
111. Ibáñez, *Mexico in Revolution*, 58–59.
112. Lawton to Secretary, July 16, 1917, DS, 812.00/21141.
113. "Weekly Border Report," March 31, 1917, MID, box 1943, 8536-207; Farmer, "Plutarco Elías Calles," 264–80.
114. Quoted in Hall and Coerver, *Revolution on the Border*, 39.
115. Enclosures in Wright to Commanding Officer, June 25, 1917, and "Weekly Report," June 19, 1917, MID, box 1941, 8534-160 and 161; "Weekly Report of General Conditions along the Mexico Border," July 21, 1917, and Lawton to Secretary,

July 16, 1917, DS, 812.00/21140 and 21141; Farmer, "Plutarco Elías Calles," 280–301.
116. Lawton to Secretary, September 12, 1917, and border report, September 29, 1917, DS, 812.00/21282 and 21312.
117. Aguilar Camín, "Antes del reino," 83.
118. "Manifiesto al pueblo de Sonora," October 24, 1917, AHGES, vol. 3117.
119. Figueroa, "La Revolución Mexicana y los indios de Sonora," 373–74.
120. Calles to Nicolás Burgos, January 2, 1918, FEC, ser. 0204, gav. 86, exp. 56, inv. 1082 "Presidentes Municipales."
121. Réñique, "Race, Region, and Nation," 226.
122. Polk to Fletcher, December 24, 1918, DS, 312.115/354.
123. FPEC, ser. 010201, exp. 2, inv. 38 "Elías Calles, Plutarco (Gral. Gob.)," legs. 9–10; Farmer, "Plutarco Elías Calles," 210–19.
124. "Informe leído por el C. gobernador constitucional del estado de Sonora Gral. Plutarco Elías Calles," April 1, 1919, DHS, reel 10.
125. Anaya, "Banco Mercantil," 1–23.
126. Schuler, *Secret Wars and Secret Policies*, 168–228.
127. Katz, *Secret War*, especially 349–78.
128. Calles to Carranza, October 22, 1917, FP, ser. 0201, gav. 83, exp. 4, inv. 713 "Elías Calles, Plutarco (Gral.) 1917"; "Special Border Report," May 2, 1917, and Lipscomb to Southern Department, February 8, 1918, MID, box 1943, 8536-237, and box 1444, 8536-297; German military attaché to Auswärtiges Amt, July 8, 1918, PAAA, R 16917. After the war, one German agent even implausibly claimed a conspiracy with Calles to attack the United States in 1918. Harris and Sadler, "Witzke Affair," 41.
129. De la Huerta, *Informe*, 9–10.
130. "Special Border Report," February 23, 1917, MID, box 1943, 8536-168; Guzmán Esparza, *Memorias*, 102–3; de la Huerta to Calles, May 11, 1918, FP, ser. 02, exp. 2, inv. 719 "Elías Calles, Plutarco (Gral.) 1918."
131. Sáenz to Obregón, August 27, 1917, FAO, ser. 020200, exp. 98, inv. 243 "Sáenz, Aarón."
132. "Special Border Report," May 2, 1917, MID, box 1943, 8536-237.
133. "Report on Conditions in Mexico," November 8, 1917, MID, box 2168, 9700-495.

4. Triumph of the Sonoran Alliance

1. Guzmán, *Caudillos y otros extremos*, 193.
2. For this term, see Fuentes Díaz, *Partidos políticos*, 199.
3. L. Meyer, "La Revolución Mexicana y sus elecciones presidenciales"; Barbosa Guzmán, *Jalisco desde la revolución*, 59–95.
4. Hall, *Obregón*, 158, 172.

5. Richmond, *Carranza's Nationalist Struggle*, 152–53; Avent, "Representing Revolution," 12.
6. Jorge Prieto Laurens, "The Moral and Political Balance of the XXX Legislature," JWFD, box 6, vol. 7.
7. Fuentes Díaz, *Partidos políticos*, 206–7. Some historians incorrectly use the name Partido Cooperatista Nacional; see P. Castro, *Obregón*, 65, and Dulles, *Yesterday in Mexico*, 133.
8. Chasteen, *Heroes on Horseback*, 2–3.
9. Gerth and Mills, *Max Weber*, 358.
10. I have made this point previously in *Last Caudillo*, 6; see also Castro Martínez, "Álvaro Obregón," 209–29.
11. "Mexico's Latest Man of the Hour," *New York Times*, March 14, 1915.
12. Francisco Castillo Nájera, "Obregón: Ingenio y humorismo," FAO, ser. 060400, exp. 19, inv. 5146 "Homenajes 1947."
13. Quoted in Ibáñez, *Mexico in Revolution*, 59–60.
14. Quoted in Ibáñez, *Mexico in Revolution*, 60–62.
15. Santos, *Memorias*, 167. I appreciate Paul Gillingham's bringing this quote to my attention.
16. Krauze, *La presidencia imperial*.
17. For example, see Meyer, Sherman, and Deeds, *Course of Mexican History*, 441.
18. Osten, *Mexican Revolution's Wake*, especially 8–10, 22.
19. Hill to Obregón, February 27, 1919, and March 13, 1919, FAO, ser. 020700, exp. H-5/138, inv. 886 "Hill, Benjamín G. (Gral.)"; and Carrillo Puerto to Obregón, July 22, 1919, ser. 030100, exp. C-7/114, inv. 1183 "Carrillo Puerto, Felipe."
20. Obregón to Calles, October 18, 1919, FAO, ser. 030100, exp. C-1/189, inv. 1158 "Calles, Plutarco Elías (Gral.)."
21. Calles to Obregón and Calles to Serrano, October 14, 1919, FAO, ser. 030100, exp. C-1/189, inv. 1158 "Calles, Plutarco Elías (Gral.)."
22. Puente, *Hombres de la revolución*, 68.
23. "Alocución pronunciada por el Gral. Álvaro Obregón," DHRM, XVII:I:5, 79–80.
24. Lieuwen, *Mexican Militarism*, 52.
25. Alvarado to Obregón, August 22, 1919, FAO, ser. 020700, exp. A-2/30, inv. 778 "Alvarado, Salvador (Gral.)."
26. "Manifiesto del C. presidente a la nación," January 15, 1919, FFT, ser. 010202, exp. 5B1, 5B2/9, inv. 106 "Obregón, Álvaro (Gral.)."
27. "Los presidenciables, sus amigos actuales y futuros," *El Universal*, March 30, 1919.
28. Quoted in Castro Martínez, *La integridad*, 21.
29. Valadés, *Las memorias*, 29.
30. Alessio Robles, *A medio camino*, 25–26; Castro Martínez, *De la Huerta y la Revolución*, 79–81.

31. Quoted in Johnson, *Heroic Mexico*, 178.
32. Copies of both letters can be found in *Campaña política*, 22–39.
33. Womack, *Zapata*, 260–68.
34. McCaa, "Missing Millions," 367–400.
35. R. Smith, *United States and Revolutionary Nationalism*, 128–32; Hall, *Oil, Banks, and Politics*, 36–48.
36. "Don Venustiano Carranza, al abrir el Congreso las sesiones ordinarias el 1o de septiembre de 1918," in González y González, *Presidentes*, 3:250.
37. Thornton, *Revolution in Development*, 19–24.
38. Pani, *Apuntes*, 1:260–64; Haynes, "Orden y Progreso," 264–65; Guzmán Esparza, *Memorias*, 137.
39. Carranza to Calles, April 29, 1919, and Calles to Carranza, April 30, 1919, FP, ser. 01, exp. 7, inv. 716 "Elías Calles, Plutarco (Gral.) 1919."
40. Obregón, *Manifiesto*, 1–5.
41. Obregón, *Manifiesto*, 6.
42. Obregón, *Manifiesto*, 15.
43. Watkins to Obregón, July 8, 1919, FAO, ser. 030100, exp. 832, inv. 1902 "Watkins, Robert A."
44. Hill to Obregón, April 20, 1919, FAO, ser. 030100, exp. H-1/355, inv. 1425 "Hill, Benjamín G. (Gral.)," vol. 1.
45. Richmond, *Carranza*, 224.
46. Calles to de la Huerta, Mexico City, December 26, 1919, in Valenzuela and Chaverri Matamoros, *Sonora y Carranza*, 75.
47. Spenser, *En el gabinete de Venustiano Carranza*, 11–15.
48. "Declaraciones," November 25, 1919, in Calles, *Pensamiento político*, 50–51.
49. Buford, "Biography of Luis N. Morones," 6–47.
50. Hall, *Obregón*, 217–18.
51. Knight, *Mexican Revolution*, 2:10.
52. Quoted in Krauze, *Biography of Power*, 392.
53. Speech in Mazatlán, November 7, 1919, in Obregón, *Discursos*, 1:70–71.
54. Quoted in Dulles, *Yesterday in Mexico*, 20.
55. Quoted in Dulles, *Yesterday in Mexico*, 22.
56. Summerlin to Secretary, January 7, 1920, DS, 812.00/23328; Stewart to Secretary, February 17, 1920, DS, 812.00/23400.
57. "El estado mayor de Carranza era cueva de coyotes, dijo Calles," *La Prensa*, November 2, 1944.
58. Calles to Carranza, February 1, 1920, FPEC, ser. 010100, exp. 5, inv. 5 "Secretario de Industria, Comercio y Trabajo."
59. Calles to de la Huerta, February 1, 1920, in Calles, *Correspondencia personal*, 1:39.
60. Hernández Enríquez, *El genio de la raza*, 258; "Weekly Report on General Conditions on the Mexican Border," May 17, 1918, DS, 812.00/21993.

61. "Report on Conditions in Mexico," November 8, 1917, MID, box 2168, 9700-495.
62. "Carta abierta a los CC. Venustiano Carranza, Álvaro Obregón, y Pablo González," in Paoli, *Alvarado*, 99–115.
63. Hill to Obregón, September 25, 1919, FAO, ser. 030100, exp. H-1/335, inv. 1425 "Hill, Benjamín G., Gral.," vol. 5.
64. Summerlin to Secretary, January 20, 1920, and Burlington to Secretary, January 26, 1920, DS, 812.00/23338 and 23350; "Gen. Alvarado Released," *New York Times*, January 30, 1920.
65. "Carta abierta al C. presidente de la república," in Paoli, *Alvarado*, 116.
66. Aldana, *Diéguez*, 15, 162–63.
67. Aldana, *Diéguez*, 19.
68. Richmond, *Carranza*, 224.
69. De la Huerta to Calles, October 14, 1919, in Calles, *Correspondencia personal*, 1:27–28; Matute, *La carrera del caudillo*, 91–92.
70. Quoted in P. Castro, *Obregón*, 74.
71. Yost to Secretary, April 7, 1920, DS, 812.00/23775; de la Huerta to Carranza, March 30 and April 4, 1920, Carranza to de la Huerta, April 2, 1920, DHS, reel 10; P. Castro, *Obregón*, 73.
72. Calles to Diéguez, April 8, 1920, DHS, reel 10.
73. Aguirre, *Memorias de campaña*, 315.
74. Dulles, *Yesterday in Mexico*, 25–27.
75. Quoted in Hall, *Obregón*, 239.
76. Quoted in Castro Martínez, *La integridad*, 37n75.
77. Dulles, *Yesterday in Mexico*, 29–32; Hall, *Obregón*, 232–41; FFT, ser. 010201, exp. 22/41, inv. 66 "Movimiento revolucionario de 1920. Chilpancingo."
78. Castro Martínez, *Soto y Gama*, 11–46; Fuentes Díaz, *Partidos políticos*, 204–10.
79. A Spanish-language copy of the plan is in DHS, reel 10.
80. P. Castro, *Obregón*, 82.
81. David C. Bailey, interview with Gilberto Valenzuela, July 20, 1973, notes in private collection of David C. Bailey, kindly shared with author by Dr. Douglas Richmond.
82. Altamirano Cozzi and Villa G., *Los sonorenses y sus alianzas*, 2–8.
83. "Esta revolución será la más rápida, la menos sangrienta y la definitiva, dijo el general Calles," *El Universal*, May 8, 1920.
84. Dulles, *Yesterday in Mexico*, 35–36.
85. P. Castro, *Obregón*, 90.
86. P. Castro, *Obregón*, 99–103; Dulles, *Yesterday in Mexico*, 41–58.
87. Quoted from the English-language text in Parker to Secretary, February 7, 1917, DS 812.011/31.
88. Alessio Robles, *Ideales de la revolución*, 69.
89. Dulles, *Yesterday in Mexico*, 38–39, 86.

90. I will use the term "cabinet" for the sake of the English-language reader.
91. Castro Martínez, *De la Huerta y la Revolución*, 45–107.
92. Alvarado to Obregón, September 17, 1920, FAO, ser. 030400, exp. A-19/30, inv. 2046 "Alvarado, Salvador (Gral.)."
93. Summerlin to Secretary, August 3, 1920, DS, 812.00/24457.
94. Alvarado, *A Message from Mexico*, 10.
95. Summerlin to Secretary, November 23, 1920, DS, 812.00/24796.
96. Alvarado to Obregón, September 17, 1920, FAO, ser. 030400, exp. A-19/30, inv. 2046 "Alvarado, Salvador (Gral.)."
97. Calles to Obregón, July 2 and 6, 1920, FAO, ser. 030400, exp. C-7 y E-03/104, inv. 2120 "Calles, Plutarco Elías (Gral.)."
98. Katz, *Pancho Villa*, 722–24; de la Huerta to Obregón, July 17 and 19, 1920, FAO, ser. 030400, exp. H-27, H-012, y VD-12/387, inv. 2403 "De la Huerta, Adolfo."
99. Obregón to de la Huerta, July 17, 1920, FAO, ser. 030400, exp. H-27, H-012, y VD-12/387, inv. 2403 "De la Huerta, Adolfo."
100. De la Huerta to Obregón, July 18 and 19, 1920, FAO, ser. 030400, exp. H-27, H-012, y VD-12/387, inv. 2403 "De la Huerta, Adolfo."
101. Katz, *Pancho Villa*, 726–27.
102. Hill and Serrano to Obregón, July 26, 1920, FAO, ser. 030400, exp. H-17 y H-03/375, inv. 2391 "Hill, Benjamín (Gral.)."
103. Obregón to Hill and Serrano, July 26, 1920, FAO, ser. 030400, exp. H-17 y H-03/375, inv. 2391 "Hill, Benjamín (Gral.)."
104. Katz, *Pancho Villa*, 727.
105. Rivera Domínguez to de la Huerta, August 4, 1920, AADH, ser. 01.03, exp. 5, "Situación actual." For a recent study of Cantú, see Werne, *Esteban Cantú*.
106. "Informe que rinde el C. general Abelardo L. Rodríguez," February 15, 1922, Archivo Particular General Abelardo L. Rodríguez, Universidad Autónoma de Baja California, Tijuana (hereafter APALR), box 1; Vanderwood, *Satan's Playground*, 112; Werne, *Cantú*, 126–27.
107. P. Castro, *Obregón*, 92.

5. The Sonorenses in Power

1. "Gen. Benjamin Hill Dies in Mexico," *New York Times*, December 16, 1920.
2. Obregón to Mexican Consulate, September 7, 1921, Obregón to Mayo Clinic, December 14, 1920, and Carmen viuda de Hill to Obregón, June 7, 1921, Benjamín Hill Jr. to Obregón, January 2, 1923, and Obregón to Secretaría de Relaciones Exteriores, January 3, 1923, P-OC, 103-H-7, 103-H-8, and 818-X-15.
3. Miguel Alessio Robles, "El festín de los Borgia," *Universal*, July 4, 1938.
4. "Recognition for Obregon," *New York Times*, February 1, 1921.
5. Harding to Obregón, February 21, 1921, Obregón to Harding, August 18, 1921, FFT, ser. 010201, exp. 48/27, inv. 52 "Harding, Warren G."

6. Quoted in Hall, *Oil, Banks, and Politics*, 52.
7. Summerlin to Secretary, February 28, 1921, DS, 812.00/24876; Hall, *Oil, Banks, and Politics*, 54–57.
8. "El señor presidente Obregón, expone un programa de paz, moral y ley," *El Universal*, April 4, 1921.
9. Secretaría de la Economía Nacional, *Anuario*, 254; Vergara, *Fueling Mexico*, 142–43.
10. Hall, *Oil, Banks, and Politics*, 27–28; de la Huerta to Obregón, June 5, 1921, FFT, ser. 010201, exp. 39/29, inv. 54 "De la Huerta, Adolfo."
11. Hall, *Oil, Banks, and Politics*, 29–32.
12. De la Huerta to Obregón, June 13, 1922, FFT, ser. 010203, exp. 5/6, "Convenio de la Huerta-Lamont," vol. 2; Obregón to de la Huerta, June 14, 1922, FFT, ser. 010203, exp. 3/22, "Huerta, Adolfo de la. Invitación a Washington"; Hall, *Oil, Banks, and Politics*, 95–100; Lomelí, "La controversia de la Huerta-Pani," 214–15.
13. Calles to de la Huerta, June 28, 1922, APEC, gav. 9 bis, exp. 56, inv. 1379 "De la Huerta, Adolfo," vol. 6.
14. Hall, *Oil, Banks, and Politics*, 131–54; Castro Martínez, *De la Huerta y la Revolución*, 78–83.
15. Quoted in P. Castro, *Obregón*, 126-27.
16. Dulles, *Yesterday in Mexico*, 298.
17. Fallaw, *Religion and State Formation*, 17.
18. P. Castro, *Obregón*, 126.
19. Quoted in Mitchell and Schell, *Women's Revolution in Mexico*, 99. For the influence of women in the social and political life of the church, see Chowning, *Catholic Women*.
20. Filippi to Obregón, June 3, 1922, P-OC, 438-F-1.
21. "No se efectuará el homenaje a Cristo Rey," *El Universal*, January 11, 1923; "Entronización de Cristo Rey en el cubilete," *El Universal*, January 12, 1923; "La ceremonia religiosa en el Cerro de Cubilete," *El Universal*, January 13, 1923; "Expulsión de Mons. Filippi, delegado apostólico en México," *El Universal*, January 14, 1923; "Monseñor Ernesto Filippi, delegado apostólico, saldrá de México mañana," *El Universal*, January 15, 1923; "El Vaticano y el gobierno de México tratan el caso de Mons. Filippi," *El Universal*, January 17, 1923.
22. Hermelinda R. de Velasco, Unión de Damas Católicas Mexicanas de Cuernavaca to Obregón, January 15, 1923, P-OC, 438-C-8, vol. 2.
23. Quoted in Dulles, *Yesterday in Mexico*, 299; see also Obregón to archbishops, January 27, 1923, AHAM, Mora y del Río, box 123, exp. 54.
24. "El clero mexicano se dirige al presidente," *Excélsior*, February 7, 1923.
25. For an article that makes this point more generally, see Fallaw, "Mexican Revolutionary Anticlericalism," 481–509.
26. "La Iglesia Católica se dispone en México entrar de lleno en el campo de la acción social," *El Universal*, September 26, 1923.

27. Dulles, *Yesterday in Mexico*, 299.
28. Spenser, *Impossible Triangle*, 56.
29. Avent, "Representing Revolution," 12.
30. De la Huerta to Obregón, May 27, 1921, P-OC, 102-S-12.
31. "La bandera socialista ondeó ayer noche en la tribuna de la Cámara de Diputados," *Excélsior*, May 14, 1921; Dulles, *Yesterday in Mexico*, 129–31.
32. "Graves cargos de la mayoría para los Sres. Calles y de la Huerta," *El Universal*, May 18, 1921.
33. Dulles, *Yesterday in Mexico*, 132–33.
34. Fuentes Díaz, *Partidos políticos*, 205; Piccato, "El parlamentarismo," 83.
35. Fuentes Díaz, *Partidos políticos*, 207–8.
36. Jeffrey A. Weldon, "El presidente como legislador," 121.
37. "El ejecutivo desconoce a los nuevos magistrados," *El Universal*, January 9, 1923.
38. P. Castro, *A la sombra*, 54–64.
39. Dulles, *Yesterday in Mexico*, 15.
40. "El Gral. Álvaro Obregón, al abrir el Congreso las sesiones ordinarias el 1o de septiembre de 1922," in González y González, *Presidentes*, 3:508; "Cuál es el efectivo del ejército actualmente," *El Universal*, October 10, 1923.
41. Camp, *Generals in the Palacio*, 18.
42. Rath, *Myths of Demilitarization*, 9.
43. Cothran, *Political Stability and Democracy*, 73.
44. Russell, *History of Mexico*, 359.
45. T. Henderson, *Worm in the Wheat*, 92–93.
46. Obregón, *El problema agrario*. Quote is on pp. 24–25.
47. Baitenmann, *Matters of Justice*, 1–16.
48. "El Gral. Álvaro Obregón, al abrir las sesiones extraordinarias del Congreso, el 7 de febrero de 1921," in González y González, *Presidentes*, 3:423.
49. INEGI, *Estadísticas Históricas*, 329.
50. Quoted in Brunk, *Posthumous Career of Emiliano Zapata*, 66.
51. "Deseo que en lo sucesivo, dijo ayer el Sr. presidente, haya más ejidos y menos política," *El Universal*, November 27, 1921.
52. T. Henderson, *Worm in the Wheat*, 94.
53. T. Henderson, *Worm in the Wheat*; Joseph, *Revolution from Without*, 228–63; Wasserman, *Persistent Oligarchs*, 146; Okada, "Compañía Constructora Richardson," 91–143; P. Castro, *Obregón*, 162–65; Paxman, *Jenkins of Mexico*, 144–46.
54. Cedillo Fernández, "La diplomacia obrera," 144.
55. Brachet-Marquez, *Dynamics of Domination*, 58–61; Ruiz, *Labor and the Ambivalent Revolutionaries*, 74–78; Bailey, "Obregón," 87; P. Castro, *Obregón*, 144.
56. Brachet-Marquez, *Dynamics of Domination*, 59–61; Ruiz, *Labor*, 89–93.
57. Quoted in Snodgrass, *Deference and Defiance*, 49.
58. Quoted in Snodgrass, *Deference and Defiance*, 128.

59. Wood, *Revolution in the Street*, 51–63.
60. Obregón to de la Huerta, May 23, 1921; de la Huerta to Obregón, June 22, 1921, P-OC, 101-S-1 and 102-S-12.
61. Krauze, *Redeemers*, ch. 3.
62. Tenorio Trillo, *I Speak of the City*, 257.
63. Vaughan, *State, Education, and Social Class*, 134–48 and 165–89; Padilla, *Unintended Consequences*.
64. Rockwell, *Hacer escuela, hacer estado*, 55–56.
65. Quoted in Ruiz, *Triumph and Tragedy*, 379.
66. Vaughan, *State, Education, and Social Class*, 239–66; S. Smith, *Power and Politics of Art*.
67. "Alvaro Obregón," *Nation*, August 1, 1928, 106.
68. Mistral, *Croquis mexicanos*, 54.
69. Lacy, "1921 Centennial Celebration," 199–232; P. Castro, *Obregón*, 189.
70. Gómez, *Lealtades divididas*, 72–74.
71. Alessio, *Ideales*, 70.
72. Puente, *Calles*, 81.
73. Almada Bay, "De regidores porfiristas," 772.
74. Almada Bay, "De regidores porfiristas," 773–74.
75. Wasserman, *Pesos and Politics*, 2.
76. A. Rodríguez, *Autobiografía*, 101–5; Gómez, *Lealtades divididas*, 81–150.
77. Vanderwood, *Satan's Playground*.
78. Vanderwood, *Satan's Playground*, 148; Gómez Estrada, *Gobierno y casinos*, 38–63.
79. Vanderwood, *Satan's Playground*, 1, 119.
80. Vanderwood, *Satan's Playground*, 120; Rodríguez to Moneda, October 14, 1925, APEC, gav. 66, exp. 189, inv. 5010 "Rodríguez, Abelardo L., Gral.," vol. 5.
81. Gruening, *Mexico and Its Heritage*, 319.
82. Méndez Medina, "En los bordes de la corrupción," 209–48.
83. P. Castro, *A la sombra*, 117–26; T. Henderson, *Worm in the Wheat*, 141.
84. Collado, "Vida social y tiempo libre," 101–26.
85. Quoted in Gómez, *Lealtades divididas*, 188.
86. Gómez, *Lealtades divididas*, 186.
87. FPEC, ser. 010901, exp. 40, inv. 625 "Elías Calles, Plutarco (Gral.). Datos clínicos," and exp. 46, inv. 681 "Elías Calles, Plutarco (Gral.). Reportes Médicos."
88. Ibáñez, *Mexico in Revolution*, 52; Buchenau, *Last Caudillo*, 157; Gómez, *Lealtades divididas*, 187.
89. León to Obregón, n.d., FAO, ser. 050100, exp. 32, inv. 4828 "León, Luis L."
90. Macías Richard, *Vida y temperamento*, 269–71; FPEC, ser. 011100, gav. 72, exp. 153 "Elías Calles Ruiz, Manuel"; David C. Bailey, interview with Gilberto Valenzuela, July 20, 1973.
91. Gómez, *Gobierno y casinos*, 137; P. Castro, *A la sombra*, 90–91.
92. Sefchovich, *La suerte de la consorte*, 266.

93. Sefchovich, *La suerte de la consorte*, 225–29.
94. FPEC, ser. 010901, exp. 31, inv. 666 "Elías Calles, familia"; Macías Richard, *Vida y temperamento*, 272–78; Ramírez González, *Natalia Chacón de Elías Calles*; Buchenau, *Calles*, 19–20, 77–78, 92–93, 160–62.
95. A. Rodríguez, *Autobiografía*, 111–21; Sefchovich, *La suerte de la consorte*, 263–69.
96. P. Castro, *A la sombra*, 88–90.
97. Sefchovich, *La suerte de la consorte*, 221–22.
98. Krauze, *Biography of Power*, 376; Gómez, *Lealtades divididas*, 189–90.
99. Enclosed in Sheffield to Secretary, May 6, 1927, DS, 812.00/28405.
100. Santos, *Memorias*, 428–29.

6. The Triangle Broken

1. Quoted in Dulles, *Yesterday in Mexico*, 173–74.
2. "Conditions in Mexico," January 30, 1923, MID, box 800, 2064-354.
3. "Obregón to Pass Power to Calles," *New York Times*, March 8, 1923.
4. P. Castro, *Obregón*, 239.
5. Valenzuela, *La campaña presidencial*, 93.
6. Dulles, *Yesterday in Mexico*, 174–75.
7. "Discurso," January 20, 1921, in Calles, *Pensamiento político*, 53.
8. Osten, *Mexican Revolution's Wake*, 101.
9. Manzanilla to Obregón, November 12, 1920, FAO, ser. 030500, exp. 913, inv. 3787 "Manzanilla, D.A. (Dip.)."
10. On the anti-alcohol campaign, see Carrillo Puerto to Calles, April 3, 1922, APEC, gav. 12, exp. 25, inv. 830 "Carrillo Puerto, Felipe," vol. 3.
11. "Discurso," February 20, 1921, in Calles, *Pensamiento político*, 55–56.
12. "Discurso," February 27, 1921, in Calles, *Pensamiento político*, 57–59.
13. Calles to Carrillo Puerto, March 31, 1922, and March 8, 1923, APEC, gav. 12, exp. 25, inv. 830 "Carrillo Puerto, Felipe," vols. 3 and 5; see also the correspondence in Macías Richard, *Visiones sobre Felipe Carrillo Puerto*.
14. Carrillo Puerto to Calles, May 4, 1921, APEC, gav. 12, exp. 25, inv. 830 "Carrillo Puerto, Felipe," vol. 1.
15. Ridgeway, "Monoculture, Monopoly, and the Mexican Revolution," 143–69.
16. Martínez de Escobar to Obregón, July 28, 1919, FAO, ser. 030100, exp. M-031/452, inv. 1522 "Martínez de Escobar, Rafael (Lic.)."
17. Garrido to Calles, March 23, 1921, APEC, gav. 35, exp. 140, inv. 2312 "Garrido Canabal, Tomás (Lic.)," vol. 1.
18. Espinosa and Jaime Solís to Calles, February 15, 1923, APEC, gav. 29, exp. 68, inv. 1899 "Espinosa, Luis (Dip.)."
19. Calles to Obregón, February 19 and 21, 1923, and Obregón to Calles, February 20 and 23, APEC, gav. 56, exp. 5, inv. 4038 "Obregón, Álvaro Gral.," vol. 2.

20. Osten, *Mexican Revolution's Wake*, 79.
21. Osten, *Mexican Revolution's Wake*, 90, 122.
22. FEC, ser. 0401, exp. 5, inv. 1198 "Adhesiones a la candidatura presidencial del Gral. Plutarco Elías Calles. Chiapas."
23. "Mexico under the New Regime: General Calles and His Plans for the Reorganization of the Mexican Nation," *New York Times*, February 9, 1921.
24. Quoted in Alessio Robles, *A medio camino*, 65.
25. Puig Casauranc, *El sentido social*, 176.
26. "Declaraciones," September 6, 1923, in Calles, *Pensamiento político*, 69–71.
27. Buchenau, *Calles*, 102–9.
28. "Discurso," in Calles, *Pensamiento político*, 72–73.
29. "Discurso," in Calles, *Pensamiento político*, 78.
30. Guzmán Esparza, *Memorias*, 243–45; Valadés, *Las memorias*, 54.
31. Madrid, *Prieto Laurens*.
32. Guzmán, *Sombra del caudillo*; see also Valenzuela, *El relevo del caudillo*, 47–52.
33. Valadés, *Las memorias*, 56–58; undated fragment of de la Huerta's memoirs, AADH, ser. 01.04, exp. 4, inv. 33 "Candidatos a la presidencia."
34. Quoted in P. Castro, *Obregón*, 240n9.
35. Alessio, *Ideales*, 77–78; Castro Martínez, *La integridad*, 148.
36. Almada Bay, "De regidores porfiristas," 755–56; Dulles, *Yesterday in Mexico*, 164–65.
37. P. Castro, *Obregón*, 251.
38. Marsh to Secretary, September 29, 1921, DS, 812.00/25188; Carrillo Puerto to Calles, August 15, 1922, APEC, gav. 12, exp. 25, inv. 830 "Carrillo Puerto, Felipe," vol. 4.
39. See also Valenzuela, *El relevo del caudillo*, 47.
40. "Graves cargos de la mayoría para los Sres. Calles y de la Huerta," *El Universal*, May 18, 1921.
41. Summerlin to Secretary, March 27, 1923, DS, 812.00/26254.
42. Hall, *Oil, Banks, and Politics*, 160–62.
43. P. Castro, *Obregón*, 241–53.
44. Katz, *Pancho Villa*, 756–66.
45. Salas Barraza to Amaro, July 2 and 7, 1923, AJA, ser. 0101, exp. 50, inv. 50 "Jesús Salas Barraza," vol. 1.
46. Carriedo, "General Joaquín Amaro," 69–70.
47. Katz, *Pancho Villa*, 782.
48. Obregón to Calles, July 23 and August 2, 1923, and Calles to Obregón, July 25 and August 6, 1923, APEC, gav. 56, exp. 5, inv. 4038 "Obregón, Álvaro (Gral.)," vol. 3.
49. Castro Martínez, *De la Huerta y la Revolución*, 93–95; Lomelí, "La controversia de la Huerta-Pani," 216.

50. Osten, "Trials by Fire," 241.
51. Ankerson, *Agrarian Warlord*, 105–8; P. Castro, *Obregón*, 253–54; Osten, "Trials by Fire," 256–64.
52. "Contestación del Dip. Jorge Prieto Laurens," September 1, 1923, in González y González, *Presidentes*, 3:588.
53. "Sensacional Renuncia del Lic. Emilio Portes Gil," *El Universal*, September 4, 1923.
54. Osten, "Trials by Fire," 265–67; Dulles, *Yesterday in Mexico*, 186–88.
55. Obregón to Calles, September 25, 1923, APEC, gav. 56, exp. 5, inv. 4038 "Obregón, Álvaro, Gral.," vol. 3.
56. Alessio, *Ideales*, 86–87.
57. De la Huerta to Calles, September 25, 1923, APEC, gav. 22, exp. 56, inv. 1379 "De la Huerta, Adolfo," vol. 9.
58. Calles to de la Huerta, September 25, 1923, APEC, gav. 22, exp. 56, inv. 1379 "De la Huerta, Adolfo," vol. 9.
59. De la Huerta to Calles, October 4, 1923, FP, ser. 02, exp. 7, inv. 724 "Elías Calles, Plutarco (Gral.) 1923."
60. Quoted in Dulles, *Yesterday in Mexico*, 192.
61. Obregón to Calles, September 25, 1923, APEC, gav. 56, exp. 5, inv. 4038 "Obregón, Álvaro, Gral.," vol. 3.
62. "Declaración," n.d., APEC, gav. 22, exp. 56, inv. 1379 "De la Huerta, Adolfo," vol. 9.
63. Quoted in P. Castro, *Obregón*, 261–62.
64. Lomelí, "Pani-de la Huerta," 217–47; Dulles, *Yesterday in Mexico*, 192–96.
65. Guzmán Esparza, *Memorias*, 245–49.
66. "'Lion' Not Dead, Say Orbegon [sic]," *New York Times*, December 7, 1923.
67. Quoted in Castro Martínez, *La integridad*, 209.
68. Castro Martínez, *La integridad*, 210.
69. Buchenau and Henderson, *Mexican Revolution*, 186–88.
70. A U.S. intelligence agent quoting a conversation with Madero, "General Raoul [sic] Madero," December 18, 1923, MID, box 1660, 2657-G-432/29.
71. Castro Martínez, *La integridad*, 211.
72. Plasencia de la Parra, *Escenarios y personajes*; Piña, "Rebellious Citizens," 27–54.
73. "El Gral. Alvaro Obregón, al abrir el Congreso las sesiones ordinarias, el 1o de septiembre de 1924," in González y González, *Presidentes*, 3:621–22.
74. G-2 Reports, December 8 and 15, 1923, MID, box 1660, 2657-G-432/14 and 24; Summerlin to Department of State, January 1, 1924, DS, 812.00/26768; Lieuwen, *Mexican Militarism*, 76.
75. Garrido to Calles, December 23, 1923; APEC, gav. 35, exp. 140, inv. 2312 "Garrido Canabal, Tomás (Lic.)," vol. 2; Martínez Assad, *El laboratorio de la revolución*, 160–61.
76. Osten, *Mexican Revolution's Wake*, 118–20.
77. Calles to Puig Casauranc, in Calles, *Declaraciones y discursos políticos*, 79.

78. Calles to Arturo M. Elías, January 7, 1924, APEC, gav. 26, exp. 53, inv. 1717 "Elías, Arturo M.," vol. 9.
79. León to Puig Casauranc, July 3, 1924, FEC, ser. 0407, exp. 10, inv. 1317 "León, Luis L. (Ing. y Dip.)."
80. "Current Mexican Revolutionary Movement," December 22, 1923, MID, box 1660, 2657-G-432/26.
81. "Activities of General Plutarco Elías Calles," January 17, 1924, MID, box 1660, 2657-G-432/85.
82. "Mexican Disorders Not a Revolution, Obregón Declares," *Transcript*, January 6, 1924, in AADH, ser. 01.05, exp. 11, inv. 53 "Recortes de prensa norteamericana," vol. 2.
83. Calles to Obregón, January 19, 1924, P-OC, 101-R2-B-1.
84. "Asks Obregon to Resign," *New York Times*, December 15, 1923.
85. "General Raoul [sic] Madero," December 18, 1923, MID, box 1660, 2657-G-432/29.
86. Quoted in Hall, *Oil, Banks, and Politics*, 169. Obregón and Calles held a favorable view of Hughes after the Bucareli Agreement. See Calles to Gruening, August 31, 1923, APEC, gav. 38, exp. 64, inv. 2516 "Gruening, Ernest (Dr.)."
87. "Gompers Spurns Rebels," *New York Times*, January 31, 1924.
88. Castro Martínez, *De la Huerta y la Revolución*, 108–9; V. E. Dillon memorandum for Obregón, March 5, 1924, P-OC, 101-R2-I-1.
89. Quoted in Castro Martínez, *De la Huerta y la Revolución*, 118.
90. Zubarán Capmany to Palacios, May 22, 1924, AADH, ser. 01.05, exp. 15, inv. 57 "Palacios Macedo, Miguel."
91. L. Meyer, *Su majestad británica*, 347–48.
92. "Weekly Survey of Mexican Revolutionary Situation, February 1, 1924," MID, box 1661, 2657-G-432/60.
93. Ramírez de Aguilar, *Desde el tren amarillo*, 83–86.
94. Calles to Elías, January 7, 1924, APEC, gav. 26, exp. 53, inv. 1717 "Elías, Arturo M.," vol. 9.
95. Hernández Enríquez, *El genio de la raza*, x–xi.
96. Pérez Montfort, *Cárdenas*, 1:275.
97. "Manifiesto a la nación," February 20, 1924, APEC, gav. 22, exp. 56, inv. 1379 "De la Huerta, Adolfo," vol. 10.
98. Garrido to Calles, April 1, 1924, APEC, gav. 35, exp. 140, inv. 2312 "Garrido Canabal, Tomás (Lic.)," vol. 2; Osten, *Mexican Revolution's Wake*, 127–28.
99. No author, "viaje," January 19, 1925, P-OC, 104-E-57; Montgelas to Auswärtiges Amt, December 12, 1923, PAAA, R 28501; Pascual Ortiz Rubio to Auswärtiges Amt, March 12, 1924, and Ortiz Rubio to Stresemann, June 4, 1924, PAAA, R 79598.
100. Crespi to Segreteria di Stato, June 7, 1923, ASCAES, Quarto Periodo (hereafter QP), fasc. 16, pos. 493.
101. Crespi to Segretaria, February 8, 1924, ASCAES, QP, fasc. 16, pos. 493.

102. Crespi to Segreteria, November 16, 1923, ASCAES, QP, fasc. 16, pos. 493.
103. Crespi to Segreteria, March 12, 1924, ASCAES, QP, fasc. 16, pos. 493.
104. Shutan to Acting Chief of Staff, May 3, 1926, FEC, ser. 0905, exp. 1, inv. 1513 "Actividades revolucionarias mexicanas en Cuba."
105. Summerlin to Secretary, May 11, 1924, DS, 812.00/23990; Aldana, *Diéguez*, 543–45.
106. Castro Martínez, *De la Huerta y la Revolución*, 120; Plasencia, *Personajes*, 266–69.
107. "De la Huerta Funds Given to Wife," *New York Times*, January 17, 1924.
108. Castro Martínez, *De la Huerta y la Revolución*, 130–31.
109. P. Castro, *A la sombra*, 77–88.
110. "Rebel Deputies' Manifesto," *New York Times*, December 24, 1923.
111. "Morones Threatens Foes in the Chamber," *New York Times*, January 17, 1924.
112. See Obregón to Morones, January 25, 1924, FAO, ser. 010400, exp. 154, inv. 4690 "Morones, Luis N."
113. Castro Martínez, *De la Huerta y la Revolución*, 109–10.
114. Quoted in Cameron, *Mexico in Revolution*, 203.
115. Quoted in Justin Castro, *Radio in Revolution*, 1.
116. A. Rodríguez, *Autobiografía*, 123–26.
117. Obregón to Rodríguez, December 6, 1923, FFT, ser. 010214, exp. 88, inv. 1201 "Rodríguez, Abelardo L., General."
118. Rodríguez to Calles, December 29, 1923, APEC, gav. 66, exp. 189, inv. 5407 "Rodríguez, Abelardo L., General," vol. 4; Pani to Rodríguez, January 4, 1924; Rodríguez to Lubbert, January 14, 1924; Rodríguez to Obregón, February 3, 1924; Obregón to Rodríguez, February 5, 1924, APALR, box 3, exp. "Presidencia de la República"; Gómez, *Gobierno y casinos*, 146.
119. P. Castro, *Obregón*, 302.
120. Buchenau, *Calles*, 127.
121. "Declaraciones," December 8, 1923, in Calles, *Pensamiento político*, 85–87.
122. Crespi to Gasparri, May 5, 1924, ASCAES, QP, fasc. 16, pos. 493.
123. "Discurso," April 11, 1923, in Calles, *Pensamiento político*, 97.
124. Carr, *Marxism and Communism in Twentieth-Century Mexico*, 40–41.
125. "Discurso," May 24, 1924, in Calles, *Pensamiento político*, 130.
126. "Discurso," May 14, 1924, in Calles, *Pensamiento político*, 122.
127. Crespi to Gasparri, May 22, 1924, ASCAES, QP, fasc. 16, pos. 493.
128. "Informe confidencial relativo a la candidatura del general Calles," May 20, 1924, APEC, gav. 33, exp. 38, inv. 2210 "Gamio, Manuel."
129. Calles to Obregón, July 25, 1923, APEC, gav. 56, exp. 5, inv. 4038 "Obregón, Alvaro (Gral.)," vol. 3.
130. "Alocución radiofónica," April 12, 1924, in Calles, *Pensamiento político*, 95.
131. Dulles, *Yesterday in Mexico*, 265.
132. Buchenau, *Calles*, 111–12.

7. On Trial before the World

1. "Obregón President Four Hard Years," *New York Times*, November 30, 1924.
2. "D.," "Mexican Presidential Dilemma," 84.
3. Meyer, Krauze, and Reyes, *Estado y sociedad*, 97.
4. Antonio Ríos Zertuche, "La muerte del general Obregón," *El Universal*, July 29, 1963. According to Ríos, this pact committed Calles to providing the CROM with public funds. It also entailed the replacement of the federal army with CROM battalions and support for a Morones presidential candidacy in 1928. Seeking to prove Calles's and Morones's complicity in Obregón's assassination, Ríos's version must be read with great caution.
5. Cline, "Mexico," 86.
6. "Present Executive and Ministry," January 28, 1925, MID, box 1661, 2657-G-547/1.
7. "Las economías en el gobierno llegarán a más de cien millones," *Excélsior*, December 25, 1924.
8. Haber, *Industry and Underdevelopment*, 151.
9. "Present Executive and Ministry," April 20, 1925, MID, box 1661, 2657-G-547/3.
10. The law and congressional debate can be found in Archivo General de la Nación, *Boletín*.
11. Calles to Obregón, July 24, 1925, P-OC, 104-O-41.
12. Sheffield to Wadsworth, March 4, 1924, JRSP, series I, box 5, vol. 49.
13. Sheffield to Butler, November 17, 1925, JRSP, series I, box 5, vol. 49.
14. Kellogg, declaration to the press, June 12, 1925, DS, 711.12/546a.
15. Calles to Herbert Bayard Swope, June 18, 1925, APEC, gav. 18 bis, exp. 28, "Declaraciones del general Calles."
16. The English version quoted here is in *FRUS*, 1925, 2:518–20.
17. James M. Reeves, "Memorandum for the Chief of Staff," June 18, 1925, MID, box 1661, 2657-G-569/3.
18. L. Meyer, "La Revolución Mexicana y las potencias anglosajonas," 325.
19. Buford, "Morones," 98.
20. Clark, *Organized Labor in Mexico*, 109, 177.
21. Quoted in Buford, "Morones," 110.
22. Porter, *Flowering Judas and Other Stories*, 139–60.
23. Nacional Financiera, *Statistics on the Mexican Economy*, 350.
24. Dulles, *Yesterday in Mexico*, 282–85; Maurer, *Power and the Money*, 176–77.
25. Calles to Obregón, October 1, 1925, FFT, ser. 010206, exp. 16, inv. 437 "Obregón, Álvaro (Gral.) y Fernando Torreblanca," vol. 4; Calles to Torreblanca, July 1, 1925, and Calles to Obregón, July 22, 1925, FFT, ser. 010213, exp. 32, inv. 1099 "Obregón, Álvaro (Gral.)," vol. 2.
26. Pani, *Apuntes*, 2:47–53; Krauze et al., *La reconstrucción económica*, 83–84.

27. Meyer, Krauze, and Reyes, *Estado y sociedad*, 15.
28. Loyo, *Amaro*, 123–49.
29. Bess, *Routes of Compromise*, 19–38; Krauze et al., *La reconstrucción económica*, 98–107.
30. Hamilton, *State Autonomy*; Haber, *Industry and Underdevelopment*, 139–44; Salmerón Sanginés, *Aarón Sáenz Garza*, 25–103.
31. INEGI, *Estadísticas Históricas*, 329.
32. On Cedillo's eclectic approach to land reform, see Falcón, "Charisma, Tradition, and Caciquismo," 439–47.
33. Quoted in Knight, "Mexican Revolution," 25.
34. Dulles, *Yesterday in Mexico*, 282–87.
35. "Declaraciones," May 28, 1926, in Calles, *Pensamiento político*, 188.
36. Vaughan, *State, Education, and Social Class*, 100–279.
37. Marak, *From Many, One*, 11–12.
38. Quoted in J. Meyer, "Revolution and Reconstruction in the 1920s," 209.
39. Vaughan, *Cultural Politics in Revolution*, especially 3–30; Padilla, *Unintended Consequences*, 28.
40. Vaughan, *State, Education, and Social Class*, 146.
41. Bliss, *Compromised Positions*, 1–5.
42. Quoted in T. Henderson, *Mexican Wars for Independence*, 216.
43. Bailey, *Viva Cristo Rey*, 50–53.
44. "Varios mexicanos" to Crespi, March 2, 1925, enclosed in Crespi to Segreteria, March 9, 1925, ASCAES, QP, fasc. 21, pos. 499.
45. Butler, "Sotanas rojinegras," 535–58, and Butler, *Mexico's Spiritual Reconquest*.
46. Obregón to Calles, May 13, 1925, in Calles, *Correspondencia personal*, 1:145–46.
47. Bailey, *Viva Cristo Rey*, 57–61.
48. Quoted in Dulles, *Yesterday in Mexico*, 301.
49. Quoted in Gauss, *Made in Mexico*, 41.
50. J. Meyer, *Cristero Rebellion*, 37.
51. Andes, "Catholic Alternative to Revolution," 529–62.
52. J. Meyer, "Idea of Mexico," 282.
53. Weis, *For Christ and Country*.
54. "The Religious Crisis in Mexico," enclosed in Morrow to Secretary, February 27, 1928, DS, 812.404/867, 3–4. Hereafter cited as Lagarde memorandum.
55. Aldana, *Diéguez*, 154.
56. Scott, *Domination and the Arts of Resistance*, 18.
57. See Mora y del Río to Gasparri, July 25, 1917, ASCAES, Terzo Periodo (hereafter TP), fasc. 138, pos. 769; Quirk, *Mexican Revolution and the Catholic Church*, 100.
58. Quoted in Bailey, *Viva Cristo Rey*, 62.
59. "Habla el episcopado," *El Universal*, February 8, 1926.
60. Crespi to Segretaria, August 10, 1923, ASCAES, QP, fasc. 16, pos. 493.

61. Caruana to Pietro Fumasoni-Biondi, March 30, 1926, ASCAES, QP, fasc. 29, pos. 505.
62. Quoted in J. Meyer, *Cristero Rebellion*, 37.
63. Quoted in Russell, "Mexico: Political," February 8, 1926, MID, box 1664, 2657-G-616.
64. Bailey, *Viva Cristo Rey*, 63.
65. Bailey, *Viva Cristo Rey*, 64–66.
66. Bantjes, "Regional Dynamics," 112–14.
67. On Tejeda, see Wood, "Tejeda." On Amaro, see Loyo, "Amaro."
68. Sheffield to Secretary, February 23 and 26, 1926, DS, 812.404/294, 295, and 324; Weddell to Secretary, March 20, 1926, DS, 812.404/399; Early to Sheffield, March 26, 1926, DS 812.404/409.
69. Memorandum by Caruana, May 16, 1926, JRSP, series I, box 5, v. 50; Lagarde memorandum, 40–42.
70. Mora y del Río to Calles, May 18, 1926, and Calles to Mora y del Río, May 22, 1926, FFT, ser. 010215, exp. 22, inv. 1254 "Mora y del Río, José."
71. Calles to Mora y del Río, June 2, 1926, AHAM, Mora y del Río, box 123, exp. 53.
72. *Diario Oficial*, July 2, 1926, 1–4.
73. Quoted in "El estado y la iglesia en México," n.d., AJA, ser. 030703, inv. 291 "Correspondencia con el presidente Pascual Ortiz Rubio."
74. Lagarde memorandum, 68.
75. Bailey, *Viva Cristo Rey*, 82–85.
76. Lagarde memorandum, 16.
77. Butler, "Revolution in Spirit?," 1.
78. Lagarde memorandum, 5.
79. Quoted in Bailey, *Viva Cristo Rey*, 65.
80. Mora y del Río and Díaz to Calles, August 16, 1926, and Calles to Mora y del Río and Díaz, August 19, 1926, FFT, ser. 010215, exp. 22, inv. 1254 "Mora y del Río, José."
81. "Entrevista del presidente Calles con los obispos Leopoldo Ruiz y Pascual Díaz," August 21, 1926, APEC, gav. 3, exp. 137, inv. 364, "Arzobispos," vol. 1.
82. Morrow, "Memorandum of conversation with Lic. Mestre," March 8, 1929, DWMP, series X, reel 17; Bailey, *Viva Cristo Rey*, 91–93.
83. "Laymen of Mexico Plead for Church," *New York Times*, October 13, 1926.
84. The best scholarly explanation of campesino Cristero mobilization, as well as that of their agrarista opponents, is Butler, *Popular Piety*.
85. Purnell, *Popular Movements and State Formation in Revolutionary Mexico*, 79–102.
86. L. González, *Pueblo en vilo*, 201–8; Lagarde memorandum, 72.
87. Hernández Hurtado, *¡Tierra de cristeros!*, 82–91.
88. AGN, Secretaría de Gobernación, Dirección General de Investigaciones Políticas y Sociales (hereafter DGIPS), box 225, exp. 15.
89. There is no good scholarly biography of Gorostieta. For a popular treatment, see Grabman, *Gorostieta and the Cristiada*.

90. J. Meyer, *Cristero Rebellion*, 48–200.
91. Buchenau and Henderson, *Mexican Revolution*, 212–14.
92. Miller, "Role of Women," 303–23.
93. L. Meyer, *Mexico and the United States*, 107–14; Santiago, *Ecology of Oil*, 280–81.
94. L. Meyer, *Oil Controversy*, 110.
95. Horn, "U.S. Diplomacy and the Specter of 'Bolshevism,'" 32–33.
96. "Confidential Memorandum," initialed REO [Robert E. Olds], 1926 (no date), Yale University Library, New Haven CT, Arthur Bliss Lane Papers, box 56a, v. 986.
97. Burleigh, "Memorandum to the Military Attaché, Mexico City: The Policy of the War Department toward Mexico," July 20, 1926, AGN, Ramo Fondos Incorporados, Fondo Particular Emilio Portes Gil, box 321, exp. 3.
98. Bailey, *Viva Cristo Rey*, 100–102; Sheffield to Chandler P. Anderson, May 14, 1926, JRSP, series I, box 5, vol. 50.
99. Lane to Weddell, September 23, 1926, FEC, ser. 0901, exp. 4, inv. 1417 "Bliss Lane, Arthur y Alexander W. Weddell."
100. Buchenau, *In the Shadow of the Giant*, 165–74.
101. "A Concise Review of the Year 1926 in Mexico," December 31, 1926, FEC, ser. 0905, exp. 22, inv. 1534 "México-General."
102. Ovey to Foreign Office, November 4, 1926, FO 371, 11156.
103. Sheffield to William H. Taft, February 9, 1927, JRSP, series I, box 5, folder 52; Eugenia Meyer, interview with Gruening, November 4, 1969, PHO/4/3.
104. Horn, "Invasion of Mexico in 1927?," 454–71; Sheffield to Kellogg, July 1, 1926, JRSP, series I, box 5, vol. 51.
105. "Distribution of Troops," May 31, 1926, FEC, ser. 0905, exp. 8, inv. 1520 "México-Combate. Distribución de tropas"; Emilio Portes Gil, *Autobiografía*, 397; Sáenz to Kellogg, March 2, 1927, FFT, ser. 010213, exp. 14, inv. 1081 "Elías Calles, Plutarco (Gral.)," vol. 7.
106. For some of the consular correspondence regarding these rebels, see AHSRE, L-E-822 to 824.
107. Intercepted letters enclosed in Carrillo to Mexican Consulate, Los Angeles, October 7, 1927, AHSRE, L-E-852.
108. De la Huerta to Managing Editor, August 9, 1926, AADH, ser. 01.06.05, exp. 4, inv. 242 "Publicaciones de diferentes periódicos."
109. Kay, confidential memorandum enclosed in Arturo M. Elías to Soledad González, August 17, 1925, P-OC, 101-R2-I-1.
110. Kay, confidential memorandum.
111. Kay, confidential memorandum.
112. Dodson, *Fanáticos, Exiles, and Spies*, 69–73.
113. De la Huerta to Lt. Col. Juan Martínez in Rodríguez to Calles, January 19, 1927, FFT, ser. 010207, exp. "6"/223, inv. 674 "Rodríguez, Abelardo L." Quote in the original English.

114. Young, "Calles Government and Catholic Dissidents," 63–91; for the broader context of the Cristiada as a transnational event, see Young, *Mexican Exodus*.
115. Castro Martínez, *De la Huerta y la Revolución*, 128.
116. Plasencia de la Parra, "El exilio delahuertista," 117–18.
117. Dodson, *Fanáticos*, 87; Grijalva Dávila, "El ejército de Estrada," 165–210; Ferreira to Secretario, March 11, 1927, AHSRE, L-E-852.
118. Plasencia de la Parra, "El exilio," 107.
119. Dodson, *Fanáticos*, 87.
120. Capetillo, *La rebelión sin cabeza*.
121. González to Maytorena, February 14, 1927, JMMP, box 6, vol. 13.
122. Lubbert to Secretary, January 3, 1927, AHSRE, L-E-852.
123. L. Meyer, *Mexico and the United States*, 129.
124. INEGI, *Estadísticas históricas*, 333.
125. Haber, *Industry and Underdevelopment*, 150–56; Haber, "Assessing the Obstacles to Industrialisation," 28–29; INEGI, *Estadísticas históricas*, 666.
126. Antonio Villarreal, quoted in Krauze, *Biography of Power*, 399.
127. Obregón to Calles, October 12, 1926, FFT, ser. 010207, exp. "22"/174, inv. 625 "Obregón, Álvaro, Gral."; Davis to War Department, October 28, 1926, FEC, ser. 0905, exp. 2, inv. 1514 "Combinación política Calles-Obregón."
128. Obregón to Calles, January 17 and 20, 1927, FFT, ser. 010213, exp. 14, inv. 1081 "Elías Calles, Plutarco (Gral.)," vol. 2–3.
129. "Declaraciones del Gral. Obregón," *El Universal*, August 3, 1926; Obregón to Calles, August 15, 1926, FFT, ser. 010213, exp. 14, inv. 1081 "Elías Calles, Plutarco (Gral.)," vol. 1.
130. P. Castro, *Obregón*, 319–25; Meyer, Krauze, and Reyes, *Estado y sociedad*, 262–70.
131. Collado, *Dwight W. Morrow*; Calles to Burke, April 4, 1928, APEC, gav. 3, exp. 137, inv. 363, "Arzobispos," vol. 2.
132. Melzer, "Dwight Morrow's Role," 120–27.
133. Morrow to Sheffield, December 2, 1927, JRSP, series I, box 6, vol. 54–55.
134. Morrow to Sheffield, April 2, 1928, JRSP, series I, box 6, vol. 56.
135. Quoted in Dulles, *Yesterday in Mexico*, 356.

8. Almost Porfirio

1. This joke was related to the author by Luis Anaya Merchant.
2. Quoted in Krauze, *Biography of Power*, 392.
3. Krauze, *Biography of Power*, 399.
4. Juan de Dios Bojórquez, "El espíritu revolucionario de Obregón," in Romero et al., *Obregón*, 163–64.
5. Quoted in Buchenau, *Last Caudillo*, 138.
6. "Comment on Current Events," July 17, 1925, MID, box 800, 2064-489.

7. Francisco V. Bay to Fernando Torreblanca, December 9, 1930, FAO, ser. 060200, exp. 11, inv. 5063 "Bonificación Amigos Gral. Álvaro Obregón."
8. Gómez, *Lealtades divididas*; Ignacio P. Gaxiola to Rodríguez, April 9, 1925; Rodríguez to Gaxiola, April 17 and May 30, 1925, APALR, box 1, "Oficina comercial de Álvaro Obregón."
9. José Ramón García Jr., "Álvaro Obregón, you can love him or hate him, but he initiated his successful run for the Mexican presidency in Nogales, Sonora, Mexico," unpublished ms., 3. I appreciate the willingness of the FAPEC director, Norma Mereles de Ogarrio, to let me consult this manuscript in her personal possession.
10. For a refusal to pay the caudillo's debts, see Obregón to Torreblanca, January 19, 1925, FFT, ser. 010215, exp. 24, inv. 1256 "Obregón, Álvaro; Fernando Torreblanca."
11. Calles to Obregón, July 22, 1925, FFT, ser. 010213, exp. 32, inv. 1099 "Obregón, Álvaro (Gral.)," vol. 2.
12. Calles to Obregón, October 1, 1925, FFT, ser. 010206, exp. 16, inv. 437 "Obregón, Álvaro (Gral.) y Fernando Torreblanca," vol. 4; Calles to Torreblanca, July 1, 1925, and Calles to Obregón, July 22, 1925, FFT, ser. 010213, exp. 32, inv. 1099 "Oficina comercial de Álvaro Obregón," v. 2; Rodríguez to Gaxiola, May 30, 1925, APALR, box 1, vol. 5.
13. Interview with Alejandro Elías Calles Lacy, July 17, 2015.
14. Obregón to Bay, August 19, 1925, CDFVB, exp. 1, inv. 1 "Correspondencia con el general Álvaro Obregón," vol. 3.
15. Rodríguez to Obregón, June 17, 1926, APALR, box 1, "Construcción de tanque de guerra"; Obregón to Pani, Jan. 23, 1927, FFT, ser. 010207, exp. "5"/173, inv. 624 "Obregón, Álvaro (Gral.)."
16. Speech, November 3, 1925, FFT, ser. 010202, exp. 5D/14, inv. 111 "Obregón, Álvaro (Gral.) Discursos, Artículos," vol. 31.
17. Speech, March 14, 1926, FFT, ser. 010202, exp. 5D/14, inv. 111 "Obregón, Álvaro (Gral.) Discursos, Artículos," vol. 32.
18. Obregón to Bay, June 11, July 2, and July 13, 1926, CDFVB, exp. 1, inv. 1 "Correspondencia con el general Álvaro Obregón," vol. 4; Okada, "La Compañía Constructora Richardson," 132–36. Regarding the Mayo communities and irrigation techniques on the Fuerte River, see Mestaz, *Strength from the Waters*.
19. Gómez, *Gobierno y casinos*, 155; Gaxiola to Rodríguez, June 26, 1926, APALR, box 1, "Construcción de tanque de guerra"; Gaxiola to Rodríguez, March 23, 1927, and February 14, 1928, APALR, box 1, "Oficina comercial de Álvaro Obregón."
20. García, "Obregón," 3–4.
21. Interview with Alejandro Elías Calles Lacy, July 17, 2015.
22. Figueroa, "La Revolución Mexicana y los indios de Sonora," 367–78.
23. Figueroa, "La Revolución Mexicana y los indios de Sonora," 376; "Political and Economic Conditions in Mexico," September 8, 1926, FEC, ser. 0903, exp. 17, inv. 1489 "Weddell, Alexander W.," vol. 2.

24. Castro to "M," September 20, 1926, AADH, ser. 01.06.01, exp. 31, inv. 88 "Castro, Luis G.," vol. 1.
25. Matus to de la Huerta, December 10, 1926, AADH, ser. 01.06.01, exp. 91, inv. 148 "Matus, Luis"; Maxwell to Secretary, September 15, 1926, FEC, ser. 0902, exp. 17, inv. 1458 "Maxwell."
26. Memoranda, Edward Davis, December 14, 1926, and January 18, 1927, FEC, ser. 0905, exp. 9, inv. 1521 "México-Combate. Distribución de tropas. La campaña Yaqui."
27. Castro to "M," June 19, 1927, AADH, ser. 01.06.01, exp. 31, inv. 88 "Castro, Luis G.," vol. 1.
28. Unsigned memorandum, May 24, 1927, AADH, ser. 01.06.01, exp. 9, inv. 224 "Movimientos armados"; Achondo to Secretary, December 6, 1926, and Matus to de la Huerta, April 11, 1927, AHSRE, L-E-851; Dodson, *Fanáticos, Exiles, and Spies*, 73–84; P. Castro, *Obregón*, 321, 330; Plasencia, "El exilio," 124.
29. "Testamento," March 27, 1927, FAO, ser. 060300, exp. 18, inv. 5118 "Obregón, Alvaro (Gral.): Testamento."
30. Tobler, "La burguesía revolucionaria," 216, 221.
31. Sheffield to Secretary, April 6, 1926, DS, 812.00/27754.
32. Quoted in Daniel Cazes, interview with Luis Sánchez Pontón, April 1961, PHO/1/20.
33. "Political and Economic Conditions in Mexico," April 3, 1926, FEC, ser. 0903, exp. 17, inv. 1489 "Weddell, Alexander W.," vol. 1.
34. "National Elections," April 4, 1926, FEC, ser. 0905, exp. 23, inv. 1535 "México-Político. Elecciones."
35. Obregón to Torreblanca, March 6, 1926, FFT, ser. 010215, exp. 24, inv. 1256 "Obregón, Álvaro; Fernando Torreblanca."
36. Quoted in Meyer, Krauze, and Reyes, *Estado y sociedad*, 124.
37. Osten, *Mexican Revolution's Wake*, 205.
38. "Boletín para la prensa," August 3, 1927, FFT, ser. 010212, exp. 24, inv. 880 "Boletines de Prensa," vol. 1.
39. M. Rodríguez, *Movements after Revolution*.
40. "Political and Economic Conditions in Mexico," April 3, 1926, FEC, ser. 0903, exp. 17, inv. 1489 "Weddell, Alexander W.," vol. 1; P. Castro, *A la sombra*, 69–88, 127–48.
41. Santos, *Memorias*, 318.
42. See also "La muerte del general Obregón," *El Universal*, July 29, 1963; Edward Davis, G-2 reports, April 23 and October 29, 1926, MID, box 1665, 2657-G-622/2 and 6.
43. David C. Bailey, interview with Gilberto Valenzuela, July 20, 1973.
44. "El Sr. presidente Calles no aprueba la reelección," *Excélsior*, October 20, 1925; see also "M" to Samuel Belden, October 6, 1925, AADH, ser. 01.06.01, exp. 15, inv. 72 "Belden, Samuel."

45. "M" to Palafox, July 4, 1925, AADH, ser. 01.06.01, exp. 104, inv. 161 "Palafox, Ismael."
46. "Political and Economic Conditions in Mexico," April 3, 1926, FEC, ser. 0903, exp. 17, inv. 1489 "Weddell, Alexander W."; see also "National Elections," April 4, 1926, FEC, ser. 0905, exp. 23, inv. 1535 "México-Político. Elecciones."
47. For example, see the episode recounted in Dulles, *Yesterday in Mexico*, 332–33.
48. "La muerte del general Obregón," *El Universal*, July 29, 1963, quoting Antonio Ríos Zertuche.
49. "Acuerdo privado provisional entre el General de División Álvaro Obregón, por sus propios derechos, y el señor Arturo de Saracho como representante del Sr. Luis N. Morones," February 10, 1926, FEC, ser. 0903, exp. 17, inv. 1489 "Weddell, Alexander W.," vol. 2.
50. "National Elections," April 23, 1926, FEC, ser. 0905, exp. 23, inv. 1535 "México-político. Elecciones."
51. Quoted in Guillermo Fárber, "Francisco R. Serrano: La sombra del caudillo o de las armas a las urnas," CFRS, box 1, exp. 4, "Estudios y datos biográficos," 4.
52. Obregón to Bay, October 5, 1926, CDFVB, exp. 1, inv. 1 "Correspondencia con el general Álvaro Obregón," vol. 4; Gómez, *Lealtades divididas*, 179.
53. "El Gral. Francisco Serrano emprenderá hoy el viaje de regreso a tierra mexicana," *Excélsior*, April 25, 1926; Serrano to Micaela Jáuregui, June 28 and August 3, 1925, CFRS, box 1, exps. 20 and 21, "Asuntos personales"; "Equipment: Acquisitions," January 28, 1927, FEC, ser. 0905, exp. 7, inv. 1519 "México-combate. Adquisiciones militares."
54. P. Castro, *A la sombra*, 92; no author to Adalberto Tejeda, February 1, 1926, DGIPS, box 106, exp. 44; Gómez, *Lealtades divididas*, 182.
55. "Probable Presidential Candidates," April 12, 1927, MID, box 1664, 2657-G-622/11.
56. "La muerte del general Obregón," *El Universal*, July 29, 1963.
57. P. Castro, *A la sombra*, 111–12.
58. P. Castro, *A la sombra*, 128–42.
59. "Probable Presidential Candidates," April 12, 1927, MID, box 1664, 2657-G-622/11; P. Castro, *Obregón*, 335.
60. "National Elections," April 4 and 23, 1926, FEC, ser. 0905, exp. 23, inv. 1535 "México-político. Elecciones."
61. "Political and Economic Conditions in Mexico, April 1926," FEC, ser. 0903, exp. 17, inv. 1489, "Weddell, Alexander W.," vol. 1.
62. Agente Especial no. 7 to Oficina Confidencial, July 3, 1927, DGIPS, box C2046-B, exp. 3.
63. "La próxima convención," *El Universal*, June 14, 1927, "El programa de gobierno del Gral. Arnulfo R. Gómez," *El Universal*, June 24, 1927; "Plataforma de acción política del partido nacional antirreeleccionista," *Excélsior*, July 2, 1927.
64. "La muerte del general Obregón," *El Universal*, July 30, 1963.

65. P. Castro, *A la sombra*, 127–28.
66. "Crueles enseñanzas de la política," *El Universal*, June 5, 1939; see also Marte R. Gómez, letter to John W. F. Dulles, December 2, 1955, cited in Dulles, *Yesterday in Mexico*, 354.
67. "La tragedia de Huitzilac," *El Universal*, April 13, 1937.
68. Speech in Mexico City, June 25, 1927, in Obregón, *Discursos*, 2:68–83.
69. "Discurso," July 1, 1927, in Obregón, *Discursos*, 2:85–93.
70. "Discurso," July 16, 1927, in Obregón, *Discursos*, 2:129.
71. Agente Especial no. 7 to Oficina Confidencial, July 3, 1927; DGIPS, box C2046-B, exp. 3.
72. Quoted in Fárber, "Francisco R. Serrano," CFRS, box 1, exp. 4, "Estudios y datos biográficos," 10.
73. "GG" to anonymous, August 27, 1927, AADH, ser. 01.06.01, exp. 60, inv. 117 "GG."
74. Richkarday, *60 años en la vida de México*, 152.
75. Rodríguez to Platt, May 14, 1927, APALR, box 2, exp. "Juan R. Platt."
76. Rodríguez to Platt, July 11, 1927, APALR, box 2, exp. "Juan R. Platt."
77. For these efforts, see Osten, *Mexican Revolution's Wake*, 209–14.
78. Serrano to Vidal, September 23, 1927, FFT, ser. 010212, exp. 204, inv. 1060, "Vidal, Carlos A. (Gral.)."
79. "Discurso," July 2, 1927, in Obregón, *Discursos*, 2:97.
80. "Manifiesto a la nación," CFRS, box 1, exp. 6, "Documentos de campaña para la presidencia."
81. FFT, ser. 010207, exp. 50, inv. 906, "Discursos serranistas."
82. "Protesta ante la nación," August 24, 1927, FFT, ser. 010212, exp. 24, inv. 889 "Boletines de prensa," vol. 1.
83. "El Gral. Gómez en Tampico y Cd. Victoria," *El Universal*, August 1, 1927.
84. Quoted in Lieuwen, *Mexican Militarism*, 64–65.
85. P. Castro, *Obregón*, 351–52.
86. Castro to "M," August 21, 1927, AADH, ser. 01.06.01, exp. 31, inv. 88 "Castro, Luis G.," vol. 1.
87. Dulles, *Yesterday in Mexico*, 240–44; Schoenfeld to Secretary, September 3, 1927, DS, 812.00/28708.
88. For example, FEC, ser. 0902, exp. 17, inv. 1489 "Weddell, Alexander W.," and FEC, ser. 0906, exp. 14, inv. 1561 "Informes confidenciales emitidos por 10-B."
89. P. Castro, *Obregón*, 361.
90. "El brindis del Sr. general Arnulfo R. Gómez," FFT, ser. 010207, exp. 50, inv. 906 "Discursos serranistas."
91. Quoted in Miguel Alessio Robles, "La paloma y el gavilán," *El Universal*, April 19, 1937.
92. Quoted in "Sensacional declaración del Gral. Álvarez," *El Universal*, February 18, 1938.

93. P. Castro, *A la sombra*, 182, and *Obregón*, 363–64. The letters referenced above that informed Calles of insurrectionary activities also contained the outlines of this plot: "San Pedro" to Calles, September 21 and 24, 1927, FFT, ser. 010207, exp. "105"/246, inv. 697 "Serrano, Francisco R. (Gral.); Arnulfo R. Gómez (Gral.)." For an eyewitness account, see "Cómo iban a ser fusilados Obregón, Calles, y Amaro," *La Prensa*, October 25, 1945.
94. Undated, unsigned memorandum, FFT, ser. 010207, exp. "86"/245, inv. 696 "Serrano, Francisco R. (Gral.); Arnulfo R. Gómez (Gral.)"; "San Pedro" to Calles, September 21 and 24, 1927, FFT, exp. "105"/246, inv. 697 "Serrano, Francisco R. (Gral.); Arnulfo R. Gómez (Gral.)"; Villavicencio, memorandum for Fernando Torreblanca, September 1927, exp. "181"/292, inv. 743 "Villavicencio, Leonel."
95. Schoenfeld to Secretary, September 27, 1927, DS, 812.00/28767.
96. Schoenfeld to Secretary, October 3 and 4, 1927, DS, 812.00/28817 and 28776; "El Sr. Presidente habla de la sublevación militar," *El Universal*, October 4, 1927.
97. Osten, "Out of the Shadows," 181.
98. Schoenfeld to Secretary, October 24, 1927, DS, 812.00/28919.
99. Schoenfeld to Secretary, October 24, 1927, DS, 812.00/28919.
100. Richkarday, *60 años*, 208.
101. Richkarday, *60 años*, 210; Fox quoted in "Cómo fueron asesinados el general Serrano y sus 13 acompañantes en Huitzilac," *El Nacional*, November 12, 1937.
102. Quoted in "Obregón ajeno al sacrificio de Fco Serrano," *Excélsior*, August 16, 1938.
103. P. Castro, *Obregón*, 374.
104. G-2 report, October 5, 1927, MID, box 1665, 2657-G-622/22.
105. Almada, "¿Cuál triángulo sonorense?," 202. Alfonso había ayudado a su hermano — Alfonso had helped his brother provision Yaqui rebels with arms and ammunition, and authorities in Arizona had prepared to arrest him in mid-September. Achondo to Consul in El Paso, Sep. 19, 1927, AHSRE, L-E-851.
106. "Gomez and Huerta in Alliance," *New York Times*, October 8, 1928.
107. Dulles, *Yesterday in Mexico*, 353.
108. Quoted in "El general Luis Garfias Magaña reproduce el oficio de Calles con la orden de matar al general Serrano," CFRS, box 1, "Sucesos de Huitzilac," exp. 36.
109. Quoted in P. Castro, *Obregón*, 376–77.
110. Quoted in P. Castro, *Obregón*, 373. The reference is to Serrano's name day.
111. Luis Cabrera, *Veinte años después*, 135–36.
112. Francisco R. Serrano Méndez to Ernesto Zedillo, July 31, 1997, CFRS, box 1, "Sucesos de Huitzilac," exp. 38.
113. Speech in Orizaba, Veracruz, April 20, 1928, in *Discursos*, 2:382.
114. Juan Manuel Álvarez de Castillo to Obregón, October 6, 1927, FAPEC, Archivo Plutarco Elías Calles Anexo, Fondo Soledad González, exp. 540, inv. 471 "Obregón, Alvaro (Gral.)."

115. Dulles, *Yesterday in Mexico*, 313–15, 356.
116. Quoted in Krauze, *Biography of Power*, 402.
117. Weis, *For Christ and Country*, 2–6.
118. Almada Bay, "De regidores porfiristas," 768.
119. Ramón Puente, "Obregón," in *La dictadura, la revolución y los hombres*, 181.
120. Nemesio García Naranjo, open letter to the Duke of Alba, "Los verdaderos alteradores de la paz mexicana," August 28, 1928, AADH, ser. 01.05, exp. 11, inv. 53 "Prensa," vol. 2.
121. Almada Bay, "Las dos mitades de Plutarco Elías Calles," 1162.
122. León, *Crónica del poder*, 272.
123. Quoted in Serrano Álvarez, "La muerte de un caudillo," 275.
124. Manuel Ramos to Soto y Gama, May 18, 1928; anonymous to Soto y Gama, [June 27, 1928?], FFT, ser. 010207, exp. "234"/182, inv. 633 "Obregón, Álvaro (Gral.)."
125. Meyer, Segovia, and Lajous, *Los inicios*, 18. For an excellent summary of the various theories, see P. Castro, *Obregón*, 394–414.
126. "La muerte del general Obregón," *El Universal*, July 29, 30, 31, and August 1, 1963; "Plutarco Elías Calles fue quien ordenó el asesinato del Gral. Álvaro Obregón," *La Prensa*, December 6, 1985.
127. Eulogy by Luis L. León, October 19, 1964, FPEC, ser. 011400, exp. 20 "Homenajes 1964."
128. "El Gral. Plutarco Elías Calles, al abrir las sesiones ordinarias el Congreso, el 10 de septiembre de 1928," in González y González, *Presidentes*, 3:805.
129. Manjarrez, *La jornada institucional*, 1:24; "La Junta de Jefes de Operaciones," *El Universal*, September 6, 1928.
130. FFT, ser. 010213, gav. 45, exp. 26, inv. 1093 "Junta de los generales," vol. 1, 5–6.
131. "El ejército actual ante la historia," *El Universal*, September 6, 1928.
132. Dulles, *Yesterday in Mexico*, 393.
133. G-2 report, October 30, 1928, MID, box 1665, 2657-G-657/5.
134. Portes Gil, *Emilio Portes Gil*, 119.
135. Puig, *Galatea rebelde*, 309.
136. Dulles, *Yesterday in Mexico*, 386.

9. From Caudillos to Institutions

1. Córdova, *La revolución en crisis*, 23.
2. Quoted in Dulles, *Yesterday in Mexico*, 358.
3. Garrido, *El Partido de la Revolución institucionalizada*, 103–232.
4. León, *Crónica del poder*, 294–96.
5. "Discurso," December 6, 1928, in Calles, *Pensamiento político*, 280–81.
6. "Comunicado," December 7, 1928, APEC, gav. 21, exp. 28, inv. 1353 "Declaraciones del General Plutarco Elías Calles," vol. 3.

7. Garrido, *El Partido de la Revolución institucionalizada*, 99–102.
8. Osten, *Mexican Revolution's Wake*, 234–64.
9. Quoted in Meyer, Segovia, and Lajous, *Los inicios*, 47.
10. "Programa de Trabajo del PNR," FPEC, ser. 010801, exp. 6, inv. 393 "Plano Nacional, El," vol. 1.
11. "Planes radicales," *El Nacional Revolucionario*, May 27, 1929.
12. Buchenau, *Calles*, 149–51.
13. Agente 24, "Memorandum," January 22, 1929, DGIPS, box 54, exp. 11.
14. Saragoza, *Monterrey Elite*, 120–25; Dulles, *Yesterday in Mexico*, 415.
15. Santos, *Memorias*, 349.
16. Meyer, Segovia, and Lajous, *Los inicios*, 59–63; Ortiz Rubio, *Memorias*, 209.
17. Fowler-Salamini, *Agrarian Radicalism in Veracruz*; Ginzberg, *Revolutionary Ideology*, 34–37.
18. Garrido, *El Partido de la Revolución institucionalizada*, 103.
19. Medin, *El minimato presidencial*, 41.
20. Cárdenas to Calles, December 8, 1928, AGN, Archivo Particular de Lázaro Cárdenas, reel 15:1.
21. "Discurso pronunciado por el Lic. Aarón Sáenz," July 17, 1929, FAO, ser. 060400, gav. 33, exp. 2, inv. 5129 "Homenaje 1929."
22. Dulles, *Yesterday in Mexico*, 673, attributes the term to Abelardo Rodríguez.
23. Benjamin, *La revolución*, 131; Buchenau, "Arm and Body of a Revolution," 179–206; Olsen, *Artifacts of Revolution*, 77–84.
24. "Homenaje al Gral. Obregón," *El Universal*, July 18, 1931.
25. "Solemne Velada de Homenaje al Gral. Obregón," *El Universal*, July 18, 1932.
26. "Plan de Hermosillo," in Iglesias, *Planes políticos*, 956–60.
27. G-2 reports, February 21 and March 5, 1929, MID, box 1665, 2657-G-657/8 and 11.
28. Rodríguez, "Soldiers of the Army in Sonora," March 8, 1929, MID, box 1660, 2657-G-605/161. Translated by U.S. intelligence agent.
29. Vanderwood, *Satan's Playground*, 302.
30. FPEC, ser. 010802, exp. 1, inv. 395 "Rebelión escobarista."
31. "Movimiento rebelde en Sonora y Veracruz," *El Universal*, March 4, 1929.
32. De la Huerta to Escobar, June 27, 1925, APEC, gav. 22, exp. 56, inv. 1388 "De la Huerta, Adolfo," vol. 10.
33. "Recado telefónico," February 22, 1929, in Calles, *Correspondencia personal*, 1:210–11.
34. De la Huerta to Calles, June 9, 1929, APEC, gav. 22, exp. 56, inv. 1388 "De la Huerta, Adolfo," vol. 10.
35. Agente 24, "Actividades sediciosas. Movimiento rebelde Escobar-Manzo y socios," April 1, 4, and 20, 1929, DGIPS, box 54, exp. 11.
36. Ragsdale, *Wings over the Mexican Border*, 3–57.

37. Camp, *Generals in the Palacio*, 20.
38. "Declaraciones," May 22, 1929, in Calles, *Pensamiento político*, 289–92; Camp, *Generals in the Palacio*, 67.
39. "Declaraciones," May 22, 1929, 288.
40. Rodríguez to Portes Gil, October 1, 1929; Portes Gil to Rodríguez, December 31, 1929, AALR, 01.01.03, exp. "Renuncia al cargo de gobernador y exposición de motivos."
41. For this term, see Amaya, *Los gobiernos de Obregón, Calles y regímenes peleles*. Amaya was a participant in the Escobar rebellion. As an example of scholarly views, see Gonzales, *Mexican Revolution*, 220.
42. Portes Gil, *Portes Gil*, 125.
43. G-2 report, May 8, 1929, MID, box 1664, 2657-G-616/26.
44. Quirk, *Mexican Revolution and the Catholic Church*, 238–39.
45. Morrow, draft statements for Ruiz and Portes Gil, May 11 and June 13, 1929, DWMP, series X, reel 17.
46. G-2 reports, June 25 and July 3, 1929, MID, box 1664, 2657-G-616/31; Bailey, *Viva Cristo Rey*, 255.
47. Nicolson, *Dwight Morrow*, 347.
48. Nacional Financiera, *Statistics on the Mexican Economy*, 358.
49. Pérez Treviño to Calles, undated, and Calles to Pérez Treviño, September 30, 1929, FFT, ser. 010803, exp. 38, inv. 433 "Pérez Treviño, Manuel."
50. INEGI, *Estadísticas Históricas*, 329.
51. Cárdenas to Amaro, January 25 and February 2, 1929, AJA, ser. 030123, "Cárdenas del Río, Lázaro."
52. Pani, *Apuntes*, 2:111.
53. Pérez Treviño to Calles, August 30, 1929, FFT, ser. 010803, exp. 38, inv. 433 "Pérez Treviño, Manuel."
54. APEC, gav. 58, exp. 51, inv. 4239 "Ortiz Rubio, Pascual (Ing.)," vol. 1.
55. Córdova, *La revolución en crisis*, 119.
56. Spenser, *Impossible Triangle*, 183–88.
57. Córdova, *La revolución en crisis*, 75–86.
58. Skirius, *Vasconcelos*.
59. Agente 24, "Memorandum," January 22, 1929, DGIPS, box 54, exp. 11.
60. Skirius, *Vasconcelos*, 30–69, 114.
61. Skirius, *Vasconcelos*, 43.
62. Vasconcelos to Ugarte, July 23, 1929, in Ugarte, *Epistolario de Manuel Ugarte*, 76–77.
63. Vasconcelos, *Mexican Ulysses*, 52 and 119.
64. A. Rodríguez, *Autobiografía*, 138–39.
65. Skirius, *Vasconcelos*, 60–79; Dulles, *Yesterday in Mexico*, 351, 422.

66. Garrido, *El Partido de la Revolución institucionalizada*, 164–66.
67. Vasconcelos, *Mexican Ulysses*, 248–49.
68. Yankelevich, "El exilio argentino de José Vasconcelos," 27.
69. Dulles, *Yesterday in Mexico*, 481–87; Ortiz Rubio, *Memorias*, 215; G-2 Report, September 13, 1932, MID, box 1664, 2657-G-605/328.
70. Fallaw, "Eulogio Ortiz," 153; Taracena, *Los vasconcelistas sacrificados en Topilejo*.
71. Meyer, Segovia, and Lajous, *Los inicios*, 105–45; Santos, *Memorias*, 389–511.
72. Dulles, *Yesterday in Mexico*, 492; FPEC, ser. 010901, exp. 23, inv. 658 "Casa de Anzures. Menaje de casa."
73. Interview with Alejandro Elías Calles Lacy, July 17, 2015.
74. Cárdenas to Calles, October 10, 1930, in Calles, *Correspondencia personal*, 1:241–42.
75. Gómez, *Lealtades divididas*, 211.
76. "Hay que apoyar al gobierno y arrojar a malos elementos," *Excélsior*, October 5, 1930.
77. "Ortiz Rubio y Calles en amigable compañía," *Excélsior*, March 19, 1931.
78. Puig Casauranc, *Galatea rebelde a varias pigmaliones*, 407–13; N. Cárdenas, *La reconstrucción*, 139–40.
79. Gómez, *Lealtades divididas*, 220–31; Medin, *El minimato presidencial*, 104–5; Vanderwood, *Satan's Playground*, 302–3.
80. Córdova, *La revolución en crisis*, 113.
81. Loyo, *Amaro*, 173–76; Córdova, *La revolución en crisis*, 117; Dulles, *Yesterday in Mexico*, 524–27.
82. G-2 Report, December 21, 1931, MID, box 1664, 2657-G-605/314; Fallaw, *Religion*, 17.
83. "Historical Notes: Lunch with Lic. Ez. Padilla 5/16/56," JWFD, box 3, v. 8.IV.
84. Haber, *Industry and Underdevelopment*, 149–54; Nacional Financiera, *Statistics on the Mexican Economy*, 351; Tutino, *Mexican Heartland*, 329; INEGI, *Estadísticas históricas*, 666.
85. Haber, *Industry and Underdevelopment*, 154–55.
86. Pani, *Apuntes*, 2:143–44; Pani to Calles, August 6, 1931, in Calles, *Correspondencia personal*, 1:246–47.
87. Pani, *Apuntes*, 2:148–52; Haber, *Industry and Underdevelopment*, 174–75.
88. "Informe relativo al ejercicio del año 1929," APEC, gav. 14, exp. 119, inv. 975 "Compañía Azucarera Almada, S.C.," vol. 1.
89. "Se retira el general D. Abelardo Rodríguez," *Excélsior*, August 10, 1930.
90. Interview with Portes Gil in Wilkie and Wilkie, *México visto en el siglo XX*, 540–41.
91. Krauze et al., *La reconstrucción económica*, 166–70.
92. L. Meyer, *La Revolución Mexicana*, 200.
93. Quoted in Córdova, *La revolución en crisis*, 127.

94. Nacional Financiera, *Statistics on the Mexican Economy*, 107; G-2 reports, February 21 and June 6, 1930, and "Memorandum on the Mexican Agrarian Situation," September 30, 1930, MID, box 1662, 2657-G-561/10-12.
95. Córdova, *La revolución en crisis*, 134–35.
96. "Has Mexico Betrayed Her Revolution?," *New Republic*, July 22, 1931.
97. "Mexico Turns to Fascist Tactics," *Nation*, January 28, 1931.
98. For example, see Meyer, Krauze, and Reyes, *Estado y sociedad*, 283–90.
99. *Ley Federal de Trabajo*.
100. Quoted in Sherman, *Mexican Right*, 53.
101. Interview with Vicente Lombardo Toledano in Wilkie and Wilkie, *México visto en el siglo XX*, 307–11; L. Meyer, *El conflicto social*, 148–54; Spenser, *In Combat*, 43, 71–73.
102. "Agreement signed on Mexican debt," *New York Times*, July 26, 1930; Pani, *Apuntes*, 2:129–32; Bazant, *Historia de la deuda exterior de México*, 207–10.
103. Estrada, *Obras completas*, 2:144–45.
104. Córdova, *La revolución en crisis*, 171–83; Spenser, *Los primeros tropiezos*, 267–80.
105. Herrera León, *México en la Sociedad de Naciones, 1931–1940*.
106. Sacristán, "'La locópolis de Mixcoac,'" 212.
107. Dulles, *Yesterday in Mexico*, 533–40; G-2 Report, Sep. 5, 1932, MID, box 1664, 2657-G-605/329.
108. Some textbooks still report this story as fact. See Meyer, Sherman, and Deeds, *Course of Mexican History*, 570; and Sherman, *Mexico*, 163.
109. Quoted in Dulles, *Yesterday in Mexico*, 537.
110. "La renuncia de Ortiz Rubio," September 5, 1932, in Calles, *Pensamiento político*, 298.
111. A. Rodríguez, *Autobiografía*, 143.
112. "Mexican Information," August 8, 1932, MID, 2657-G-657, box 1665.
113. For Rodríguez's own assessment, see "La personalidad revolucionaria del Gral. Abelardo L. Rodríguez," *El Nacional*, September 22, 1932.
114. A. Rodríguez, *Autobiografía*, 161–70.

10. The End of an Era

1. Sherman, *Mexico*, 163.
2. Córdova, *La revolución en crisis*, 313–15.
3. A. Rodríguez, *Autobiografía*, 144.
4. Meyer, Segovia, and Lajous, *Los inicios*, 158–87; Córdova, *La revolución en crisis*, 307.
5. FPEC, ser. 010901, exp. 40, inv. 625 "Elías Calles, Plutarco (Gral.). Datos clínicos," and exp. 46, inv. 681 "Elías Calles, Plutarco (Gral.). Reportes médicos"; interviews with Plutarco Elías Calles Llorente, May 31, 2004; and Norma Torreblanca Elías Calles, June 1, 2004.

6. Pérez Montfort, *Cárdenas*, 1:456; APEC, gav. 66, exp. 189, inv. 5010 "Rodríguez, Abelardo L. (Gral.)," Calles to Rodríguez, March 29, 1933.
7. Daniels to Secretary, April 17, 1934, DS, 812.00/30040; "Partió rumbo a Sinaloa el Gral. Calles," *Excélsior*, April 14, 1934.
8. Eugenia Meyer, interview with Alicia Calles, July 3, 1975, PHO/4/45.
9. Calles, *La rehabilitación de la plata como moneda*.
10. INEGI, *Estadísticas históricas*, 333, 666; E. Cárdenas, "Great Depression and Industrialization," 230–31.
11. Russell, *History of Mexico*, 360.
12. Hernández Chávez, *La mecánica cardenista*, 197; Spenser, *In Combat*, 77–79.
13. Quoted in Dulles, *Yesterday in Mexico*, 547.
14. G-2 Report, January 1933, DS, 812.00/29828.
15. Daniels, *Shirt-Sleeve Diplomat*, 52–54. For Rodríguez's take on these events, see *Autobiografía*, 155–60.
16. "El balance político del estadista," in Calles, *Pensamiento político*, 303–9.
17. Rodríguez to Calles, June 19, 1933, in Calles, *Correspondencia personal*, 1:290.
18. Daniels to Secretary, September 29, 1933, DS, 812.00/29926.
19. Gaxiola, *El presidente Rodríguez*, 119.
20. Partido Revolucionario Nacional, *Plan sexenal* (Mexico City: n.p., 1934); Garrido, *El Partido de la Revolución institucionalizada*, 156–57.
21. "San Angel se denominará Villa Obregón," *El Universal*, December 19, 1931.
22. Bantjes, *As If Jesus Walked on Earth*, 10–11.
23. Pius XI, *Acerba animi*, September 29, 1932, http://www.vatican.va/content/pius-xi/en/encyclicals/documents/hf_p-xi_enc_29091932_acerba-animi.html.
24. "La encíclica papal y el gobierno de la república," *La Prensa*, October 2, 1932.
25. Outside the presidency, Rodríguez never expressed an opinion of the subject. He adored his mother, a devoted Catholic. Gaxiola, *El presidente Rodríguez*, 58.
26. Dulles, *Yesterday in Mexico*, 559–60; Lerner, *La educación socialista*, 39–42; Sherman, *Mexican Right*, 38.
27. Quoted in Meyer, Segovia, and Lajous, *Los inicios*, 178.
28. Sherman, *Mexican Right*, 39.
29. Aguilar Camín and Meyer, *In the Shadow*, 126.
30. Gaxiola, *El presidente Rodríguez*, 506–10.
31. Quoted in Olsen, *Artifacts of Revolution*, 94.
32. *Diario oficial de la Federación*, November 4, 1933, 73; A. Rodríguez, *Autobiografía*, 152–54.
33. "Conferencia radiofónica del presidente Abelardo L. Rodríguez sobre el salario mínimo," accessed April 16, 2020, http://www.memoriapoliticademexico.org/Textos/6revolucion/1934ism.html.
34. INEGI, *Estadísticas históricas*, 329.

35. Rodríguez, "Segundo informe de gobierno," September 1, 1934, in González y González, *Presidentes*, 3:1282.
36. Rodríguez, "Primer informe de gobierno," September 1, 1933, in González y González, *Presidentes*, 3:1211.
37. Rodríguez, "Segundo informe de gobierno," September 1, 1934, in González y González, *Presidentes*, 3:1269.
38. Gaxiola, *El presidente Rodríguez*, 245–48; Córdova, *La revolución en crisis*, 339–41.
39. Antonio Juárez to Rodríguez, November 11, 1933, AALR, Presidencia de la República.
40. Bowman to Rodríguez, October 24, 1932, AALR, Presidencia de la República, "Bowman, Wirt."
41. "Gral. Abelardo L. Rodríguez," *La Prensa*, November 17, 1938.
42. Russell, *History of Mexico*, 341.
43. Rivera León, "Understanding Constitutional Amendments in Mexico," 7–8.
44. Portes Gil, *Quince años*, 462.
45. Dulles, *Yesterday in Mexico*, 569.
46. Pérez Montfort, *Cárdenas*, 1:453–57; Becker, *Setting the Virgin on Fire*.
47. Brenner and Deighton, *Wind That Swept Mexico*, 89.
48. Ginzberg, *Revolutionary Ideology*, 157–75; Pérez Montfort, *Cárdenas*, 1:453.
49. Pérez Montfort, *Cárdenas*, 1:457–61.
50. Rodríguez to Calles, May 30, 1933, in Calles, *Correspondencia personal*, 1:283–86.
51. Pérez Montfort, *Cárdenas*, 1:461–62; Pérez Treviño to Calles, Mexico City, June 7, 1933, in Calles, *Correspondencia personal*, 1:287–88.
52. "Elogio del General Cárdenas," in Calles, *Pensamiento político*, 314.
53. "Interview with Sr. Ing. Plutarco Elías Calles, Jr., Jan. 19, 1959," JWFD, box 3, vol. 8.
54. "Interview with Lic. Francisco Javier Gaxiola, Jan. 14, 1959"; and "Interview with Sr. Carlos Riva Palacio, Jan. 22, 1959," JWFD, box 3, vol. 8.
55. "Breakfast with Dr. Ezequiel Padilla, Jan. 16, 1959," JWFD, box 3, vol. 8.
56. Córdova, *La política de masas*, 16–36.
57. Krauze, *Reformar desde el origen*, 131–33.
58. Dulles, *Yesterday in Mexico*, 578–86.
59. Dulles, *Yesterday in Mexico*, 586–89.
60. "Discurso del general Lázaro Cárdenas," November 30, 1934, in González y González, *Presidentes*, 4:11–15.
61. A. Rodríguez, *Autobiografía*, 146.
62. L. González, *Los días del presidente Cárdenas*, 13; "Mexico's President Has Turned the Presidential Palace into a Museum," *Washington Post*, December 1, 2018.
63. Pérez Montfort, *Cárdenas*, 2:94.
64. Quoted in Dulles, *Yesterday in Mexico*, 630.
65. Yepis to Daniels, January 15, 1935, and Ray to Secretary, March 15, 1935, MID 2657-G-768/15.

66. Quoted in Dulles, *Yesterday in Mexico*, 622.
67. Sherman, *Mexican Right*, 62.
68. Cárdenas to Calles, April 17 and 23, 1935; Calles to Cárdenas, April 24, 1935, APEC, gav. 12, exp. 206, inv. 280 "Cárdenas, Lázaro (Gral.)."
69. L. Cárdenas, *Apuntes*, May 3, 1935, 1:318–19; Torreblanca to Alicia Elías Calles, January 15, 1935, FPEC, ser. 010901, exp. 44, inv. 679 "Elías Calles, Plutarco (Gral.) Operación vesícula."
70. Pérez Montfort, *Cárdenas*, 2:102.
71. "Sensacionales declaraciones del General Calles," *El Universal*, June 12, 1935.
72. Flores Romero, *La obra constructiva de la Revolución Mexicana*, 3:55–57.
73. Portes Gil, *Quince años*, 504; Dulles, *Yesterday in Mexico*, 643.
74. G-2 report, August 2, 1935, MID 2657-G-768/22.
75. Knight, "Cardenismo," 79.
76. Portes Gil, *Autobiografía de la Revolución Mexicana*, 699–700.
77. Calles to Pérez Treviño, October 29, 1935, FPEC, ser. 011000, exp. 159, inv. 1359 "Pérez Treviño, Manuel."
78. G-2 report, December 5, 1935, MID 2657-G-768/36.
79. Osten, "Out of the Shadows," 169–99; "La Sangre de Huitzilac," *Excélsior*, October 6, 1937; "Calles y Amaro presuntos autores de la muerte de Serrano," *Excélsior*, October 8, 1938.
80. G-2 reports, December 16 and 20, 1935, MID 2657-G-768/50 and 53; Calles, *Correspondencia personal*, 1:318–19.
81. Daniels, *Shirt-Sleeve Diplomat*, 62; Knight, "Cardenismo: Juggernaut or Jalopy," 79–80, 103; APALR, box 10, exp. G, Guillermo Flores Muñoz to Rodríguez, December 18, 1936.
82. "Discurso a los trabajadores del país," APEC, gav. 12, exp. 208, inv. 280 "Cárdenas, Lázaro, Gral.," vol. 9.
83. "La huelga de electricistas," *El Nacional*, January 8, 1936; Olcott, *Revolutionary Women*, 1–2.
84. Bantjes, *As If Jesus Walked on Earth*, 23–122.
85. Dulles, *Yesterday in Mexico*, 674–75.
86. Quoted in Dulles, *Yesterday in Mexico*, 679–80.
87. G-2 report, April 10, 1936, MID 2657-G-768/88; Daniels, *Shirt-Sleeve Diplomat*, 62–65; "Mexican Workers Hail Calles Exile," *New York Times*, April 13, 1936.
88. Calles to Sáenz, March 17, 1936, APEC, gav. 15, exp. 120, inv. 976 "Compañía Azucarera el Mante," vol. 16; FPEC, ser. 011303, exp. 28 "Inventario," exp. 31 "Testamento."
89. "Calles Dominated Mexico 11 Years," *New York Times*, April 11, 1936.
90. INEGI, *Estadísticas históricas*, 329.
91. Knight, "Cardenismo," 73–107.

92. "Calles y la CROM fueron objetos de nuevos cargos," *Excélsior*, June 15, 1936.
93. "Las garras demoniacas del Maquiavelo negro," *La Prensa*, July 22, 1936.
94. "Calles no piensa regresar por hoy," *El Gráfico*, February 14, 1936.
95. "Calles, enfermo y taciturno, es sólo un espectro," *La Prensa*, October 20, 1938.
96. Loyo, "El Partido Revolucionario Anticomunista," 145–78; Calles to Amaro, October 10, 1939, FPEC, ser. 011000, gav. 69, exp. 6, inv. 1208 "Amaro, Joaquín (Gral.)." Rodríguez denied his involvement; see *Autobiografía*, 181 and 405–7.
97. Meyer, "Calles vs. Calles," 1005–44; Schuler, *Mexico between Hitler and Roosevelt*, 7–8, 186–87; Calles to Ortega, April 18, 1939, FPEC, ser. 011000, gav. 70, exp. 145 "Ortega, Melchor."
98. Calles to Ortega, April 18 and May 22, 1940, FPEC, ser. 011000, gav. 70, exp. 145 "Ortega, Melchor."
99. Quoted in Castro Martínez, *De la Huerta y la Revolución*, 132.
100. JMMP, box 6, folder 23.
101. O'Gorman, "Discovery of Pluralistic Ignorance," 333–47.
102. Kuran, *Private Truths, Public Lies*.
103. Quoted in Dulles, *Yesterday in Mexico*, 672–73.
104. Knight, "Mexican Revolution," 17; Hamilton, *Limits of State Autonomy*, 137–39.

Epilogue

1. Ankerson, *Agrarian Warlord*, 85.
2. "La llegada de Calles y nuestro temperamento," *La Prensa*, May 28, 1941.
3. "Calles, el enemigo núm. 1 de los católicos, celebró ayer su santo," *La Prensa*, June 29, 1942.
4. "Así viven ahora los poderosos," *La Prensa*, March 19, 1942; "El Gral. Calles supo ayer quiénes fueron sus amigos," *Excélsior*, June 29, 1944; Buchenau, *Calles*, 192–96.
5. "Calles, el enemigo," *La Prensa*, June 29, 1942.
6. Rodríguez to Calles, August 15, 1942, FPEC, ser. 011100, exp. 94, inv. 1540 "Comité Director de Acercamiento Nacional"; press clippings in FPEC, ser. 011100, exp. 264, inv. 1710 "Prensa"; interview with Alicia Almada de Calles, July 4, 1975, PHO/4/45.
7. L. Cárdenas, *Apuntes*, September 15, 1942, 2:90.
8. "Murió el Gral. Calles," *El Universal*, October 20, 1945.
9. "No hagan nada, es inútil, dijo casi en agonía," *Excélsior*, October 20, 1945.
10. Fernando Torreblanca to Rodolfo Elías Calles Chacón, October 11, 1945, FPEC, ser. 011100, exp. 133, inv. 1579 "Elías Calles, Plutarco (Gral.), Enfermedades"; León, "Elogio del Gral. Plutarco Elías Calles," FPEC, ser. 011400, exp. 1 "Homenajes 1945."
11. L. Cárdenas, *Apuntes*, October 19, 1945, 2:191.
12. De la Huerta to Dulles, August 25, 1954, JWFD, box 3, folder 6.
13. De la Huerta to Dulles, June 22, 1954, JWFD, box 3, folder 7.
14. Castro Martínez, *De la Huerta y la Revolución*, 137.

15. "Humano y limpio," *El Nacional*, July 11, 1969.
16. Rodríguez to Cárdenas, September 1, 1937, AALR, Correspondencia, 1934–1942; Daniels to Secretary, March 21, 1938, DS, 812.6363/3109.
17. "La Cámara de Diputados de acuerdo con los senadores," *Últimas Noticias*, October 22, 1938; "A. L. Rodríguez es calificado como fascista," *Excélsior*, November 8, 1938; "Abelardo Rodríguez no volverá a la política," *La Prensa*, November 16, 1938.
18. "¿Puede el general Rodríguez explicar públicamente el origen de su fortuna?," *El Popular*, July 16, 1943.
19. "Existe profunda oposición en la C.N.C. a la candidatura de Abelardo Rodríguez en Sonora," *El Popular*, November 20, 1942; "Declaraciones del Gral. Abelardo L. Rodríguez," *El Nacional*, February 13, 1943.
20. "Nada de experimentos basados en teorías exóticas; Hay que acabar con la demagogia," *El Nacional*, July 11, 1969.
21. Luis A. González, "The Five Possible Candidates," July 23, 1956, JWFD, box 4, vol. 6.
22. See, for example, "Las verdades del Gral. Rodríguez," *Excélsior*, October 29, 1960.
23. Vanderwood, *Satan's Playground*, 328.
24. AALR, Fondo Familiar, "Asociaciones, empresas, e industria," and A. Rodríguez, *Autobiografía*, 161–201.
25. A. Rodríguez, *Autobiografía*, 161–70; Paxman, *Jenkins of Mexico*, 207, 296, 312–13.
26. Guzmán, *Caudillos*, 75.
27. "Discurso," July 17, 1935, FAO, ser. 060400, exp. 8, inv. 5135 "Homenaje 1935."
28. Bórquez, *Crónica del constituyente*.
29. Niblo, *Mexico in the 1940s*, 1–74.
30. Alfonso Romandía Ferreira, "Discurso," July 18, 1941, FAO, ser. 060400, exp. 13, inv. 5140 "Homenaje 1941."
31. David C. Bailey, interview with Gilberto Valenzuela, July 20, 1973.
32. Almada, *La conexión Yocupicio*.
33. "Obregón y el sonorismo, aspecto de la revolución," *El Universal*, July 17, 1980.
34. Lomnitz-Adler, *Death and the Idea of Mexico*, 286–91.
35. Katz, *Pancho Villa*, 729–30.

Bibliography

ARCHIVES/MANUSCRIPT MATERIALS

Germany

Politisches Archiv des Auswärtigen Amtes (PAAA)

Mexico

Archivo de la Secretaría de la Defensa Nacional, Mexico City (AHSDN)
    Archivo de Cancelados
Archivo General de la Nación, Mexico City (AGN)
    Fondos Incorporados
        Colección Francisco R. Serrano (CFRS)
        Archivo Particular de Lázaro Cárdenas
        Fondo Particular Emilio Portes Gil
    Fondo Presidentes
        Obregón-Calles (P-OC)
    Secretaría de Gobernación
        Dirección General de Investigaciones Políticas y Sociales (DGIPS)
Archivo Histórico del Arzobispado de México, Mexico City (AHAM)
Archivo Histórico General del Estado de Sonora, Hermosillo (AHGES)
Archivo Histórico General y Licenciado Aarón Sáenz, Mexico City
Biblioteca Nacional de Antropología e Historia, Mexico City
    Archivo Histórico en Micropelícula
        Documentos para la Historia de Sonora (DHS)
    Programa de Historia Oral (PHO)
Centro de Estudios de la Historia de México Carso, Mexico City
    Archivo Venustiano Carranza (AVC)
Fideicomiso Archivos Plutarco Elías Calles y Fernando Torreblanca
Archivo Abelardo L. Rodríguez (AALR)
    Archivo Adolfo de la Huerta Marcor (AADH)
    Archivo Fernando Torreblanca
        Fondo Alvaro Obregón (FAO)
        Fondo Fernando Torreblanca (FFT)
        Fondo Plutarco Elías Calles (FPEC)
    Archivo Joaquín Amaro (AJA)

Archivo Plutarco Elías Calles
    Fondo Archivo Plutarco Elías Calles (APEC)
    Fondo Archivo Plutarco Elías Calles Anexo
    Fondo Presidentes (FP)
    Fondo Soledad González
    Fondo Elías Calles (FEC)
Colección Documental Francisco V. Bay (CDFVB)
Secretaría de Relaciones Exteriores, Mexico City
    Archivo Histórico (AHSRE)
Universidad Autónoma de Baja California, Tijuana
    Archivo Particular General Abelardo L. Rodríguez (APALR)

United Kingdom

National Archives, Kew
    Foreign Office (FO)

United States

Amherst College Library, Amherst MA
    Dwight Morrow Papers (DWMP)
Claremont College, Claremont CA
    José María Maytorena Papers (JMMP)
National Archives, College Park MD
    RG 59: General Records of the Department of State (DS)
    RG 165: Records of the Army General and Special Staffs. Military Intelligence Division (MID)
    John Watson Foster Dulles Papers (JWFD)
Yale University Library, New Haven CT
    James R. Sheffield Papers (JRSP)
    Arthur Bliss Lane Papers

Vatican

Archivio della Sacra Congregazione degli Affari Ecclesiastici Straordinari, Vatican City (ASCAES)

PUBLISHED WORKS

Acuña, Rodolfo F. *Sonoran Strongman: Ignacio Pesqueira and His Times*. Tucson: University of Arizona Press, 1974.

Aguilar Camín, Héctor. "Antes del reino: Plutarco Elías Calles y Adolfo de la Huerta: Un ensayo de gobierno, 1915–1920." *Trimestre político* 1, no. 4 (1976): 60–89.

———. *La frontera nómada: Sonora y la Revolución Mexicana*. Mexico City: Siglo Veintiuno Editores, 1977.

———. "The Relevant Tradition: Sonoran Leaders in the Revolution." In Brading, *Caudillo and Peasant in the Mexican Revolution*, 92–123.

———. *Saldos de la revolución: Cultura y política de México, 1910–1980*. Mexico City: Nueva Imagen, 1980.

Aguirre y Santiago, Amado. *Mis memorias de campaña*. Mexico City: Instituto Nacional de Estudios Históricos de la Revolución Mexicana, 1985.

Alarcón Menchaca, Laura. *José María Maytorena: Una biografía política*. Hermosillo: Colegio de Sonora, 2008.

Aldana Rendón, Mario. *Manuel M. Diéguez y la Revolución Mexicana*. Zapopan: El Colegio de Jalisco, 2006.

Alessio Robles, Miguel. *A medio camino*. Mexico City: Stylo, 1949.

———. *Historia política de la revolución*. Mexico City: Instituto Nacional de Estudios sobre la Revolución Mexicana, 1985.

———. *Ideales de la revolución*. Mexico City: Editorial Cultura, 1935.

Alexander, Ryan M. *Sons of the Revolution: Miguel Alemán and His Generation*. Albuquerque: University of New Mexico Press, 2017.

Almada Bay, Ignacio. *Breve historia de Sonora*. Mexico City: Fideicomiso Historia de las Américas, 2000.

———. "¿Cuál triángulo sonorense?" *Región y sociedad* 20 (2008): 199–205.

———. "De regidores porfiristas a presidentes de la república en el periodo revolucionario: Explorando el ascenso y la caída del 'sonorismo.'" *Historia mexicana* 60, no. 2 (2010): 729–89.

———. *José María Maytorena: Trayectoria y gobierno*. Boletín 29. Mexico City: Fideicomiso Archivos Plutarco Elías Calles y Fernando Torreblanca, 1998.

———. *La conexión Yocupicio: Soberanía estatal y tradición cívico-liberal en Sonora, 1913–1939*. Mexico City: Colegio de México, 2009.

———. "Las dos mitades de Plutarco Elías Calles." *Historia mexicana* 58, no. 3 (2009): 1155–69.

Altamirano Cozzi, Graziella, and Guadalupe Villa G. *Los sonorenses y sus alianzas: La capitalización del poder*. Boletín 7. Mexico City: FAPEC, 1991.

Alvarado, Salvador. *A Message from Mexico*. New York: American Exchange National Bank, 1920.

———. *Pensamiento revolucionario*. Mérida: Instituto de Seguridad Social de los Trabajadores del Estado de Yucatán, 1980.

Amaya, Juan Gualberto. *Los gobiernos de Obregón, Calles y regímenes peleles derivados del callismo, tercera etapa de 1920 a 1935*. Mexico City: n.p., 1947.

Anaya, Luis. "Calles, fundador de instituciones bancarias: El Banco Mercantil y Agrícola de Sonora, 1917–1935." *América Latina en la historia económica* 27, no. 3 (2020): 1–23.

Andes, Stephen J. C. "A Catholic Alternative to Revolution: The Survival of Social Catholicism in Postrevolutionary Mexico." *Americas* 68, no. 4 (2012): 529–62.

Ankerson, Dudley. *Agrarian Warlord: Saturnino Cedillo and the Mexican Revolution in San Luis Potosí*. DeKalb: Northern Illinois University Press, 1984.

Archivo General de la Nación. *Boletín del Archivo General de la Nación*. Mexico City: Archivo General de la Nación, 1977.

Avent, Glenn J. "Representing Revolution: The Mexican Congress and the Origins of Single-Party Rule, 1916–1934." PhD diss., University of Arizona, 2004.

Ávila Espinosa, Felipe Arturo. *Las corrientes revolucionarias y la Soberana Convención*. Mexico City: Instituto Nacional de Estudios Históricos de las Revoluciones en México, 2014.

Azuela, Mariano. *The Underdogs: A Novel of the Mexican Revolution*. Translated by E. Munguía. New York: Signet, 1996.

Bailey, David C. "Revisionism and the Recent Historiography of the Mexican Revolution." *Hispanic American Historical Review* 58, no. 1 (1978): 62–79.

———. *Viva Cristo Rey: The Cristero Rebellion and the Church-State Conflict in Mexico*. Austin: University of Texas Press, 1974.

Baitenmann, Helga. *Matters of Justice: Pueblos, the Judiciary, and Agrarian Reform in Revolutionary Mexico*. Lincoln: University of Nebraska Press, 2020.

Bantjes, Adrian A. *As If Jesus Walked on Earth: Cardenismo, Sonora, and the Mexican Revolution*. Wilmington DE: Scholarly Resources, 1998.

———. "The Regional Dynamics of Anticlericalism and Defanatization in Revolutionary Mexico." In Butler, *Faith and Impiety in Revolutionary Mexico*, 111–30.

———. "Saints, Sinners, and State Formation: Local Religion and Cultural Revolution in Mexico." In Vaughan and Lewis, *Eagle and the Virgin*, 137–56.

Barbosa Guzmán, Francisco. *Jalisco desde la revolución*. Vol. 6, *La Iglesia y el gobierno civil*. Guadalajara: Gobierno del Estado & Universidad de Guadalajara, 1988.

Bazant, Jan. *Historia de la deuda exterior de México, 1823–1946*. Mexico City: El Colegio de México, 1968.

Becker, Marjorie. *Setting the Virgin on Fire: Lázaro Cárdenas, Michoacán Peasants, and the Redemption of the Mexican Revolution*. Berkeley: University of California Press, 1996.

Beezley, William H. *Insurgent Governor: Abraham González of Chihuahua*. Lincoln: University of Nebraska Press, 1973.

———. *Judas at the Jockey Club and Other Episodes of Porfirian Mexico*. Lincoln: University of Nebraska Press, 1987.

———. "Madero, the 'Unknown' President and His Political Failure to Organize Rural Mexico." In *Essays on the Mexican Revolution: Revisionist Views of the Leaders*, edited by George Wolfskill and Douglas W. Richmond, 1–24. Austin: University of Texas Press, 1979.

Benjamin, Thomas. *La revolución: Mexico's Great Revolution as Memory, Myth, and History*. Austin: University of Texas Press, 2000.

———. "Leviathan on the Zócalo: Recent Historiography on the Postrevolutionary Mexican State." *Latin American Research Review* 20, no. 3 (1985): 195–217.
Bess, Michael K. *Routes of Compromise: Building Roads and Shaping the Nation in Mexico, 1917–1952*. Lincoln: University of Nebraska Press, 2014.
Blancarte, Roberto. "Closing Comment: 'Personal Enemies of God': Anticlericals and Anticlericalism in Revolutionary Mexico, 1915–1940." *Americas* 65, no. 4 (2009): 589–99.
Blasco Ibáñez, Vicente. *Mexico in Revolution*. New York: E. P. Dutton, 1920.
Bliss, Katherine E. *Compromised Positions: Prostitution, Public Health, and Gender Politics in Revolutionary Mexico City*. University Park: Penn State University Press, 2001.
Boletín oficial: Órgano del gobierno constitucionalista de Sonora. Hermosillo: n.p., 1916–17.
Bórquez, Djed [pseud.]. *Crónica del constituyente*. Mexico City: Ediciones Botas, 1938.
Boyer, Christopher R. *Becoming Campesinos: Politics, Identity, and Agrarian Struggle in Postrevolutionary Michoacán, 1920–1935*. Stanford CA: Stanford University Press, 2003.
Brachet-Marquez, Viviane. *The Dynamics of Domination: State, Class, and Social Reform in Mexico, 1910–1990*. Pittsburgh: University of Pittsburgh Press, 1994.
Brading, D. A., ed. *Caudillo and Peasant in the Mexican Revolution*. Cambridge, UK: Cambridge University Press, 1980.
Breceda, Alfredo. *México revolucionario, 1913–1917*. 2 vols. Madrid: Tipografía Artística, 1920–41.
Brenner, Anita, and George R. Leighton. *The Wind That Swept Mexico*. New York: Harper, 1943.
Brown, Jonathan C. *Oil and Revolution in Mexico*. Berkeley: University of California Press, 1995.
Brown, Lyle C. "The Calles-Cárdenas Connection." In *Twentieth-Century Mexico*, edited by W. Dirk Raat and William H. Beezley, 146–58. Lincoln: University of Nebraska Press, 1986.
Brunk, Samuel. *Emiliano Zapata! Revolution and Betrayal in Mexico*. Albuquerque: University of New Mexico Press, 1995.
———. *The Posthumous Career of Emiliano Zapata: Myth, Memory, and Mexico's Twentieth Century*. Austin: University of Texas Press, 2010.
Buchenau, Jürgen. "The Arm and Body of the Revolution: Remembering Mexico's Last Caudillo, Alvaro Obregón." In *Death, Dismemberment, and Memory: Body Politics in Latin America*, edited by Lyman Johnson, 179–206. Albuquerque: University of New Mexico Press, 2004.
———. *In the Shadow of the Giant: The Making of Mexico's Central America Policy, 1876–1930*. Tuscaloosa: University of Alabama Press, 1996.
———. "'La Bola': Corruption and Power in Revolutionary Mexico, 1920–1934." *Südost-Forschungen* 77, no. 1 (2018): 51–73.

———. *The Last Caudillo: Alvaro Obregón and the Mexican Revolution.* Chichester: Wiley Blackwell, 2011.

———. *Plutarco Elías Calles and the Mexican Revolution.* Lanham MD: Rowman Littlefield, 2007.

Buchenau, Jürgen, and Timothy Henderson, eds. and tr. *The Mexican Revolution: A Documentary History.* Indianapolis: Hackett, 2022.

Buford, Camile Nick. "A Biography of Luis N. Morones, Mexican Labor and Political Leader." PhD diss., Louisiana State University, 1972.

Butler, Matthew, ed. *Faith and Impiety in Revolutionary Mexico.* London: Palgrave, 2007.

———. *Mexico's Spiritual Reconquest: Indigenous Catholics and Father Pérez's Revolutionary Church.* Albuquerque: University of New Mexico Press, 2023.

———. *Popular Piety and Political Identity in Mexico's Cristero Rebellion.* London: Oxford University Press, 2004.

———. "A Revolution in Spirit? Mexico, 1910–1940." In Butler, *Faith and Impiety in Revolutionary Mexico*, 1–20.

———. "Sotanas rojinegras: Catholic Anticlericalism and Mexico's Revolutionary Schism." *Americas* 65, no. 4 (2012): 535–58.

Cabrera, Luis. *Obras completas.* Mexico City: Ediciones Oasis, 1975 [1911].

Cabrera, Luis [Blas Urrea]. *Veinte años después.* 3rd ed. Mexico City: Ediciones Botas, 1938.

Calles, Plutarco Elías. *Correspondencia personal, 1919–1945.* 2 vols. Edited by Carlos Macías Richard. Mexico City: FAPEC, 1991–93.

———. *Declaraciones y discursos políticos.* Mexico City: Cuadernos de causa, 1979.

———. *Decretos, circulares y demás disposiciones dictadas por el C. Gobernador y Comandante Militar del Estado de Sonora, General Plutarco Elías Calles, durante el año de 1915.* Hermosillo: Imprenta de Gobierno, 1915.

———. *Decretos, circulares y demás disposiciones dictadas por el C. Gobernador y Comandante Militar del Estado de Sonora, General Plutarco Elías Calles, durante el año de 1916.* Hermosillo: Imprenta de Gobierno, 1916.

———. *La rehabilitación de la plata como moneda: Entrevista exclusiva con 'El Nacional'.* Mexico City: Secretaría de Relaciones Exteriores, 1933.

———. *Partes oficiales de la campaña de Sonora.* Mexico City: Talleres Gráficos de la Nación, 1932.

———. *Pensamiento político y social: Antología, 1913–1936.* Edited by Carlos Macías Richard. Mexico City: FAPEC and Fondo de Cultura Económica, 1988.

Cameron, Charlotte. *Mexico in Revolution: An Account of an English Woman's Experiences and Adventures in the Land of Revolution, with a Description of the People, the Beauties of the Country and the Highly Interesting Remains of Aztec Civilisation.* London: Seeley, Service, 1925.

Camp, Roderic A. *Generals in the Palacio: The Military in Modern Mexico.* Oxford: Oxford University Press, 1992.

Campaña política del C. Álvaro Obregón, candidato a la presidencia de la República, 1920–1924. Mexico City: n.p., 1923.

Capetillo, Alonso. *La rebelión sin cabeza: Génesis y desarrollo del movimiento delahuertista*. Mexico City: Botas, 1925.

Cárdenas, Enrique. "The Great Depression and Industrialization: The Case of Mexico." In *Latin America in the 1930s: The Role of the Periphery in World Crisis*, edited by Rosemary Thorp, 222–41. New York: Palgrave, 1984.

Cárdenas, Lázaro. *Obras: Apuntes*. 3 vols. Mexico City: Universidad Nacional Autónoma de Mexico, 1972.

Cárdenas, Nicolás. *La reconstrucción del estado mexicano: Los años sonorenses, 1920–1935*. Mexico City: Universidad Autónoma Metropolitana, 1992.

———. "'Lo que queremos es que salgan los blancos y las tropas': Yaquis y mexicanos en tiempos de revolución (1910–1920)." *Historia mexicana* 66, no. 4 (2017): 1863–921.

Caro, Brígido. *Plutarco Elías Calles, dictador bolcheviki de México: Episodios de la Revolución Mexicana desde 1910 al 1924*. Los Angeles: n.p. 1924.

Carr, Barry. "Las peculiaridades del norte mexicano: Ensayo de interpretación." *Historia Mexicana* 22 no. 3 (1973): 320–46.

———. *Marxism and Communism in Twentieth-Century Mexico*. Lincoln: University of Nebraska Press, 1992.

Carranza, Venustiano. *Adiciones al Plan de Guadalupe*. Veracruz: n.p., 1914.

Carriedo, Robert. "The Man Who Tamed Mexico's Tiger: General Joaquín Amaro and the Professionalization of Mexico's Revolutionary Army." PhD diss., University of New Mexico, 2005.

Castro, Justin. *Apostle of Progress: Modesto C. Rolland, Global Progressivism, and the Engineering of Revolutionary Mexico*. Lincoln: University of Nebraska Press, 2019.

———. *Radio in Revolution: Wireless Technology and State Power in Mexico, 1897–1938*. Lincoln: University of Nebraska Press, 2016.

Castro, Pedro. *A la sombra de un caudillo: Vida y muerte del general Francisco R. Serrano*. Mexico City: Plaza y Janés, 2005.

———. *Álvaro Obregón: Fuego y cenizas de la Revolución Mexicana*. Mexico City: Era, 2009.

Castro Martínez, Pedro. *Adolfo de la Huerta: La integridad como arma de la revolución*. Mexico City: Siglo XXI Editores, 1998.

———. *Adolfo de la Huerta y la Revolución Mexicana*. Mexico City: Instituto Nacional de Estudios Históricos de la Revolución Mexicana, 1992.

———. "Álvaro Obregón: El último caudillo." *Polis* 3, no. 2 (2003): 209–29.

———. "La campaña presidencial de 1927–1928 y el ocaso del caudillismo." *Estudios de historia moderna y contemporánea de México* 23 (2002): 113–34.

———. *Soto y Gama: Genio y figura*. Mexico City: Universidad Autónoma Metropolitana, 2002.

Cedillo Fernández, Sergio Miguel. "La diplomacia obrera: La estrategia sindical y las relaciones México–Estados Unidos durante los años posrevolucionarios." *Historia mexicana* 72, no. 1 (2022): 131–64.

Chao Romero, Robert. *The Chinese in Mexico, 1882–1940.* Tucson: University of Arizona Press, 2010.

Chasteen, John C. *Heroes on Horseback: A Life and Times of the Last Gaucho Caudillos.* Albuquerque: University of New Mexico Press, 1995.

Chowning, Margaret. *Catholic Women and Mexican Politics, 1750–1940.* Princeton NJ: Princeton University Press, 2023.

Clark, Marjorie R. *Organized Labor in Mexico.* Chapel Hill: University of North Carolina Press, 1934.

Cline, Howard F. "Mexico: A Mature Latin-American Revolution, 1910–1960." *Annals of the American Academy of Political and Social Science* 334 (1961): 84–94.

Collado Herrera, María del Carmen. *Dwight W. Morrow: Reencuentro y revolución en las relaciones entre México y Estados Unidos.* Mexico City: Secretaría de Relaciones Exteriores, 2005.

———. "Vida social y tiempo libre de la alta clase capitalina en los tempranos años veinte." *Historias* 28 (1992): 101–26.

Córdova, Arnaldo. *La ideología de la Revolución Mexicana: La formación del nuevo régimen.* Mexico City: Era, 1973.

———. *La política de masas del cardenismo.* Mexico City: Ediciones Era, 1974.

———. *La revolución en crisis: La aventura del maximato.* Mexico City: Cal y Arena, 1995.

Cothran, Dan A. *Political Stability and Democracy in Mexico.* Westport CT: Greenwood Press, 1994.

Cruz Rivas, Miguel Angel, Lorenza Remigio Marcial, and Laura U. Lizárraga Cano. *Un recorrido por el archivo del general Abelardo L. Rodríguez, a 50 años de su fallecimiento.* Boletín 83. Mexico City: FAPEC, 2016.

Curley, Robert. *Citizens and Believers: Religion and Politics in Revolutionary Jalisco.* Albuquerque: University of New Mexico Press, 2018.

"D." "The Mexican Presidential Dilemma." *Foreign Affairs* 3, no. 1 (1924): 78–89.

Dabdoub, Claudio. *Historia del Valle del Yaqui.* Mexico City: Porrúa, 1964.

Daniels, Josephus. *Shirt-Sleeve Diplomat.* Chapel Hill: University of North Carolina Press, 1947.

Deeds, Susan M. "José María Maytorena and the Mexican Revolution in Sonora (Part 1)." *Arizona and the West* 18, no. 1 (1976): 21–40.

———. "José María Maytorena and the Mexican Revolution in Sonora (Part 2)." *Arizona and the West* 18, no. 2 (1976): 125–48.

de la Huerta, Adolfo. *Informe que rinde al H. Congreso del Estado, el gobernador provisional de Sonora . . . por el periodo de su gobierno, comprendido entre el 19 de mayo de 1916 y el 18 de junio de 1917.* Hermosillo: Imprenta del Gobierno del Estado, 1917.

Delpar, Helen. *The Enormous Vogue of Things Mexican*. Tuscaloosa: University of Alabama Press, 1992.
Departamento de la Estadística Nacional. *Censo general de habitantes, 30 de noviembre de 1921: Estado de Sonora*. Mexico City: Talleres Gráficas de la Nación, 1925.
———. *Resumen del censo general de habitantes de 30 de noviembre de 1921*. Mexico City: Talleres Gráficas de la Nación, 1928.
Diario de los debates del Congreso Constituyente. 2 vols. Mexico City: Secretaría de Gobernación, 1917.
Diéguez, Manuel M. "Informe rendido el día 10 de febrero de 1919 a la XXVIa legislature del Estado por el C. Gobernador Constitucional Gral. Manuel M. Diéguez." In *Jalisco, testimonio de sus gobernantes*, edited by Aída Urzúa Orozco and Gilberto Hernández Zaragoza, 203–303. Guadalajara: Gobierno de Jalisco, 1987.
Dillon, E. J. *President Obregón: A World Reformer*. Cambridge MA: Small, Maynard, 1923.
Dios Bojórquez, Juan de. "El espíritu revolucionario de Obregón." In *Obregón: Aspectos de su vida*, edited by José Rubén Romero et al., 45–92. Mexico City: Cultura, 1935.
———. *Forjadores de la Revolución Mexicana*. Mexico City: Instituto Nacional de Estudios Históricos de la Revolución Mexicana, 1960.
Dodson, Julian F. *Fanáticos, Exiles, and Spies; Revolutionary Failures on the U.S.-Mexican Border*. College Station: Texas A&M University Press, 2019.
Dulles, John W. F. *Yesterday in Mexico: A Chronicle of the Revolution, 1919–1936*. Austin: University of Texas Press, 1961.
Estrada, Genaro. *Obras completas*. Mexico City: Siglo XXI Editores, 1988.
Estupiñán Munguía, Víctor. *Los sonorenses y su identidad cultural*. Hermosillo: Sonora Marketing y Asociados, 1999.
Fabela, Isidro, ed. *Documentos históricos de la Revolución Mexicana*. Mexico City: Fondo de Cultura Económica, 1960 (DHRM).
Falcón, Romana. "Charisma, Tradition, and Caciquismo: Revolution in San Luis Potosí." In *Riot, Rebellion, and Revolution: Rural Social Conflict in Mexico*, edited by Friedrich Katz, 417–47. Princeton NJ: Princeton University Press, 1988.
Fallaw, Ben. "Eulogio Ortiz: The Army and the Antipolitics of Post-Revolutionary State Formation." In *Forced Marches: Soldiers and Military Caciques in Modern Mexico*, edited by Ben Fallaw and Terry Rugeley, 136–71. Tucson: University of Arizona Press, 2012.
———. *Religion and State Formation in Postrevolutionary Mexico*. Durham NC: Duke University Press, 2013.
———. "Varieties of Mexican Revolutionary Anticlericalism: Radicalism, Iconoclasm, and Otherwise, 1914–1935." *Americas* 65, no. 4 (2009): 481–509.
Farmer, Edward M. "Plutarco Elías Calles and the Revolutionary Government in Sonora, Mexico, 1915–1919." PhD diss., Cambridge University, 1997.

Figueroa Valenzuela, Alejandro. "La Revolución Mexicana y los indios de Sonora." In *Historia general de Sonora*, vol. 4, *Sonora moderno, 1880–1929*, 355–80. Hermosillo: Gobierno del Estado de Sonora, 1997.

———. "Los indios de Sonora ante la modernización porfirista." In *Historia general de Sonora*, 4:140–66.

Flores Romero, Jesús, ed. *La obra constructiva de la Revolución Mexicana: Anales históricos de la Revolución Mexicana*. Mexico City: Libro-Mex Editores, 1960.

Flores Vizcarra, Jorge, and Otto Granados Roldán. *Salvador Alvarado y la Revolución Mexicana*. Culiacán: Universidad Autónoma de Sinaloa, 1980.

Folsom, Raphael. *The Yaquis and the Empire: Violence, Spanish Imperial Power, and Native Resilience in Colonial Mexico*. New Haven CT: Yale University Press, 2014.

Fowler, Will. *The Grammar of Civil War: A Mexican Case Study, 1857–1861*. Lincoln: University of Nebraska Press, 2022.

Fowler-Salamini, Heather. *Agrarian Radicalism in Veracruz, 1920–1938*. Lincoln: University of Nebraska Press, 1971.

Fuentes Díaz, Vicente. *Los partidos políticos en México*. 2nd ed. Mexico City: Editorial Altiplano, 1969.

Garcíadiego, Javier. "¿Cuándo, cómo, por qué, y quiénes hicieron la Constitución de 1917?" *Historia mexicana* 66, no. 3 (2017): 1183–270.

———, ed. *La Revolución Mexicana: Crónicas, documentos, planes y testimonios*. Mexico City: UNAM, 2008.

Garner, Paul. "Autoritarismo revolucionario en el México provincial: El carrancismo y el gobierno preconstitucional en Oaxaca, 1915–1920." *Historia mexicana* 34, no. 2 (1984): 238–99.

———. *Porfirio Díaz*. London: Longman, 2001.

Garrido, Luis Javier. *El Partido de la Revolución institucionalizada: La formación del nuevo estado en México (1928–1945)*. Mexico City: Siglo Veintiuno Editores, 1982.

Gauss, Susan M. *Made in Mexico: Regions, Nation, and the State in the Rise of Mexican Industrialism*. University Park: Penn State University Press, 2010.

Gaxiola, Francisco J. *El presidente Rodríguez (1932–1934)*. Mexico City: Editorial Cultura, 1938.

Gerhard, Peter. *The North Frontier of New Spain*. Princeton NJ: Princeton University Press, 1982.

Gerth, Hans H., and C. Wright Mills, eds. and tr. *From Max Weber: Essays in Sociology*. New York: Oxford University Press, 1947.

Gillingham, Paul. *Unrevolutionary Mexico: The Birth of a Strange Dictatorship*. New Haven CT: Yale University Press, 2021.

Gilly, Adolfo. *El cardenismo: Una utopia mexicana*. Mexico City: Cal y Arena, 1994.

———. *La revolución interrumpida*. Mexico City: Caballito, 1972.

Ginzberg, Eitan. *Revolutionary Ideology and Political Destiny in Mexico, 1928–1932: Lázaro Cárdenas and Adalberto Tejeda*. Brighton, UK: Sussex Academic Press, 2015.

Gómez Estrada, José Alfredo. *Gobierno y casinos: El origen de la riqueza de Abelardo L. Rodríguez*. Mexicali: Universidad Autónoma de Baja California, 2002.

———. *Lealtades divididas: Camarillas y poder en México, 1913–1932*. Mexico City: Instituto de Investigaciones Históricas José Luis Mora, 2012.

Gonzales, Michael J. *The Mexican Revolution, 1910–1940*. Albuquerque: University of New Mexico Press, 2002.

———. "United States Copper Companies, the State, and Labour Conflict in Mexico, 1900–1910." *Journal of Latin American Studies* 26, no. 3 (1994): 651–81.

González, Luis. *Historia de la Revolución Mexicana, 1934–1940: Los días del presidente Cárdenas*. Mexico City: Colegio de México, 1981.

———. *Pueblo en vilo: Una microhistoria de San José de Gracia*. Mexico City: Colegio de México, 1968.

González de Reufels, Delia. *Siedler und Filibuster in Sonora: Eine mexikanische Region im Interesse ausländischer Abenteurer und Mächte (1821–1860)*. Cologne, Germany: Böhlau Verlag, 2003.

González y González, Luis, ed. *Los presidentes de México ante la nación*. 4 vols. Mexico City: Cámara de Diputados, 1966.

Grabman, Richard. *Gorostieta and the Cristiada: Mexico's Catholic Insurgency, 1926–1929*. Mazatlán, Sinaloa: Editorial Mazatlán, 2012.

Gramsci, Antonio. *Selections from the Prison Notebooks*. Edited and translated by Quintin Hoare and Geoffrey N. Smith. New York: International Publishers, 1971.

Grijalva Dávila, Miguel Ángel. "El ejército de Estrada: Disección de una rebelión frustrada en la frontera norte, 1926–1927." *Historia mexicana* 72, no. 1 (2022): 165–210.

Gruening, Ernest. *Mexico and Its Heritage*. New York: Century, 1928.

Guzmán, Martín Luis. *Caudillos y otros extremos*. Mexico City: Universidad Nacional Autónoma de México, 1995.

———. *The Eagle and the Serpent*. Translated by Harriet de Onís. Garden City NJ: Doubleday, 1965 [1928].

———. *La sombra del caudillo*. Translated by Gustavo Pellón as *The Shadow of the Strongman*. (Indianapolis IN: Hackett, 2017).

Guzmán Esparza, Roberto. *Memorias de don Adolfo de la Huerta, según su propio dictado*. Mexico City: Ediciones Guzmán, 1957.

Haber, Stephen H. "Assessing the Obstacles to Industrialisation: The Mexican Economy, 1830–1940." *Journal of Latin American Studies* 24, no. 1 (1992): 1–32.

———. *Industry and Underdevelopment: The Industrialization of Mexico, 1880–1940*. Stanford CA: Stanford University Press, 1989.

Hall, Linda B. "Alvaro Obregón and the Agrarian Movement, 1912–1930." In Brading, *Caudillo and Peasant in the Mexican Revolution*, 127–30.

———. *Alvaro Obregón: Power and Revolution in Mexico, 1911–1920*. College Station: Texas A&M University Press, 1981.

———. *Oil, Banks, and Politics: The United States and Postrevolutionary Mexico*. Austin: University of Texas Press, 1995.

Hall, Linda B., and Don M. Coerver. *Revolution on the Border: The United States and Mexico, 1910–1920*. Albuquerque: University of New Mexico Press, 1988.

Hamilton, Nora. *The Limits of State Autonomy: Post-Revolutionary Mexico*. Princeton NJ: Princeton University Press, 1982.

Harris, Charles H., and Louis R. Sadler. *The Plan de San Diego: Tejano Rebellion, Mexican Intrigue*. Albuquerque: University of New Mexico Press, 2013.

———. "The Witzke Affair: German Intrigue on the Mexican Border, 1917–18." *Military Review* 59 (1979): 36–46.

Hart, Paul. *Emiliano Zapata: Mexico's Social Revolutionary*. New York: Oxford University Press, 2017.

Haynes, Keith A. "Orden y progreso: The Revolutionary Ideology of Alberto J. Pani." In *Los intelectuales y el poder en México: Memoria de la VI Reunión de Historiadores Mexicanos y Estadounidenses*, 259–79. Mexico City: Colegio de México, 1991.

Henderson, Peter V. N. *In the Absence of Don Porfirio: Francisco León de la Barra and the Mexican Revolution*. Wilmington DE: Scholarly Resources, 2000.

———. "Un gobernador maderista: José María Maytorena y la revolución en Sonora." *Historia Mexicana* 51, no. 1 (2001): 151–86.

Henderson, Timothy J. *The Mexican Wars for Independence*. New York: Hill and Wang, 2009.

———. *The Worm in the Wheat: Rosalie Evans and Agrarian Struggle in the Puebla-Tlaxcala Valley of Mexico, 1906–1927*. Durham NC: Duke University Press, 1998.

Hernández Chávez, Alicia. *Historia de la Revolución Mexicana, periodo 1934–1940: La mecánica cardenista*. Mexico City: Colegio de México, 1979.

———. "Militares y negocios en la Revolución Mexicana." *Historia mexicana* 34, no. 2 (1984): 181–212.

Hernández Enríquez, Gustavo Abel. *El genio de la raza: La concepción ética de la Revolución Mexicana*. Culiacán, Sinaloa: Consejo Ciudadano para el Desarrollo Cultural Municipal de Salvador Alvarado, 2009.

Hernández Hurtado, Juan Francisco. *¡Tierra de cristeros! Historia de Victoriano Ramírez y de la revolución cristera en Los Altos*. Mexico City: CEMCA, 2003.

Herrera León, Fabián. *México en la Sociedad de Naciones, 1931–1940*. Mexico City: Secretaría de Relaciones Exteriores, 2014.

Hobbes, Thomas. Excerpt from *Leviathan*. In *Classics in Moral and Political Theory*, edited by Michael L. Morgan, 4th ed. Indianapolis IN: Hackett, 1992.

Hobsbawm, E. J. "Revolution." In *Revolution in History*, edited by Roy Porter and Mikulás Teich, 5–46. Cambridge, UK: Cambridge University Press, 1986.

Horn, James J. "Did the United States Plan an Invasion of Mexico in 1927?" *Journal of Inter-American Studies and World Affairs* 15, no. 4 (1973): 454–71.

---. "U.S. Diplomacy and the 'Specter of Bolshevism' in Mexico (1924–27)." *Americas* 32, no. 1 (1975): 31–45.

Hu-DeHart, Evelyn. "La comunidad china en el desarrollo de Sonora." In *Historia general de Sonora*, 4:195–211.

---. *Missionaries, Miners, and Indians: Spanish Contact with the Yaqui Nation of Northwestern New Spain, 1533–1820*. Tucson: University of Arizona Press, 1981.

---. *Yaqui Resistance and Survival: The Struggle for Land and Autonomy, 1821–1910*. Madison: University of Wisconsin Press, 1984.

Humboldt, Alexander von. *Political Essay on the Kingdom of New Spain*. Edited by Mary Maples Dunn and translated by John Black. Norman: University of Oklahoma Press, 1972.

Iglesias González, Román, ed. *Planes políticos, proclamas, manifiestos y otros documentos de la independencia al México moderno, 1812–1940*. Mexico City: Universidad Nacional Autónoma de Mexico, 1998.

Instituto Nacional de Estadística, Geografía e Informática. *Estadísticas históricas de México*. 4th ed. Aguascalientes: El Instituto Nacional de Estadística y Geografía, 1999.

Jiménez Ornelas, Roberto, and Iván Figueroa Acuña. "Colegio de Sonora: Un intento de terciarización de la educación." In *La educación superior en el proceso histórico de México*. Edited by David Piñera Ramírez, 147–55. Tijuana: Universidad Autónoma de Baja California, 2001.

Johnson, William W. *Heroic Mexico: The Violent Emergence of a Modern Nation*. New York: Doubleday, 1968.

Joseph, Gilbert M. *Revolution from Without: Yucatán, Mexico, and the United States, 1880–1924*. Cambridge, UK: Cambridge University Press, 1982.

Joseph, Gilbert M., and Jürgen Buchenau. *Mexico's Once and Future Revolution: Social Upheaval and the Challenge of Rule since the Late Nineteenth Century*. Durham NC: Duke University Press, 2013.

Joseph, Gilbert M., and Daniel Nugent, eds. *Everyday Forms of State Formation: Revolution and the Negotiation of Rule in Mexico*. Durham NC: Duke University Press, 1994.

Katz, Friedrich. *The Life and Times of Pancho Villa*. Stanford CA: Stanford University Press, 1998.

---. *The Secret War in Mexico: Europe, the United States, and the Mexican Revolution*. Chicago: University of Chicago Press, 1981.

Kiddle, Amelia M., and María L. O. Muñoz, eds. *Populism in Twentieth Century Mexico: The Presidencies of Lázaro Cárdenas and Luis Echeverría*. Tucson: University of Arizona Press, 2010.

Kirchhoff, Paul. *Mesoamérica: Sus límites geográficos, composición étnica y caracteres culturales*. 3rd ed. Mexico City: Instituto Nacional de Antropología e Historia, 1967.

Knight, Alan. "Cardenismo: Juggernaut or Jalopy." *Journal of Latin American Studies* 24 (1994): 73–107.

———. "Corruption in Twentieth-Century Mexico." In *Political Corruption in Europe and Latin America*, edited by Walter Little and Eduardo Posada-Carbó, 219–36. London: Macmillan, 1996.

———. "The End of the Mexican Revolution? From Cárdenas to Ávila Camacho, 1937–1941." In *Dictablanda: Politics, Work, and Culture in Mexico, 1938–1968*, edited by Paul Gillingham and Benjamin T. Smith, 47–69. Durham NC: Duke University Press, 2014.

———. "Forjar Constitución, 1916–1917." *Jahrbuch für Geschichte Lateinamerikas* 54 (2017): 11–38.

———. "The Mentality and Modus Operandi of Revolutionary Anticlericalism." In Butler, *Faith and Impiety in Revolutionary Mexico*, 21–56.

———. *The Mexican Revolution*. 2 vols. Cambridge, UK: Cambridge University Press, 1986.

———. "The Mexican Revolution: Bourgeois? Nationalist? Or Just a 'Great Rebellion'?" *Bulletin of Latin American Research* 4, no. 2 (1985): 1–37.

Krauze, Enrique. *La presidencia imperial: Ascenso y caída del sistema político mexicano, 1940–1994*. Mexico City: Tusquets, 2002.

———. *Mexico: Biography of Power*. Translated by Hank Heifetz. New York: Harper Collins, 1997.

———. *Redeemers: Ideas and Power in Latin America*. Translated by Hank Heifetz. New York: Harper Collins, 2011.

Krauze, Enrique, Jean Meyer, and Cayetano Reyes. *Historia de la Revolución Mexicana, periodo 1924–28: La reconstrucción económica*. Mexico City: El Colegio de México, 1977.

Kuran, Timur. *Private Truths, Public Lies: The Social Consequences of Preference Falsification*. Cambridge MA: Harvard University Press, 1994.

Lacy, Elaine C. "The 1921 Centennial Celebration of Mexico's Independence: State Building and Popular Negotiation." In *¡Viva México, Viva la independencia! Celebrations of 16 September*, edited by William H. Beezley and David E. Lorey, 199–232. Wilmington DE: Scholarly Resources, 2001.

Lajous, Alejandra. *Los orígenes del partido único en México*. Mexico City: Universidad Nacional Autónoma de Mexico, 1979.

Lear, John. *Workers, Neighbors, and Citizens: The Revolution in Mexico City*. Lincoln: University of Nebraska Press, 2001.

León, Luis L. *Crónica del poder: En los recuerdos de un político en el México revolucionario*. Mexico City: Fondo de Cultura Económica, 1987.

Lerner, Victoria. *Historia de la Revolución Mexicana, periodo 1934–1940: La educación socialista*. Mexico City: Colegio de México, 1979.

Levitsky, Steven, and Lucan Way. "The Durability of Revolutionary Regimes." *Journal of Democracy* 24, no. 3 (2013): 5–17.

Ley Federal de Trabajo. Mexico City: Talleres Gráficos de la Nación, 1931.
Lieuwen, Edwin. *Mexican Militarism: The Political Rise and Fall of the Revolutionary Army, 1910–1940*. Albuquerque: University of New Mexico Press, 1968.
Lomelí Vanegas, Leonardo. "La controversia de la Huerta-Pani: ¿Crisis fiscal o artificio político?" *Historia Mexicana* 72, no. 1 (2022): 211–50.
Lomnitz-Adler, Claudio. *Death and the Idea of Mexico*. Brooklyn NY: Zone Books, 2005.
Loyo, Martha Beatriz. "El Partido Revolucionario Anticomunista en las elecciones de 1940." *Estudios de historia moderna y contemporánea de México* 23 (2002): 145–60.
———. *Joaquín Amaro y el proceso de institucionalización del ejército mexicano, 1917–1931*. Mexico City: Universidad Nacional Autónoma de Mexico, 2003.
Loyola Díaz, Rafael. *La crisis Obregón-Calles y el estado mexicano*. 3rd ed. Mexico City: Siglo Veintiuno Editores, 1987.
Macías Richard, Carlos, ed. *Vida y temperamento: Plutarco Elías Calles, 1877–1920*. Mexico City: FAPEC and Fondo de Cultura Económica, 1995.
———. *Visiones sobre Felipe Carrillo Puerto: Correspondencia con Plutarco Elías Calles y otros testimonios*. Mexico City: Conaculta, 2014.
Madero, Francisco I. *La sucesión presidencial: El Partido Nacional Democrático*. Mexico City: Secretaría de Hacienda, 1960 [1908].
Madrid Mulia, Héctor. *Jorge Prieto Laurens: Biografía política de un revolucionario*. Mexico City: Porrúa, 2010.
Manjarrez, Froylán C. *La jornada institucional*. 2 vols. Mexico City: Talleres Gráficos de la Nación, 1930.
Marak, Andrae M. *From Many, One: Indians, Peasants, Borders, and Education in Callista Mexico, 1924–1935*. Calgary, Alberta: University of Calgary Press, 2009.
Martínez, Ignacio. *The Intimate Frontier: Friendship and Civil Society in Northern New Spain*. Tucson: University of Arizona Press, 2019.
Martínez Assad, Carlos R. *El laboratorio de la revolución: El Tabasco garridista*. Mexico City: Siglo Veintiuno, 1979.
Matute, Alvaro. *Historia de la Revolución Mexicana, 1917–1924: La carrera del caudillo*. Mexico City: El Colegio de México, 1980.
Maurer, Noel. *The Power and the Money: The Mexican Financial System, 1876–1932*. Stanford CA: Stanford University Press, 2002.
McCaa, Robert. "Missing Millions: The Demographic Costs of the Mexican Revolution." *Mexican Studies / Estudios mexicanos* 19, no. 2 (2003): 367–400.
Mecham, Lloyd. *Church and State in Latin America: A History of Politico-Ecclesiastical Relations*. Chapel Hill: University of North Carolina Press, 1934.
———. "The Jefe Político in Mexico." *Southwestern Social Science Quarterly* 13, no. 4 (1933): 333–52.
Medin, Tzvi. *El minimato presidencial: Historia política del maximato*. Mexico City: Era, 1982.

Melzer, Richard A. "Dwight Morrow's Role in the Mexican Revolution: Good Neighbor or Meddling Yankee?" PhD diss., University of New Mexico, 1979.

Méndez Medina, Diana Lizbeth. "En los bordes de la corrupción: Análisis de la conformación, funcionamiento y expropiación de la Compañía Azucarera del Mante (1930–1939)." *Región y sociedad* 27 (2015): 209–48.

Mestaz, James V. *Strength from the Waters: A History of Indigenous Mobilization in Northwest Mexico*. Lincoln: University of Nebraska Press, 2022.

Meyer, Jean. *The Cristero Rebellion: The Mexican People between Church and State, 1926–1929*. Translated by Richard Southern. Cambridge, UK: Cambridge University Press, 1976.

———. "An Idea of Mexico: Catholics in the Revolution." In *The Eagle and the Virgin: Nation and Cultural Revolution in Mexico, 1920–1940*, edited by Mary Kay Vaughan and Stephen Lewis, 281-96. Durham NC: Duke University Press.

———. "Revolution and Reconstruction in the 1920s." In *Mexico since Independence*, edited by Leslie Bethell, 201–40. Cambridge, UK: Cambridge University Press, 1991.

Meyer, Jean, Enrique Krauze, and Cayetano Reyes. *Historia de la Revolución Mexicana, 1924–1928: Estado y sociedad con Calles*. Mexico City: El Colegio de México, 1977.

Meyer, Lorenzo. *Historia de la Revolución Mexicana, 1928–1934: El conflicto social y los gobiernos del maximato*. Mexico City: Colegio de México, 1978.

———. "La Revolución Mexicana y las potencias anglosajonas: El final de la confrontación y el inicio de la colaboración, 1925–1927." *Historia mexicana* 34, no. 2 (1984): 300–352.

———. "La Revolución Mexicana y sus elecciones presidenciales: Una interpretación (1911–1940)." *Historia Mexicana* 32, no. 2 (1982): 143–97.

———. *Mexico and the United States in the Oil Controversy, 1917–1942*. Translated by Lidia Lozano. Austin: University of Texas Press, 1972.

———. *Su majestad británica contra la Revolución Mexicana, 1900–1950*. Mexico City: Colegio de México, 1992.

Meyer, Lorenzo, Rafael Segovia, and Alejandra Lajous. *Historia de la Revolución Mexicana, 1928–1934: Los inicios de la institucionalización*. Mexico City: Colegio de México, 1978.

Meyer, Michael C. *Huerta: A Political Portrait*. Lincoln: University of Nebraska Press, 1972.

———. *Mexican Rebel: Pascual Orozco and the Mexican Revolution, 1910–1915*. Lincoln: University of Nebraska Press, 1967.

Meyer, Michael C., John L. Sherman, and Susan Deeds. *The Course of Mexican History*. 9th ed. Oxford: Oxford University Press, 2011.

Middlebrook, Kevin J. *The Paradox of Revolution: Labor, the State, and Authoritarianism in Mexico*. Baltimore: Johns Hopkins University, 1995.

Mijangos Díaz, Eduardo N. *La dictadura enana: Las prefecturas del porfiriato en Michoacán*. Morelia, Michoacán: Universidad Michoacana de San Nicolás de Hidalgo, 2008.

Miller, Barbara. "The Role of Women in the Mexican Cristero Rebellion: Las señoras y Las religiosas." *Americas* 40, no. 3 (1984): 303–23.

Mistral, Gabriela. *Croquis mexicanos*. Santiago de Chile: Nascimento, 1979.

Mitchell, Stephanie, and Patience A. Schell. *The Women's Revolution in Mexico, 1910–1953*. Lanham MD: Rowman and Littlefield, 2007.

Montaño, Diana J. *Electrifying Mexico: Technology and the Transformation of a Modern City*. Austin: University of Texas Press, 2021.

Moore, Walter. "Adolfo de la Huerta: His Political Role in Sonora, 1906–1920." PhD diss., University of California, San Diego, 1982.

Mora, Gregorio. "Sonora al filo de la tormenta: Desilusión con el porfiriato, 1900–1911." In *The Revolutionary Process in Mexico: Essays on Political and Social Change, 1880–1940*, edited by Jaime E. Rodríguez, 57–80. Los Angeles: UCLA Latin American Center Publications, 1990.

Morris, Stephen D. "Continuity and Change in Mexican Politics: The Legacies of the Mexican Revolution." *Latin Americanist* 54, no. 4 (2010): 183–99.

Nacional Financiera. *Statistics on the Mexican Economy*. Mexico City: Nacional Financiera, 1977.

Naylor, Thomas H. "Massacre at San Pedro de la Cueva: The Significance of Pancho Villa's Disastrous Sonora Campaign." *Western Historical Quarterly* 8, no. 2 (1977): 125–50.

Niblo, Stephen R. *Mexico in the 1940s: Modernity, Politics, and Corruption*. Wilmington DE: Scholarly Resources, 1999.

Nicolson, Harold G. *Dwight Morrow*. New York: Harcourt, Brace, 1935.

Niemeyer, E. Victor, Jr. *Revolution at Querétaro: The Mexican Constitutional Convention of 1916–1917*. Austin: The University of Texas Press, 1974.

O'Gorman, Hubert J. "The Discovery of Pluralistic Ignorance: An Ironic Lesson." *Journal of the History of the Behavioral Sciences* 22, no. 4 (1986): 333–47.

Obregón, Álvaro. *Discursos del general Alvaro Obregón*. 2 vols. Mexico City: Dirección General de Educación Militar, 1932.

———. *El problema agrario: Versión taquigráfica del cambio de impresiones tenido por el presidente electo con un numeroso grupo de diputados al Congreso de la Unión, octubre de 1920*. Mexico City: n.p., 1920.

———. *Manifiesto a la nación lanzado por el C. Álvaro Obregón*. Hermosillo: Imprenta Moderna, 1919.

———. *Ocho mil kilómetros en campaña*. 2nd ed. Mexico City: Fondo de Cultura Económica, 1959 [1917].

Okada, Atsumi. "El impacto de la Revolución Mexicana: La Compañía Constructora Richardson en el Valle del Yaqui (1905–1928)." *Historia mexicana* 50, no. 1 (2000): 91–143.

Olcott, Jocelyn. *Revolutionary Women in Postrevolutionary Mexico*. Durham NC: Duke University Press, 2005.

Olsen, Patrice Elizabeth. *Artifacts of Revolution: Architecture, Society, and Politics in Mexico City, 1920–1940*. Lanham MD: Rowman and Littlefield, 2008.

Olson, Mancur. *Power and Prosperity: Outgrowing Communist and Capitalist Dictatorships*. New York: Basic Books, 2000.

Ortiz Rubio, Pascual. *Memorias, 1925–1928*. Morelia: Universidad Michoacana de San Nicolás, 1981.

Osten, Sarah. *The Mexican Revolution's Wake: The Making of a Political System*. Cambridge: Cambridge University Press, 2018.

———. "Out of the Shadows: Violence and State Consolidation in Postrevolutionary Mexico, 1927–1940." *Latin Americanist* 64, no. 2 (2020): 169–99.

———. "Trials by Fire: National Political Lessons from Failed State Elections in Post-Revolutionary Mexico, 1920–1925." *Mexican Studies / Estudios mexicanos* 29, no. 1 (2013): 238–79.

Padilla, Tanalís. *Unintended Consequences of Revolution: Student Teachers and Political Radicalism in Twentieth-Century Mexico*. Durham NC: Duke University Press, 2021.

Padilla Ramos, Raquel, and Ana Luz Ramírez Zavala. "Los yaquis en la revolución carrancista, 1913–1915: Pactos y rupturas." In *De los márgenes al centro: Sonora en la independencia y la revolución: Cambios y continuidades*, edited by Ignacio Almada Bay and José Marcos Medina Bustos, 185–210. Hermosillo: Colegio de Sonora, 2010.

Pani, Alberto J. *Apuntes autobiográficos*. 2 vols. Mexico City: Porrúa, 1950.

Paoli, Francisco J., ed. *Salvador Alvarado*. Mexico City: Editorial Terra Nova, 1985.

Partido Revolucionario Nacional. *Plan sexenal*. Mexico City: n.p., 1934.

Paxman, Andrew. *Jenkins of Mexico: How a Southern Farmboy Became a Mexican Magnate*. Oxford: Oxford University Press, 2017.

Pérez Montfort, Ricardo. *Lázaro Cárdenas: Un mexicano del siglo XX*. 2 vols. Mexico City: Debate, 2018–19.

Piccato, Pablo. "El parlamentarismo en la Cámara de Diputados, 1912–1921, entre la opinión pública y los grupos de choque." In Piccato Rodríguez et al., *El poder legislativo en las décadas revolucionarias, 1908–1934*, 65–116.

Piccato Rodríguez, Pablo Atilio, et al., eds. *El poder legislativo en las décadas revolucionarias, 1908–1934*. Mexico City: Cámara de Diputados, 1997.

Piña, Ulices. "Rebellious Citizens: National Reforms and the Practice of Local Governance in Jalisco, 1914-1940," PhD diss., University of California at San Diego, 2017.

Plasencia de la Parra, Enrique. "El exilio delahuertista." *Estudios de historia moderna y contemporánea de México* 43 (2012): 105–34.

———. *Escenarios y personajes de la rebelión delahuertista*. Mexico City: Miguel Porrúa, 1998.

Porter, Katherine Anne. *Flowering Judas and Other Stories*. New York: Harcourt, Brace, 1935.

Portes Gil, Emilio. *Autobiografía de la Revolución Mexicana: Un tratado de interpretación histórica*. Mexico City: Instituto Mexicano de Cultura, 1964.

———. *Emilio Portes Gil: Un civil en la Revolución Mexicana*. Tampico: Instituto Tamaulipeco de Cultura, 1989.

———. *La dictadura, la revolución y los hombres*. Mexico City: Imprenta Manuel León Sánchez, 1938.

———. *Quince años de política mexicana*. 2nd ed. Mexico City: Ediciones Botas, 1941.

Puente, Ramón. *Hombres de la revolución: Calles*. Mexico City: Fondo de Cultura Económica, 1994 [1933].

Puig Casauranc, José Manuel. *El sentido social del proceso histórico de México*. Mexico City: Ediciones Botas, 1936.

———. *Galatea rebelde a varias pigmaliones: De Obregón a Cárdenas*. Mexico City: Impresores Unidos, 1938.

Purnell, Jennie. *Popular Movements and State Formation in Revolutionary Mexico: The Agraristas and Cristeros of Michoacán*. Durham NC: Duke University Press, 1999.

Quirk, Robert E. *The Mexican Revolution and the Catholic Church, 1910–1929*. Bloomington: Indiana University Press, 1973.

———. *The Mexican Revolution, 1914–1915: The Convention of Aguascalientes*. Bloomington: Indiana University Press, 1960.

Radding de Murrieta, Cynthia. "El triunfo constitucionalista y las reformas en la región, 1913–1919." In *Historia general de Sonora*, 4: 215–311.

Ragsdale, Kenneth Baxter. *Wings over the Mexican Border: Pioneer Military Aviation in the Big Bend*. Austin: University of Texas Press, 2010.

Ramírez de Aguilar, Fernando. *Desde el tren amarillo: Crónicas de guerra*. Mexico City: Botas, 1924.

Ramírez González, Beatriz. *En la pobreza y en la riqueza: Biografía de doña Natalia Chacón de Elías Calles*. Mexico City: Documentación y Estudio de Mujeres, 2008.

Ramírez Plancarte, Francisco. *La Ciudad de México durante la revolución constitucionalista*. 2nd ed. Mexico City: Ediciones Botas, 1941.

Rath, Thomas. "Modernizing Military Patriarchy: Gender and State-Building in Postrevolutionary Mexico, 1920–1960." *Journal of Social History* 52, no. 3 (2019): 807–30.

———. *Myths of Demilitarization in Postrevolutionary Mexico, 1920–1960*. Chapel Hill: University of North Carolina Press, 2013.

Reff, Daniel T. *Disease, Depopulation, and Cultural Change in Northwestern New Spain, 1518–1764*. Salt Lake City: University of Utah Press, 1991.

Richkarday, Ignacio A. *60 años en la vida de México*. Mexico City, n.p., 1963.

Richmond, Douglas. *Venustiano Carranza's Nationalist Struggle, 1893–1920*. Lincoln: University of Nebraska Press, 1983.

Ridgeway, Stan. "Monoculture, Monopoly, and the Mexican Revolution: Tomás Garrido Canabal and the Standard Fruit Company in Tabasco, 1920–1935." *Mexican Studies / Estudios mexicanos* 17, no. 1 (2001): 143–69.

Rivera, Antonio G. *La revolución en Sonora*. Hermosillo: Gobierno de Sonora, 1981.

Rivera León, Mauro Arturo. "Understanding Constitutional Amendments in Mexico: Perpetuum Mobile Constitution." *Mexican Law Review* 9, no. 2 (2017): 3–27.

Rockwell, Elsie. *Hacer escuela, hacer estado: La educación posrevolucionaria vista desde Tlaxcala*. Mexico City: Centro de Investigaciones y Estudios Superiores en Antropología Social, 2007.

Rodríguez, Abelardo L. *Autobiografía*. Mexico City: n.p., 1962.

Rodríguez, Miles. *Movements after Revolution: A History of People's Struggles in Mexico*. New York: Oxford University Press, 2022.

Romero, Matías. "Mexico a Central American State." *Journal of the American Geographical Society* 26 (1894): 32–37.

Ruiz, Ramón Eduardo. *Labor and the Ambivalent Revolutionaries: Mexico, 1911–1923*. Baltimore: Johns Hopkins University Press, 1976.

———. *The People of Sonora and Yankee Capitalists*. Tucson: University of Arizona Press, 1988.

———. *Triumph and Tragedy: A History of the Mexican People*. New York: W.W. Norton, 1993.

Russell, Philip L. *The History of Mexico: From Pre-Conquest to Present*. London: Routledge, 2010.

Sacristán, Cristina. "'La locópolis de Mixcoac' en una encrucijada política: Reforma psiquiátrica y opinion pública, 1929–1933." In *Actores, espacios y debates en la historia de la esfera pública en México*, edited by Cristina Sacristán and Pablo Piccato, 199–232. Mexico City: Instituto Mora, 2005.

Salmerón Sanginés, Pedro. *Aarón Sáenz Garza: Militar, diplomático, político, empresario*. Mexico City: Editorial Porrúa, 2001.

Sánchez Aguilar, Juan Bernardino. "La integración del Congreso Constituyente en 1917." *Historia mexicana* 66, no. 3 (2017): 1271–322.

Santiago, Myrna I. *The Ecology of Oil: Environment, Labor, and the Mexican Revolution*. Cambridge, UK: Cambridge University Press, 2006.

Santos, Gonzalo N. *Memorias*. 4th ed. Mexico City: Grijalbo, 1984.

Saragoza, Alex. *The Monterrey Elite and the Mexican State, 1880–1940*. Austin: University of Texas Press, 1988.

Schell, William B. *Integral Outsiders: The American Colony in Mexico City, 1876–1910*. Wilmington DE: Scholarly Resources, 2001.

Schuler, Friedrich E. *Mexico between Hitler and Roosevelt: Mexican Foreign Relations in the Age of Lázaro Cárdenas, 1934–1940*. Albuquerque: University of New Mexico Press, 1998.

———. *Secret Wars and Secret Policies in the Americas, 1842–1929*. Albuquerque: University of New Mexico Press, 2010.

Scott, James C. *Domination and the Arts of Resistance: Hidden Transcripts*. New Haven CT: Yale University Press, 1990.

Secretaría de la Economía Nacional. *Anuario estadístico 1938*. Mexico City: Talleres Gráficos de la Nación, 1939.

Sefchovich, Sara. *La suerte de la consorte: Las esposas de los gobernantes de México, historia de un olvido y relato de un fracaso*. Mexico City: Océano, 1999.

Serrano Álvarez, Pablo. "La muerte de un caudillo." In *Álvaro Obregón: Ranchero, caudillo, empresario y político*, edited by Carlos Silva, 263–78. Mexico City: Cal y Arena, 2020.

Sherman, John W. *The Mexican Right*. Westport CT: Praeger, 1997.

———. *Mexico: A Concise Illustrated History*. Lanham MD: Rowman and Littlefield, 2020.

Simpson, Eyler N. *The Ejido: Mexico's Way Out*. Chapel Hill: University of North Carolina Press, 1937.

Simpson, Lesley B. *Many Mexicos*. Rev. 4th ed. Berkeley: University of California Press, 1967.

Skirius, John. *José Vasconcelos y la cruzada de 1929*. Mexico City: Siglo XXI, 1978.

Slattery, Matthew. *Felipe Angeles and the Mexican Revolution*. Parma Heights OH: Greenbriar Books, 1982.

Smith, Peter H. *Labyrinths of Power: Political Recruitment in Twentieth Century Mexico*. Princeton NJ: Princeton University Press, 1979.

———. "La política dentro de la revolución: El Congreso Constituyente de 1916–1917." *Historia Mexicana* 22, no. 4 (April 1973): 363–95.

Smith, Robert F. *The United States and Revolutionary Nationalism in Mexico, 1916–1932*. Chicago: University of Chicago Press, 1972.

Smith, Stephanie J. *Gender and the Mexican Revolution: Yucatán Women and the Realities of Patriarchy*. Chapel Hill: University of North Carolina Press, 2009.

———. *The Power and Politics of Art in Postrevolutionary Mexico*. Chapel Hill: University of North Carolina Press, 2017.

Snodgrass, Michael. *Deference and Defiance in Monterrey: Workers, Paternalism, and Revolution in Mexico, 1890–1950*. Cambridge, UK: Cambridge University Press, 2003.

Spenser, Daniela. *En el gabinete de Venustiano Carranza*. Boletín 30. Mexico City: FAPEC, 1999.

———. *The Impossible Triangle: Mexico, Soviet Russia, and the United States in the 1920s*. Durham NC: Duke University Press, 1999.

———. *In Combat: The Life of Lombardo Toledano*. Leiden, Netherlands: Brill, 2020.

———. *Los primeros tropiezos de la internacional comunista en México*. Mexico City: Centro de Investigaciones y Estudios Superiores en Antropología Social, 2009.

Spicer, Edward H. *Cycles of Conquest: The Impact of Spain, Mexico, and the United States on Indians of the Southwest, 1533–1960*. Tucson: University of Arizona Press, 1962.

Tannenbaum, Frank. *Mexico: The Struggle for Peace and Bread*. New York: Knopf, 1950.

Taracena, Alfonso. *Los vasconcelistas sacrificados en Topilejo*. Mexico City: Editora Librera, 1958.

Tenorio Trillo, Mauricio. *I Speak of the City: Mexico City at the Turn of the Century*. Chicago: University of Chicago Press, 2012.

Thornton, Christy. *Revolution in Development: Mexico and the Governance of the Global Economy*. Berkeley: University of California Press, 2020.

Tinker Salas, Miguel. *In the Shadow of the Eagles: Sonora and the Transformation of the Border During the Porfiriato*. Berkeley: University of California Press, 1997.

Tobler, Hans Werner. "La burguesía revolucionaria en México: Su origen y su papel, 1915–1935." *Historia mexicana* 34, no. 2 (1984): 213–37.

Turner, John Kenneth. *Barbarous Mexico*. New York: Cassell, 1912.

Tutino, John. *The Mexican Heartland: How Communities Shaped Capitalism, a Nation, and World History, 1500–2000*. Princeton NJ: Princeton University Press, 2017.

Ugarte, Manuel. *El epistolario de Manuel Ugarte (1896–1951)*. Buenos Aires: Archivo General de la Nación, 1999.

Valadés, José C. *Las memorias de don Adolfo de la Huerta, ex-presidente de México*. Mérida: Talleres de la Compañía Tipográfica Yucateca, 1930.

Valenzuela, Clodoveo, and Amado Chaverri Matamoros. *Sonora y Carranza: Obra de la más amplia información gráfica y periodística del último movimiento libertario, respaldada por gran número de valiosos documentos, hasta hoy desconocidos, que entregamos a la historia*. Mexico City: Casa Editorial Renacimiento, 1925.

Valenzuela, Georgette José. *El relevo del caudillo: De cómo y por qué Calles fue candidato presidencial*. Mexico City: El Caballito, 1982.

———. *La campaña presidencial de 1923–1924 en México*. Mexico City: Instituto Nacional de Estudios Históricos de la Revolución Mexicana, 1998.

Valvo, Paolo. *La Cristiada: Fe, guerra y diplomacia en México (1926–1929)*. Translated by Chiara Serafini. Mexico City: Universidad Nacional Autónoma de México, 2023.

Vanderwood, Paul J. *Satan's Playground: Mobsters and Movie Stars at America's Greatest Gaming Resort*. Durham NC: Duke University Press, 2010.

Vasconcelos, José. *La tormenta*. Mexico City: Trillas, 2000.

———. *A Mexican Ulysses: An Autobiography*. New York: Greenwood Press, 1963.

Vaughan, Mary Kay. "Cultural Approaches to Peasant Politics in the Mexican Revolution." *Hispanic American Historical Review* 79, no. 2 (1999): 269–305.

———. *Cultural Politics in Revolution: Teachers, Peasants, and Schools in Mexico, 1930–1940*. Tucson: University of Arizona Press, 1998.

———. "Rural Women's Literacy During the Mexican Revolution: Subverting a Patriarchal Event?" In *Women of the Mexican Countryside, 1850–1990*, edited by Heather Fowler-Salamini and Mary Kay Vaughan, 106–24. Tucson: University of Arizona Press, 1994.

———. *The State, Education, and Social Class in Mexico, 1880–1924*. DeKalb: Northern Illinois University Press, 1982.

Vaughan, Mary Kay, and Stephen Lewis, eds. *The Eagle and the Virgin: Nation and Cultural Revolution in Mexico, 1920–1940*. Durham NC: Duke University Press, 2005.

Vergara, Germán. *Fueling Mexico: Energy and Environment, 1850–1950*. Cambridge, UK: Cambridge University Press, 2021.

Voss, Stuart F. *On the Periphery of Nineteenth-Century Mexico: Sonora and Sinaloa, 1810–1877*. Tucson: University of Arizona Press, 1982.

Wakild, Emily. *Revolutionary Parks: Conservation, Social Justice, and Mexico's National Parks, 1910–1940*. Tucson: University of Arizona Press, 2011.

Wasserman, Mark. *Capitalists, Caciques, and Revolution: The Native Elite and Foreign Enterprise in Mexico, 1854–1911*. Chapel Hill: University of North Carolina Press, 1984.

———. *Persistent Oligarchs: Elites and Politics in Chihuahua, Mexico, 1910–1940*. Durham NC: Duke University Press, 1993.

———. *Pesos and Politics: Business, Elites, Foreigners, and Government in Mexico, 1854–1940*. Stanford CA: Stanford University Press, 2015.

———. "You Can Teach an Old Revolutionary Historiography New Tricks: Regions, Popular Movements, Culture, and Gender in Mexico, 1820–1940." *Latin American Research Review* 43, no. 2 (2008): 260–71.

Weis, Robert. *For Christ and Country: Militant Catholic Youth in Post-Revolutionary Mexico*. Cambridge, UK: Cambridge University Press, 2019.

Weldon, Jeffrey A. "El presidente como legislador." In Piccato Rodríguez et al., *El poder legislativo en las décadas revolucionarias, 1908–1934*, 117–46.

Werne, Joseph R. *Esteban Cantú and the Mexican Revolution in Baja California Norte, 1910–1921*. Fort Worth: Texas Christian University Press, 2020.

Wilkie, James W., and Edna Monzón de Wilkie. *México visto en el siglo XX: Entrevistas de historia oral*. Mexico City: Instituto Mexicano de Investigaciones Económicas, 1969.

Wilkins, Mira, and Frank E. Hill. *American Business Abroad: Ford on Six Continents*. Detroit: Wayne State University Press, 1964.

Womack, John. *Zapata and the Mexican Revolution*. New York: Knopf, 1968.

Wood, Andrew G. "Adalberto Tejeda: Radicalism and Reaction in Revolutionary Veracruz." In *Governors of the Mexican Revolution: Conflict, Corruption, and Survival*, edited by Jürgen Buchenau and William H. Beezley, 77–94. Lanham MD: Scholarly Resources, 2009.

———. *Revolution in the Street: Women, Workers, and Urban Protest in Veracruz, 1870–1927*. Wilmington DE: Scholarly Resources, 2001.

Yankelevich, Pablo. "El exilio argentino de José Vasconcelos." *Iberoamericana* 6, no. 24 (2006): 27–42.

Young, Julia G. D. "The Calles Government and Catholic Dissidents: Mexico's Transnational Projects of Repression, 1926–1929." *Americas* 70 (2013): 63–91.

———. *Mexican Exodus: Emigrants, Exiles, and Refugees of the Cristero War*. Oxford: Oxford University Press, 2015.

Index

Italicized page numbers refer to figures.

Acapulco, 120, 198
acarreado strategy, 261
Acerba animi (Pius XI), 280–81
ACJM (Asociación Católica de la Juventud Mexicana), 138, 203
Acosta, José María, 56
acuerdos colectivos, 266–67, 269, 278
AF of L (American Federation of Labor), 99, 114, 165, 179
agrarian code, 96, 275, 284, 296, 308
Agrarian Law of October 1915, 85
agrarian leaders, 110, 220, 287
agrarian reform, 63, 66, 90–91, 92, 143–44, 194, 198–99, 235, 269–70, 279, 280, 289
agrarians, 120, 141, 150, 152, 154, 165
agraristas, 121, 144, 163, 209, 287, 310
agribusinesses, 35, 52, 113, 222–25, 268
agricultural policy. *See* smallholding
agriculture, 2, 10, 20, 22, 30–32, 77, 90, 144–45, 165, 189, 269. *See also* Garbanzo League
Agua Caliente casino, 153–54, 266, 268, 285, 304
Agua Prieta, 42–44, 51, 67, 73, 78, *121*, 157. *See also* Plan de Agua Prieta
Aguascalientes, 64–65, 70. *See also* Convention of Aguascalientes
Aguilar, Cándido, 117
Aguilar Camín, Héctor, 10–13
Aguirre Berlanga, Manuel, 109
Álamos, 23, 24, 36, 39

alcohol, 78, 156–57, 165–66, 200
Alemán Valdés, Miguel, 12
Alessio Robles, Miguel, 120, 133
Alessio Robles, Vito, 263
Alfaro Siqueiros, David, 149
Alien Land Law, 202, 211–12
Allende, Salvador, 9
alliances, 2, 4, 11, 32, 60, 62–66, 68–69, 72, 100–101, 103, 111, 120, 142, 146, 154. *See also* Jacobins
Almada, Ignacio, 10, 236–37
Almada, Jorge, 296
Almazán, Juan Andreu, 12, 155, 243, 252, 257, 258, 265–66
Alvarado, Salvador, 5–6, 8, 31, 35, 36–38, 50–51, *55*, 56–57, 62–63, 66, 72, 86–91, 93, 96, 101, 109, 116–17, 121, 124–26, 129, 146, 165–68, 169–71, 181, 182–83, 241, 308
Amaro, Joaquín, 172, 181, 197–98, 205, 209, 236–38, 257, 261, 265–67, 294, 297
American Federation of Labor (AF of L), 99, 114, 165, 179
AMLO. *See* López Obrador, Andrés Manuel
amparo, 145, 219, 269, 284, 311
anarcho-syndicalism, 36, 87, 94. *See also* Casa del Obrero Mundial (COM); Partido Liberal Mexicano
Ángeles, Felipe, 39, 57–59, 62, 64, 66
Angel of Independence, 200
anticlericalism, 6, 85–90, 137–40, 160, 182, 200, 203–8, 311; Calles's early,

383

anticlericalism (*cont.*) 79–80; and the Carranza-era party system, 104; in constitutional provisions, 134; in the Constitution of 1857, 203–4; and the Constitution of 1917, 95–96; and the Cubilete incident, 140; and Francisco R. Serrano, 230–32; and Jacobins, 93; and James R. Sheffield, 212; and the Ortiz Rubio administration, 269; and schismatic churches, 200–201; and Tomás Garrido Canabal, 166; and the Vasconcelista coalition, 262
anticorruption measures, 198
anti-reelectionism, 34–38, 43, 232, 235, 237, 310–11
Antonio Páez, José, 105
Apaches, 23–25, 29–30, 43
Arango, Doroteo. *See* Villa, Pancho
Arbenz, Jacobo, 303–4
arbitration, 83, 196, 217–18, 270–71, 283. *See also* Junta Federal de Conciliación y Arbitraje (JFCA)
Argentina, 264, 299
Arizona, 28, 30, 34–35, 37, 50, 53, 55, 99, 159, 216, 225–26, 273, 348n105
Arizona Mining Journal, 112–13
Arizona Rangers, 32
Arizpe, Sonora, 24, 43
arms and ammunition, 37, 54–55, 67, 179–81, 348n105
arms embargo, 59, 212, 214
army, 1, 32, 48–57, 60, 70, 87, 93, 105, 143, 177, 180–81, 209, 225–26, 339n4. *See also* Federales
Asociación Católica de la Juventud Mexicana (ACJM), 138, 203
Asociación Cívica General Álvaro Obregón, 307
assassinations, 8, 10, 49, 87, 110, 123, 143, 171–72, 180, 183, 184, 240, 241–45, 249, 254, 263–64, 293, 295, 309, 310

Ateneo de la Juventud, 148
authoritarianism, 9, 11, 32, 96, 107, 196, 262, 264, 274, 307, 310–11
Ávila Camacho, Manuel, 297, 302–3, 306
Ávila Camacho, Maximino, 12, 264–65, 304
Azuela, Mariano, 47

Baja California, 21, 128, 153, 161, 185, 216, 259, 273–74, 277, 283, 285
Bajío, 61, 77, 87, 260, 269
Balboa Park, 295
Banco de México (Banxico), 197, 223, 268
Banco Mercantil y Agrícola de Sonora, 100
Banco Nacional de Crédito Agrícola (BNCA), 197, 223–24, 284
banditry, 12, 39, 60, 62, 77
banquet of December 1920, 133–34, 308
Barragán, Juan, 116, 237–38
Bassols, Narciso, 279, 282, 291
batallones rojos. *See* Red Battalions
Battle of Agua Prieta, 171
Battle of Jiménez, 258
Battle of Ocotlán, 180–81
Battle of Puebla (1867), 27–28
Battle of San Julián (Jalisco), 209
Bay Valenzuela, Alejo, 152, 222, 228
Beals, Carleton, 150, 213, 270
Benedict XV (pope), 138
Beneficencia Pública, 266, 272
Berkeley, 305
Berlin, Germany, 188–89, 230
Bernal López, Amada, 160
Bierce, Ambrose, 150
Blanco, Lucio, 143
Blasco Ibáñez, Vicente, 26, 98, 150
BNCA (Banco Nacional de Crédito Agrícola), 197, 223–24, 284
Bolsheviks/Bolshevism, 4, 96, 125–26, 140, 164–66, 211–13
Bonaparte, Napoleon, 106, 270

Bonillas Frajio, Ignacio, *115*, 116, 117, 120, 164
Border Barons, 154
Bórquez, Flavio, 94
boss rule, 103, 250, 259
Bourbon Reforms, 23–24
Bowman, Wirt, 154, 285
Brenner, Anita, 286–87
bribery, 135–37, 198, 257, 266, 271
Britain, 140
British government, 134, 180
bronco Yaqui, 29, 56, 81, 83–84, 99
brothels, 128, 157, 230
Brownsville TX, 295
Bucareli Agreement, 137, 152, 170–72, 179–80, 194–95, 211
Buenavista train station, 120, 277
Burke, John J., 218

Cabral, Juan G., 35, 37–38, 50–51, 56, 63, 313n19
Cabrera, Luis, 68, 91, 109–10, 239, 289
caciques, 2, 42, 74, 77, 193, 254, 270, 275
Cajemé. *See* Leyva, José María
California, 25, 136, 216, 224
Calles, Alicia Elías, 277, 303
Calles, Hortensia, 154, 159–60, 240, 292, 295
Calles, Juan Bautista, 43
Calles, Plutarco Elías, 4, 5–6, 8–12, 26, 30–32, 37, 41–45, 54–57, 62–64, 78–85, 118–23, 133–34, 146–47, 193–94, 204–17; and the aftermath of Obregón's assassination, 241–45; and anticlericalism, 137; and an auspicious beginning, 194–202; and the Calles-Cárdenas split, 306; in the Carranza era, 98–101; and the Carranza-era party system, 108; and the Constituyente, 93, 96; death of, 303; and the De la Huerta Rebellion, 176–82; and de la Huerta's interim presidency, 124–29; and endeavor to create a national party, 249–55; and the end of Sonorismo, 291–99; and the Escobar Rebellion, 256–59; and the Huerta coup, 51–52; and the Huitzilac massacre, 237–39; illustration of, *253*; inauguration of, *188*; and José Vasconcelos, 262–63; in Mexico City, 156–61; and Obregón's encore, 226–34; and Obregón's investments, 221–25; and Obregón's presidential campaign, 111–16; and occupation of the Chamber of Deputies, 141–42; as official candidate of the presidential election of 1924, 163–66; and opposition to the Catholic Church, 307; and the Ortiz Rubio administration, 264–74; photograph of, *51*, *55*, *80*, *121*, *125*, *164*, *184*; and the Portes Gil administration, 259–61; and the presidential election of 1924, 169–75, 186–89; and the presidential election of 1927, 226–41; and presidential succession, 163; and reform, 85–91; and retrenchment from the reform drive, 217–20; and the rise of Cárdenas, 286–89; and the Rodríguez presidency, 275, 276–85; and Salvador Alvarado, 89–91; and structure of the Sonorense coalition, 151–55; and the War of the Winners, 67–74
Calles, Plutarco Elías, Jr., 168, 288, 292, 296
Calles, Rodolfo Elías, 101, 153, 159, 224–25, 265, 280, 290, 292, 296
Calles Chacón, Plutarco "Aco" Elías, 154, 252
Calles Law, 206–7, 209, 218, 260
Calles Plan, 268
Calles Ruiz, Manuel, 157

Index 385

Callismo, 297
Callistas, 193, 252, 256, 265, 267, 290, 292–93, 295, 297
Calvo Clause, 270
Cámara Obrera, 98–99, 152, 196
camarilla, 151–55, 309, 310
Camisas Rojas, 291
Campeche, 74
campesinos, 2, 5, 8, 54, 90, 144, 168–69, 179, 209, 233, 251, 253, 260–61, 274, 276, 277–78, 283, 294
Canadian Mennonites, 145
Cananea, 30–32, 34–35, 37–39, 44, 50, 54, 87, 98–99
Cananea Cattle Company, 32, 35
Cananea Consolidated Copper Company (CCCC), 30, 32, 62, 91, 98–99
Cantú, Esteban, 128, 135
Canutillo, Durango, 127
Capistrán Garza, René, 209
capitalist system, 9–10, 83, 90, 96, 112, 115, 187–89, 307
Cárdenas del Rio, Lázaro, 10–12, 72, 74, 79, 213–14; and Abelardo L. Rodríguez, 304; and Álvaro Obregón Tapia, 307; and the Calles-Cárdenas split, 306; and the De la Huerta Rebellion, 181; and the end of Sonorismo, 291–99; and the Escobar Rebellion, 257–58; and expropriations, 284; and land distribution, 285; and land reform, 261, 270, 308; and the Ortiz Rubio administration, 266; and personality cults, 107; photograph of, *281*; and the *plan sexenal*, 279–80; and Plutarco Elías Calles, 291–99, 303; and reforms, 275; rise of, 286–91; and the War of the Winners, 67–68
Cardenismo, 11, 280, 295, 299, 306, 308
Cardenista populism, 307
Cardenista radicalism, 304
Cardenistas, 10–11, 286, 291–92, 299
Carrancistas, 53, 62–68, 70, 72, 104, 118, 122–23, 309
Carranza de la Garza, José Venustiano, 3–4, 10, 12, 49, 52–54, 55, 57–61, 62–66, 77–78, 80–85, 128–29, 134–35, 140–41, 144–46, 148, 156, 161, 164–65, 174–75, 177, 185, 237, 313n19; and the Constitution of 1917, 92–95; and diplomatic relations, 272; and Obregón's presidential campaign, 109–16; and parties and leaders in the Carranza administration, 103–10; photograph of, *115*; and reform, 85–89; and the revolutionary family, 254; and the road to Agua Prieta, 116–23; and Sonorenses in the Carranza era, 97–101; and the War of the Winners, 66–74
Carranza Doctrine, 111
Carrillo Puerto, Elvia, 108
Carrillo Puerto, Felipe, 89, 107–8, 141, 145, 164–67, 170, 171, 177–78, 180, 183–84
Caruana, George, 204–6, 212
Caruso, Enrico, Jr., 183
Casa del Obrero Mundial (COM), 61, 69, 83, 95, 113–14, 120
Casa de los Azulejos, 61, 104
Casino de la Selva, 304
casinos, 69, 128–29, 154, 185. *See also* Agua Caliente casino
Caso, Antonio, 202
casta divina, 88, 117
Castro Morales, Carlos, 89
catastrophic equilibrium, 5
Catholic Association of Mexican Youth. *See* Asociación Católica de la Juventud Mexicana (ACJM)
Catholic associations, 201
Catholic Church, 2, 8, 28, 68, 79–81, 86, 88, 95–96, 137–40, 148, 150, 177, 186,

194, 202–11, 218, 220, 262, 276, 307.
   See also anticlericalism
Catholic Party, 59
Catholic place names removed, 280
CCCC (Cananea Consolidated Copper Company), 30, 32, 62, 91, 98–99
Cedillo, Saturnino, 173, 179, 193, 199, 252, 257, 258, 266, 287
Cejudo, Roberto F., 119
Central America, 21, 146, 212
Centralists, 24
centralization, 2, 6, 27–28, 68, 142, 194, 202, 209
central Mexico, 3, 6, 22, 24, 33, 67, 70, 74, 99, 118
Centro Recreativo Sonora-Sinaloa, 161, 170
CGT (Confederación General de Trabajo), 146, 196, 253
Chacón Amarillas, Natalia, 159
Chamber of Deputies, 97, 103, 141–42, 144, 159, 163, 164, 167, 169, 171–74, 183–84, 209, 227–28, 238, 243–45, 258, 292–93
Chamorro, Emiliano, 212
Chao, Manuel, 182
Chapultepec Castle, 161, 221, 238, 265, 290, 292
charismatic leadership, 106
Chiapanecan Socialist Party, 167
Chiapas, 25, 74, 117, 166–67, 181, 280
Chihuahua, 3, 6, 21, 29, 34–35, 41–42, 49, 53–54, 59, 63–64, 66, 68, 73–74, 81, 92, 127, 145, 182, 209
Chile, 9
Chilpancingo, 59
Chinameca, 110
Chinese community, 30–31, 99, 265
"Christ the King" shrine, 139
church-state conflict, 8, 79–81, 85–88, 137–40, 199–212, 235, 259–60, 265, 280–82, 307, 310

church strike, 207–8, 219, 249, 259–60
CIDOSA (textile conglomerate), 198
científico faction, 31, 222, 262
Cinco de Mayo, 27
Ciudad Juárez, 38, 256. *See also* Treaty of Ciudad Juárez
Ciudad Obregón, 222, 265
civic liberalism, 308
civilian authoritarianism, 107
civilians, 109, 134, 152, 168
Clemente Jacques food cannery, 101
Clemente Orozco, José, 149
clergy, 58–59, 68, 80–81, 84, 86–88, 95–96, 138–40, 149, 200–201, 203–8, 260, 280–81
Club Reyista of Guaymas, 33
Coahuila, 3, 49, 52–53, 55, 59, 103, 127, 178, 236, 296
Coatepec, Veracruz, 238–39
Cold War, 5, 303, 305
Colegio de Sonora, 31
Colegio Militar, 53, 198
Colima, 173, 209–10
collective bargaining, 2, 83, 95, 113, 270, 280
Cologne Cathedral, 230
Colombia, 264
Colonia Roma, 292
Colorado River, 82
Columbus, New Mexico, 81
COM. *See* Casa del Obrero Mundial (COM)
Comarca Lagunera, 236, 296
Comintern, 187
commercial agriculture, 29, 144, 269, 284, 296
Committee of Five, 136
commodity prices, 98, 224, 268
communal land, 25, 40, 79, 98, 144, 296
Communist International, 165
Communist Party (PCM), 94, 186–87, 211, 261–62, 289

Index   387

Compañía Azucarera El Mante, 154, 199, 268, 295–96
Compañía Constructora Richardson, 30, 32, 87, 145, 222–25
Compañía Operadora de Teatros S.A., 305
Compañía Telefónica y Telegráfica Mexicana, 69
compensation for expropriated land, 137, 144–45
concessions, 30, 34, 64, 79, 135, 136–37, 145, 152, 172, 211, 213, 266, 284
conciliation and arbitration boards, 283. *See also* arbitration
Confederación de Trabajadores Mexicanos (CTM), 296, 305
Confederación General de Obreros y Campesinos Mexicanos (CGOCM), 278, 290, 296
Confederación General de Trabajo (CGT), 146, 196, 253
Confederación Nacional Campesina, 304–5
Confederación Regional Obrera Mexicana (CROM), 114, 137, 140, 145–47, 152, 163, 165, 171, 178, 187, 194–96, 202, 253, 307, 339n4; and anticlerical policies, 205; and Arnulfo R. Gómez, 232; disintegration of, 277–78; and Francisco R. Serrano, 230; laws directed at weakening, 220; and the Obregonistas, 242; and the Portes Gil administration, 259
Confederación Revolucionaria, 68
Conferences of American States, 272
Congress, 2, 39, 49, 52, 93, 103–4, 108, 113, 123, 141–42, 144–46, 152, 163, 173, 178, 183, 193, 195, 208–9, 211, 226–27, 232, 233, 236, 242, 243–44, 260, 264–65, 267, 268, 270, 273, 279, 282–85, 290, 292, 294, 310, 311. *See also* Chamber of Deputies

Constitutionalist Rebellion, 58–59
Constitutionalists, 3, 54–56, 58–60, 66–74, 77, 78–85, 86–88, 100, 101, 103–4, 106, 110, 114, 140, 143, 159
Constitutionalist victory in 1915, 249
Constitutional Progressive Party. *See* Partido Constitucional Progresista (PCP)
Constitution of 1857, 53, 203–4, 206, 210
Constitution of 1917, 2, 91–97, 99–101, 113, 141, 148, 176, 185, 208, 244, 260, 310–11; article 3, 95, 148, 282; article 5, 95; article 24, 95, 139; article 27, 94–95, 111–12, 117, 134, 136–37, 168, 172, 194–95, 211, 235, 251; article 33, 95–96, 139, 194; article 82, 168; article 83, 226–27, 234–35, 242, 285–86; article 123, 94–96, 99, 113–14, 117, 146, 168, 169, 194, 251, 270, 283; article 130, 95, 104; constitutional reforms, 141–42, 194–95, 208–9, 227–28, 285–86
Constituyente, 92–96, 177, 228, 306
consulates, 214, 298
Conventionists, 66–74, 87
Convention of Aguascalientes, 64–66, 120, 291
Coolidge, Calvin, 137, 179, 214, 217
Cooperatistas, 141, 163, 172
copper, 30–31, 51, 62, 78–79, 91, 94, 96, 98–99, 135
Córdoba, Veracruz, 65
cordonazo de San Francisco, 224
Córdova, Arnaldo, 10–11
Corps of the Army of the Northeast (Cuerpo de Ejército del Noreste), 54, 59
Corps of the Army of the Northwest (Cuerpo de Ejército del Noroeste), 54, 57
Corpus Christi church, 201
Corral, Luz, 64
Corral, Ramón, 21, 29, 31, 33, 170

388 Index

corruption, 9, 12–13, 107, 154, 175, 198, 200, 262, 272–73, 305
Council of Ministers, 124
coups, 4–5, 48–54, 103, 123, 236, 303
Creelman, James, 33
Crespi, Tito, 182, 187
Cristeros, 209–11, *210*, 217, 225, 243, 259–61, 286
Cristiada, 10, 209–11, 217–20, 260, 269, 309
Crofton, James, 154
CROM. *See* Confederación Regional Obrera Mexicana (CROM)
CROMistas, *164*
Cruz, Roberto, 238
Cruz Gálvez school, 79, *80*
CTM (Confederación de Trabajadores Mexicanos), 296, 305
Cuautla, Morelos, 38
Cuba, 9, 181–82, 237, 264
Cuban Revolution, 305
Cubilete Hill incident, 139–40, 203
Cuernavaca, 9, 41, 60, 155, 236–38, 264, 276–77, 278, 292, 304
Cuerpo de Ejército del Noreste, 54, 59
Cuerpo de Ejército del Noroeste, 54, 57

Daniels, Josephus, 278–79, 297
Davis, James J., 215
debt, 134–36, 175, 196–97, 219, 271
"Decena Trágica," 48
defanaticization, 85, 89, 280
de la Huerta, Alfonso, 214, 216, 238, 241, 348n105
de la Huerta Oriol, Adolfo, 4–6, 11, 13, 26, 31–32, 36–37, 39, 42–43, 53–54, 55, 58, 85, 133–37, 143, 146–48, 160–61, 195, 196, 214–16, 308, 310–11; and the beginning of the Maximato, 82; and the Cámara Obrera, 82–83; in the Carranza era, 100–101; and the Carranza-era party system, 108–9; and the congressional elections of 1918, 103; and constitutional reform, 141; and the Constituyente, 94, 96; death of, 304; and the De la Huerta Rebellion, 176–89; and the end of Sonorismo, 298; and the Escobar Rebellion, 257; and the Huerta coup, 48, 51; interim presidency of, 124–29; and *jefe máximo* moniker, 254–55; in Mexico City, 155–56; and the Obregón group, 116; and Obregón's presidential campaign, 109, 112–13; and parliamentary rule, 310–11; photograph of, *80*, *119*, *125*; and the Plan de Veracruz, 228; and Plutarco Elías Calles, 98; and the presidential election of 1924, 169–75; and presidential succession, 163; and the road to Agua Prieta, 116–23; after Sonorismo, 302–4; and structure of the Sonorense coalition, 151–53; and the War of the Winners, 72; and the Yaqui, 83–84; and the Yaqui War, 225
De la Huerta Rebellion, 6, 163, 176–89, 214–15, 238, 239, 255, 260, 286, 308–9
Delahuertistas, 170, 180, 181–82, 184, 186, 225, 235
de la O, Genovevo, 120
democracy/democratic rule, 48, 52–53, 58, 298, 301, 308
Dewey, John, 79, 199
DGIPS (Dirección General de Investigaciones Políticas y Sociales), 214–15
Díaz, Félix, 48, 74, 117, 122, 126–27, 143, 155, 214–16
Díaz, Pascual, 201, 208
Díaz, Porfirio, 3–4, 12, 27–29, 31, 33–39, 52–53, 61, 95–96, 103, 106, 150, 157, 193, 218

Index 389

Diéguez, Manuel M., 5–6, 8, 31, 36–39, 50, 56, 59–60, 65, 67, 71, 72–74, 86–88, 93, 96, 109, 116, 118–19, 129, 168, 177, 182–83, 241, 308
Dios Bojórquez, Juan de, 93–94, 298, 306
diplomatic recognition, 73, 124, 127, 134–37, 145, 202, 271
Dirección General de Investigaciones Políticas y Sociales (DGIPS), 214–15
divisional generals (*divisionarios*), 93, 117, 127, 143, 184, 185, 197–98, 228, 232, 243, 258, 266–67, 302, 308; rank, 60
División del Norte, 54, 60, 62, 64, 70
Doheny, Edward L., 134–37
Dorados, 291
dotación, 144
Dulles, John W. F., 9, 303–4
Durango, 44, 69, 127, 155, 172

Ebert, Friedrich, 189
economy, 27, 77, 196, 275, 277, 305–6; and boycott, 88, 206–7; economic crisis, 110–13, 219, 267–68, 271; economic nationalism, 104, 113, 124, 135–36, 169, 176, 213, 284; economic reforms, 36, 58, 101; economic sovereignty, 111; economic status quo, 35–36, 171, 176, 304; growth and development of, 24, 28, 30–32, 153, 195–98, 280; and production, 194
Ecuador, 264
education, 2, 5, 31, 39, 79, 89, 91, 95–96, 138, 147–49, 165, 189, 269, 279, 280; and reform, 167–68, 199–200. *See also* Secretaría de Educación Pública (SEP)
"Ejército Libertador," 214
ejidatarios, 290
ejidos, 144–45, 177–78, 199, 269, 279, 289, 296

El Águila Mexican Petroleum Co., 122, 181–82, 283, 290
El desmoronamiento de Morones (skit), 251
El Dictamen (newspaper), 176
election clubs, parties as, 105, 107–8
electrical workers union, 69, 294
El Hormiguero, Tabasco, 183
Elías, Arturo M., 181
Elías, Francisco S., 147, 153, 228, 265
El Mante. *See* Compañía Azucarera El Mante
El Mundo (newspaper), 174
El Nacional (newspaper), 304
El Paso TX, 47, 53
El Sauzal, Baja California, 277, 286
El Tambor, Sinaloa, 277, 288, 291
El Tigre copper mine, 98
El Universal (newspaper), 109, 203–4, 309
embargos, 59–60, 179, 212, 214
emigration to the United States, 111
ENP (Escuela Nacional Preparatoria), 36, 148
Ensenada fishers, 274
entrepreneurs, 10, 30, 34, 69, 88, 129, 153, 155, 197, 198, 231, 235, 270, 283, 285, 308
epidemics, 22–23, 110–11
Episcopal Committee, 205–6, 208
episcopate, 137, 139–40, 203–4, 206–9
Escobar Rebellion, 6–8, 153, 249, 256–59, 261, 269, 286, 295
Escuela Nacional Preparatoria (ENP), 36, 148
Esperanza, Veracruz, 180
Estadio Nacional, 193, 264, 289
Estrada, Enrique, 168, 177, 180, 182, 216, 271, 298, 309
Estrada Doctrine, 271–72
Europe, 181, 188, 230
European social democracy, 2, 107, 188

Evans, Rosalie, 145
Excélsior (newspaper), 110, 235, 268
executions, 8, 29, 87, 99, 178–79, 182, 237–39, 293
executive branch, 142, 151, 193, 251, 255
exile, 34, 52, 60, 73–74, 103, 117, 120, 128, 143, 148, 182, 209, 215–17, 241, 263–64, 295–98, 308
experimental farm, 265
export commodities, 135, 199
exports, 97–98, 110, 124, 135, 179–80, 218, 267–68, 277; and export economies, 32, 77, 90, 145, 166; and export tax, 124, 135–36
expropriations, 10, 73, 100, 137, 144, 211, 262, 269, 284, 287, 295–96, 304

Falangist government (Spain), 297
Fall, Albert B., 111, 134–36
familism, 25–26
Faure, Gloria, 197
Faustino Sarmiento, Domingo, 81
Feast of Christ the King, 203
Federal Board of Conciliation and Arbitration. *See* Junta Federal de Conciliación y Arbitraje (JFCA)
Federal District. *See* Mexico City
Federales, 1, 38, 41, 48–52, 55, 56–57, 60, 87
federal government, 6, 49, 54, 56–58, 87, 94, 118, 120, 153, 185, 215, 257, 259–60, 270, 273
Federalists, 24
Felicistas, 117, 122, 215
feminist congress, 90
Fernández Ruiz, Tiburcio, 128, 166–67
Field Jurado, Francisco, 184
fiesta patria, 151
Filippi, Ernesto, 138–39, 182
Flores, Ángel, 128, 179, 186–88, 228
Flores, Daniel, 264

Flores Magón brothers, 36
food production, 26, 77, 90, 98, 269
Ford Motor Company, 198
Foreign Affairs, 193
foreign-born in Mexico, 32, 48, 94–96, 181, 204; and ownership of land, 211
Foreign Club, Mexico City, 304
foreign investments and companies, 28, 30, 78, 92, 94, 111–12, 124, 194, 198, 202, 235, 270, 284–85, 310
foreign policy, 217–20, 271
Fourth Irregular Battalion, 42
Fox, Claudio, 237–39, 293
Fox Quesada, Vicente, 301
France, 49, 259, 264
Franco, Francisco, 297
French Intervention, 3, 24, 27, 60–61
Fronteras, 43, 67, 74
Fuerte River, 224

Gadsden Purchase (1853), 24
Galván, Úrsulo, 253, 287
Gálvez, Cruz, 79
gambling, 89, 161
Gamboa, Federico, 21–22
Gamio, Manuel, 187
garbanzo, 12, 30, 97–98, 224
Garbanzo League, 97–98
García Correa, Bartolomé, 250
Garci-Crespo of Tehuacán, 285
Garrido Canabal, Tomás, 165, 166, 171, 178, 181, 183, 193, 205, 207, 251, 280, 290, 291, 292
Gasparri, Pietro, 206
Gaxiola, Ignacio P., 151, 222, 224
General Directorate of Political and Social Investigations, 214–15
General Workers' Confederation. *See* Confederación General de Trabajo (CGT)
Genossenschaften, 189

gente alta, 156
Germany, 49, 94, 100–101, 188–89, 285
Gerónimo, 29–30
Gila River, 23
Gilly, Adolfo, 9–10
gold, 25, 86–87, 135, 171, 268
Gold Shirts, 291
Gómez, Arnulfo R., 5–6, 8, 10, 27, 36, 38, *51*, 52, 67, 93, 116, 122, 151, 156, 161, 171, 175, 183–86, *188*, 228, 231–41, 263, 308, 310–11
Gómez, Marte R., 287
Gómez Morín, Manuel, 202
Gompers, Samuel, 145–46, 165, 180
González, Abraham, 49
González, Manuel, 28, 193
González, Soledad "Cholita," 154
González Garza, Pablo, 53–55, 59–60, 78, 104, 109–10, 116, 117, 122, 126–27, 214–16
González Hermosillo, José María, 24
Gonzalistas, 104, 215
Gonzalo Escobar, José, 238–39, 243, 256–58, 313n19
Gorostieta Velarde, Enrique, 210, 260
government revenue, 194, 202, 217
governors, 2, 6, 29, 49, 54, 74, 78–88, 91, 94, 96, 118–19, 122, 152–53, 172–74, 178, 185, 294–95, 304–5
Gramsci, Antonio, 5
Gran Confederación Nacional Católica de Trabajo, 138, 146
grassroots mobilization, 53, 68, 89, 107, 138, 234, 250–51, 287
Great Britain, 49, 111, 196, 218
Great Depression, 8, 267–68, 272, 274, 275–77
Greene, William, 30, 32
Gruening, Ernest, 150, 154, 200, 213
Grupo Sonora, 129, 186

Guadalajara, 59–60, 80, 86–88, 96, 181, 198, 205, 207, 233, 277, 282
Guajardo, Jesús, 123
Guanajuato, 70–71, 139, 209
Guatemala, 25, 166, 198, 212, 303
Guaymas, 6, 24, 30–31, 33–34, 37, 42–43, 49, 55–56, 87, 263, 298
gubernatorial elections, 33, 52, 84, 116, 172–74
Guerrero, 59, 120, 145, 173, 176
Guerrero (warship), 128
Guerrero, Vicente, 200
guerrilla warfare, 29, 42, 66
Guggenheims, 30
Gulf Coast military region, 304
Gutiérrez, Eulalio, 65, 148
Gutiérrez de Lara, Lázaro, 99
Guzmán, Martín Luis, 8, 169, 174, 239, 306

hacendados, 53, 61, 144, 154, 177, 179, 187, 262
Hacienda de Santa Rosa, 56
haciendas, 4, 12, 39, 41, 90, 98, 169, 276–77, 296. *See also* land reform
Harding, Warren G., 134, 137
Havana, 272
Hawaii, 293
Haya de la Torre, Victor, 150
henequen, 32, 72, 88–91, 145, 177, 180, 183, 222
Hermosillo, 36–37, 43, 56–58, 74, 80, 118, 225, 298
Herrero, Rodolfo, 123
Hidalgo, Miguel, 150–51, 200
Hill, Benjamín G., 5–6, 8, 31, 35–36, 39, 56, 63–64, 101, 113, 116, 120, 122–23, 133–34, 161, 171, 307–8; and the Carranza-era party system, 104, 108–9; and the Constituyente, 93; death of, 141, 241; and de la Huerta's interim

presidency, 127–29; and the Huerta coup, 50–51; photograph of, *105, 125*; and the road to Agua Prieta, 116–17; and the War of the Winners, 67, 72
Hobbes, Thomas, 5
Holy See, 134, 137–39, 182, 187, 201, 204, 206, 209
Hoover, Herbert, 258
Hospital Inglés, 303
Hotel Regis, 243
House of the World's Worker. *See* Casa del Obrero Mundial (COM)
Huasteca Petroleum Company, 180, 283, 290
Huasteca region, 122, 154, 180
Huatabampo, 38, 41–42
Huerta, Victoriano, 3, 12, 26, 41–42, 48–62, 63, 68, 70, 80, 95–96, 103, 114, 119, 155, 157, 176, 208, 210
Huertistas, 48, 55–56, 104, 262
Hughes, Charles Evans, 179–80, 187
Huitzilac, Morelos, 237–39, 241, 264, 293, 309, 310
Humboldt, Alexander von, 24

Ibáñez, Blasco, 26, 98, 150
ICAM (Iglesia Católica Apostólica Mexicana), 200–201
ICBM (International Committee of Bankers on Mexico), 136, 171, 197, 217, 271
Iglesia Católica Apostólica Mexicana (ICAM), 200–201
Iguala, Guerrero, 120
immigration, 24, 99, 215, 267, 284–85
Impulsora de Cines Independientes, 305
Indigenous communities, 2, 22–26, 29–33, 34, 69, 79, 199, 201, 289, 296
industrialization, 27, 77, 111, 198, 218
Industrial Workers of the World, 99, 146
Inés Novelo, José, 108, 133

infalsificables, 87
informe, 236, 284, 304
infrastructure, 2, 28, 98, 185, 198–99, 252, 265, 279
Iniquis afflictisque (Pius XI), 209
Institutional Revolutionary Party. *See* Partido Revolucionario Institucional (PRI)
intellectuals, 92–93, 213
intelligence reports, 82–83, 164, 218, 222, 230, 262
interim governments, 5, 39, 54, 65, 66, 123, 124–29, 152–53, 236, 242–44
International Committee of Bankers on Mexico (ICBM), 136, 171, 197, 217, 271
International Harvester, 88–90
international law, 111, 271, 290
investments, 28, 30, 69, 153, 221–25
irrigation, 29, 30, 33–34, 78–79, 113, 155, 199, 224, 265; canals, 222
Iturbide, Eduardo, 26, 150, 200
Iturbide, Agustín de, 26, 150
Izábal, Rafael, 29, 41

Jacobins, 92–93, 95, 118, 202, 301, 306
Jalisco, 6, 59–60, 67, 72, 78, 86–88, 91–92, 101, 118, 176, 180, 207, 209, 259
Japanese minister, 221–22
Javier Gaxiola, Francisco, 288
jefaturas políticas, 86
jefe de operaciones, 36, 81–83, 99, 109, 122, 128, 143, 153, 172, 185, 231, 243–44
jefe máximo moniker, 4, 8, 254–55, 299
jefes municipales, 29
jefes políticos, 29
jefe supremo de la revolución, 176, 255
Jenkins, William O., 145, 305–6
Jesuit order, 23
JFCA (Junta Federal de Conciliación y Arbitraje), 217, 270–71

Jockey Club, 61
José Ríos, Juan, 273
Juárez, Benito, 3, 25, 27–28, 104, 157, 195
Junta Federal de Conciliación y Arbitraje (JFCA), 217, 270–71
Junta Revolucionaria, 34, 37

Kellogg, Frank B., 195–96, 211–13, 215, 217–18
kinship ties, 26, 28, 157, 159, 252
Knight, Alan, 11–12
Knights of Columbus, 200, 212
Knights of Guadalupe, 200
Kropotkin, Peter, 38
Krumm-Heller, Arnold, 182

La Bombilla, 240
labor, 2, 11, 23, 32, 77, 90, 95–96, 98; and activism, 278, 290–91; and conflicts, 82–83, 113–14, 217, 270–71, 276; and labor law, 100; and the labor market, 267; and labor movements, 145–47; and leaders, 146–47, 196, 220; and organizations/unions, 61, 80, 113–14, 143, 146–47, 152, 187, 196, 205, 220, 270–71, 277–78, 290, 292, 294–96, 310; and reform, 279, 280, 282–83, 308
Laborde, Hernán, 289
Laboristas, 121, 242, 250–51
Lagarde, Ernest, 203, 207–8
Laguna area in the Northeast, 179
La Malinche, 155
Lamont, Thomas W., 136, 152, 172, 197, 271
landowners, 25–26, 40–43, 49, 53, 55–56, 79, 98, 145, 176–77, 199, 211, 262, 268–69, 284
land reform, 2, 12, 39–41, 48, 53, 68–69, 72, 77, 79, 113, 144–45, 155, 165, 209, 233, 253, 261, 262, 265, 269–70, 277, 279, 284, 295, 296, 308, 310; and
land distributions, 5, 8, 10, 73, 90, 94, 96, 137, 144–45, 185, 199, 261–62, 269, 279, 280, 289–90, 296
La Prensa (newspaper), 44–45, 242, 285, 297
La rebelión sin cabeza (Capetillo), 216
Laredo TX, 143
La Regeneración (newspaper), 32, 37
La sombra del caudillo (Guzmán), 169, 239
La sucesión presidencial de 1910 (Madero), 34, 154
Law of Agrarian Credit, 284
Lawrence, D. H., 150
League of Nations, 272
Legion of Merit, 305
legislature, 50, 54, 83, 86, 92, 96, 103–4, 108, 119, 141–42, 173–74, 175, 178, 201, 220, 227, 236
Leo VIII (pope), 80
León, Luis L., 72, 151, 241, 250, 255, 265, 294–99
León de la Barra, Francisco, 38, 215
León Toral, José de, 240, 242
Lerdo de Tejada, Sebastián, 28
Ley Agraria, 100
Ley de Ejidos, 144–45
Ley de Gobierno, 100
Ley de Trabajo, 100
Ley Federal de Trabajo, 270, 283
ley seca, 78, 84
Leyva, José María, 25
liberal anticlericalism, 96
Liberal Constitutionalist Army, 121
Liberal Constitutionalist Party. *See* Partido Liberal Constitucionalista (PLC)
liberal democracy, 310
Liberal Reform of the 1850s, 29
Liberals and Liberal Party, 25, 28, 35, 112
Liège, 230
Liga Nacional Campesina (LNC), 228, 253, 261

Liga Nacional Campesina "Úrsulo Galván," 287
Liga Nacional Defensora de la Libertad Religiosa (LNDLR), 205–11, 260
Liga Nacional de la Defensa Religiosa (LNDR), 201, 205–6
ligas de resistencia, 89, 165–66
Lindbergh, Charles, 219
literacy, 31, 89, 148, 194, 199
Llorente, Leonor, 160, 276
LNC (Liga Nacional Campesina), 228, 253, 261
LNDLR (Liga Nacional Defensora de la Libertad Religiosa), 205–11, 260
LNDR (Liga Nacional de la Defensa Religiosa), 201, 205–6
loans, 60, 77, 97, 111, 124–25, 136–37, 181, 197, 223–24, 284
Lombardo Toledano, Vicente, 271, 277–78, 292, 296–97, 305
Long, Baron, 153–54
López de Santa Anna, Antonio, 105, 297
López Mateos, Adolfo, 305
López Obrador, Andrés Manuel, 107, 290, 301–2
López Portillo, José, 12
Los Angeles CA, 159, 183, 230, 295
Los Pinos, 290
loyalists, 12, 104, 150, 234, 270, 290

machine guns, 70, 230
machine politics, 263, 301
macho archetype, 72, 156, 241
Maderismo, 104, 141, 263, 308
Maderistas, 6, 38, 40, 43, 92, 104, 168, 170–71, 185, 262
Madero, Francisco I., 3, 6, 8, 10, 12, 33–36, 38–45, 40, 48–49, 52–53, 93, 96, 103, 104, 114, 118, 154, 155, 176, 234–35, 254, 262–63, 295
Madero, Raúl, 177

Madrazo, Arturo, 139
Magaña, Gildardo, 120, 122
Magdalena, 99
manifestos, 50–51, 66, 72–73, 99, 112, 118, 122, 176, 181, 183–84, 209, 234–35
Manrique, Aurelio, 141, 173–74, 244, 258
manso Yaqui, 29, 83–84
Manuel de Rosas, Juan, 105
Mapache faction, 166
map of Mexico, *18*
map of Sonora, *7*
María Morelos, José, 200
María Tapia, José, 151, 266
marriages, 27, 157–60
martial law, 45, 61
Martínez, Eugenio, 236–37
massacre in Huitzilac, 237–39, 309
massacre of San Pedro de la Cueva, 73–74
massacre of Yaqui, 25
Matamoros, 119
Matus, Luis, 225, 313n19
Maximato, 4, 8, 10–11, 82, 249–99, 308, 310
Maximilian, Emperor, 24–25, 27–28, 41, 290
Maya, 21, 88–90
Maycotte, Fortunato, 120, 177
Mayo, 22, 25, 29, 42, 50, 56, 98
Mayo River, 6, 21, 224
Mayo Valley, 29, 35, 38, 41
Maytorena Tapia, José María "Pepe," 5–6, 33–45, 40, 49–50, 52, 53, 55–58, 62–66, 67, 72–73, 79, 103, 241, 298, 302, 308
Mazatlán, Sinaloa, 37, 59, 115, 128, 159
Medina, Julián, 87
Mennonites, 145
Mérida, Yucatán, 90, 165
Mesoamerica, 21
mestizaje, 148

Index 395

Mestre Ghigliazza, Eduardo, 218–19
Mexicali, 156–57, 185, 259, 283
Mexican Catholic Apostolic Church, 200–201
Mexican Labor Party. *See* Partido Laborista Mexicano (PLM)
Mexican Regional Workers' Confederation. *See* Confederación Regional Obrera Mexicana (CROM)
Mexican Socialist Party, 170
Mexican Telephone and Telegraph Company, 292
Mexican Workers' Confederation. *See* Confederación de Trabajadores Mexicanos (CTM)
Mexico City, 1, 11, 22, 26, 28, 36, 48, 57, 59–61, 64, 66–67, 69, 80, 82, 88, 94, 96, 99, 104, 109, 111, 119, 128, 135–37, 140, 145, 146, 155–61, 165–67, 183, 187, 198, 201, 205, 226, 231, 232, 233, 237, 250, 266, 283, 290, 291–94, 304
Michoacán, 122, 143, 209, 280, 286–87. *See also* Morelia, Michoacán
middle class, 6, 27, 30, 32, 169, 262
Middle East, 136, 285
military: budget of, 260; downsizing of, 177; and Gulf Coast, 304; intelligence documents, 235; leaders, 54, 62–66, 92–96, 122, 209, 242–44; militarism, 62, 93; militias, 41–42, 45, 50, 68, 81, 104–5, 253; officers, 134; reform of, 143; role of in national politics, 6, 262; service in, 179
minimum wage, 83, 86, 275, 279, 283–84, 308
mining and miners, 32, 40, 77–79, 98–99, 296
Mistral, Gabriela, 150
mobilization, 4, 11, 50–51, 52–53, 68, 89, 107, 165, 166, 178, 208
Moctezuma, Emperor, 22

Moctezuma brewery, 114
Moctezuma Copper Company, 99
modernization, 2, 10, 31, 61, 106–7, 197, 274
Modotti, Tina, 150
Monclova, 49
Monclova Convention, 54, 148
Monetary Commission, 183
monetary policy, 268, 291
Monroe Doctrine, 272
Monterrey, 33–34, 59, 159, 198, 243, 256, 266
Montes de Oca, Luis, 219, 271
Montijo Hugues, Luisa, 160
Monumento a la Revolución, 255
Monumento al General Álvaro Obregón, 255, 306
Monzón, Luis G., 94, 228
moralization, 89, 128, 153–54, 304
Mora y del Río, José, 61, 203–4, 206, 208–9
Morelia, Michoacán, 187, 205, 208
Morelos, 3, 34, 38, 39, 45, 53, 110, 145, 209, 237
Morena party, 302
Morgan, J. P., 30
Morones, Luis Napoleón, 114, 120, 146–47, 171, 183–84, 193, 194–97, 201, 205, 211–13, 226, 232, 235; and anticlericalism, 137; in Calles's power base, 164–65; and the end of Sonorismo, 293–95; excesses of, 157; and the Maximato, 310; and Obregón's assassination, 242; as Obregón's rival, 228; and the Partido Revolucionario Anti-Comunista (PRAC), 297; photograph of, *164*; and the PNR organizing committee, 250–51; speech of, 219–20
Morrow, Dwight W., 217, 219, 242, 260, 263, 269, 271, 278
Motul, 178

movie theaters, 305–6
Múgica, Francisco J., 85, 92, 128, 177
multilateral diplomacy, 272
municipio, 69, 100
murals/muralists, 149, 187, 228, 255
Murguía, Francisco, 72, 143

Nacional Financiera, 284
Naco, 51–52, 54, 67, 72, 171
Nacozari, 99
Nacozari Manifesto, 51
Náinari, 222, 225, 236
Natera, Pánfilo, 64
Nation, 270
National Agrarian Party. *See* Partido Nacional Agrarista (PNA)
National Agricultural Credit Bank. *See* Banco Nacional de Crédito Agrícola (BNCA)
National Anti-reelectionist Party (Partido Nacional Antirreleccionista), 104, 141, 231, 263, 289
National Campesino League. *See* Liga Nacional Campesina (LNC)
National Catholic Party. *See* Partido Católico Nacional (PCN)
national commission of fisheries, 305
national commission of roadways, 198
National Cooperatist Party. *See* Partido Nacional Cooperatista (PNC)
National Eucharistic Congress, 140
nationalism, 2, 96, 203. *See also* economy: economic nationalism
nationalization, 287, 303–4; of land, 104–5
National League for Religious Defense. *See* Liga Nacional de la Defensa Religiosa (LNDR)
National League for the Defense of Religious Liberty. *See* Liga Nacional Defensora de la Libertad Religiosa (LNDLR)

national minimum wage commission, 283–84
National Palace, 11, 48, 66, 69, 149, 264
National Revolutionary Party. *See* Partido Nacional Revolucionario (PNR)
National University (UNAM), 262–63
Navojoa, 35–36, 38, 42, 50, 67, 255
Nayarit, 153
Nazi Germany, 285, 291
Neutrality Act, 124
New Deal, 280
New Spain, 23–24
New York City, 117, 124, 136, 152, 197, 214–15
New York Daily Mirror, 197
New York Times, 134, 164, 167, 193, 296
Nicaragua, 9, 166, 212, 217, 269
Nineteenth Amendment (U.S.), 138
Nogales AZ, 28, 34, 36, 44–45, 51, 54, 62, 67, 74, 97, 112, 159, 225, 233, 238, 257–58
Nogales Manifesto, 112–13, 118
nonconsecutive terms (presidency), 226–28
normal schools for teachers (*normales*), 79, 148, 199
Northwest, 22, 24, 25, 32, 65, 128, 198, 222, 277
notables, 24–25, 28–29, 33, 42–43
Nueva Andalucía, 23
Nuevo León, 33, 153, 159, 168, 174, 252, 292, 296

Oaxaca, 3, 32, 74, 155, 176
Oaxaca (military transport), 37
Obrecallista, 193
Obregón, Francisco, 24
Obregón, José J., 84–85, 238
Obregón, Lamberto, 41, 230
Obregonistas, 65, 66–67, 77, 117–19, 193, 234, 242, 244, 252, 256, 297, 306, 309

Index 397

Obregón Tapia, Álvaro, 1, 3–6, 8, 10–13, 26, 31, 41–44, 54–66, 80–85, 116–23, 133–34, 164–69, 193–94, 195, 201, 205, 306–9; aftermath of the death of, 241–45; assassination of, 240–41, 249; in the Carranza era, 97–101; and the Carranza-era party system, 103, 104–9; and the Constituyente, 93–94, 96; cult of, 255–56; and the De la Huerta Rebellion, 176–86; and de la Huerta's interim presidency, 124–29; and diplomatic recognition, 134–40; and the Escobar Rebellion, 256–57; and government finances, 197–98; and the Huerta coup, 50–52; and the Huitzilac massacre, 237–39; investments of, 221–25; and *jefe máximo* moniker, 254–55; and land distribution, 285; in Mexico City, 155–61; photograph of, *55, 71, 105, 158, 184*; policies of, 140–51; and policies of the Calles administration, 218–20, 294; and the presidential campaign of 1920, 109–16; and the presidential election of 1924, 169–75; and presidential succession, 163; in public memory, 306; resignation of, 64; and retrenchment from the reform drive, 218–20; and the revolutionary family, 254; second term campaign of, 226–41; and structure of the Sonorense coalition, 151–55; and the War of the Winners, 66–74; and the Yaqui, 225–26, 295

Obregón y Cía, 224

oficial mayor, 58, 118

Oficina Comercial de Álvaro Obregón, 222

oil companies, 10, 77, 122, 134–35, 177, 202, 213–15; and Arnulfo R. Gómez, 232; and article 27, 94, 194–95; and controversy, 217–19; and economic nationalism, 284; expropriation of, 304; and labor activism, 290; and Mexico's economy, 267; and the Petroleum Law, 211–13; and U.S. assistance, 180

Old Regime, 32, 38, 40, 80, 221

Ópata, 22–23

Orendaín, Jalisco, 60

Oriol Ortiz de la Torre, Clara, 160–61

Orizaba, Veracruz, 113, 240

Orozco, Pascual, 3, 6, 10, 34, 38, 40–41, 49, 51, 53, 63, 209, 236

Orozco y Jiménez, José Francisco, 86, 203, 209

Orozquistas, 34–35, 41–45

Ortega, Melchor, 295

orthodox anticlericalism, 96

Ortiz, Eulogio, 235–36

Ortiz Rubio, Francisco, 272

Ortiz Rubio, Pascual: as example of political divisions, 292; crisis in the presidency of, 264–74; and crisis management, 276; and land distribution, 284, 285; and limits on the number of priests, 280; and the Obregón cult, 255–56; and Obregón's succession, 244; as presidential candidate, 252; and presidential elections, 261, 263; and the rise of Cárdenas, 288–89

Ortizrubistas, 265

Osten, Sarah, 11

pacification committee, 64

Padilla, Ezequiel, 279, 288

Palacio de Bellas Artes, 283

Palacio de Gobierno, 157

Palacio Nacional, 133, 255, 264

Palavicini, Félix, 109

Panama Canal, 218

Pan-American Federation of Labor, 145–46
Pan-American Highway, 198
Pan-American Workers Confederation, 165
Pan-American Workers Federation, 114
Pani, Albert J., 136, 175, 193, 195, 196–97; and alliance with the COM, 69; and anticyclical monetary policies, 277; and centennial celebrations, 156; and Obregón's investments, 224; and the Ortiz Rubio administration, 265, 268; and the Paris Peace Conference, 111; resignation of, 212; and the Rodríguez presidency, 279, 282–83
papal delegates, 138–39, 182, 207–8, 282
Paris, France, 148, 160, 254, 259–61
Paris Peace Conference of 1919, 111
Parral, 171–72
Partido Católico Nacional (PCN), 86, 104, 202–3
Partido Comunista Mexicano. *See* Communist Party (PCM)
Partido Constitucional Progresista (PCP), 104
Partido de la Revolución Mexicana (PRM), 108, 297, 301
Partido Laborista Mexicano (PLM), 114, 141, 142, 146, 164, 171, 202, 205, 235, 242, 251
Partido Liberal Constitucionalista (PLC), 104, 108, 112, 116–17, 134, 141–42, 171, 250
Partido Liberal Mexicano, 32, 37–38, 120
Partido Nacional Agrarista (PNA), 120–21, 141–42, 146, 164, 171, 173, 175, 227–28, 233
Partido Nacional Antirreleccionista, 104, 141, 231, 263, 289
Partido Nacional Cooperatista (PNC), 104–5, 142, 165, 169, 172–75, 183–84, 250

Partido Nacional Revolucionario (PNR), 108, 231, 250–54, 256, 261, 270, 273, 275, 278–80, 286–89, 292, 294, 297, 301
Partido Radical Tabasqueño, 251
Partido Revolucionario Anti-Comunista (PRAC), 297
Partido Revolucionario Institucional (PRI), 11, 243, 270, 301
Partido Socialista Chiapaneco, 167
Partido Socialista del Sureste (PSS), 141, 164–66, 251
Partido Socialista de Yucatán (PSY), 89, 107–8
Partido Socialista Fronterizo, 251
Partido Socialista Obrero, 89
Pascua Hiaki, 23
Paseo de la Reforma, 200
pax priista, 301
PCM. *See* Communist Party (PCM)
PCN (Partido Católico Nacional), 86, 104, 202–3
PCP (Partido Constitucional Progresista), 104
Peláez, Manuel, 77, 122, 135, 155
Pemex, 284
pequeña propiedad, 79, 199, 279, 296
Pérez Budar, Joaquín, 200
Pérez Treviño, Manuel, 243, 250, 253, 257, 260–61, 265, 269, 286, 288, 293, 297
Permanent Commission, 142
Peronismo, 299
persecution of the church, 8, 265. *See also* church-state conflict
personality cults, 105–7, 301–2
Pesqueira, Ignacio L., 5–6, 24–25, 28–29, 31–32, 35–36, 50–51, 54, 56, 81–82, 84, 94, 112, *115*, 116, 118–19, 241, 308
Pesqueira, José, 28
Pesqueira, Roberto V., 54
Petroleum Law, 195, 197, 202, 211–13, 219

Petromex, 284
Pima, 22
Pino Suárez, José María, 48–49
Pius X (pope), 59
Pius XI (pope), 138, 209, 280–81
Plan de Agua Prieta, 121–22, 128, 143, 152, 161, 166–68, 177, 182, 244
Plan de Ayala, 39, 65, 69, 99
Plan de Caborca, 35
Plan de Guadalupe, 52–53, 54, 68–69, 92, 122
Plan de Hermosillo, 122, 256
Plan de la Empacadora, 41
Plan de Los Altos, 210
Plan de San Luis Potosí, 34
Plan de Veracruz, 176, 228
plan sexenal, 278–80
PLC. *See* Partido Liberal Constitucionalista (PLC)
PLM. *See* Partido Laborista Mexicano (PLM)
pluralistic ignorance, 298
PNA. *See* Partido Nacional Agrarista (PNA)
PNC. *See* Partido Nacional Cooperatista (PNC)
PNR. *See* Partido Nacional Revolucionario (PNR)
political stability, 8, 13, 22, 61, 249, 258, 271, 274, 280, 301
populism: Calles and, 168–69; Cárdenas and, 307
Porfiriato/Porfirians, 3, 27–29, 31–32, 33, 36–39, 57, 74, 77, 112, 153, 198
Porter, Katherine Anne, 150, 196
Portes Gil, Emilio, 8, 165; and the end of Sonorismo, 293; and the Escobar Rebellion, 258; and land distribution, 285; and Luis Napoleón Morones, 251; and Obregón's succession, 243–44; and the Ortiz Rubio administration, 264–65, 269–74; and the Partido Socialista Fronterizo, 251; and the Plan de Hermosillo, 256; and the PNR organizing committee, 250; and political stability, 249; and presidential elections, 252; as puppet president, 259–62; resignation of, 173; and the rise of Cárdenas, 286–87; and supporters in Congress, 265
Positivism, 282
PRAC (Partido Revolucionario Anti-Comunista), 297
presidente municipal, 42, 99
presidential elections, 252–54, 261; of 1913, 59; of 1920, 103, 109–16; of 1924, 134, 163–75, 186–89, 228; of 1928, 183, 226–41, 309; of 1929, 261–63; of 1934, 286–89; of 1958, 305
presidio, 23–24
PRI. *See* Partido Revolucionario Institucional (PRI)
Prieto Laurens, Jorge, 104, 163, 165, 169, 173–75, 176, 215–16, 308
PRM (Partido de la Revolución Mexicana), 108, 297, 301
Pro, Miguel, 240
Proal, Herón, 147, 179
Prohibition, 78, 89, 128, 154, 200, 273
proletariat, 44, 84–85, 100, 187, 188, 306–7
property rights, 12, 96, 112–13, 122, 195, 217
Provincias de Sonora, Ostimuri y Sinaloa, 23
PSY (Partido Socialista de Yucatán), 89, 107–8
public health, 194; and hygiene, 148, 200
Puebla, 66–67, 74, 123, 143, 145, 155, 177, 198, 205, 231, 235, 236, 285, 286, 287
Puig Casauranc, 265
Punitive Expedition, 81

Quas primas (Pius XI), 202
Querétaro, 92, 93, 178, 251–52, 288, 311
Quintana Roo, 185

radical policies and movements, 137–38, 140, 185, 261, 287, 304
railroads, 28, 30, 57, 59, 90, 185, 196–98, 290, 296
railroad workers, 120; strike of, 146, 166, 217; union of, 147, 232
ranchería people, 22
Red Battalions, 69, 113
redemptive anticlericalism, 96, 138
redistribution of land, 3–5, 10, 41, 50, 69, 73, 90, 94, 96, 144–45, 185, 199, 269, 289–90, 296
Red Shirts, 280, 291
Reed, John, 150
reforms, 2, 4–5, 13, 88–91, 202, 275; and anti-Communist backlash, 97; and the Cámara Obrera, 82–83; in the Carranza era, 99–101; of the constitution, 141–42, 194–95, 208–9, 227–28, 285–86; and the De la Huerta Rebellion, 185–86; and government debt, 196–97; national context of, 85–91; retrenchment from, 219–20; of Rodolfo Elías Calles, 265; and the Rodríguez presidency, 282–86. *See also* Bourbon Reforms
religion, 187; and conflict, 218; and fanaticism, 137; holidays celebrating, 86–87, 95; liberty of, 225, 235; and persecution, 209, 231; and political activism, 104; practice of, 201, 206. *See also* church-state conflict
renovadores, 93
rent strikes, 187; in Veracruz, 147
repression, 8–9, 13, 29, 31, 78, 79–80, 118, 143–44, 146, 178, 186, 196, 263
Republican exiles (from Spain), 297

Republican Party (U.S.), 111, 134–35
Rerum novarum (Leo VIII), 80, 202
revolutionary family, 254–55, 299, 303
Revolutionary Junta for Aid to the Poor, 69
revolutionary regimes, 4, 10, 163, 203, 210
revolution by administration, 3, 45, 73
Reyes, Bernardo, 33–34
Reyes, Rodolfo, 33–34, 48–49, 52
Richkarday, Ignacio A., 234, 238
Rio de Janeiro, 244
Río Lerma, 181
Río Sonora, 118
Ríos Zertuche, Antonio, 230–31
Riva Palacio, Carlos, 286, 288
Rivera, Diego, 149, 228, 255
Riveros, Felipe, 56
road building, 198, 280
Robles Domínguez, Alfredo, 124
robolución, 12
Rodríguez, Abelardo L., 4–5, 6, 8–9, 12, 44–45, 121, 160–61, 302–6, 309, 310; administration of, 275–86; and the agrarian code, 296; and Baja California, 216; and civil service, 290; and the Constituyente, 93; and the De la Huerta Rebellion, 183, 185–86; and de la Huerta's interim presidency, 128–29; and the end of Sonorismo, 293–94; and the Escobar Rebellion, 257–59; excesses of, 156–57; fortunes of, 153–55; and the Huerta coup, 51; and José Vasconcelos, 262–63; letter to Juan de Dios Bojórquez, 298–99; loyalties of, 234; and Obregón's assassination, 241; and Obregón's investments, 222–24; and Obregón's succession, 243; and the Ortiz Rubio administration, 266–69, 273–74; and the Partido Revolucionario Anti-Comunista (PRAC), 297; photograph of, *159, 281*; and presidential

Index   401

Rodríguez (*cont.*) succession, 286; and the rise of Cárdenas, 287–88; as substitute president, 308; and the War of the Winners, 72
Rodríguez, Fernando, 285
Rodríguez Triana, Pedro, 261–62
Romero, Matías, 21–22
Romero Rubio, Carmen, 28
Roosevelt, Franklin D., 278, 280
Ross, Ramón, 94, 170
Rouaix, Pastor, 69, 94
roving bandits, 12
Royal Dutch and Shell Transport, 181
Ruiz, Amanda, 157
Ruiz Cortines, Adolfo, 304
Ruiz y Flores, Leopoldo, 208–9, 218, 260, 282
ruling party, 5, 8, 10–11, 231, 249–50, 274
rural education, 5, 147, 148, 199, 280
rural workers, 165, 196
Russian Revolution, 4, 107

Sacasa, Juan Bautista, 212
Sáenz, Aarón, 151, 155, 198–99, 250, 252, 255, 257, 265, 273, 283, 288, 290, 292, 306, 309
Sáenz, Moisés, 199, 252
Sáenz Garza, Aarón, 57, 154
Sagrada Familia, 205
Sahuaripa, 35
Salas Barraza, Jesús, 172
Salinas de Gortari, Carlos, 12
Saltillo, 60
San Angel, 240
San Antonio TX, 34, 52, 209, 215, 219
Sánchez, Guadalupe, 119, 123, 168, 175, 176–82, 186
San Diego CA, 216, 295
San Francisco CA, 170, 216, 227
San José de Gracia, Michoacán, 209
San José de Guaymas, 44
San Juan Bautista, 85
San Juan hacienda, Chinameca, 110
San Luis Potosí, 74, 169, 172–74, 178–79, 205, 287
San Pedro de la Cueva, 74
San Rafael paper mill, 198
Santa Ana de Trinidad, Guanajuato, 71
Santa Bárbara hacienda, 276, 294–96
Santa María, 56
Santiago Tlatelolco prison, 119
Santos, Gonzalo N., 107, 161, 228
Sea of Cortez, 21, 100
Sección de Guerra, 39–41, 50
Second Cristiada, 280
Secretaría de Educación Pública (SEP), 147–50, 199
Secretaría de Hacienda, 111
Secretariat of Labor, 114
Secretariat of the Interior (Gobernación), 58, 84, 181
Secretariat of Public Education. *See* Secretaría de Educación Pública (SEP)
Secretariat of War and the Navy, 57, 143, 181
secular education, 140, 148–49
secular nationalism, 200, 202
Senate, 103, 134–35, 141, 173–75, 214, 217, 227, 293–94
Senate Foreign Relations Committee (U.S.), 111
SEP (Secretaría de Educación Pública), 147–50, 199
separation of church and state, 95–96, 232
Serranistas, 232–33
Serrano, Francisco R., 5–6, 8, 10, 31, 36, 41–42, 52, 56–57, 61, 63–64, 81–83, 96, 103, 105, 116, 121, 134, 142–44, 160–61, 171, 221; and anti-reelectionism, 38, 232, 310–11; assassination of, 238–41; and

church-state conflict, 310; and
the Constituyente, 93; and the De
la Huerta Rebellion, 177, 179, 183,
185–86; and de la Huerta's interim
presidency, 127–28; entrepreneurial
success of, 155; excesses of, 157; and
the Huitzilac murders, 237–39, 293;
importance of, 309; photograph
of, *184, 229*; and the presidential
election of 1927, 228–37; and the
Sonoran Triangle, 151; spouse of,
160; and the War of the Winners,
72–73
Serranos, 27
settler elite. *See* notables
sex education, 282
sexenio, 107, 295
Sheffield, James R., 195–96, 211–14,
217, 219
silver, 23–24, 31–32, 83, 87–88, 124, 135,
171, 217, 268, 277
Sinaloa, 6, 23–24, 30–31, 37–38, 56–57,
59, 97–98, 113, 128, 153, 160, 269, 277,
293, 296
Sinaloa and Sonora Land Irrigation
Company, 30
Sinclair, Harry S., 134–37
síndico, 35
smallholding, 79, 90, 144, 169, 209
Smoot-Hawley Tariff Act, 268
soberanista movement, 63, 67
Sochiloa, 6
social Catholicism, 80, 202–3
social democratic parties, 189, 275
Socialism, 9, 11, 89–90, 140, 163–67, 178,
189; propaganda, 171
Socialist education, 280, 282, 290
Socialist parties, 107, 108, 114, 250–51
Socialist Party of the Frontier, 251
Socialist Party of the Southeast. *See* Partido Socialista del Sureste (PSS)

Socialist Workers' Party, 89
social justice, 9, 48, 104, 199
social movements, 2, 8, 202
social reforms, 2, 9, 36, 39, 48, 58, 68, 78,
90, 93, 101, 140, 165, 202, 220, 268,
274, 296, 304
social rights, 2, 91, 93–94, 96, 101, 141,
206, 310
social unrest, 49, 134, 275, 310
Sociedad Agrícola Cooperativa de Sonora
Sinaloa, 97
Soledad de la Mota, Nuevo León, 168
Soledad de Santa Cruz, 200–201
Somme River, 101
Sonoran Triangle, 134, 142–43, 151–52,
163, 174, 310
Sonora-Sinaloa Recreational Center, 161
Sonora y Sinaloa, 23–24
Sonorismo, 8, 11, 103, 274, 291–99, 302–
6, 307, 309
Son-Sin. *See* Centro Recreativo
Sonora-Sinaloa
Soriano, Cesáreo, 99
Soto y Gama, Antonio Díaz, 65, 120, 141,
144–45, 163, 186, 193, 227, 233, 242,
244, 255, 258
southeastern Socialism, 11, 107, 141, 163–
67, 171, 178, 250–51
Southern Pacific Railroad, 30, 38
sovereignty, 13, 50, 54, 59, 62, 63, 134–40,
181, 213; national, 2, 111, 118, 169, 218,
272; state, 50, 54, 68, 174
Soviet Union, 4, 96–97, 140, 262, 271–
72, 282, 304
Spain, 24, 49, 264, 297
Spaniards, 22–23, 31, 99
Spanish flu, 110–11, 200
Standard Fruit Company, 166
stationary bandits, 12
statolatry, 11–12
stolen documents, 214, 217, 235–36

Index   403

strikes, 32, 37–38, 40, 83, 99, 146–47, 166, 187, 194, 196, 217, 249, 259–60, 271, 278, 283, 290, 292, 294
Sturmabteilung (SA), 291
Sullivan Coya, Aida, 160
Supreme Court of Mexico, 136, 219

Tabasco, 74, 85, 117, 143, 166, 180, 181, 183, 201, 237, 280, 291, 292
Taft, William H., 48
Tamaulipas, 153, 154, 178, 199, 250, 259, 287
Tampico, 67, 180, 263
Tannenbaum, Frank, 9, 150
Tapia Monteverde, María, *158*, 158–59
taxes/taxation, 2, 25, 69, 73, 78–79, 83, 90, 96, 98, 118, 135–36, 147, 196, 198
Teapot Dome WY scandal, 136–37, 213
Teatro Hidalgo, 242
Teatro Olimpia, 140
Tehuantepec, 67, 86
Tejeda, Adalberto, 128, 137, 147, 171, 175, 177, 193, 199, 204–5, 209, 212, 231, 250, 252–53, 270, 275, 287, 289
Tenochtitlán, 22
Tepic, 59
Terrazas, Luis, 29, 41, 145
Tetabiate, 29
Texcoco, 237
textile industry, 194, 198, 218, 253
Third Congress of the Pan-American Federation of Labor, 145–46
Tijuana, 128, 154, 274, 283, 304
Tlalpan, 114, 157
Tlaxcala, 149, 155, 173
Tlaxcalantongo, 123
Tobar Doctrine, 271
Tohono O'odham, 22
Topete Almada, Fausto, 153, 256
Topilejo, 264

Torreblanca, Fernando, 151, 154, 160, 222–23, 229, 293
Torregrosa Pact, 164–65
Torreón, Coahuila, 59, 256
Torres, Luis E., 29
tourism, 128–29, 153–54
transnational capital. *See* Carranza Doctrine
Treaty of Ciudad Juárez, 39
Treaty of Guadalupe Hidalgo, 24
Treaty of Teoloyucan, 60
Tucson AZ, 50, 216, 225–26

UDCM (Unión de Damas Católicas Mexicanas), 138–40
UNAM (National University), 262–63
The Underdogs (Azuela), 47
Unión de Damas Católicas Mexicanas (UDCM), 138–40
Unión de Militares de Origen Revolucionario 1910–1913, 168, 170–71, 175
Unión Liberal Humana, 38
Union of Catholic Mexican Ladies, 138–40
Union of Military Leaders of the Origins of the Revolution (Unión de Militares), 168, 170–71, 175
United Fruit Company, 303
United States, 5, 9–10, 22, 24, 27–28, 30, 57, 59, 73, 86, 100–101, 111, 116, 120, 124–25, 135, 138, 140, 145, 165, 167, 172, 182, 188, 201, 224, 241, 264, 293; armed forces of, 197; assistance of, 180, 195; and banks, 111, 172; and border, 67; citizens of, 31, 153; and claims, 111, 124; consuls and consular reports of, 50, 67, 87, 227–28, 230, 291; culture of, 44; currency of, 268; and diplomatic relations, 271–72; and election of 1920, 134; and the Escobar

Rebellion, 258; and fighter pilots, 180; government of, 81, 111, 124, 127, 134, 137, 179–81, 187, 194, 195–96, 211–15; and immigration, 267; and intelligence agents, 97; and intelligence reports, 82–83, 164, 218, 222, 230; and investors, 112, 127, 152; and José Vasconcelos, 262; and law enforcement, 215–16; Mexican consulates in, 214, 298; and military academies, 159; military attaché of, 161, 213; and military intelligence officers, 84, 101, 194; and the New Deal, 280; and pilots, 258; and the Smoot-Hawley Tariff Act, 268; support of, 62, 113; territory of, 55, 67, 124, 202; and the U.S. Department of Justice, 216; and the U.S. embassy, 214, 235; and U.S.-held property, 211; and U.S. Marines, 59, 66, 122, 212–13; and U.S.-Mexican relations, 11, 217–20, 233, 307; and U.S. Progressivism, 2, 107; and the U.S. Senate, 213; and the U.S. State Department, 100, 134, 202, 211–12, 217, 218, 304; and warships, 180

Universidad Autónoma Nacional de México, 278
Urbalejo, Francisco, 56, 62, 256, 313n19
urban labor, 2, 114, 146
Urrea, Refugio, 157–58
Uruchurtu, Ernesto P., 305

Valenzuela, Gilberto, 122, 193, 204, 228, 298, 307, 313n19
Valle Nacional, Oaxaca, 32
Vargas Lugo, Bartolomé, 275
Vasconcelistas, 262–64
Vasconcelos, Eduardo, 282
Vasconcelos, José, 8, 147–51, 239, 249, 261–64, 289, 298

Venezuela, 136, 194
Veracruz, 122–23, 175, 186; and the Constitutionalists, 66; and the De la Huerta Rebellion, 180; and the Escobar Rebellion, 256; grassroots activism in, 287; and industrialization, 198; and insurrection, 236–38; invasion of 1914, 278; labor dispute in, 113–14; and the Liga Nacional Campesina (LNC), 253; and limits on the number of priests, 280; and Obregón's assassination, 240–41; occupation of, 59; and the Partido Nacional Antirreeleccionista, 231; and the Plan de Veracruz, 176; rent strikes in, 147, 187; U.S. occupation of, 62; and the War of the Winners, 66–74
Veracruz Decrees, 69, 73, 77, 90, 92, 94, 144
Vera Meier, Earthyl, 160
vice tourism, 128–29, 153
Vidal, Carlos A., 165, 167, 227, 234, 235–37
Villa, Pancho, 3–4, 9, 12, 52–54, 57, 58–61, 62–66; and alliance with Zapata, 124–29; assassination of, 171–72; and de la Huerta's interim presidency, 126–28; and José Venustiano Carranza de la Garza, 103; and the presidential election of 1924, 169; and the Punitive Expedition, 81; and the revolutionary family, 254; and Villismo, 81; and the War of the Winners, 66–74
Villahermosa, 85, 178
Villarreal, Antonio J., 142, 289
Villistas, 57, 60, 62–66, 70, 72–74, 77, 81, 87, 171
violence, 4–5, 8, 12, 41, 47, 49–50, 77, 122, 156, 172–73, 198, 200, 207, 235,

Index 405

violence (*cont.*) 237–39, 245, 249, 264, 280–81, 302, 304. *See also* assassinations; executions

war against Huerta, 50, 56, 68
War Department (U.S.), 180
War of the Winners, 3–4, 66–74, 77, 87, 113, 260
Wars of Independence, 24, 77, 150
war with the United States (1846–48), 24
Washington DC, 28, 101
Weber, Max, 106
Western Europe, 2
Wilson, Henry Lane, 48
Wilson, Woodrow, 49, 54–55, 59, 73, 81, 97, 101, 107, 124, 134–35
wives of the Sonorenses, 157–58
women, 25, 31; Alvarado's approach to, 89–90; campesina, 294; and conspicuous consumption, 157; and lay associations, 138; and *normales*, 148; participation in plebiscites, 210; in political leadership, 108; rights of, 165, 187; suffrage, 176, 231–32, 262; workers, 200
Workers' Chamber. *See* Cámara Obrera
working classes, 54, 68–69, 82–83, 86, 90, 94–96, 97–101, 113–15, 141, 144, 146–47, 165, 168–69, 185, 189, 194, 196, 200, 233, 251, 260–61, 270–71, 274, 283, 289–90, 294–96
working conditions, 2, 32, 48, 73, 80–81
World War I, 77, 79, 100–101
World War II, 5, 272, 302

xenophobia, 31, 99, 285

Yaqui, 1, 22–26, 29–36, 40, 50, 55–56, 62–63, 81–85, 88, 91, 99–100, 112, 118, 123, 145, 147, 152, 215, 217, 265, 295
Yaqui River, 21, 23, 37, 224
Yaqui Valley, 29–30, 32, 35, 87, 222, 224, 265, 296
Yaqui War, 225–26, 257
Yesterday in Mexico (Dulles), 9
Yocupicio Valenzuela, Román, 295
Yori, 25–31, 40, 43, 56, 81, 83, 85, 99, 123
Yucatán, 32, 72, 78, 86, 88–91, 101, 117, 125, 145, 165, 177–78, 181, 183

Zacatecas, 60, 64, 122, 209
Zapata, Emiliano, 3–4, 9, 34, 39, 53–54, 57, 60, 65–74, 110, 120, 155, 186, 209, 254; land reform of, 144–45
Zapatistas, 38, 52, 59, 65, 66, 99, 110, 122
Zimmermann Telegram, 100
Zócalo, 11, 303
Zurbarán, Pedro, 42

In the Confluencias series:

*The Sonoran Dynasty in Mexico:
Revolution, Reform, and Repression*
By Jürgen Buchenau

*The Enlightened Patrolman: Early
Law Enforcement in Mexico City*
By Nicole von Germeten

*Strength from the Waters: A
History of Indigenous Mobilization
in Northwest Mexico*
By James V. Mestaz

To order or obtain more
information on these or other
University of Nebraska Press titles,
visit nebraskapress.unl.edu.

www.ingramcontent.com/pod-product-compliance
Lightning Source LLC
Chambersburg PA
CBHW030602230426
43661CB00053B/1802